THE FATHERS
OF THE CHURCH

A NEW TRANSLATION

VOLUME 137

THE FATHERS OF THE CHURCH

A NEW TRANSLATION

EDITORIAL BOARD

David G. Hunter
University of Kentucky
Editorial Director

Andrew Cain
University of Colorado

William E. Klingshirn
The Catholic University of America

Brian Daley, S.J.
University of Notre Dame

Joseph T. Lienhard, S.J.
Fordham University

Mark DelCogliano
University of St. Thomas

Rebecca Lyman
Church Divinity School of the Pacific

Susan Ashbrook Harvey
Brown University

Wendy Mayer
Australian Catholic University

Robert A. Kitchen
Sankt Ignatios Theological Academy

Trevor Lipscombe
Director, The Catholic University of America Press

FORMER EDITORIAL DIRECTORS

Ludwig Schopp, Roy J. Deferrari, Bernard M. Peebles,
Hermigild Dressler, O.F.M., Thomas P. Halton

Carole Monica C. Burnett
Staff Editor

ST. CYRIL OF ALEXANDRIA

GLAPHYRA ON THE PENTATEUCH, VOLUME 1

GENESIS

Translated by

NICHOLAS P. LUNN

Spurgeon's College

With introduction by

GREGORY K. HILLIS

Bellarmine University

THE CATHOLIC UNIVERSITY OF AMERICA PRESS
Washington, D.C.

Copyright © 2018
THE CATHOLIC UNIVERSITY OF AMERICA PRESS
All rights reserved

Library of Congress Cataloging-in-Publication Data
Names: Cyril, Saint, Patriarch of Alexandria, approximately 370–444, author.
| Lunn, Nicholas P., translator. | Hillis, Gregory K., 1975– author
of introduction.
Title: Glaphyra on the Penteteuch / St. Cyril of Alexandria ;
translated by Nicholas P. Lunn, Spurgeon's College ; with introduction
by Gregory K. Hillis, Bellarmine University.
Description: Washington, D.C. : The Catholic University of America Press,
2018. | Series: Fathers of the Church: a new translation ; volume 137 |
In English; translated from Greek. | Includes bibliographical
references and index.
Identifiers: LCCN 2018024041 | ISBN 978-0-8132-3591-2 (pbk)
Subjects: LCSH: Bible. Pentateuch.—Commentaries. | Cyril, Saint,
Patriarch of Alexandria, approximately 370–444. | Jesus Christ—Person
and offices. | Typology (Theology)
Classification: LCC BS1225 .C975 2018 | DDC 222/.107—dc23
LC record available at https://lccn.loc.gov/2018024041

CONTENTS

Acknowledgments	vii
Abbreviations	ix
Select Bibliography	xi

INTRODUCTION   1

Encountering Cyril of Alexandria the Exegete	3
Biography of Cyril	6
The Purpose and Structure of the *Glaphyra*	10
The Bishop as Exegete and Enlightener	15
The *Glaphyra* and Jewish-Christian Relations in Alexandria	19
Theological Themes in the *Glaphyra*	23
Conclusion	36

PREFACE   37

The Text	39
The Translation	40
Key Terms	42
Format	45
Footnotes	46
Sources Consulted	46

GLAPHYRA ON THE PENTATEUCH, VOLUME 1: GENESIS   49

Book One: Genesis 1–5	51
Book Two: Genesis 6–14	81

CONTENTS

Book Three: Genesis 15–27	131
Book Four: Genesis 27–30	185
Book Five: Genesis 30–35	225
Book Six: Genesis 36–48	272
Book Seven: Genesis 49	313

Indices for both volumes will appear in Volume 2.

ACKNOWLEDGMENTS

I would like to thank those whom I consulted in linguistic matters, namely Theodore Zachariades and Eirini Artemi. Thanks are especially due to Gregory Hillis for his contributions: the introduction and a number of informative notes on the text. With regard to certain more specific theological concerns, I gladly acknowledge the assistance of Matthew Crawford and Matthew Bates.

NPL

ABBREVIATIONS

AcT	*Acta theologica*
AnBib	Analecta Biblica, Pontificio Istituto Biblico, Rome
CCR	*Coptic Church Review*
FOTC	The Fathers of the Church, Washington, DC: The Catholic University of America Press
JTS	*The Journal of Theological Studies*
LXX	Septuagint
MT	Masoretic Text
NASB	New American Standard Bible
NIV	New International Version
NJB	New Jerusalem Bible
NKJV	New King James Version
NLT	New Living Translation
NRSV	New Revised Standard Version
OT	Old Testament
PG	Patrologia Graeca, ed. J.-P. Migne, Paris, 1857–66
PL	Patrologia Latina, ed. J.-P. Migne, Paris, 1878–90
RA	*Recherches augustiniennes*
VC	*Vigiliae Christianae*
Vg	Vulgate

SELECT BIBLIOGRAPHY

Artemi, Eirini. "Cyril of Alexandria Speaks for God in his Interpretation of the Holy Bible." *AcT* 34.1 (2014): 1–16.
Blackburn, B. Lee. "The Mystery of the Synagogue: Cyril of Alexandria on the Law of Moses." PhD dissertation, University of Notre Dame, 2009.
Boulnois, Marie-Odile. "Le souffle et l'Esprit: Exégèses patristiques de l'insufflation originelle de Gn 2, 7 en lien avec celle de Jn 20, 22." *RA* 24 (1989): 3–37.
Cassel, J. David. "Cyril of Alexandria as Educator." In *In Dominico Eloquio—In Lordly Eloquence: Essays on Patristic Exegesis in Honor of Robert Louis Wilken*, ed. Paul M. Blowers, Angela R. Christman, David G. Hunter, and Robin D. Young, 348–68. Grand Rapids: Eerdmans, 2002.
Crawford, Matthew R. "The Preface and Subject Matter of Cyril of Alexandria's *De adoratione*." *JTS* 64.1 (2013): 154–67.
———. *Cyril of Alexandria's Trinitarian Theology of Scripture*. Oxford: Oxford University Press, 2014.
Cyril of Alexandria. *Select Letters*. Edited by Lionel Wickham. Oxford Early Christian Texts. Oxford: Oxford University Press, 1983.
Hill, Robert C., trans. *St. Cyril of Alexandria. Commentary on the Twelve Prophets, Volume 1*. FOTC 115. Washington, DC: The Catholic University of America Press, 2007.
———, trans. *St. Cyril of Alexandria. Commentary on the Twelve Prophets, Volume 2*. FOTC 116. Washington, DC: The Catholic University of America Press, 2008.
———, trans. *Cyril of Alexandria. Commentary on Isaiah, Volume 1: Chapters 1–14*. Brookline, MA: Holy Cross Orthodox Press, 2008.
———, trans. *Cyril of Alexandria. Commentary on Isaiah, Volume II: Chapters 15–39*. Brookline, MA: Holy Cross Orthodox Press, 2008.
———, trans. *Cyril of Alexandria. Commentary on Isaiah, Volume III: Chapters 40–50*. Brookline, MA: Holy Cross Orthodox Press, 2008.
———, trans. *St. Cyril of Alexandria. Commentary on the Twelve Prophets, Volume 3*. FOTC 124. Washington, DC: The Catholic University of America Press, 2012.
Keating, Daniel A. *The Appropriation of the Divine Life in Cyril of Alexandria*. Oxford: Oxford University Press, 2004.
Kerrigan, Alexander. *St. Cyril of Alexandria: Interpreter of the Old Testament*. AnBib 2. Rome: Pontificio Istituto Biblico, 1952.

de Margerie, SJ, Bertrand. *An Introduction to the History of Exegesis, Volume 1: The Greek Fathers*. Translated by Leonard Maluf. Petersham, MA: Saint Bede's Publications, 1993.

McGuckin, John A. "Moses and 'The Mystery of Christ' in Cyril of Alexandria's Exegesis, Part 1." *CCR* 21.1 (2000): 24–32.

———. "Moses and 'The Mystery of Christ' in Cyril of Alexandria's Exegesis, Part 2." *CCR* 21.2 (2000): 98–114.

———. "Cyril of Alexandria: Bishop and Pastor." In *The Theology of St Cyril of Alexandria: A Critical Appreciation*, ed. Thomas G. Weinandy and Daniel A. Keating, 205–36. London: T&T Clark, 2003.

McKinion, Steven A. *Words, Imagery, and the Mystery of Christ: A Reconstruction of Cyril of Alexandria's Christology*. Leiden: Brill, 2000.

Meunier, Bernard. *Le Christ de Cyrille d'Alexandrie: L'Humanité, Le Salut, et la Question Monophysite*. Paris: Beauchesne, 1997.

O'Keefe, J. J. "Christianizing Malachi: Fifth-Century Insights from Cyril of Alexandria." *VC* 50.2 (1996): 136–58.

Peloquin, Andy. "The Exegesis of Cyril of Alexandria and Theodore of Mopsuestia: A Play in Three Acts." Unpublished paper. Western Seminary, April 2010.

Quasten, Johannes. *Patrology, Volume 3: The Golden Age of Greek Patristic Literature from the Council of Nicaea to the Council of Chalcedon*. Notre Dame, IN: Ave Maria, 1983.

Russell, Norman. *Cyril of Alexandria*. The Early Christian Fathers. Abingdon, Oxon: Routledge, 2000.

———. *The Doctrine of Deification in the Greek Patristic Tradition*. Oxford: Oxford University Press, 2004.

Weinandy, Thomas G., and Daniel A. Keating, eds. *The Theology of St Cyril of Alexandria: A Critical Appreciation*. London: T&T Clark, 2003.

Wilken, Robert L. *Judaism and the Early Christian Mind: A Study of Cyril of Alexandria's Exegesis and Theology*. New Haven, CT: Yale University Press, 1971.

———. "St. Cyril of Alexandria: Biblical Expositor." *CCR* 19.1–2 (1998): 30–41.

———. "Cyril of Alexandria as Interpreter of the Old Testament." In *The Theology of St Cyril of Alexandria: A Critical Appreciation*, ed. Thomas G. Weinandy and Daniel A. Keating, 1–21. London: T&T Clark, 2003.

———. "Cyril of Alexandria, Biblical Exegete." In *Handbook of Patristic Exegesis: The Bible in Ancient Christianity*, ed. Charles Kannengiesser, 840–69. Leiden: Brill, 2006.

Yanney, Rudolph. "Life and Work of St. Cyril of Alexandria." *CCR* 19 (1998): 17–29.

Young, Frances M. *From Nicea to Chalcedon: A Guide to the Literature and its Background*. London: SCM, 1983.

———. *Biblical Exegesis and the Formation of Christian Culture*. Peabody, MA: Hendrickson, 1997.

Zachariades-Holmberg, Evie. *Saint Cyril of Alexandria, Commentary on the Book of Exodus, First Discourse*. Patristic and Ecclesiastical Texts and Translations. Rollinsford, NH: Orthodox Research Institute, 2010.

INTRODUCTION

INTRODUCTION

Encountering Cyril of Alexandria the Exegete

Cyril of Alexandria (d. 444) has not enjoyed a favorable reputation in the English-speaking world. In *The Decline and Fall of the Roman Empire*, Edward Gibbon refers to Cyril as the "tyrant of Alexandria," describing him as a ruthless politician and dogmatician.[1] In the nineteenth century, Charles Kingsley wrote a historical novel in which he laid the blame for the massacre of Hypatia, a female philosopher in Alexandria, squarely at the feet of Cyril. Although Kingsley's "lurid rendering of the story owes more to his polemic against Edward Pusey and the Tractarian movement than to a sober assessment of the ancient sources,"[2] it was at least partly due to Kingsley's novel that Cyril's writings were omitted from a well-known series of late Victorian translations of patristic texts, the Library of Nicene and Post-Nicene Fathers.[3] Depictions of Cyril as an unscrupulous politician of questionable character continue to prevail in modern scholarly treatments of the period,[4] as well as in pop-

---

1. Edward Gibbon, *The Decline and Fall of the Roman Empire, Volume II: 395 A.D.–1185 A.D.* (New York: Modern Library, n.d.), 825.

2. Christopher Haas, *Alexandria in Late Antiquity: Topography and Social Conflict* (Baltimore: Johns Hopkins University Press, 1997), 307.

3. Andrew Louth, "Cyril of Alexandria," in *The Cambridge History of Early Christian Literature*, ed. Lewis Ayres, et al. (New York: Cambridge University Press, 2006), 353; John A. McGuckin, "Cyril of Alexandria: Bishop and Pastor," in *The Theology of St Cyril of Alexandria: A Critical Appreciation*, ed. Thomas G. Weinandy and Daniel A. Keating (New York: T & T Clark, 2003), 208 n. 9.

4. For example, in his introduction to patristic theology, Maurice Wiles describes Cyril as "unscrupulous." See *The Christian Fathers* (Oxford: Oxford University Press, 1982), 77. In a popular collection of primary texts frequently used in introductory courses on the history of Christianity, William C. Placher refers to Cyril as "[a]mbitious and scheming." See *Readings in the History*

ular accounts; a 2009 film, *Agora*, depicts Cyril as a ruthless schemer drunk with ambition.

Until relatively recently, modern English translations of Cyril focused almost entirely on his christological writings, due of course to the undeniable and pivotal role Cyril played in the development of christology during the Nestorian controversy. But however important Cyril's christological contributions, his anti-Nestorian writings comprise only a fraction of his enormous literary corpus. Had Cyril not become involved in the Nestorian controversy, it is likely that he would have been known primarily as an exegete. Of the ten volumes of J.-P. Migne's Patrologia Graeca that contain Cyril's works, a full seven volumes are devoted to works of biblical exegesis. These works include commentaries on Isaiah, the minor prophets, the gospel of John, a collection of homilies on the gospel of Luke preserved largely in Syriac, and numerous fragments of commentaries on both the Old and the New Testaments. Cyril also wrote two substantial commentaries on the Pentateuch, *De adoratione et cultu in spiritu et veritate* and the *Glaphyra*.

Before this century, the only English translations of Cyril's exegetical writings were done in the nineteenth century, and these included only a translation of his homilies on Luke[5] and a two-volume translation of his commentary on John, the first volume of which is translated so literally as to be practically unreadable.[6] In 2007, the late Robert C. Hill published the first

---

of Christian Theology, Volume 1: From its Beginnings to the Eve of the Reformation (Philadelphia: Westminster Press, 1988), 71. And in a more recent collection of primary texts, Bart Ehrman and Andrew S. Jacobs, while acknowledging Cyril to be brilliant, define him principally in terms of the violent events that occurred during the early years of his episcopacy. See *Christianity in Late Antiquity 300–450 C.E.: A Reader* (Oxford: Oxford University Press, 2004), 182. In his popular book on the history of Christianity, Diarmaid MacCulloch is more nuanced in his approach to Cyril, though he still damns Cyril with faint praise: "Cyril, though unlikely to have been a pleasant man to know, was more than simply an unscrupulous party boss." See *Christianity: The First Three Thousand Years* (New York: Viking, 2009), 224.

5. *A Commentary upon the Gospel according to S. Luke by S. Cyril, Patriarch of Alexandria*, trans. R. Payne Smith (Oxford: Oxford University Press, 1859).

6. *Commentary on the Gospel according to St. John by S. Cyril, Archbishop of Alexandria*, vol. 1, trans. P. E. Pusey (Oxford: James Parker, 1874); *Commentary on*

of three volumes of a translation of Cyril's commentary on the minor prophets,[7] and the remaining two volumes were released by 2012. In the following year (2008) he published three volumes of Cyril's commentary on Isaiah.[8] In 2013 and 2015, two volumes were published of a new translation of Cyril's commentary on John by David Maxwell.[9] Cyril's exegetical writings are therefore more accessible to a general readership than ever before, although much work remains to be done. Until now, however, there have existed no English translations of either of Cyril's commentaries on the Pentateuch. This translation of the *Glaphyra* is the first.

Broader access to Cyril's vast exegetical corpus allows for an understanding of Cyril as a theologian beyond the narrow lens of the Nestorian controversy, enabling us to see the theological ideas and concepts that animated him throughout his career, rather than just during a narrow span of time. Moreover, these texts give us a means by which to comprehend more fully the theological and societal issues of pastoral concern to Cyril as the shepherd of the church in Alexandria. They also provide us with the means by which to assess Cyril's method of exegesis, as well as to see the ways in which Cyril's theology was intertwined with his reading of scripture.

In what follows, in addition to situating the *Glaphyra* in Cyril's biographical and literary context, I will address the purpose and structure of the work, focusing particularly on what Cyril sought to draw out of the Pentateuch and why he was convinced

---

the Gospel according to St. John by S. Cyril, Archbishop of Alexandria, vol. 2, trans. Thomas Randall (London: Walter Smith, 1885).

7. *Commentary on the Twelve Prophets, Volume 1,* trans. Robert C. Hill (Washington, DC: The Catholic University of America Press, 2007); *Commentary on the Twelve Prophets, Volume 2,* trans. Robert C. Hill (Washington, DC: The Catholic University of America Press, 2008); *Commentary on the Twelve Prophets, Volume 3,* trans. Robert C. Hill (Washington, DC: The Catholic University of America Press, 2012).

8. *Commentary on Isaiah, Volume I: Chapters 1–14; Commentary on Isaiah, Volume II: Chapters 15–39; Commentary on Isaiah, Volume III: Chapters 40–50,* trans. Robert Charles Hill (Brookline, MA: Holy Cross Orthodox Press, 2008).

9. *Commentary on John, Volume 1,* trans. David Maxwell (Downers Grove, IL: InterVarsity Press, 2013); *Commentary on John, Volume 2,* trans. David Maxwell (Downers Grove, IL: InterVarsity Press, 2015).

not only that he, as a bishop, was most suited to undertake such a task but also that it was incumbent upon him to do so. I will also touch upon the most prominent theological themes and ideas articulated in the *Glaphyra*, all of which remain important themes in Cyril's corpus as a whole, and which give us a broader picture of the scope of Cyril's theology. At the same time, while the *Glaphyra* provides an important lens through which to understand Cyril's thought more fully, peppered throughout the text are deeply anti-Jewish arguments that should be troubling to modern readers. I will assess what Cyril's anti-Jewish rhetoric tells us about his understanding of Judaism and the Jewish community in Alexandria, as well as what it tells us about Jewish-Christian relations in fifth-century Alexandria.

Biography of Cyril

Born c. 378, Cyril was seven years old, the age at which children were first sent to school, when his uncle Theophilus was made archbishop of Alexandria.[10] Little is known about the specifics of Cyril's early life and education, although various attempts have been made to reconstruct his intellectual and spiritual formation on the basis of our knowledge of educational structures in the fourth and fifth centuries and from Cyril's own writings.[11] As with other children from prosperous families, both Christian and non-Christian, Cyril's primary education would have consisted of a rigorous regimen of memorization as a means of attaining literacy and proficiency in arithmetic.[12] His secondary education would have focused on the study of classical Greek literature, including Homer, Euripides, Menander, and Demosthenes.[13] After

---

10. See H. I. Marrou, *A History of Education in Antiquity*, trans. George Lamb (New York: Sheed and Ward, 1956), 142.

11. See E. R. Hardy, "The Further Education of Cyril of Alexandria (412–444): Questions and Problems," *Spirit* 17 (1982), 116–22; John A. McGuckin, *St Cyril of Alexandria: The Christological Controversy* (Crestwood, NY: St Vladimir's Seminary Press, 2004), 4; Norman Russell, *Cyril of Alexandria* (New York: Routledge, 2000), 5.

12. This process is described in Marrou, *A History of Education in Antiquity*, 150–59.

13. Russell, *Cyril of Alexandria*, 5; Marrou, *A History of Education in Antiquity*,

secondary school Cyril would have undertaken higher education in rhetoric, a key facet of higher studies at the time.[14] It is also likely that Cyril studied philosophy as part of his higher education.[15] As Robert Grant has demonstrated, however, much of his knowledge of philosophy was mediated through Christian sources, such as Eusebius of Caesarea's *Chronicon* and *Praeparatio evangelica* and Clement of Alexandria's *Protrepticus* and *Stromata*.[16] Cyril also underwent a thorough immersion in the scriptures and in the writings of the church fathers. This Cyril received through a monastic education in the desert, where he likely studied for five years between 394 and 399.[17] Here he studied the scriptures in depth; I shall have more to say about Cyril's understanding of scriptural interpretation below. Relatedly, Cyril was also exposed to the writings of church fathers, including Clement of Alexandria, Origen, Didymus the Blind (who himself died in the year when Cyril likely began his formal education),[18] the Cappadocian Fathers, Athanasius, Jerome, and John Chrysostom.[19]

161–64. For more on the classical Greek literature and Christian education, see Robert A. Kaster, *Guardians of Language: The Grammarian and Society in Late Antiquity* (Los Angeles: University of California Press, 1988), 76–81.

14. Marrou, *A History of Education in Antiquity*, 194–205.

15. Ibid., 206–16. Marrou here points out that philosophy was often a component of higher education.

16. Robert Grant, "Greek Literature in the Treatise *De Trinitate* and Cyril *Contra Julianum*," *The Journal of Theological Studies* 15 (1964): 265–99.

17. For more on this period of Cyril's life see Pierre Évieux's introduction to *Cyrille d'Alexandrie: Lettres Festales, I–VI* (Paris: Les Éditions du Cerf, 1991), 15–17. Évieux's introduction provides an excellent overview of Cyril's biography.

18. McGuckin, *Christological Controversy*, 4.

19. That Cyril expresses cordial familiarity with Chrysostom is somewhat surprising given that the former accompanied Theophilus to the Synod of the Oak in 403, a synod that deposed Chrysostom from the episcopal throne of Constantinople. For more on this synod and Cyril's involvement in it, see J. N. D. Kelly, *Golden Mouth: The Story of John Chrysostom: Ascetic, Preacher, Bishop* (Grand Rapids: Baker, 1995), 211–27, 287–88. For the influence of the other fathers listed above on Cyril's thought, particularly in terms of his exegesis of scripture, see McGuckin, *Christological Controversy*, 3; Russell, *Cyril of Alexandria*, 16; Robert Louis Wilken, "Cyril of Alexandria as Interpreter of the Old Testament," in *The Theology of St Cyril of Alexandria*, ed. Keating and Weinandy, 16; Lawrence J. Welch, *Christology and Eucharist in the Early Thought of Cyril of Alexandria* (San Francisco: Catholic Scholars Press, 1994), 10–12.

Amidst great tumult, Cyril ascended to the episcopal throne of St. Mark three days after the death of Theophilus in 412, having been groomed for the position by his uncle.[20] The first years following his elevation were stormy. He embarked on a campaign to seize Novatianist churches and played a role in the temporary expulsion of Jews from Alexandria after they attacked a group of Christians, about which I shall have more to say below. Moreover, as already mentioned, he was implicated in the mob violence that culminated in the slaying of Hypatia in 415. Opinion varies regarding Cyril's involvement in the latter two events. Socrates Scholasticus, a supporter of Nestorius and one of the historians upon whom we rely for our knowledge of these incidents, expresses strong animosity toward Cyril in his rendering.[21] That Cyril was antipathetic towards heretics, Jews, and pagans cannot be gainsaid, and that these events occurred under his tenure is indisputable. As Wickham argues, however, the picture that the facts "yield is not of a fanatical priest, hungry for power, heading a howling mob, but of an untried leader attempting, and initially failing, to master popular forces."[22] After his tumultuous election to the archbishopric in a city of numerous communal groups where outbreaks of violence were a prominent feature of everyday life,[23] Cyril may have wanted to consolidate his position and that of the church in Alexandria. Cyril's vocal opposition to heretics, Jews, and paganism in his early years might thus have been an expression of a sense of political vulnerability. Cyril appears, moreover, to have been incapable of harnessing violent expressions of this opposition among the Christian populace. The violent incidents of his early episcopacy may therefore speak more to Cyril's lack of prudence as a young archbishop than to his moral character, although I will address this point in greater detail below, particularly re-

20. The tumultuous circumstances of Cyril's election are recounted by Haas, *Alexandria in Late Antiquity*, 297–98.
21. Haas, *Alexandria in Late Antiquity*, 308; McGuckin, *Christological Controversy*, 7; Lionel Wickham, ed., *Select Letters*, Oxford Early Christian Texts (Oxford: Oxford University Press, 1983), xvi.
22. Wickham, ed., *Select Letters*, xvi.
23. See Haas, *Alexandria in Late Antiquity*, 8–12.

garding the many references Cyril makes in the *Glaphyra* to Jews and Judaism.

Despite their tumultuousness, Cyril's early episcopal years witnessed to a substantial literary output.[24] Between 412, when he was consecrated as archbishop, and 423, Cyril devoted himself to extensive exegetical work. It was during this period that he composed his two major commentaries on the Pentateuch, including the *Glaphyra*; a massive five-book commentary on Isaiah; and a commentary of similar size on the minor prophets.[25] Between 423 and 428, the year when the Nestorian controversy erupted, Cyril focused his attention on the refutation of Arianism, perhaps as a rhetorical exercise or perhaps due to the continued influence of Arianism among simpler believers in Alexandria.[26] Three substantial works emerge from this period, all devoted in large part to the doctrine of the Trinity: *Thesaurus de sancta et consubstantiali Trinitate* (written between 423 and 425), *De Trinitate Dialogi* (423–25), and *In Joannem* (425–28), a twelve-book commentary on the gospel of John. Cyril probably also began *Contra Julianum* during this period, a work written as a refutation of paganism.[27]

After 428 Cyril focused almost all his attention on Nestorianism, writing numerous letters and treatises, the largest of which was *Adversus Nestorii blasphemias*, composed during the spring of 430.[28] Political factors undoubtedly played some role in the controversy that erupted between Nestorius and Cyril. Henry Chadwick, however, has convincingly demonstrated that Cyril's concerns were primarily theological, and that he was genuinely troubled by the soteriological ramifications of Nestorius's chris-

24. For a listing of Cyril's early works see Robert L. Wilken, *Judaism and the Early Christian Mind: A Study of Cyril of Alexandria's Exegesis and Theology* (New Haven: Yale University Press, 1971), 5.

25. See Georges Jouassard, "L'activité littéraire de Saint Cyrille d'Alexandrie jusqu'à 428," in *Mélanges E. Podechard* (Lyons: Facultés Catholiques, 1945), 159–74.

26. See Russell, *Cyril of Alexandria*, 21–22.

27. See ibid. as well as Georges Jouassard, "La date des écrits antiariens de saint Cyrille d'Alexandrie," *Revue Bénédictine* 87 (1977): 172–78; Wickham, ed., *Select Letters*, xvii–xviii n. 19.

28. Russell, *Cyril of Alexandria*, 130.

tology, specifically in terms of the Eucharist.[29] What began as an exchange of polemical letters between Cyril and Nestorius, regarding whether Mary could be called *Theotokos* ("God-bearer"), developed into a full-blown christological confrontation, culminating in the Council of Ephesus in 431. While Nestorius was formally condemned by the council, it took two more years after the council before formal reconciliation occurred between Alexandria and Antioch.[30] Cyril spent the remaining years of his life clarifying his teachings (particularly for those who disagreed with his reconciliation with Antioch) and composing small treatises on such topics as christology, the Nicene Creed, and anthropology.[31] He died on June 27, 444, leaving behind a tremendous corpus of writings.

The Purpose and Structure of the Glaphyra

Cyril wrote two large commentaries on the Pentateuch. The first, to which he makes brief reference in the *Glaphyra*, is *De adoratione et cultu in spiritu et veritate*. Unlike Cyril's other exegetical works, including the *Glaphyra*, *De adoratione* is not a verse-by-verse commentary, but is written in a dialogical form and is arranged around broad themes.[32] The *Glaphyra* is a much different work

29. Henry Chadwick, "Eucharist and Christology in the Nestorian Controversy," *The Journal of Theological Studies*, NS 2 (1951): 145–61. See also Wickham, ed., *Select Letters*, xix–xxviii; McGuckin, *Christological Controversy*, 21: "In the great conflict that was now to unfold, the issues cannot be reduced merely to the level of personality clashes, or even to the complex issue of the precedence of sees, or the involved political machinations of the imperial court ... for what was about to clash was no less than two great schools of ecclesiastical reflection, piety, and discourse."

30. For an in-depth account of the Nestorian crisis, see McGuckin, *Christological Controversy*, 20–125; Russell, *Cyril of Alexandria*, 31–58. See also Rodolph Yanney, "Life and Work of Saint Cyril of Alexandria," *Coptic Church Review* 19 (1998): 24–26.

31. Russell, *Cyril of Alexandria*, 56–58.

32. See Wilken, *Judaism and the Early Christian Mind*, 69, for a list of themes in *De adoratione*. For more on the purpose and structure of *De adoratione*, see Mark W. Elliott, "What Cyril of Alexandria's *De Adoratione* is All About," *Studia Patristica* 50 (2011): 245–52, and Matthew R. Crawford, "The Preface and Subject Matter of Cyril of Alexandria's *De Adoratione*," *The Journal of Theological Studies*, NS 64.1 (2013): 154–67.

from *De adoratione*, as Cyril himself acknowledges in book 8 when commenting on how his treatment of Exodus differs from that which he had provided in *De adoratione*:

> For, if God wills and grants the wisdom, we will now deal with the sections in Exodus which can be seen to have been omitted when we composed our moral exhortation [*De adoratione*]. It was then thought best to avoid lengthy discourse, as we wanted to show how we are to understand the manner of worship in spirit and in truth. For having delineated each of the sections that comprise the five books of Moses, and having first carefully considered the matter in them intended for our contemplation, we conveniently gathered together those things in some way necessary for moral guidance and things that were especially profitable, in what I would say was the most appropriate order for each matter. Yet those things by means of which the mystery of Christ seems to some degree to be depicted in advance, albeit in shadows relating to the law, we reserved for the work to be written later [the *Glaphyra*].[33]

The primary focus of *De adoratione* was not specifically doctrinal, though he does not ignore doctrine in this work. Rather, as Cyril writes, his focus was on deriving moral guidance from the Pentateuch. The *Glaphyra* is different in that Cyril is focused specifically on drawing out "the mystery of Christ" hidden in the text.

Cyril's exegetical method and style have been the subject of numerous studies, particularly in relation to his interpretation of the Hebrew scriptures.[34] My purpose here is simply to high-

---

33. PG 69: 385B–388A. All translations from the *Glaphyra* are by Nicholas Lunn. All references to the text will be to Migne's Patrologia Graeca.

34. One of the best and most recent treatments of Cyril's understanding of scripture is Matthew R. Crawford's book, *Cyril of Alexandria's Trinitarian Theology of Scripture* (Oxford: Oxford University Press, 2014). Other treatments of Cyril's exegesis of the Old Testament include Alexander Kerrigan, *St Cyril of Alexandria: Interpreter of the Old Testament* (Rome: Pontificio Istituto Biblico, 1952); Robert Wilken, *Judaism and the Early Christian Mind;* Bertrand de Margerie, "L'exégèse christologique de saint Cyrille d'Alexandrie," *Nouvelle Revue de Théologie* 102 (1980): 400–435; Robert L. Wilken, "St. Cyril of Alexandria: The Mystery of Christ in the Bible," *Pro Ecclesia* 4 (1995): 454–78; John J. O'Keefe, "Christianizing Malachi: Fifth-Century Insights from Cyril of Alexandria," *Vigiliae Christianae* 50.2 (1996): 136–58; John A. McGuckin, "Moses and the Mystery of Christ in Cyril of Alexandria's Exegesis, Part I," *Coptic Church Review* 21.1 (2000): 24–32; idem, "Moses and the Mystery of Christ in Cyril of Alexandria's Exegesis, Part II," *Coptic Church Review* 21.2 (2000): 98–114; J. David Cassel, "Key principles in Cyril of Alexandria's exegesis," *Studia Patristica* 37

light key facets of how Cyril goes about interpreting the Pentateuch in the *Glaphyra*. As is the case in most of his Old Testament commentaries, Cyril's focus in the *Glaphyra* is on what he refers to as the spiritual meaning of the text, which he contrasts with the literal meaning of the text. This does not mean, as we shall see, that Cyril neglects the literal sense of the text as unimportant. Rather, Cyril is convinced that, above and beyond the literal sense of scripture is a higher sense, a spiritual sense. Matthew Crawford points out that "Cyril displays a remarkable consistency in describing the higher sense of Scripture as 'spiritual,'" and the word he uses most frequently to denote the spiritual sense is θεωρία, sometimes pairing it with an adjective, such as in the phrase θεωρία πνευματική.[35] We see Cyril using such terminology in the *Glaphyra* with regularity when describing the spiritual sense.[36] For example, referring to what he hopes to accomplish in his exploration of the story of Noah, Cyril writes: "Come then, and let us describe, as we are able, each detail concerning him, refining the earthiness of the literal sense and skillfully transforming the things that occurred visibly into matter for spiritual contemplation [θεωρίαν τὴν πνευματικὴν]."[37] For Cyril, this spiritual sense always points to the mystery of Christ.[38] Again, with

---

(2001): 413–20; Robert L. Wilken, "Cyril of Alexandria as Interpreter of the Old Testament," in *The Theology of St Cyril of Alexandria*, ed. Weinandy and Keating, 1–21; Matthew R. Crawford, "Scripture as 'One Book': Origen, Jerome, and Cyril of Alexandria on Isaiah 29:11," *The Journal of Theological Studies*, NS 64.1 (2013): 137–53. The late Robert C. Hill's introductions to his translations of Cyril's *Commentary on the Twelve Prophets* and his *Commentary on Isaiah* are also helpful; references are in nn. 7–8, above. See especially "Introduction," in *St. Cyril of Alexandria: Commentary on the Twelve Prophets, Volume 1*, 2–22, and "Introduction," in *Cyril of Alexandria: Commentary on Isaiah, Volume I: Chapters 1–14*, 1–14. The most thorough survey of biblical exegesis during the patristic period as a whole is Frances M. Young, *Biblical Exegesis and the Formation of Christian Culture* (Cambridge: Cambridge University Press, 1997).

35. Crawford, *Cyril of Alexandria's Trinitarian Theology of Scripture*, 217. This point is also made by Kerrigan, *St Cyril of Alexandria: Interpreter*, 112–15, and by de Margerie, "L'exégèse christologique," 401.

36. For example, see PG 69: 149B; PG 69: 181B; PG 69: 293B; PG 69: 664D.

37. PG 69: 49C.

38. de Margerie, "L'exégèse christologique," 401; Crawford, *Cyril of Alexandria's Trinitarian Theology of Scripture*, 220–21; O'Keefe, "Christianizing Malachi," 140–41; Robert L. Wilken, "St. Cyril of Alexandria: The Mystery of Christ in the

reference to the story of Noah, Cyril writes: "So let us now go over the things that have been said to bring out the hidden, inner, spiritual meaning [θεωρίαν], and let us trace out the mystery of Christ and present Noah himself and the ingenious and mysterious arrangement relating to the ark as a picture of the salvation that comes through Christ."[39]

Therefore, when Cyril refers to "the extraordinary beauty of the spiritual contemplation (θεωρίας),"[40] he means the beauty of the text when interpreted christologically. According to Cyril, this deeper christological meaning of the text is hidden within the literal sense of the texts. "This can be likened," he writes, "to the most fragrant flowers in the meadows, which are wrapped around with ordinary leaves on the outside. If one cuts them open, he will find and lay bare what is good and profitable."[41] Christ is to be found on almost every page of the law. He is the pearl hidden in the text,[42] although to the one who looks carefully, Christ is found everywhere: "It is the intent of inspired Scripture to indicate to us the mystery of Christ through innumerable objects. Someone might compare it to a magnificent and illustrious city which does not have just one image of its king, but very many, set up everywhere and visible to all."[43]

As can be seen, the spiritual sense is for Cyril the primary and most important sense for understanding the true meaning of the scriptures. Cyril, however, does not disregard the literal meaning of the text in the *Glaphyra*, but devotes extensive attention to it, acknowledging that not everything in the scriptures can or should be interpreted spiritually. "One should realize," Cyril writes in book 4, "that some things that happened at the literal level are just as they are in themselves."[44] And even for those passages in the scriptures that do lend themselves to a spiritual interpretation, Cyril is still at pains to provide a careful explanation

---

Bible," 459; McGuckin, "Moses and 'The Mystery of Christ' in Cyril of Alexandria's Exegesis, Part 1," 25.

39. PG 69: 60A. See also PG 69: 149B.
40. PG 69: 293B.
41. PG 69: 140A.
42. PG 69: 13A.
43. PG 69: 308C.
44. PG 69: 192B. See also O'Keefe, "Christianizing Malachi," 138–39.

of the literal meaning of the text before proceeding to a spiritual exegesis. In his *Commentary on Isaiah*, Cyril explains why it is that he devotes such attention to the literal meaning. Acknowledging the preeminence of the spiritual over the literal, Cyril nevertheless argues that a true understanding of the spiritual sense can occur only through careful examination of the literal meaning first: "I say that those who wish to make clear the subtle and hidden breath of spiritual insights must hasten to consider thoroughly, with the eye of the mind, especially, on the one hand, the exact literal meaning [τῆς ἱστορίας τὸ ἀκριβές] and, on the other hand, the interpretation resulting from spiritual contemplation [τῆς πνευματικῆς θεωρίας]."[45] Cyril makes a similar comment at the beginning of the *Glaphyra* while explaining his methodology: "Now we shall first present the literal events in a helpful way, making them suitably clear. Then, refashioning the narrative by bringing it out of type and shadow, we shall explain it with reference to the mystery of Christ, having him as the goal, since it is true that Christ is the end of the law and the prophets."[46] In order to comprehend the deeper meaning of the text, in order to be able to draw out the christological nuances present in the scripture, it is necessary to have a thorough understanding of the literal level itself.[47] Thus, one will find in the *Glaphyra* that Cyril always follows the same method when going through the text. He first provides an explanation of the literal meaning of the passage under question, and only after doing so does he delve into the spiritual meaning of the text.

---

45. PG 70: 9A. This is a slight modification of the translation provided in O'Keefe, "Christianizing Malachi," 139.

46. PG 69: 16A.

47. Drawing on Frances Young's work, John J. O'Keefe argues that the exegetical methods of the ancient grammatical schools were an influence on Cyril's approach to exegeting scriptures, as they were an influence on the Antiochene approach. The grammatical method involved a number of steps—checking the accuracy of the text as well as examining difficult names and historical details—before delving more deeply into the meaning of the text. See O'Keefe, "Christianizing Malachi," 138–39, and Frances Young, "The Rhetorical Schools and their Influence on Patristic Exegesis," in *The Making of Orthodoxy: Essays in Honour of Henry Chadwick,* ed. Rowan Williams (Cambridge: Cambridge University Press, 1989), 182–99.

The Bishop as Exegete and Enlightener

Divine assistance, however, is necessary if one is to comprehend this spiritual meaning. This point Cyril makes in the *Glaphyra* while commenting on Exodus 34.33–34, which refers to the veil that Moses put on in the presence of the Israelites to obscure the radiance of his face but that he removed when entering the presence of God. Cyril, reading the text spiritually, interprets this event as follows:

> For the law contains a shadow, the earthiness of the letter, and the not very great brightness of the literal sense. When, however, he entered into the presence of God, it says that Moses removed the veil. This same thing we find also to be true with respect to our own selves. For when we have been brought, as it were, into the presence of God the Father, being led there by Christ, we will see the glory of Moses without any obscuring shadows, as we will understand the law spiritually, for "we are being transformed from one degree of glory to another," as it is written.[48]

To understand the law spiritually, we need to be transformed spiritually, brought into relationship with God the Father through Christ himself. And for this to occur, we must be transformed by the Holy Spirit, given to Christians through Christ. In his recent book on Cyril's exegesis, Matthew Crawford demonstrates that Cyril understands the divine life to be communicated in and through the scriptures. That is to say, for Cyril exegesis is inseparable from transformative contemplation of the Son revealed in the scriptures: "[T]he practice of exegesis results in growth in virtue and understanding of the Christological mystery. In other words, exegesis takes place in the Spirit, proceeds through contemplation of the Son, and leads ultimately to the Father."[49] The goal of exegesis is the Spirit-led vision of Christ in the scripture, through which one ultimately beholds the Father.[50] Crawford argues that Cyril's theology of scriptural exegesis has a close correlation to his sacramental theology in that, just as believers are brought into transforma-

---

48. PG 69: 537B. See n. 33 above. Also *Glaphyra*, vol. 2, trans. Lunn (forthcoming).
49. Crawford, *Cyril of Alexandria's Trinitarian Theology of Scripture*, 183–84.
50. Ibid., 229.

tive immediacy with the Spirit and the Son through baptism and the Eucharist, so the scriptures bring us to an analogous participation in the divine life. Exegesis can thus bring one to a "Spirit-enabled contemplation of the Son in scripture, by which believers are led onwards to a vision of the Father."[51]

According to Cyril, the ability to contemplate the Son in the scriptures, to comprehend the mystery of Christ, is given to all who possess the Spirit. But it is a gift particularly given to those who guide the church, the bishops. As successors to the apostles, bishops are elucidators of the scriptures, drawing out the mystery of Christ in the scriptures for those under their care. This point Cyril makes in the *Glaphyra* both with reference to the apostles themselves and to bishops as their successors. In a number of places in the *Glaphyra*, Cyril refers to the disciples' reception of the Holy Spirit. Their reception of the Holy Spirit is significant both because they became the first fruits of a renewed and transformed humanity through the Holy Spirit and because, through the Spirit, they became enlightened so as to interpret the scriptures christologically. Cyril describes this enlightenment as follows:

For when Christ was raised to life from the dead, having trampled down death and plundered Hades, "saying to those in bonds, 'Come out,' and to those in darkness, 'Show yourselves,'" [Is 49.9] and then beautifying human nature by the Holy Spirit as the firstfruits of the human race and of those being restored to holiness, he breathed upon the apostles and said, "Receive the Holy Spirit" [Jn 20.22]. Then the eyes of our minds were opened, and then we were enlightened, and we came to understand the law that had remained obscure since ancient times, that which had been unknown to any of those of old. We were also then gathered together from the corners of the earth to the place he chose, which is the church, and for us who have come to that place, the elected sacred instructors and teachers interpret the law with its types and shadows.[52]

Here we see Cyril describe the disciples as enlighteners, capable through the Holy Spirit of reading the law christologically. Notably, Cyril also includes the bishops among those whose eyes were opened and who are now teachers of mysteries. Cyril understands that he and his fellow bishops participate in the enlightenment of the Holy Spirit in an analogous manner as

51. Ibid., 4.
52. PG 69: 676C–D.

did the disciples, and that his primary task as a bishop is to teach the flock to understand clearly the christological meaning of the law, a meaning "expressed in types and shadows."[53]

He expresses similar ideas elsewhere in the *Glaphyra*. In book 7, commenting on Genesis 49.20, which he reads as "Asher's bread is rich, and he will provide food for rulers," Cyril discusses the role of bishops as teachers. He uses the reference to bread in this verse to talk about the "life-giving bread" that is particularly given to bishops who teach their flock. Christ feeds the leaders of his flock on earth with food of a spiritual nature, namely, "the revelation of divine mysteries and the knowledge of all virtue."[54] The reason why these leaders are fed in this way is in order that they themselves might "feed those people under their authority with teachings that lead to life."[55] These teachings, as Cyril has made clear, are christological in nature, so his reference here is to the role the bishops play in opening up the christological import of the scriptures to their flock. Indeed, Cyril directly connects the work of the bishops to that done by the Spirit-filled apostles: "We shall find the teachers of the churches engaged in this task [the task of teaching], and before them the holy apostles especially did so."[56] And both the apostles and the bishops are able to do this through the "provisions granted through the Spirit."[57]

One other passage from the *Glaphyra* is worth noting as a way of demonstrating the emphasis Cyril places on the bishops as interpreters of the scriptures. He uses the story of Jacob as a shepherd caring for Laban's flocks as a springboard for expounding on the disciples and later on the bishops as shepherds of those belonging to the church, focusing particularly on the importance of interpreting the scriptures christologically. He points first to the disciples, who through the Holy Spirit became "spiritual shepherds, skilled in divine instruction."[58] This divine instruction revolved around the scriptures, as Cyril makes clear when referring to those whom the disciples appointed as shepherds in their stead:

53. Ibid.
54. PG 69: 369A.
55. Ibid.
56. Ibid.
57. PG 69: 369B.
58. PG 69: 197A.

So passing through each land and town, they appointed countless other shepherds to lead the people and to care for the spiritual sheep, to feed them, as it were, in good pasture, in a fertile place, and to bring them to the most wonderful grass, namely, the inspired Scripture. For the word of God is life-giving food for the soul.[59]

As the section proceeds, Cyril focuses more attention on the central role scriptural interpretation plays in a bishop's leadership. Pointing to the text from Genesis, Cyril notes that a very heavy stone was placed over a well and only Jacob was able to lift it to allow for others to drink from the waters. Similarly, the Jewish scriptures are covered with a heavy stone that leads most to be unable to drink from the life-giving water embedded in the text. This is why it is so important that the bishops lift this stone: "So much labor and sweat are necessary on the part of those tending the spiritual flocks in order to take the word out from its obscurity, to draw it from the depths, as it were, and bring it up into the open, and so to set it forth clearly for the life-giving benefit of their listeners."[60]

Cyril's emphasis in the *Glaphyra* and elsewhere on the absolute importance of comprehending the christological import of the Hebrew scriptures, and particularly on the role bishops play in aiding their flocks to see and understand the deeper meaning of the scriptures,[61] goes some way to explaining why Cyril devoted himself so thoroughly to the task of writing this commentary on the Pentateuch, and explains further why he devoted so much of his literary output to scriptural interpretation. Cyril is convinced that a tremendous amount rides on how the Hebrew scriptures are interpreted, arguing that the disciples were themselves given the Holy Spirit in John 20 specifically so that they could attain to an understanding of the christological meaning of those scriptures. And that which the disciples were called to do has passed to the bishops themselves, whose primary job, according to Cyril,

---

59. PG 69: 197B.
60. PG 69: 200A–B.
61. For more on the emphasis Cyril placed on the role of bishops in the proper interpretation of scripture see Crawford, *Cyril of Alexandria's Trinitarian Theology of Scripture*, 96–103, 160–73, 197–98; Bertrand de Margerie, "L'exégèse christologique de saint Cyrille d'Alexandrie," 403–5; Gregory K. Hillis, "The Holy Spirit and Episcopal Teaching Authority according to Cyril of Alexandria," *Theoforum* 40.3 (2009): 187–208.

is to draw out the christological nuances of those scriptures, nuances that are denied by the Jews and not immediately seen by the faithful. It is indeed likely that Cyril wrote this commentary, as well as his other commentaries on scripture, primarily to educate and train clergy in the proper interpretation of scripture.[62]

The Glaphyra *and Jewish-Christian Relations in Alexandria*

In addition to providing a means by which to understand Cyril's theology of scriptural interpretation as well as a means to examine Cyril's theology beyond the narrow confines of the Nestorian controversy, the *Glaphyra* gives us a glimpse into the tumultuous relationship between Jews and Christians in Alexandria in the fifth century. As already noted, Cyril's focus in the *Glaphyra* is on elucidating the christological meaning of the scriptures, and as shall be seen, Cyril's focus on discovering Christ in the Pentateuch leads him to expound on christology, pneumatology, and soteriology in ways that should be of interest to those wanting to know more about the development of Cyril's theology beyond the narrow confines of his specifically doctrinal works. His emphasis, however, on discovering Christ in the text also comes with pronounced denunciation of Jews, who, to Cyril's mind, obstinately refuse to recognize Christ in their own scriptures. Peppered throughout the *Glaphyra*, therefore, are screeds against the Jews and their (alleged) ignorance. For just as Cyril is able to locate Christ in the letter of the law, so he is able also to find evidence for what he perceives to be the ultimate downfall of the Jews for their rejection of Christ.

An unfortunately typical example of this can be found in Cyril's interpretation of Joseph's treatment at the hands of his brothers. Consistent with his methodology, Cyril first provides for the reader an account of the literal meaning of the text, but delves more deeply into it to draw out the spiritual meaning. According to Cyril, therefore, the tale of Joseph points to the treat-

62. See J. David Cassel, "Cyril of Alexandria as Educator," in *In Dominico Eloquio—In Lordly Eloquence: Essays on Patristic Exegesis in Honor of Robert Louis Wilken,* ed. Paul M. Blowers, Angela Russell Christman, David G. Hunter, and Robin Darling Young (Grand Rapids: Eerdmans, 2002), 348–68.

ment Jesus himself would receive at the hands of the Jews. Just as Joseph's brothers took offense to notions that Joseph would one day rule over them, the "Jews too were incited and not a little vexed when they learned that Emmanuel would be superior to the holy patriarchs themselves."[63] Therefore, Cyril writes that the Jews showed "cruel and unrestrained envy" of Christ and so became "intolerable and murderous."[64] Consequently, "those wretched men killed [Christ] and, as it were, put him into a pit—the deep, dark pit of death, which is Hades."[65]

These words are not easy to read, reflecting as they do an often-expressed animosity towards Jews in the *Glaphyra*. Cyril accuses the Jews of killing Christ and argues that they are ignorant,[66] stupid,[67] and spiritually lame,[68] utterly incapable of reading and understanding their own scriptures.[69] Whatever may be the benefits of reading Cyril's christological interpretations of the Pentateuch for understanding his theology and biblical hermeneutics, we also have to reckon with the pervasive anti-Jewish rhetoric found throughout the pages of the *Glaphyra*. In his introduction to the English translation of Cyril's *Festal Letters*, John O'Keefe endeavors to explain the anti-Jewish venom present in those letters, arguing that this rhetoric needs to be read in the context of the cultural and theological battles being waged in fifth-century Alexandria between Christians and Jews. For Christians, this rhetoric emerged out of the fundamental question as to why vibrant Jewish communities continue to exist after the coming of the Messiah.[70] Given that Christians had appropriated the Jewish scriptures for themselves, they found themselves having to make sense of these texts given the continued presence of Jewish communities that interpreted those

63. PG 69: 304A.
64. PG 69: 304B.
65. PG 69: 305B.
66. PG 69: 456A–D.
67. PG 69: 80A.
68. PG 69: 272B–D.
69. PG 69: 41B–D; 533B–C.
70. John J. O'Keefe, "Introduction," in *St. Cyril of Alexandria: Festal Letters 1–12*, trans. Philip R. Amidon (Washington, DC: The Catholic University of America Press, 2009), 20.

texts very differently.[71] In Alexandria this battle was particularly intense, partly because it was only in the fifth century that Christians began outnumbering Jews in the general population.[72]

The *Glaphyra* was written during the tumultuous years of Cyril's early episcopacy, which witnessed to a prominent conflict between Cyril and the Alexandrian Jewish community, leading to the purported expulsion of Jews from Alexandria. The details of this conflict, recounted by the historian Socrates in his *Historia ecclesiastica*, need not occupy us here.[73] It suffices to say that, after a particularly violent event—apparently a group of Jews tricked Christians into believing that their church was on fire and then attacked them when they came out of their homes—Socrates writes that Cyril gathered a large group of Christians to drive Jews from their synagogues and homes, plundering them of their possessions. There are reasons to think that Socrates exaggerated the scope of the Jewish expulsion from Alexandria. It is unlikely, even impossible, that Cyril would have been able to expel most of the Jewish population from Alexandria. Not only would this have been logistically difficult to accomplish, but an expulsion of the Jewish population would have had devastating economic ramifications on Alexandria. Nevertheless, there is no reason to doubt the basic outline of Socrates's story, which tells us that Cyril had direct contact with the Jewish population and that clashes, even violent clashes, marked the relationship between the Christian and Jewish communities of Alexandria.

If we take this tumultuous relationship into account, Cyril's anti-Jewish rhetoric in the *Glaphyra* takes on a somewhat different light. Given that Jews and Christians were in open conflict in Alexandria, it is unsurprising, albeit regretful, that Cyril's commentary on the Pentateuch would contain venom. Whatever may be the cultural reasons for Jewish-Christian conflict, the theological reasons revolved principally around the person of Jesus Christ and, relatedly, around how to interpret the Jews' own scriptures. From Cyril's perspective, as we will see, Christ is

71. Ibid., 21
72. Ibid., 21–22.
73. See Wilken, *Judaism and the Early Christian Mind*, 54–58, for a detailed account and analysis of this conflict.

present on each page of the Hebrew scriptures, available to be seen by any who partake of the Holy Spirit bestowed by Christ himself. That the Jews fail to see Christ in their very own scriptures is an endless source of bafflement and frustration to Cyril, which he continually expresses in his commentary on those scriptures. That the Jews fail to see what is, to him, so clear indicates for Cyril a tremendous failure on the part of the Jews. And given the constant fighting between Christians and Jews in Alexandria, Cyril wastes no opportunities in his commentary to assert Christian superiority over Jews in the interpretation of the Jewish community's very own scriptures.

This was a rhetorically effective move for Cyril to make in the context of Jewish-Christian animosity. But this rhetorical advantage is gained by using language that, read through the prism of centuries of Christian anti-Semitism culminating in the Holocaust, is troubling. The ferocity of his venom demonstrates an animosity toward Jews and Judaism that is without excuse regardless of the context. At the same time, I would be remiss were I not also to direct attention to the many references Cyril makes in the *Glaphyra* to the ultimate salvation of the Jews. In due course, Cyril writes, the Jews "will repent and be accepted. They will obtain mercy from the Father above, as they acknowledge the Savior and Redeemer of all. This too the sacred Scripture reveals."[74] While he holds nothing back in his anti-Jewish vitriol, Cyril still looks forward to the ultimate salvation of those whom he attacks, a salvation promised in scripture. This does not excuse his anti-Jewish rhetoric, but it does contextualize that rhetoric more fully. Regardless of his animosity toward the Jews in Alexandria and elsewhere, Cyril acknowledges, without reluctance and on the basis of scripture, that God's plan of salvation ultimately includes those with whom God originally made a covenant.

Cyril's anti-Jewish rhetoric suggests that the *Glaphyra* emerged, at least in part, in response to Jewish-Christian conflict in Alexandria. That said, Cyril's purpose for the *Glaphyra* cannot and

---

74. PG 69: 136A. See also 261A–C and 324D–325C. For more on this facet of Cyril's theology, see Daniel Keating, "Supersessionism in Cyril of Alexandria," *Studia Patristica* 68 (2013): 122–23.

should not be limited solely to his anti-Jewish agenda. Central to Cyril's task as exegete is to appropriate the Pentateuch for the church, that is, to assert that the Hebrew scriptures are, first and foremost, *Christian* scriptures to be interpreted and understood christologically, and his anti-Jewish rhetoric is born in part out of this purpose. At the same time, we should not forget that Cyril took his role as elucidator of scriptural mysteries seriously. Cyril's primary focus is thus on breaking open the nuances of the spiritual sense of scripture for his flock so that they might contemplate the Son fully in the text. Cyril's purpose in the *Glaphyra* is ultimately pedagogical and pastoral.

Theological Themes in the Glaphyra

Cyril's focus on the specifically Christian content of the Pentateuch necessarily leads him to develop and expound upon theological ideas and themes. While many of these are more thoroughly developed in later writings, their presence in the *Glaphyra* demonstrates that the theological concerns he had later in his career were already in his mind at an early date. I want to focus some attention on a few of these ideas and themes as a means not only of introducing the reader to Cyril's early theology, but also of demonstrating that Cyril took with great seriousness his task of enlightening his flock theologically. I will first examine Cyril's christology in the *Glaphyra*, focusing particularly on his account of Christ as the Second Adam, as well as his treatment of the relationship between the human and the divine in Christ. I will then devote some space to his pneumatology, which is a neglected facet of Cyril's thought and one that merits more thorough attention. Again, although his pneumatology is more thoroughly developed in later works, particularly in his *Dialogues on the Trinity* and *Commentary on John*, already in the *Glaphyra* the Spirit figures prominently. Finally, and related to both his christology and pneumatology, I will examine Cyril's soteriology as articulated throughout the *Glaphyra*, paying particular attention to his frequent references to 2 Peter 1.4 and his emphasis on salvation as divine filiation through the Spirit, who conforms us to the likeness of the Son.

Jesus Christ as the Second Adam

In his *Judaism and the Early Christian Mind*, as well as in numerous articles, Robert Wilken demonstrated that Cyril frequently appeals to the Pauline notion of Christ as the Second Adam in his interpretation of both the Hebrew Scriptures and the New Testament. For example, when faced with the complicated task of interpreting Jesus Christ's baptismal reception of the Holy Spirit in a manner that preserved christological orthodoxy—that is, by interpreting it so as to emphasize that Christ received the Holy Spirit without actually needing the Spirit, given his divine unity with the Third Person—Cyril argues in his *Commentary on John* and elsewhere that Christ received the Spirit as the Second Adam. The first Adam received the Spirit when God breathed his Spirit upon him (Genesis 2.7).[75] Adam, however, lost it through sin, and because of this, the Son of God became human in order to be for us the Second Adam who could receive the Spirit as the sinless one and therefore preserve the Spirit's indwelling in humanity for our sake.[76]

We see Cyril similarly appeal to Christ as the Second Adam in his interpretation of Christ's conception through the Holy Spirit. Faced with the question of why Jesus was conceived by the power of the Holy Spirit, Cyril chooses to interpret this event soteriologically, arguing that he was conceived through the Spirit not for his own sake but for ours. As he writes in *On the Unity of Christ*, a work written near the end of his life, Christ was conceived by the power of the Spirit in order that we too shall be-

---

75. For an account of the anthropological and pneumatological weight Cyril rests on Genesis 2.7, see Marie-Odile Boulnois, "Le souffle et l'Esprit: Exégèses patristiques de l'insufflation originelle de Gn 2, 7 en lien avec celle de Jn 20, 20," in *RA* 24 (1989): 3–37.

76. Cyril offers this interpretation of Christ's baptismal reception of the Spirit in numerous places, but most prominently in his exegesis of John 1.32–33 in his *Commentary on John*. For an English translation of this passage of exegesis, see *Cyril of Alexandria: Commentary on John, Volume 1*, trans. Maxwell, 77–85. For more on Cyril's interpretation of Christ's baptism, see Daniel A. Keating, "The Baptism of Jesus in Cyril of Alexandria: The Re-Creation of the Human Race," *Pro Ecclesia* 8 (1999): 201–22; Robert L. Wilken, "The Interpretation of the Baptism of Jesus in the Later Fathers," *Studia Patristica* 11 (1967): 268–77; idem, *Judaism and the Early Christian Mind*, 127–42.

come born of the Spirit because in him [Christ] human nature attained this state first.[77]

The Second Adam typology thus provides for Cyril a way in which he could interpret potentially problematic New Testament texts in a christologically orthodox manner. But the typology does more than that for Cyril. It is at the heart of the way in which he characterizes the meaning and purpose of the Incarnation throughout his entire corpus, and is central to his soteriology. In the *Glaphyra* we see that the typology of Christ as the Second Adam was a prominent theme for Cyril early in his writing career. Perhaps predictably, this typology emerges in the very first book of the *Glaphyra* with reference to the first Adam and the fall of humanity in a subsection entitled "Concerning Adam." Cyril sets the tone of his treatment of Adam by immediately referring to Ephesians 1.9–10, focusing particularly on God's promise "to gather up all things in [Christ], things in heaven and things on earth." Cyril understands this verse to refer to the "recapitulation" of all things, by which he means the restoration of all things to what they were at the beginning. This for Cyril is a central component of his soteriology, characterizing human salvation primarily in terms of a retrieval of that which Adam possessed when he was created.[78] For Cyril, the Son of God became incarnate in order that humanity might regain its original created state. "For in Christ," he writes, "we have been transformed and have become a new creation."[79]

Given that human salvation is for Cyril a return to our original state of being, he proceeds to "examine the old state of affairs."[80] Cyril points specifically to Genesis 2.7 as being central to

77. See *Cyril of Alexandria: On the Unity of Christ*, trans. John A. McGuckin (Crestwood, NY: St Vladimir's Seminary Press, 2000), 62–63. For more on Cyril's interpretation of the Spirit's role in Christ's conception, see Gregory K. Hillis, "New Birth through the Second Adam: The Holy Spirit and the Miraculous Conception in Cyril of Alexandria," *Studia Patristica* 48 (2010): 47–51.

78. See Robert L. Wilken, "Exegesis and the History of Theology: Reflections on the Adam-Christ Typology in Cyril of Alexandria," *Church History* 35 (1966): 142–43, and (1971): 93–142. See also Walter J. Burghardt, *The Image of God in Man according to Cyril of Alexandria* (Washington, DC: The Catholic University of America Press, 1957), 160–65.

79. PG 69: 16D.
80. PG 69: 17A.

human creation, interpreting the "breath of life" to be the Holy Spirit.[81] We were created to partake of the Holy Spirit, to have unity with God through the Spirit. As such, humanity "was the image of the highest glory."[82] But humanity, endowed with free will, fell into sin, and Cyril describes the consequences of this fall primarily in terms of death and mortality. Cyril, however, emphasizes that humanity's fall was not absolute, for God intended to renew humanity:

> Yet the living creature was not consigned to complete destruction, but rather to renewal and, if we might say it thus, to a refashioning in the same way that a vessel which has been smashed is later made whole. That in the meantime the living creature would in fact experience corruption, the Maker was not unaware, but he well knew that together with this there would be deliverance from those things that were improper and the removal of corruption, as well as the return to a better state and the restoration of those good things that were there in the beginning.[83]

Here Cyril posits that God intended to return humanity to its original state, but, more than that, to bring humanity to an even better state than it had at its beginning.

This God did through Christ, and to describe how Christ accomplished this, Cyril appeals to Christ as the Second Adam. He writes:

> So, as the image of the first man taken from the ground was imprinted upon us, which had to suffer death and be ensnared in the cords of corruption, thus also in the case of our second beginning after that first one, that is to say, Christ, in whose likeness we are made through the Spirit, incorruptible nature is impressed upon us.[84]

Thus, Cyril writes one paragraph later, Christ has "become a second Adam for us."[85] Just as we experienced death in and through the first Adam, so we attain to incorruptibility in and through the Second Adam, who becomes for humankind a new beginning. In this way, the story of humanity's creation in Genesis provides for us a representation of the mystery of Christ: "For Adam was the beginning of the race, with respect to death,

81. PG 69: 20B–C.
82. PG 69: 20C.
83. PG 69: 24D–25A.
84. PG 69: 28D.
85. PG 69: 29B.

the curse, and condemnation. But Christ was the complete reverse, bringing life, blessing, and justification."[86] By using Second Adam typology, Cyril effectively "Christianizes" the story of human creation, using the Genesis account to elaborate on the salvation made possible through Christ.

Another example suffices to demonstrate the prevalence of Second Adam typology in the *Glaphyra*. In book 3, he interprets the blessing Isaac gave to Jacob by using the typology of Christ as the Second Adam, arguing that the blessing bestowed upon Jacob was not fulfilled in Jacob but was wholly fulfilled in Christ as the Second Adam: "[Christ] is also considered to be a second Adam, and he was born as a second root of humanity. For what is in Christ is a new creation, and we are renewed in him for sanctification, incorruption, and life."[87] To illustrate this point, Cyril hearkens to Isaac's comment that Jacob smells like a "full-grown field," and he proceeds to interpret this with reference to Christ:

> The words of the blessing, I believe, denote the spiritual aroma in Christ, like that of a field or a meadow blooming abundantly, spreading a beautiful and pleasant fragrance from its spring flowers. So Christ described himself to us in the Song of Songs, saying, "I am a flower of the plain, a lily of the valleys." [Song 2.1] He was, indeed, a lily and a rose sprung up from the earth, for the sake of humankind. Since he knew no sin, he was the most Godlike of those inhabiting the whole world, bringing forth a pleasing aroma through the perfection of his deeds. Therefore, it likens Christ to a field blessed by God, and rightly so, as he is the fragrance of the knowledge of God the Father.[88]

Using the typology of Christ as the Second Adam, Cyril takes the original text about Isaac's blessing of Jacob, and transforms it to become an explicitly Christian text with an explicitly Christian interpretation. The blessing was not actually about Jacob; its actual meaning revolves around Jesus Christ and the salvation made possible through him.

Emphasis on Christ as the Second Adam is prevalent in the *Glaphyra*. Apart, however, from the numerous references to Christ as the Second Adam, Cyril does not tend to delve into christology itself. Therefore, we do not find in the *Glaphyra* much in the way

---

86. PG 69: 29D.
87. PG 69: 172B.
88. PG 69: 172B–C.

of detailed christological formulation, such as what we find in his specifically Trinitarian works, all of which have Arian christology as a target, or what we find in his later anti-Nestorian writings. In one place Cyril does make comments that prefigure his christological insights during the Nestorian controversy. They occur in the context of Cyril's interpretation of the cutting of the animals into two to solidify God's covenant with Abraham (Genesis 15.7–17). After providing a literal interpretation, Cyril proceeds to interpret this event spiritually, in a way that, as we have seen, revolves around the mystery of Christ. Cyril argues that the animals represent Christ, and he uses the opportunity to elaborate on the divine and human natures of Christ. The bull, "owing to its great strength and invincibility in a fight," represents Christ's divine nature.[89] The heifer represents his human nature. At this point, Cyril does not comment on the union of these natures. This he does when referring specifically to the separation of the animals. Cyril asks his readers to remember that, although all the animals were cut into pieces, the two birds were not. This has significance when interpreted christologically, according to Cyril:

The Only-Begotten Word of God became flesh, as if he were divided in two, and the matter we have to consider concerning him extends into two parts. For on the one hand we perceive his divine and ineffable generation from the Father, while on the other we speak also of the mystery of his Incarnation. This is the profundity of the divine economy—we both make separate and take as one, thereby imparting knowledge to those who do not understand this mystery. Although our consideration of him has become twofold, however, he himself is wholly one, not capable of being divided into two following his union with flesh. Nor can he be separated into two sons, for Christ is one and undivided.[90]

As he will do against Nestorius, Cyril emphasizes the absolute unity of the divine and human after the Incarnation. He does not, however, elaborate on this point, likely for two reasons. First, christological issues were, at least to Cyril's mind, relatively uncontroversial at the time he was writing the *Glaphyra*. That he makes a brief comment against the notion of "two Christs" indicates that he thought there were some making such a claim. He does not, however, identify who these people are, and the fact that he devotes so little attention to it indicates that he under-

89. PG 69: 128B.
90. PG 69: 129B–C.

stood the threat posed by such people to be minimal. Second, Cyril's focus in the *Glaphyra* is on enunciating the "mystery of Christ," and for him this means focusing on the salvation made possible in and through Christ. What this means for Cyril is that he devotes far less attention to issues of doctrine than he does to the particularities of human salvation. Of course, in Cyril's specifically doctrinal treatises and his anti-Nestorian writings, soteriology is never off his radar. Trinitarian and christological doctrine is, for Cyril, inherently soteriological insofar as distorted conceptions of the Triune God and of Christ threaten what he perceives to be the orthodox Christian understanding of human salvation. The converse is also true. In the *Glaphyra*, although the focus is soteriological, Cyril will devote some space to doctrine. But far less attention is given to doctrinal concerns in the *Glaphyra* than we find in his later works.

The Holy Spirit

One of the gifts of this soteriological focus is that Cyril devotes an extended amount of attention to the person and work of the Holy Spirit. For those familiar with Cyril's corpus, this might not come as much of a surprise. Recent work has brought attention to Cyril's pneumatology, particularly as articulated in his doctrinal works.[91] This research demonstrates that, although he is considered by many to be primarily a theologian of christology, Cyril had a vibrant and nuanced pneumatology that was pivotal to his thought as a whole.

The *Glaphyra* demonstrates that Cyril was focused on the person and work of the Holy Spirit from very early in his writing

---

91. See, for example, Crawford, *Cyril of Alexandria's Trinitarian Theology of Scripture*; Daniel A. Keating, *The Appropriation of Divine Life in Cyril of Alexandria* (Oxford: Oxford University Press, 2004); Brian E. Daley, "The Fullness of the Saving God: Cyril of Alexandria on the Holy Spirit," in *The Theology of St Cyril of Alexandria*, ed. Weinandy and Keating, 113–48; Gregory K. Hillis, "Pneumatology and Soteriology according to Gregory of Nazianzus and Cyril of Alexandria," *Studia Patristica* 67 (2013): 187–97. Some recent work has been done on Cyril's pneumatology in his exegetical work; see David Kneip, "The Holy Spirit in Cyril of Alexandria's Commentary on Isaiah," in *The Old Testament as Authoritative Scripture in the Early Churches of the East*, ed. Vahan S. Hovhanessian (New York: Peter Lang, 2010), 43–50.

career. In the *Glaphyra* Cyril does not—as he will in the *Thesaurus, Dialogues on the Trinity*, and the *Commentary on John*—provide a defense of the Spirit's divinity, nor does he delve into the intertrinitarian relationships of the Spirit with the Father and the Son. He devotes significant attention, however, to two issues, both of which revolve in large part around the Holy Spirit. First, Cyril is at pains throughout the text to demonstrate the superiority of the Gospel over the Mosaic Law, and so the superiority of Christianity over Judaism. The Holy Spirit is central to Cyril's argument on this point. Second, and less polemically, Cyril's focus in the *Glaphyra* on the mystery of Christ and so on salvation through Christ leads him to elaborate on the Spirit's role in human salvation. I will address the former first.

Throughout the text, Cyril emphasizes that the Mosaic Law has been superseded by the salvation made possible through Christ. This is part of Cyril's anti-Jewish rhetoric, to which I have already referred. The salvation made possible through Christ is, according to Cyril, so far superior to the Mosaic Law, regardless of the benefits the law bestowed before Christ, that continued adherence to the law makes no sense to him. Central to the salvation made possible through Christ is the bestowal of the Holy Spirit, which the Jews did not and do not possess through the law.

That the Jews lacked, and continue to lack, the Holy Spirit is a point Cyril makes often. For example, Cyril uses Jacob's departure from Laban as a launching point for a discussion of soteriology, focusing particularly on the fact that the Jews did not have the Spirit prior to Christ. Cyril argues that Jacob's two wives represent different soteriological trajectories, as it were. Leah is a type of the "synagogue of the Jews," and Rachel is a type of the "church of the Gentiles."[92] Cyril notes that Jacob kept quiet after Leah gave birth, as well as after his maidservants gave birth to his children, but after Rachel gave birth to Joseph, Jacob desired to leave and establish his own house. Cyril also notes that Joseph's name means "added by God." All of this for Cyril points to the eventual adding of Gentiles to the company of believers: "[O]nce the Gentile church had given birth to the new people of

---

92. PG 69: 232D.

God, that is, those who were 'added,' the Savior then prepared his own house for himself."[93] By this Cyril refers to the indwelling of Christ in believers through the Holy Spirit, an indwelling not experienced by the Jews before Christ and not experienced by them now: "So he [Christ] dwells within us through the Spirit ... and not in Israel. That the Jews who lived before Christ's advent did not partake of the Spirit, speaking in a manner corresponding to the type, the most-wise John would make clear in saying, 'For there was as yet no Spirit, because Jesus had not yet been glorified' [John 7.39]."[94] The implications for the Jews' lack of the Spirit are twofold. Not only do they lack the "Spirit of adoption" (Romans 8.15) by whom believers are made children of God, but they lack the ability even to comprehend their own scriptures. On this latter point, Cyril cites Paul's reference to the veil that continues to lie upon the hearts of Jews when Moses is read (2 Corinthians 3.14–18), arguing that it is the Holy Spirit that enables Christians to interpret the scriptures correctly, that is, to see the mystery of Christ in them.

The presence of the Holy Spirit in Christians is so central for Cyril precisely because of the soteriological weight Cyril hangs on the Spirit in the *Glaphyra*. In the passage just examined, we saw that Cyril refers both to the indwelling of Christ and to the adoption of believers as children of God, both occurring through the Holy Spirit. As various studies have demonstrated, Cyril's soteriology as articulated in works written after the *Glaphyra* focuses particular attention on the role the Spirit plays in transforming believers into the image of Christ.[95] The *Glaphyra* demonstrates that this emphasis on the Holy Spirit was a constant in Cyril's thought from the beginning. Already in book 1, we find Cyril, in the midst of describing Christ in terms of the typology of the Second Adam, recounting human salvation in terms of being conformed to Christ through the Holy Spirit:

---

93. PG 69: 233A.
94. PG 69: 233B.
95. In particular, see Keating, *The Appropriation of Divine Life in Cyril of Alexandria,* and Hillis, "Pneumatology and Soteriology according to Gregory of Nazianzus and Cyril of Alexandria."

So, as the image of the first man taken from the ground was imprinted upon us, which had to suffer death and be ensnared in the cords of corruption, thus also in the case of our second beginning after that first one, that is to say, Christ, *in whose likeness we are made through the Spirit*, incorruptible nature is impressed upon us.[96]

And throughout the entire *Glaphyra*, Cyril reiterates over and over that we are united to Christ through the Holy Spirit. Believers "enjoy abundant union with [Christ] through partaking of the Holy Spirit by the goodwill of the Father."[97] A "complete Christ dwells in each one through their partaking of the Holy Spirit,"[98] and those "who have been sealed by the divine Spirit" are "fashioned according to the beauty of the Son."[99]

Cyril thus connects the salvific work of the Spirit to the task of bringing us into transformative contact with Christ himself, often using the language of participation to illustrate the kind of union we have with the incarnate Word. And to do so, Cyril often cites 2 Peter 1.4 with its reference to becoming "partakers of the divine nature." This is a verse to which Cyril had a deep connection, citing it throughout his works more frequently than any other patristic writer does.[100] 2 Peter 1.4 does not pop up as frequently in the *Glaphyra* as it does in later writings, but it still comes up with enough regularity to demonstrate how central it is to Cyril's soteriological vision. Of particular interest is that, despite the fact that the Holy Spirit appears nowhere near 2 Peter 1.4, Cyril consistently associates partaking of the divine nature with the Holy Spirit in all of his works, including the *Glaphyra*. And in the *Glaphyra*, as he does elsewhere, he specifically associates our partaking of the divine nature through the Spirit with our partaking of Christ. "[W]e have also been united with [Christ] in another way," Cyril writes, "because we have become 'partakers of' his 'divine nature' through the Spirit."[101] Elsewhere he writes that the Word has

96. PG 69: 28D. Emphasis mine.
97. PG 69: 148A.
98. PG 69: 425B.
99. PG 69: 409A.
100. Norman Russell, *The Doctrine of Deification in the Greek Patristic Tradition* (Oxford: Oxford University Press, 2004), 192, and "Partakers of the Divine Nature (2 Peter 1.4) in the Byzantine Tradition," in J. Chrysostomides, ed., *Kathegetria: Essays Presented to Joan Hussey* (Camberley: Porphyrogenitus, 1988), 52.
101. PG 69: 29C.

"been given to us according to our participation in him through the Spirit, and through [the Spirit] we have become 'partakers of the divine nature.'"[102] Twice in book 10, Cyril reiterates this point. He writes: "The real mediator is Christ, to whom we are firmly joined, since it is true that he came down into our estate and became a man, so that we ourselves 'might become partakers of' his 'divine nature,' being united to him by sharing in the Holy Spirit and by the grace of God."[103] Later in the book, he again emphasizes our participation in Christ through the Spirit, citing 2 Peter 1.4: "For having become partakers of [Christ] through the Spirit, we have been united with God the Father through him, since we are indeed 'partakers of the divine nature,' in accordance with the Scriptures."[104] Finally, in book 12, Cyril cites 2 Peter 1.4, writing that we partake of the divine nature through "the Spirit of Christ dwelling in us" through the grace of baptism.[105]

These references to 2 Peter 1.4 in the *Glaphyra* point to three ideas I want to draw out. First, the fact that Cyril always associates 2 Peter 1.4 with the work of the Holy Spirit in the *Glaphyra*—an association he makes in his other writings—illustrates the centrality of the Spirit in his soteriology. That Cyril cites 2 Peter 1.4 more frequently than any other patristic writer does tells us how central this verse is in his soteriology; and that he almost always references the Holy Spirit in relation to this verse tells us of the key role the Spirit plays in his understanding of human salvation.

Second, Cyril emphasizes that it is by the Holy Spirit that believers are brought into transformative contact with Christ, and this emphasis indicates something of the particular focus Cyril places on the relationship between the Holy Spirit and the Son in his trinitarian theology. Admittedly, this is a relationship to which he draws much greater attention in his later writings, where he goes so far as to use the language of procession with reference to the Spirit's relationship with the Son.[106] Nevertheless, the *Glaphyra* shows that Cyril, from early in his career,

102. PG 69: 172D.
103. PG 69: 497C–D.
104. PG 69: 517B.
105. PG 69: 625C.
106. As Marie-Odile Boulnois notes, while Cyril's theology of the Spirit's procession is not developed sufficiently to allow definitive conclusions to be

draws particular attention to the Spirit's relationship to the Son through his focus on the way the Spirit, to whom he refers above as the "Spirit of Christ," draws us to the incarnate Word such that we partake of him. Although he would develop his trinitarian theology in later works like the *Thesaurus, Dialogues on the Trinity*, and his *Commentary on John*, we see in the *Glaphyra* insights he will express in these later works, particularly in drawing his readers' attention to the way the Spirit brings us to Christ.

Third, this emphasis on the Spirit's soteriological role vis-à-vis the incarnate Word plays out in one other way in the *Glaphyra*. In no small part because of his frequent references to 2 Peter 1.4 throughout his corpus, Cyril has been described as representing "the pinnacle in the development of teaching on *theosis*."[107] Without denying that *theosis* is an important facet of Cyril's soteriology, I want to draw attention to the way in which he fleshes out the notion of *theosis* in terms of divine filiation in the *Glaphyra*. Such an examination illuminates the soteriological nuances present in the text, and so in Cyril's thought as a whole.

In book 1, deciphering the spiritual meaning of Enosh, Cyril writes the following:

> Though being of the earth, we have been called to adoption as children of the Master of all and to be brothers of Christ, who for our sakes became one of us, so that thanks to him we may possess a better estate, transcending that which is human, and through his grace and love for humankind become 'gods,' and enjoy his glory. For he declares, "I said, 'You are gods, and you are all sons of the Most High'" [Ps 82.6].[108]

---

reached regarding the Son's precise role in the procession of the Spirit, he certainly "went further than many of his predecessors in affirming the dependence of the Spirit on the Son." See Marie-Odile Boulnois, "The Mystery of the Trinity according to Cyril of Alexandria: The Deployment of the Triad and its Recapitulation into the Unity of Divinity," in *The Theology of St Cyril of Alexandria*, ed. Weinandy and Keating, 75–111. For more on Cyril's understanding of the Spirit's relationship to the Son, see Hillis, "Pneumatology and Soteriology according to Gregory of Nazianzus and Cyril of Alexandria," 192–93, and idem, "The Holy Spirit and Episcopal Teaching Authority according to Cyril of Alexandria," 191–93.

107. P. B. T. Bilaniuk, "The Mystery of *Theosis* or Divinisation," in *The Heritage of the Early Church*, Orientalia Christiana Analecta 195 (1973): 351.

108. PG 69: 48B.

This is, in essence, a summary of Cyril's soteriology. He describes human salvation in terms of being drawn into a new relationship with God through Christ. This new relationship is not merely extrinsic, but is itself deeply transformative. This Cyril emphasizes when he writes that, through Christ, we "possess a better estate, transcending that which is human." Adoption as children of God is not for Cyril simply a matter of being called children of God, but of actually becoming children of God and brothers and sisters of Christ. And it is through the Holy Spirit that we are made children of God, as Cyril writes in book 3: "We were set free in Christ, through whom and in whom we are made rich with the divine Spirit from above. We have been assigned a place among the children of God, and 'we cry out *Abba*, Father' [Romans 8.15]."[109] Later in the same book he writes that "we are included among the children of God through the Spirit of freedom" and "are admitted to Christ as to one who is like us, a brother."[110]

This transformation to become children of God through the Holy Spirit revolves around Cyril's understanding that it is by the Spirit that we partake of Christ himself, and that through this partaking we become like Christ. This point Cyril makes particularly clearly in book 9. There, citing Psalm 22.22—"I will declare your name to my brothers, in the midst of the assembly I will sing praises to you"—Cyril expounds on the psalmist's reference to brothers, placing these words in the mouth of Christ: "For having taken human nature upon himself, and having brought himself down to our level, he is not ashamed to call us brothers, since through him we have been called to adoption."[111] This adoption as children of God occurs because we are "enriched by way of conformity with [Christ] through sanctification in the Spirit."[112] When in book 1 Cyril writes that Christ's "incorruptible nature is impressed upon us" through the Holy Spirit, it would appear that Cyril understands this transformation to translate into our becoming children of God through this union.[113] As he writes in book 8, "Christ encompassed us in light

109. PG 69: 125D–128A.
110. PG 69: 176B.
111. PG 69: 436B–C.
112. PG 69: 436C.
113. PG 69: 28D.

through the Holy Spirit, and through the Spirit he is within us, and in him we cry, '*Abba*, Father' [Romans 8.15]."[114]

In later works, Cyril elaborates in much more detail about the Spirit's role in our adoption as children of God. In those texts he places heavy emphasis on the Spirit's relationship with the Son to explain how the Spirit conforms us to Christ to make us Christ's brothers and fellow children of God. In the *Glaphyra*, we see that divine filiation characterizes his soteriology early in his career. We see as well that the Holy Spirit plays a prominent and vital role in his soteriology, and that, as he will in his later writings, Cyril characterizes the Spirit primarily in terms of its relationship with the Son, to whom the Spirit draws the believer into transformative contact.

Conclusion

In the *Glaphyra* we find the reflections of a theologian and bishop near the beginning of his career, concerned with the continued presence and influence of Alexandria's Jewish community but also focused on providing a thorough literal and spiritual interpretation of the Pentateuch for his Christian flock. The care and effort Cyril expends in his interpretation reveals his conviction regarding the centrality of the scriptures for the Christian life. For Cyril, the scriptures provide moral and theological insight, and, relatedly, they bring Spirit-filled Christians into transformative contact with Christ himself, by and through whom we contemplate the Father. Overemphasis on Cyril's doctrinal works and/or his role in the Nestorian controversy can translate into an inadequate comprehension of his understanding of the pedagogical role of the bishop, his theology of biblical interpretation, and the ways in which his theology and soteriology are intertwined with scripture. Without exposure to his exegetical work, one is left with, at best, an incomplete picture of Cyril of Alexandria as a bishop and as a theologian. The translation of the *Glaphyra* you have in your hands thus provides a significant piece of the Cyrilline puzzle for English readers.

Gregory K. Hillis

114. PG 69: 416A.

PREFACE

PREFACE

By way of preface to the translation presented in this volume, the following information is provided on the textual basis of the present work and, as an orientation to aid the reader, on the style of translation and its format.

The Text

As is the case with many modern translations of patristic works, no critical edition of the *Glaphyra* exists to work from. In the latter part of the nineteenth century Philip Edward Pusey produced a multi-volume edition of a number of Cyril's works,[1] yet this did not include either of the two writings on the Pentateuch or the commentary on Isaiah.[2] Where a critical text is lacking, translators are obliged to resort to Migne's monumental Patrologia volumes.[3] The present work therefore takes as its basic source the text appearing in Patrologia Graeca volume 69 (1864), where the *Gla-*

---

1. P. E. Pusey, ed., *Opera Sancti Patris Nostri Cyrilli Archiepiscopi Alexandrini*, 7 vols. (Oxford: Clarendon Press, 1868–1877). These volumes contain critical texts of the commentaries on the Minor Prophets and John's Gospel, and some shorter non-exegetical works.

2. Robert C. Hill, trans., *Cyril of Alexandria, Commentary on Isaiah, Volume 1* (Brookline, MA: Holy Cross Orthodox Press, 2008), 4.

3. Modern translations abound that of necessity rely solely upon the Patrologia Graeca version of the original text. See, for example, Christopher Stade, *The Explanation by the Blessed Theophylact of the Holy Gospel According to St. Matthew* (House Springs, MO: Chrysostom Press, 2006), 4, which has as its only source text that found in PG 123; Robert C. Hill, *St. John Chrysostom, Old Testament Homilies, Volume 1: Homilies on Hannah, David and Saul* (Brookline, MA: Holy Cross Orthodox Press, 2003), 135, n. 1, where the version published in PG 54 is identified as the basis; Hilda C. Graef, *St. Gregory of Nyssa: The Lord's Prayer, The Beatitudes*, Ancient Christian Writers 18 (New York: Paulist Press, 1954), which translates the Greek text appearing in PG 44; see p. 20.

phyra occupies columns 13–678 in alternate blocks of Greek and Latin. This edition reproduces the earlier seventeenth-century (1638) text prepared by Professor Jean Aubert of Paris.

We are fortunate, however, that with respect to the *Glaphyra* Migne and his editors decided to incorporate variant readings derived from another documentary source, a codex from the Harleian collection, which are listed at the back of the Migne volume. The quantity and manner of alternative readings in this manuscript are not substantial, many being simply minor variations in grammatical number, case, or verbal form. Nevertheless, these variants have been taken into consideration in the present work. The great majority of them would make no or only slight difference to an English rendering. Therefore, it is only those readings which differ more significantly that have been included. Yet even then, there is relatively little that is of major consequence. These variants from the Harleian Codex have been placed in footnotes (labeled as "Var."), while the body of the text follows the main text appearing in Migne. In just a handful of instances, where the Harleian reading is unmistakably the superior, this has been translated in the body of the text. Such instances have again been indicated through the presence of a footnote.

Through this close similarity of the two versions given by Migne, there is some reason to believe that the original contents of Cyril's commentary have been transmitted with reasonable accuracy.

The Translation

With regard to translation style, a deliberate attempt has been made to steer a middle course between literalness and dynamic equivalence. The reason for not wanting to depart too far from a literal rendering is in order that the scholar or student who consults the Migne volume may readily see how the English corresponds to the Greek, and so may be helped in piecing together the various semantic, syntactic, and grammatical elements within the latter. On the other hand, Greek and English are so diverse, especially in the freedom of order permitted in the former, that it is of course impossible to follow consistently the ordering of constituents present in the original. Consideration has been given, therefore, to the question of naturalness in English, though it is freely conceded that where accuracy and naturalness have proved to be in conflict, priority has been given to accuracy.

Not only is there considerable divergence between the syntax and idiom of Greek and of English, but it is widely acknowledged that Cyril of Alexandria wrote in a particularly complex style of Greek, thus making the translator's task a difficult one.[4] While some of the difficulty lies in Cyril's predilection for atticizing and neologisms, features that would not be apparent in English translation, he also has a fondness for overly long sentences and the use of doublets. This latter consists of his restating something in different, yet virtually synonymous terms, whether at the level of individual words, phrases, or entire clauses. In such cases, where English has comparably synonymous expressions—the majority of cases, in fact—the doublet has been retained in this translation. In the few cases where English lacks a suitable synonym, no effort has been made to reproduce the reduplicating form. With regard to long sentences, for the most part these have been divided into shorter units. On some occasions, however, where the flow of the Greek makes this difficult or impossible, a long sentence has necessarily been preserved.

In working through Cyril's Greek, two Latin translations were consulted. These are the Latin rendering printed alongside the Greek columns in the Migne edition, and another earlier, partial translation dating from the fifteenth century.[5] Both, however, proved to be of very limited usefulness. Not only does each of the two adopt a relatively free style of translation, but it is also apparent that in the more difficult passages the translators strug-

---

4. On the character and complexity of Cyril's Greek, see Evie Zachariades-Holmberg, *Saint Cyril of Alexandria, Commentary on the Book of Exodus, First Discourse*, Patristic Texts and Translations (Rollinsford, NH: Orthodox Research Institute, 2010), xv–xvi, where the author describes the works of Cyril as being "among the most difficult to translate."

5. This is the parchment manuscript Beinecke MS 953, housed at the Yale University Library, which contains a Latin version of Books 1–4 of the *Glaphyra*. The document is accessible online at: http://brbl-dl.library.yale.edu/vufind/Record/3838133?image_id=11075195.

gle to determine the sense, in which case they resort to questionable paraphrase. These Latin versions therefore often provide no safe guide as to Cyril's precise meaning. What makes this circumstance more significant is the unfortunate fact that several modern scholarly works that cite passages from the *Glaphyra*, and attempt to do so in English, lean heavily, and in some cases wholly, upon the sense of Migne's Latin translation.[6]

Key Terms

For Cyril, the literal meaning of the pentateuchal text (the ἱστορία, or *historia*) possesses a certain quality that he himself expresses by means of the term παχύς (*pachus*). In a physical sense, this denotes something that is "coarse" or "rough." When applied by Cyril to the Old Testament, its meaning approximates to "earthly" or "material."[7] In order to rise beyond that which was merely earthly in the text, another altogether different approach had to be adopted. So in almost every instance, once Cyril has treated a text from the literal perspective, he then moves on to what he terms θεωρία (*theôria*), which basically means "contemplation." A fuller phrase would be θεωρία πνευματική (*theôria pneumatikê*), that is, "spiritual contemplation," indicating a spiritual sense.[8] According to Cyril, this higher sense is always related to the mystery of Christ.[9]

---

6. As a case in point, the excerpts from the *Glaphyra* in the second volume on Genesis in the Ancient Christian Commentary on Scripture series, namely, *Genesis 12–50*, ed. Mark Sheridan, ACCOS 2 (Downers Grove, IL: InterVarsity Press, 2002), looking too much to the Latin as they do, regrettably do not furnish the reader with an accurate understanding of the Greek in a significant number of instances.

7. Cf. G. W. H. Lampe, *A Patristic Greek Lexicon* (Oxford: Clarendon Press, 1961), 1054a; and Alexander Kerrigan, *St. Cyril of Alexandria: Interpreter of the Old Testament*, Analecta Biblica 2 (Rome: Pontificio Istituto Biblico, 1952), 45.

8. Bertrand de Margerie, *An Introduction to the History of Exegesis, Volume 1: The Greek Fathers*, trans. Leonard Maluf (Petersham, MA: Saint Bede's Publications, 1993), 244–45; Kerrigan, *St. Cyril of Alexandria*, 238–39.

9. de Margerie, *An Introduction*, Vol. 1, 244, where the author states, "The spiritual sense is always, for Cyril, in one way or another, relative to the mystery of Christ.... A scriptural sense that has no relation to the mystery of Christ cannot be spiritual; it can only be literal."

Apart from these terms that figure prominently in Cyril's exegetical approach, several other important terms require comment, and certain lesser ones also.

As is often the case in other languages, some Greek words either do not have a precise English equivalent, or have elements of meaning falling somewhere between two, or possibly more, English terms. One such word is λατρεία (*latreia*), which Cyril employs with reasonable frequency. It is this term that forms part of the title for his other great work on the Pentateuch, represented in Latin by *cultus*. According to the standard patristic lexicon λατρεία denotes "service," "worship," or "cult," in the sense of "mode of worship."[10] There is, of course, some distinction in meaning between these English terms. In the present work, if the context allows us to determine the particular sense, then either "service" or "worship" is used accordingly. In those places where Cyril employs the word with reference to the whole Mosaic "cult" or system, then we have rendered it by "ministration."

A greater challenge is presented by the term οἰκονομία (*oikonomia*). This has found its way into English as "economy," and many translations of theological works are content to leave it that way. It is, of course, a technical term, having quite different connotations to the use of the word in modern English. The instance of οἰκονομία in Ephesians 1.10 is rendered "dispensation" (NKJV), "plan" (NLT), or "administration" (NASB), all of which capture definite components of the term. In later patristic writings, however, the usage of the word is closely associated with the Incarnation and the new era it initiated, since the divine plan centers upon that event. Perhaps the words of Frances Young, "the incarnation as an expression of God's providential and saving plan," are as helpful as any in unpacking the term.[11] In our translation it was felt that "economy" standing alone, though doubtless acceptable for those already familiar with the term, was insufficient. In those instances, therefore, where οἰκονομία is unqualified by any other descriptive term, it is here often expressed by the phrase "divine economy."

---

10. See Lampe, *A Patristic Greek Lexicon*, 793.

11. Frances M. Young, *Biblical Exegesis and the Formation of Christian Culture* (Peabody, MA: Hendrickson, 1997), 39.

For the benefit of those who are able to consult Migne's Greek text, a word of explanation is in order regarding one specific usage of the noun φύσις (*phusis*). This basically means "nature" or "essence."[12] In certain contexts, however, despite the fact that it is a feminine noun, φύσις very clearly occurs as a designation for God. In such cases the articular phrase, ἡ φύσις, appears, that is, "*the* Essence." For this we offer an English equivalent, "the Being."

When speaking of God as "Lord," Greek has the more usual κύριος (*kurios*), as well as the less frequent δεσπότης (*despotês*). Migne's Latin rendering of the *Glaphyra* represents both terms as *dominus*. In the present translation the distinction has been preserved, the former being represented by "Lord" and the latter by "Master."

Cyril makes use of a whole range of different words with reference to the types and figures of the Old Testament, including αἴνιγμα (*ainigma*), "figure, riddle"; παραβολή (*parabolê*), "parable, parallel"; τύπος (*tupos*), "type, impression"; εἰκών (*eikôn*), "image, representation"; παράδειγμα (*paradeigma*), "pattern, illustration"; and σκιά (*skia*), "shadow." Originally, in classical Greek rhetoric such terms would have had their own distinct connotations. Cyril, however, appears to treat them all as virtually synonymous.[13] No attempt has been made to achieve complete consistency in our renderings of all these different terms, except that σκιά is regularly "shadow."

Corresponding to the various nouns above, there exists a comparable series of verbs, mostly compounded with the prefix προ- ("fore-" or "pre-"). Greek is a good deal richer here than English. These terms are mostly expressed in the translation by "prefigure." Where, however, the σκια- component is present in the Greek verb, some effort has again been made to reflect the original etymology and so to render it as "foreshadow."

Lastly, in common with a host of ancient Greek writers, Cyril is fond of the term που (*pou*) when making citations. The lexicon entry for που gives its sense as "somewhere."[14] This can give the

---

12. Lampe, *A Patristic Greek Lexicon*, 1496–97.
13. Kerrigan, *St. Cyril of Alexandria*, 64.
14. E.g., Liddell and Scott, *Greek-English Lexicon*, 1261a.

English reader the impression that Cyril is citing some indefinite source, or that the location of the quoted words has escaped his mind. Neither of these, however, need be the case. The word has found its way into the New Testament at Hebrews 2.6 and 4.4. Here English versions offer various translations, such as "in a certain place" (2.6, NKJV), "in one place" (4.4, NRSV), "as one text says" (4.4, NJB). All that the term means is that the place of the citation is not being specified, not that it is unknown. In the present work, where που has been translated, we render it by phrases similar to the foregoing English versions. Yet in some instances, where the introduction to the citation is already sufficiently lengthy, encumbered with adverbial expressions or descriptive phrases, που has been omitted.

Format

In the text printed in Patrologia Graeca 69, each book of the *Glaphyra* has been divided first into headed sections. A lower level of textual organization consists of a series of numbered subsections within the larger section. This basic framework has been preserved in the present translation. In addition to this, paragraph divisions have been introduced. Both the subject matter and the structure of the Greek have contributed to making a break at a particular point. Yet the position of these is still sometimes a subjective matter, and there is no intention to claim that each of these junctures has been placed at the best location in every instance.

Reference to the *Glaphyra* in later academic literature is generally made through the column number in the Migne edition. This basic reference system has been incorporated here. Numbers in square brackets, such as [150], therefore denote the beginning of a new column in Migne. In this connection readers should be aware that since the Latin columns also possess numbers, the numbering of the Greek columns is not consecutive. It is the consistent practice in Migne to print the Greek text in the half of the page nearest the inner binding, while the outer half of every page bears the Latin. The result, of course, is that a sequence of consecutive Greek columns would be numbered 1, 4, 5, 8, 9, and so forth (where columns 2, 3, 6, 7 are all Latin).

Footnotes

Above it was stated that variant readings ("Var.") have been placed in footnotes. In addition to this information, other kinds of data have also been included in these notes. Where Cyril makes a biblical citation, the reference is provided by using the standard chapter-verse numbers as found in modern English versions. Where the LXX differs, the varying reference follows in brackets. Attention is also drawn to those places where Cyril's Old Testament text departs to any significant degree from that of the LXX. On occasion alternate renderings have been given ("Or"), that is to say, a different way of translating the same Greek word or words. Seeing that the same original text might be rendered in several ways in English, an alternative has been proposed, for the most part only where it makes some difference to the understanding of the text. When a rendering has been necessarily free, a more literal translation ("Lit.") may be provided in a note. Where it might be of interest to the reader to know the original term being used, Greek words are also sometimes noted, and where Cyril is discussing the meaning of Hebrew terms, these too are referenced in footnotes in transliterated form. Apart from the foregoing, other information considered helpful is presented, either to aid in understanding Cyril's flow of thought, or on occasion to highlight inconsistencies in it.

Nicholas P. Lunn

Sources Consulted

Graef, Hilda C., trans. *St. Gregory of Nyssa: The Lord's Prayer, The Beatitudes*. Ancient Christian Writers 18. New York: Paulist Press, 1954.

Hill, Robert C., trans. and ed. *St. John Chrysostom, Old Testament Homilies, Volume 1: Homilies on Hannah, David and Saul*. Brookline, MA: Holy Cross Orthodox Press, 2003.

———, trans. and ed. *Cyril of Alexandria, Commentary on Isaiah, Volume 1: Chapters 1–14*. Brookline, MA: Holy Cross Orthodox Press, 2008.

Kerrigan, Alexander. *St. Cyril of Alexandria: Interpreter of the Old Testament*. Analecta Biblica 2. Rome: Pontificio Istituto Biblico, 1952.

Sheridan, Mark. *Genesis 12–50*. Ancient Christian Commentary on Scripture 2. Downers Grove, IL: InterVarsity Press, 2002.

Stade, Christopher, trans. *The Explanation by the Blessed Theophylact of the*

Holy Gospel According to St. Matthew. House Springs, MO: Chrysostom Press, 2006.

Young, Frances M. *Biblical Exegesis and the Formation of Christian Culture*. Peabody, MA: Hendrickson, 1997.

Zachariades-Holmberg, Evie, ed. and trans. *Saint Cyril of Alexandria, Commentary on the Book of Exodus, First Discourse*. Patristic and Ecclesiastical Texts and Translations. Rollinsford, NH: Orthodox Research Institute, 2010.

GLAPHYRA ON THE PENTATEUCH, VOLUME 1

GENESIS

BOOK ONE: GENESIS 1–5

That throughout all the writings of Moses the mystery of Christ is signified figuratively

"YOU SEARCH THE Scriptures,"[1] Christ declared to the Jewish people. He was very evidently saying that in no other way would any be able to attain eternal life unless, by digging up the letter of the law as if for some treasure, they should diligently seek the pearl hidden in it, which is Christ, "in whom are hidden all the treasures of wisdom and knowledge,"[2] as the blessed Paul says. Concerning this most noble and most wonderful wisdom or knowledge Solomon also said, "If you seek it like silver and search for it like treasures, then you will understand the fear of the Lord and find the knowledge of God."[3]

There is nothing equal to such a thing for those who commend the blameless life, who seek to perform the greatest and most excellent deeds and to fill their minds with the divine light. One should, therefore, feel inexpressible delight in the oracles of God, and consider the sacred Scripture a lamp, as it were, as the holy psalmist proclaims, "Your law is a lamp to my feet and a light to my paths."[4]

So then, since to investigate earnestly the mystery of Christ is clearly and manifestly the means of obtaining eternal life and the way for us to attain all happiness, come, let us once again make the worthwhile effort, even before all else that concerns us, to gather together those elements through which the mys-

---

1. Jn 5.39.
2. Col 2.3.
3. Prv 2.4–5.
4. Ps 119.105 (118.105 LXX).

tery of Christ is especially [16] represented to us. Let us strive to explain thoroughly how each is to be understood, so that the things we discuss, opened up in detail, might at times be the cause of the most significant contemplations of truth, a good opportunity for those more ready to learn to do so, and be steps upwards, as it were, leading to the higher and better knowledge that is set forth in them.

Now we shall first present the literal events in a helpful way, making them suitably clear. Then, refashioning the narrative by bringing it out of type and shadow, we shall explain it with reference to the mystery of Christ, having him as the goal, since it is true that Christ is the end of the law and the prophets.[5]

If it should happen that we fail to explain the more appropriate matters through the weakness of our understanding or the presence of much obscurity, then it befits those who will read it to be forbearing. And at this point one ought to be aware that since we have composed seventeen books on the theme "Concerning Worship and Service in Spirit and in Truth,"[6] and assembled a considerable mass of thoughts in them, we have deliberately omitted the topics[7] covered there from the present work and have included what was left unexamined, though for necessary reasons it sometimes happens that mention is made of some of the same things.

So we now begin our comments[8] upon Genesis, and make our way through the five books of Moses in order. Besides this, we shall also investigate matters from the other Scriptures relevant to our set purpose.

Concerning Adam

1. The most holy Paul, who was truly an expert in the law, reflecting upon the mystery of the salvation that comes through

---

5. Cf. Rom 10.4.
6. This is a reference to Cyril's other writing on the Pentateuch, generally known by its Latin title, *De adoratione et cultu in spiritu et veritate* (found in PG 68).
7. Or "chapters."
8. Cyril here employs the term (*glaphurôterôn*, lit. "more elegant matters") from which the present work receives its title.

Christ, states that in him there has been a "recapitulation"[9] of things in heaven and things upon the earth by the good pleasure and will of God the Father.[10] By the term "recapitulation" he clearly refers to the reformation of all things and the return of what has become corrupted to how things were in the beginning. This, it is reasonable to suppose, is what was being spoken of when God said through the mouth of the prophets, "Do not remember the former things, nor consider the things of old. Behold, I will do new things, which shall now spring forth, and you will know them."[11] Accordingly Paul, who himself had been brought up on the divine oracles, also indicated that the things prophesied in them had now been fulfilled, saying, "So that if anyone is in Christ he is a new creation; the old things have passed away; behold, all things have become new."[12] For in Christ we have been transformed and have become a new creation. Also, in him alone we have become rich through the obtaining of a new name, for we are called by the name of Christ. The divine Paul further says concerning us, "Those who belong to Christ Jesus have crucified the flesh with its passions and desires,"[13] for life for those in Christ is a matter of holiness, transcending carnal passions and earthly impurity. And that the new name by which we are called in Christ would be bestowed upon us is made evident when God declares through the mouth of the saints, "Those who serve me shall be called by a new name [17], which shall be blessed upon the earth; for they will bless the true God."[14]

Nobody, then, who cares to think correctly and reasonably can doubt that new things have come into being in Christ. So let us now examine the old state of affairs that once existed, and let it be stated how, out of that which was utterly powerless and defective, that is, out of that which was corrupted and which was unexpectedly brought down to a different state from how

---

9. This word (*anakephalaiôsis*) may have the general sense of "restoration," or the more particular sense of "a bringing together under one head."
10. Cf. Eph 1.9–10.
11. Is 43.18–19.
12. 2 Cor 5.17; cf. Rv 21.5.
13. Gal 5.24.
14. Is 65.15–16.

things were in the beginning, the reformation to something better came about. In doing this, one may correctly discern the goal to which the word set before us is heading, and see how to avoid error, and so he may not in any way depart from the true sense.

2. Now the God of all, being a Master Craftsman by his own all-effecting power, that is, by the Son, with respect to everything whatsoever that was made declares, "all things came into being through him, and not one thing came to be without him."[15] In the beginning he formed heaven and earth before all else, and called them into being, though nothing then existed.

But if someone should ask how this is possible, he should hear from us well this wise and excellent saying: "Who has known the mind of the Lord? Or who has been his counselor?"[16] For if one wishes to inquire into these things, there is no doubt that he will be completely lacking in mental ability, in contrast to that[17] which God is perceived to have. That our faculties are insignificant or as absolutely nothing in comparison with God, he himself clearly states: "For my purposes are not like your purposes, neither are my ways like your ways. For as the heaven is far from the earth, so is my way far from your ways, and your thoughts from my thinking."[18] Let it be allowed, then, that extraordinariness and incomprehensibility are the touchstone concerning these things. For God creates as he himself knows how and as only he is able.

So in the beginning heaven[19] and earth were brought forth; then the mass of the waters was drawn together into one space, for this was deemed necessary by him who said, *"Let the water be gathered into one place."*[20] The land was uncovered, and thus was adorned all over with different forms of vegetation, producing the most exceptionally well-formed fruit trees.

Then the spheres of the sun and moon appeared, and there was a law from God that directed the rule of each.[21] For it was

---

15. Jn 1.3.
16. Is 40.13.
17. Var. "the mind."
18. Is 55.8–9.
19. Or "sky."
20. Gn 1.9.
21. In Gn 1.16 the sun and moon are said to have been created "for ruling" (*eis archas*).

ordained that one should be for the day-time and light, and the other for the night-time and darkness. Also, the entire expanse of heaven itself was bedecked with stars for us. And when these things came into being, God gave a law and said, *"Let them be for signs and seasons, and for days and years, and let them be for light in the firmament of heaven so as to shine upon the earth."*[22]

Since the Maker of all things is by nature life, he also wrought the same nature in the waters, the source of swimming creatures, and in the air, the source of birds.[23] He further commanded the earth to bring forth creatures of many kinds and species of wild beasts of the field. What seemed good to him he brought about instantaneously and incomprehensibly. Respecting each of the things that were made, [20] its Maker was the Word, and its origin was solely a command.

Now, though the orderly arrangement of those things that had come into being was pleasing to the Craftsman of all things, another consideration[24] at length entered upon the scene, introduced last of all, the one on account of whom those other things had been brought into existence, namely man. For it was necessary that the Maker of all things, being in nature good, or rather that which he is being goodness itself, should be known by us. It was necessary that the earth be filled with those who knew how to give him glory and, as it is written, from the beauty of created things the glory of the one who had made them was to be viewed. For as the prophet Isaiah said, "You did not make it (meaning the earth) in vain, but to be inhabited."[25] It was essential, therefore, that a rational creature be formed upon the earth, where those things that appeared earlier serve for his enjoyment and are seen to have been made for his benefit.

So, having previously caused the earth and heaven and those things in them to appear, arranged as necessary, God came to the matter of fashioning man, whose creation was conceived be-

---

22. Gn 1.14–15.
23. Both instances of "source" in this sentence translate the Greek term literally meaning "mother" (*mêtêr*).
24. The noun *skepsis* is not easily rendered into English. It may denote something visibly seen ("a view"), or something mentally conceived ("a plan").
25. Is 45.18.

fore all else. Now he had made all the rest of creation instantaneously, merely by speaking, forming it by his own word as God. Since, however, man is truly a comely[26] and godlike creature, while he may not be considered a representation of the most supreme glory, there is nothing equal to him among all that was made. God honored the making of this masterpiece with his own deliberation and personal involvement. Having sculpted man out of the soil, he made him into a rational creature, and, in order that he might replicate the rationality of his own nature, he immediately implanted within him an immortal,[27] life-giving Spirit.[28] For it is written, *And he breathed upon his face the breath of life, and the man became a living being.*[29]

God then deemed man worthy of a garden[30] and its delights, and also assigned to him dominion over all that was upon the earth. He set him as ruler over fish and birds, and yoked to him herds of wild animals. He even subjected to him the different kinds of venomous creatures, just like the others. Also, as it was fitting that man should live fearfully, he commanded that he should be obedient to the laws of nature. So then, man was the image of the highest glory, and the representation of divine authority on earth.

But then it was absolutely necessary for the man who had come into such glory and delight to understand clearly that God held a position over him as his King and Lord. Lest man should fall by the considerable prosperity that was readily available to him, possibly even wishing to be freed from the authority and supremacy of him who ruled, God immediately issued a law and accompanied it with the threat of punishment should it be transgressed. For the practice of sin did not yet exist upon the earth,

---

26. Or "well-suited."

27. Var. add "and imperishable."

28. Elsewhere in his corpus, Cyril usually interprets Gn 2.7 ("he breathed into his nostrils the breath of life") as referring to the Holy Spirit. It is likely that he is doing so here when referring to the Spirit as "immortal" and "life-giving." See Marie-Odile Boulnois, "Le souffle et l'Esprit: Exégèses patristiques de l'insufflation originelle de Gn 2, 7 en lien avec celle de Jn 20, 22," *RA* 24 (1989): 3–37.

29. Gn 2.7.

30. *paradeisos*.

as there was just one sole Being. But in order that man might also be under law, a certain manner of constraint was contrived for him, for it says, *"From every tree which is in the garden, you may eat for food. But from the tree of the knowledge of good and evil you may not eat. On the day that you eat from it you will surely die."*[31]

Next, one of Adam's ribs was taken, and the woman was formed. She served him in the bearing of children, and being of the same nature she became his wife and continued to live together with him in single-hearted devotion.

Now when [21] the woman was carried away into transgression by the trickery of the devil and ate the forbidden fruit of the trees, so did our forefather Adam also fall with her, and human nature was straightaway condemned to death. To the woman God said, *"In pain you shall bear children,"*[32] while to Adam he declared, *"Cursed shall the ground be in your labors."*[33] In addition to this, they were sent away from that most desirable estate of their former dwelling-place and from the delights of the garden. Only then did they learn that they were naked and without clothing, and in need of garments, yet God had compassion upon them, and so skins were given to them as tunics. And they were consigned to mother earth, and brought low by the cords of corruption. So there remained, it would seem, absolutely nothing for them in their extreme state of wretchedness.

3. What then? I imagine one might say that if man was going to fall into such a woeful condition, would it not reasonably be considered much better for him not to exist? Yet the one who was quickly to become wretched and pitiable, subject to a curse and punishment, God will render most eminent and admirable. So God was not in the least bit ignorant about what would happen, seeing that by nature he is the Maker. Since he acted in accordance with his knowledge, how could he not be taken as having acted harmfully rather than beneficially, if it truly was better for those who would fall into future wretchedness not to come into being, as the Savior himself said was the case with regard to the disciple who was a traitor, "It would be better for

---

31. Gn 2.16–17.
32. Gn 3.16.
33. Gn 3.17.

that man if he had not been born"?[34] In response to such things, I would say that it is extremely dangerous and approaches the point of complete madness, or rather even greatly surpasses it, not to honor the divine purposes as being just, or to suppose either that the Supreme Being perhaps had no regard for what was proper, or that he failed utterly in what was best and profitable for us humans. It would rather be more fitting to attribute to him blamelessness in his counsels and deeds, to avoid thinking beyond what one ought to think, and not to allow reprehensible meddling in these matters.

Moreover, I believe it necessary to consider whether for those who together with their existence also obtain a good portion, it were better not to have come into being. That it were better to exist and to partake of the Maker's goodness, in my opinion, nobody would doubt. While for those brought into existence who would come into a state of wretchedness, it might reasonably be taken as better and more desirable not to have obtained this existence; by the same token, I believe, to have come into existence and to live is an excellent and precious thing for those who would not at all come into such a condition.

So tell me, what is the answer? On my part, I would say in this regard that the matter is too exalted for us and even for those that are considerably higher than we are, by which I mean the blessed angels. These were, of course, made by God. Angels and archangels, thrones and authorities, powers and principalities, and also the most exalted seraphim, were brought from nonbeing into being. Even the serpent himself [24], the one who rebelled, came into being among the things that were made, and the evil powers with him. These were together with the other holy ones[35] and rational creatures; they filled the heavenly dwellings, were eminent in glory, and, having incomparable excellence, were considerably superior to us humans. And so it was said by God, "I made you with the cherubim."[36] The holy cherubim, however, have an innate glory, and they firmly maintain their own domain. Thousands upon thousands of them serve

34. Mt 26.24.
35. Var. "angels."
36. Ezek 28.14.

God, and myriads upon myriads stand before him. But Satan, along with others, fell and was deprived of his[37] glory. So, as he willingly turned away from his conflict with God and would forsake his own domain, and as fear would enter in, that is, with respect to the composition of the holy angels, Satan parted from the Maker of all things, and that most eminent and admirable creature was cast out. So how would God not be thought to have done wrong, unless there had been brought into being a multitude who stand before him and serve him, who remain true to God the Creator,[38] and who are not disposed to experience forgetfulness of their own domain?

Tell me, then, is it so very grievous if through their arrogance some utterly failed to obtain a good estate? Yet, those who are better than these stand in the presence of God and, being abundantly filled with his goodness, they honor him with long and unceasing doxologies. It was concerning these, I should think, that the blessed David said, "Blessed are all those who dwell in your house; they will praise you for ever and ever."[39]

In discussing these things in such a way, let us now bring our inquiry down also to matters that concern us humans ourselves, and let us examine these.

4. In the beginning man was made with control over his own will and with a disposition that was free to do whatever he chose, for the Deity, in whose likeness he was formed, is free. In no other way than this, it seems to me, could he obtain an excellent estate—if he was seen to be a willing doer of virtuous deeds, resolved to be fruitful, being pure in his actions, not performed as the product of natural compunction, by no means allowing himself to be drawn away from that which was good, even if he had the desire to do that which was not so.

So in the beginning man was assigned a free and unrestrained disposition of mind with respect to everything he did. But by the trickery of the serpent he was witlessly carried away into improper actions and committed transgression without any justification.

---

37. Var. add "original."
38. Or "Designer" (*tektênamenos*).
39. Ps 84.4 (83.5 LXX).

Accordingly, he was condemned to death and corruption, although in this event God, I believe, foresaw some greater good.[40]

Since man had turned aside into sin and his nature was now infirm through its inclination to commit base acts, in the same way perhaps as the unclean spirits, continual evil was to be found upon the earth. For this reason, the death of the flesh was determined. Yet the living creature was not consigned to complete destruction, but rather to renewal and, if we might say it thus, to a refashioning in the same way that a vessel which has been smashed is later made whole. [25] That in the meantime the living creature would in fact experience corruption, the Maker was not unaware, but he well knew that together with this there would be deliverance from those things that were improper and the removal of corruption, as well as the return to a better state and the restoration of those good things that were there in the beginning. For he knew that he would later send his own Son in human form to die on our behalf, and to destroy the power of death, so that he might have dominion over the dead and the living.

What then? Though not all have come to believe, the multitude of those who are saved is certainly a great number, exceeding that of those who perish. And with regard to these latter, God declares the feeling of grief to be un-worthwhile, saying in effect, "So they shall eat the fruit of their own way."[41] For it is possible for them to be saved, if they wish, and to escape the harmful things that have since entered creation, yet they do not accept the Redeemer, who is Christ.

Now tell me, if one skilled in the art of cultivation filled his garden with the most beautiful of trees, but then it happened that they did not remain free from all those various kinds of things that were damaging to them, would someone suppose that he who wished to cultivate the land did not care to cultivate it in the right way? I think that no one would criticize him. Far from it! For that man gave the necessary attention to those trees when he planted them, yet they suffered harm. So then, shall we say that it would be better for certain people not to undertake

---

40. Lit. "something more beneficial" (*lusitelesteron*).
41. Prv 1.31.

any cultivation and for the garden not to abound in the most excellent trees, but rather to leave off all manner of cultivation, lest some of those things planted should come to harm? Would it not be utterly absurd to maintain that this is right?

5. We shall not, therefore, charge the Maker with wrongdoing when he brought things into existence. Rather, if we think aright, we ourselves should be accused of being so willing to suffer harm. For God understood that, as soon as he had brought man into being, he would fall into corruption. Nor was he ignorant of the manner in which this could be cured. The divine Paul, by the foreknowledge of the Spirit, testifies unambiguously to the antiquity of salvation through Christ. For thus he wrote to his own disciple, Timothy, "So do not be ashamed of giving testimony to our Lord or of me his prisoner, but join with me in suffering for the gospel, relying on the power of God, who saved us and called us with a holy calling. This was not according to our works, but according to his own purpose and the grace that was given us in Christ Jesus before all ages and that has been revealed in the last ages through the appearing of our Savior Jesus Christ."[42] And to others he also said, "We know that for those who love God all things work together for good, for those called according to his purpose. For those whom he foreknew, he also predestined to be conformed to the image of his Son, that he should be the firstborn among many brothers. And those whom he predestined he also called; and those whom he called he also justified; and those whom he justified he also glorified."[43]

Note [28] how it says that the grace that is in Christ was given before all ages, and that those who would be conformed to the image of his Son were evidently foreknown and predestined by God the Father. For the manner of the Incarnation, as I said, was foreknown, and the deliverance from infirmity was administered at the proper time. Paul again testified to this when he wrote, "To him who is able to strengthen us according to my gospel and the proclamation of Jesus Christ, according to the revelation of the mystery which was kept secret for long ages past, but which has now been made manifest and through the prophetic Scrip-

---

42. 1 Tm 1.8–10.
43. Rom 8.28–30.

tures has been made known to all the nations by the command of the eternal God, to bring about the obedience of faith, to the only wise God, through Jesus Christ, be glory for ever. Amen."[44]

The mystery was indeed kept secret, but has now been made manifest through the law and prophets, according to the will of God the Father. For in Christ we have in fact been restored to our original estate, having been turned away from those things that have since entered in through the deceits of the devil. Paul thus said with regard to Christ the Savior of us all, "in whom we have redemption through his blood, the forgiveness of sins according to the richness of his goodness, which he lavished upon us with all wisdom and understanding. He made known to us the mystery of his will according to his good pleasure, which he purposed in Christ as a plan for the fullness of time, to bring all things in heaven and upon earth together in him under one head,[45] in Christ. In him we have also obtained an inheritance, being predestined according to the purpose of him who works all things after the counsel of his will, so that we, who were the first to put our hope in Christ, might be for the praise of his glory."[46]

Again take note that we have indeed been predestined according to the purpose of the Father. We have been made rich, as it were, through a most ancient hope, God having foreknown the matter, prescribing in his own counsels what things would later be granted to us. For when the author of sin deceived Adam in the beginning, he made him to be guilty of the charge of carelessness, and so it came about that he was brought down to death. Then the punishment passed upon all men, this condition coming forth just as things grow out of a root. "For death reigned from Adam to Moses, even over those who had not[47] sinned in the likeness of Adam's transgression."[48]

Of necessity, therefore, the Maker made prior provision for his own creatures, and prepared for us a second root, as it were, of a

---

44. Rom 16.25–27.
45. *anakephalaiôsasthai*, "recapitulate." Cf. n. 9 above.
46. Eph 1.7–12.
47. Cyril, by accident no doubt, omitted the negative.
48. Rom 5.14.

race that would raise us back up to our former incorruption. So, as the image of the first man taken from the ground was imprinted upon us, which had to suffer death and be ensnared in the cords of corruption, thus also in the case of our second beginning after that first one, that is to say, Christ, in whose likeness we are made through the Spirit, incorruptible nature is impressed upon us. And just as the disobedience found in that first man brought us into punishment, so the total surrender and complete obedience in this second man made us to be partakers of heavenly blessing from the Father. For "the first man Adam," it says, "became a living soul [29], the last Adam a life-giving spirit."[49] It also explains this to us in other words when it says, "The first man was from the dust; the second man is the Lord from heaven. As was the man of dust, so also are those who are of the dust, and as is the heavenly man, so too are those who are heavenly. And just as we have borne the image of the man of dust, so we shall also bear the image of the heavenly man."[50] And again, "Christ redeemed us from the curse of the law, having become a curse for us."[51] For "he humbled himself," as it is written.[52] And the Only-Begotten Word of God voluntarily came down into our estate, not that he might be ruled over by death along with us, through Adam transmitting deadness to him, since he himself is the one who makes all things alive, but that having manifested that nature which was subject to corruption, he might transform it into life. This is the reason he became flesh. Thus the wise Paul writes, "For since through man came death, also through man came the resurrection of the dead. As in Adam all die, even so in Christ all will be made alive."[53]

It is absurd to think that Adam, who was earthly and human, when the curse came upon him, could spread its effects upon the whole of the race, as a kind of inheritance, while Emmanuel, who was from heaven above and God by nature, who also possessed our likeness, having become a second Adam for us,

49. 1 Cor 15.45.
50. 1 Cor 15.47–49.
51. Gal 3.13.
52. Cf. Phil 2.8.
53. 1 Cor 15.22.

could not make the very ones who wished to participate in a relationship with him by faith to share abundantly in his own life. For through the mystical blessing we have indeed become fellow members of his body. Yet we have also been united with him in another way, because we have become "partakers of his divine nature"[54] through the Spirit. For he resides in the souls of the saints, as the blessed John also says, "By this we know that he is in us, by the Spirit whom he has given us."[55] He is himself, therefore, our life and our justification. Again it is written, "So then, as through the transgression of one man condemnation came upon all men, so also through the righteous act of one man there came justification and life for all men."[56] And again, "For as through the one man's disobedience many were made sinners, so also through the one man's obedience many will be made righteous."[57]

It is apparent, then, how in the first Adam the mystery of Christ was then represented. It was not that an indistinguishable sameness between them was prefigured, but there was both a difference and a contrast in form. For Adam was the beginning of the race, with respect to death, the curse, and condemnation. But Christ was the complete reverse, bringing life, blessing, and justification. Adam received the woman as one flesh with himself, and came to ruin through her. Yet Christ, uniting the church to himself through the Spirit, rescues and saves her, and accomplishes better things for her than the devil did in his deceit. Thus we are encouraged to proclaim that "we are not ignorant of his schemes."[58] Our forefather Adam, as the wages of sin and the punishment for transgression, received corruption [32]. Yet righ-

---

54. 2 Pt 1.4. Cyril cites from this verse more frequently than any other writer during the patristic period, and usually does so with reference to the Holy Spirit. See Norman Russell, *The Doctrine of Deification in the Greek Patristic Tradition* (Oxford: Oxford University Press, 2004), 213–14; Bernard Meunier, *Le Christ de Cyrille d'Alexandrie: L'humanité, le salut, et la question Monophysite* (Paris: Beauchesne, 1997), 163–65; Daniel A. Keating, *The Appropriation of Divine Life in Cyril of Alexandria* (Oxford: Oxford University Press, 2004), 144.

55. 1 Jn 3.24.
56. Rom 5.18.
57. Rom 5.19.
58. 2 Cor 2.11.

teousness was attributed to Christ, according to the insanity of the Jews, as an offense. So, because he suffered death he is crowned with honor and glory, as the blessed Paul says.[59] And while only a few things upon earth were subject to Adam, all things are subject to Christ. For to him every knee shall bow, of those in heaven, upon earth, and under the earth, and every tongue shall confess that Jesus Christ is Lord to the glory of God the Father.[60] Amen.

Concerning Cain and Abel

1. As I said above, human nature, right at the beginning of the race in Adam, became subject to death and sin, and is redeemed in no other way except through Christ alone, for, as his disciple wrote, "There is no other name under heaven given among men by which we must be saved."[61] For it was necessary that he, through whom all things were brought into existence,[62] should become the restorer[63] of what was corrupted, to nullify the debilitating effects of sin, to do away with pain, and also to bestow richly that good estate upon those who have come into being through him.

I for my part hold this wonderful restoration to be a work of divine power and authority, one that is able to bring things into existence out of that which does not exist, and to summon those things which are, to all intents and purposes, deprived of excellence and wholeness, and to bring them back to a good estate. While the outline of these things was indeed shown in Adam, one may also see the same no less depicted in those who were born to him. For in Christ, God the Father has brought together the things in heaven and the things upon earth under one head.[64] What had fallen into an unseemly condition is raised back up to its first estate. It is only through Christ, then, that those things which had intruded into creation are now gone

---

59. Cf. Heb 2.9.
60. Cf. Phil 2.10–11.
61. Acts 4.12.
62. Cf. Jn 1.3 and Col 1.16.
63. Or "renewer."
64. See n. 45 above.

into nothingness, and that those things upon the earth are being restored into a renewed creation. For in him there is "a new creation,"[65] and this word is true.

Observe, then, that the mystery of Christ, through whom we have been saved, is also present in both Abel and Cain. Thus it is written in Genesis: *Adam knew his wife Eve, and she conceived and gave birth to Cain. And she said, "I have acquired a man through God." She again gave birth to his brother Abel. Now Abel was a shepherd of sheep, while Cain worked the soil. And it happened after some time that Cain brought some of the fruit of the ground as an offering to the Lord. Abel too brought some of the firstborn of his sheep and of their fatlings. God had regard for Abel and his gifts, but he did not give heed to Cain and his offerings. Cain was greatly troubled and his face was downcast. Then the Lord God said to Cain, "Why are you grieved? And why is your face downcast? If you had offered it in the right way, yet not discerned it correctly, would you not have sinned? Be still, his attention will be on you, and you will rule over him."*[66] *After a short while Cain said to Abel his brother, "Let us go into the field." And it happened when they were in the field that Cain rose up against Abel* [33] *his brother and killed him. The Lord God said to Cain, "Where is your brother Abel?" And he said, "I do not know. Am I my brother's keeper?" God said, "What have you done? The voice of your brother's blood is crying out to me from the ground. And now you will be cursed from the earth which has opened up its mouth to receive your brother's blood from your hand. When you till the ground, it will no more yield you its strength. You will be groaning and trembling upon the earth." Cain said to the Lord, "My crime is too great for me to be forgiven! If you drive me away today from the face of the ground, I will be hidden from your presence, and I will be groaning and trembling upon the earth. And it will happen that whoever finds me will kill me." The Lord God said to him, "Not so! Whoever kills Cain will suffer sevenfold vengeance."*[67] *Then the Lord God placed a mark upon Cain, so that no one who found him would kill him. And Cain went out from the presence of God.*[68]

65. 2 Cor 5.17.
66. The pronouns "his" and "him" may also be translated as "its" and "it."
67. Or "will be punished seven times." The verb *ekdikeisthai* may mean either "be avenged" or "be punished." In the subsequent treatment, of both this text and 4.24, Cyril takes it primarily in the latter sense.
68. Gn 4.1–16.

2. So Cain and Abel were both born to Adam. They were, so to speak, tender and blossoming shoots, growing up from the first root in the beginning. The human nature that they possessed sought to bear offspring. Though the act of increasing and multiplying was barely evident at first, later it became more prevalent.

Now Cain came forth first in order of birth. Then it is stated that Abel came after him. All the while they were tender and young, they were like any youngsters brought up together by their parents. But when the young men reached their adolescence, and from there came into adulthood, they turned to different kinds of work. As for Cain, he took pleasure, I believe, in the earth bringing forth vegetation, in seeing it abundantly flourishing with trees and being fruitful, producing diverse kinds of fruit in season. It seemed that he should give the earth a more pleasant appearance by the goodness[69] of those things that were to be seen. And these things, naturally delightful in themselves, were to some degree intended for this purpose of propagating beauty, though they may indeed be the product of agricultural labor, readily coming forth to make an incomparably wonderful sight. Certainly then, Cain was suited to living a life out in the fields. Applying all his energy, he had the desire of achieving this purpose. Nature likewise gave him understanding of these matters, and an unspoken divine law to some extent inscribed upon his mind the knowledge of those things he chose to do.

While Cain considered such matters to be worthy of exertion and much labor, the wise Abel, declining to labor over trees, to dig the soil and take up the sickle, devoted himself to flocks of sheep.[70] Perhaps he was given the inclination for this task by the lambs that one moment were scarcely able to bleat and that were still echoing weakly the sounds of their mothers, and yet were shortly leaping about on legs only recently become firm and feeding themselves on the grass, as well as the bleating goats darting about effortlessly upon the highest rocks. Abel, I believe, being extremely wise, deemed the life of a shepherd to be a most worthy lot, regarding it as something that in a way was a prelim-

---

69. Var. "fitness, usefulness."
70. Lit. "rams."

inary training for being in leadership over men, and that ruling was like this. With regard to those governing peoples, nations, cities, or populations [36], it is the custom both of the inspired Scripture itself and of the speech of the Greeks to call them shepherds. Certainly then, the two young men were differently inclined, one to working the soil, and the other to shepherding, which perhaps was something better.

When some time had passed and Cain's plantations had grown full and were laden with fine fruit, he made an offering. And Abel, there being such a numerous multitude of animals that he had gathered, also rendered what was due. Now there is within us a law of divine knowledge that is innate.[71] This was drawing the men to the fact that it was necessary to present thank offerings to the Maker of all, to the God who gives us every good thing. For although the intention that men should recognize who it is that made all things has been corrupted and is perhaps not truly apprehended among those who worship idols, yet an innate and compelling law prompts us and an instinctive knowledge stirs us up, in order that we should perceive that which transcends all—the one who is incomparably greater than we humans are, that is to say, God.

So then, the holy and all-wise Abel brought the best of the flock, selected according to their quality, for it says, *he brought some of the firstborn of his sheep and of their fatlings*, that is, the most excellent and most outstanding animals. And as he was not ignorant of the manner in which to offer worship, he presented the fatlings. Cain, however, did not do this, but acted carelessly. The better part of his ripe produce he used to gratify his own excessive desires, and grieved the God of all by giving him the second best. So it was that fire came down from heaven upon Abel's gifts and consumed his offerings, but it says, *he did not give heed to Cain and his offerings*. For the expected fire did not issue forth upon the things that had been presented.

At this Cain was extremely vexed and terribly agitated. When he learned the cause of this rejection and that Abel had obtained a better outcome, he was not inclined to rectify his mistakes, but rather he became wild and unduly angry, more so than any other

---

71. Lit. "implanted," "inherent."

man, suffering the pangs of uncontrollable envy. Although he was, in effect, retaliating against the God of all for his rejection, he cunningly sought vengeance from his praiseworthy brother. He trampled the law of natural affection underfoot, and having a mind full of diabolical evil and profane scheming, he framed a fair speech, for he said, *"Let us go into the field."* Note how he calls him into the fields, as though Abel might inspect the excellence of his cultivation and so that he might enjoy a view of the many different kinds of plants. But Cain acted profanely and delivered up his blood brother as a kind of firstfruits to death. So he instructed humanity in the way to commit murder.

When God inquired, saying, *"Where is your brother Abel?"* the wretched man lied and countered the question sharply by saying, *"I do not know."* Yet once he was convicted as a murderer and subject to the curse, he believed that he himself would also die, though if God did not will this, there would be deliverance for him from the wrath of God. For he said, *"If you drive me away today from the face of the ground, I will be hidden from your presence, and I will be groaning and trembling upon the earth. And it will happen that whoever finds me will kill me."*

That Cain, however, would [37] be altogether subject to a curse and would undergo the punishment for his profane actions through spending his life on earth in a most miserable way,[72] God clearly affirmed when he said, *"Not so! Whoever kills Cain will suffer sevenfold vengeance."*[73] Here he puts "seven" instead of "many." So it is as if the one who granted Cain bodily life were saying he would freely waive the punishment of the fratricide's many profane trespasses. Yet if one should wish to say that the number of deeds to be avenged[74] was in fact seven, it would not be at all difficult to enumerate them. First there was Cain's sin when he failed to distinguish correctly and did not set apart for God the most excellent of all his produce. Secondly, in learning of his sin he was not led to a change of heart, nor was he moved to correct his failings by the desire to do better. Rather, he was stirred to anger and provoked by the good conduct of his

---

72. Lit. "thrice-unhappily."
73. See n. 67 above.
74. Or "punished."

fellow man, whom he ought rather to have altogether admired, not considering him an enemy, nor unjustly viewing him with suspicion. Thirdly, his unrestrained envy was what set him on the path, as it were, of committing savage murder. Fourthly, the words *"Let us go into the field"* show trickery and deceit. Fifthly, there is the charge of profane bloodthirstiness. The fact that Cain told lies to God may be reckoned as his sixth transgression. And for the seventh, although God did not will it, Cain supposed that he was able to escape punishment completely, and not be removed from life in the body against his will. But it says, *God placed a mark upon Cain, so that no one who found him would kill him. And Cain went out from the presence of God.* So he was immediately placed under a curse, and the life of an outcast ensued. For how indeed might that perfectly pure and most holy Being have looked upon one who had now reached the height of all evil?

3. Up till now these matters have been expressed to us in a literal way by means of earthly[75] events. Yet if we change the picture that is outlined, as it were, into one that is colored, and refashion the shadow of the letter into the reality, and, come now, if we examine each of these things in great detail, then we may say that one can perceive the mystery of Christ foreshadowed by what happened long ago. For when human nature had become disposed towards[76] sin and was unexpectedly caught by the snares of death, it was necessary that the mystery of the restoration to a better state should be announced beforehand, and that Christ, who would later die on our account and for our sakes, should not be unknown.

So our forefather Adam was made, according to the faith contained in the sacred Scriptures, *in the image and likeness of God.*[77] Then Cain was born first and came forth from Adam, and Abel was born second after him. Now Cain we take as representing Israel. Thus Christ himself considered it appropriate to indicate that the people of the Jews were of the same character as Cain. For he said to them, "If you abide in my word, you will truly be my disciples, and you will know the truth, and the truth will

---

75. *en pachei.*
76. Var. "fallen into."
77. Cf. Gn 1.26–27; 5.1.

set you free."[78] But they, although they did not understand the wonderful manner of freedom enjoyed by the patriarchs, undertook to boast of fleshly glory, saying, "We are descendants of Abraham and have never been slaves to anyone. How can you say [40], 'You will be made free'?"[79] What did Christ say in response to this? "If you were children of Abraham," he said, "you would do the deeds of Abraham. But now you seek to kill me, a man who has told you the truth which I heard from the Father.[80] This is not what Abraham did."[81] He then identifies Satan as their father, saying, "You do the deeds of your father. That one was a murderer from the beginning and does not stand in the truth. For he is a liar and the father of lies."[82] We would not in any way maintain, if we interpret this correctly, that Christ was speaking of the original demon of evil. Rather, for these raging Jews who bore feelings of such profane murderousness against him, he makes the first murderer and liar, namely Cain, to be their father, and Satan, the author of sin, to be Cain's father. We will grant that some further teach that the devil had a father, or we may say that there was some kind of archetypal form of his depravity. Yet it is to the example provided by Cain, being, as it were, a kind of pattern, that Christ ascribes those who are said to be diseased in every respect with the same profanity that was in Cain. That it was the practice of Christ the Savior to call "Satan" those who resembled him in character, we can see without the least difficulty when he said to the holy disciples, "Did I not choose the twelve of you? Yet behold, one of you is a devil."[83]

So Israel, of which it was written, "Israel is my firstborn son,"[84] is compared to Cain. Then after Israel the firstborn, second in order of time came Christ, the youngest son. He was himself also a son of Adam, and so he wisely and appropriately everywhere calls himself the Son of Man.[85] Now Israel in fact thought

78. Jn 8.31–32.
79. Jn 8.33.
80. Var. "from God" (as Jn 8.40).
81. Jn 8.39–40.
82. Jn 8.44. Lit. "the father of him."
83. Jn 6.70.
84. Ex 4.22.
85. The Hebrew name Adam means "man," "human being."

they were honoring God by offering things that were transient and temporary, things of very little account, and their whole mind was set upon earthly concerns. For Cain gave himself to tilling the soil, while Abel was a herder of sheep. So Emmanuel was leader of the spiritual flock, and he is the good shepherd, feeding the heavenly and earthly flocks in a fertile place and on good pasture, as it is written.[86] To him also the prophetic word declares, "Shepherd your people, the sheep of your inheritance, with the staff of your protection."[87]

Israel, then, actually thought it fit to honor God with what was most earthly, offering up those things prescribed in the law, and yet were dedicating these sacrifices to him in an unwilling manner. Therefore, Israel was told through the mouth of the saints,[88] "I do not desire the burnt offerings of your rams, nor the fat of sheep, nor the blood of goats and bulls, neither shall you come to appear before me. For who has required these things from your hands? You shall no more tread my courts. If you bring fine flour, it is in vain; incense is an abomination to me."[89] And again, "Why do you bring me frankincense from Sheba, and cinnamon from a distant land? Your burnt offerings are not acceptable, and your sacrifices have not been pleasant to me."[90] This is evidently the same as when God paid no heed to the offerings of Cain.

The righteous Abel, however, who is Christ [41], offers to God the firstborn of the spiritual sheep, that is, those who are tender-hearted, childlike with respect to evil, excelling in virtue, and bearing the glory of the firstborn through sharing in his image. For the multitude of those called through faith to sanctification are designated by the divine Paul as "the assembly[91] of the firstborn, whose names are registered in heaven."[92]

So Christ has now become the officiating priest of this holy

---

86. Cf. Ezek 34.14.
87. Mi 7.14. The addition of *phulakês sou*, "of your protection," to the citation is unique to Cyril.
88. Var. "saint." By this term Cyril means the holy prophets.
89. Is 1.11–13.
90. Jer 6.20.
91. Or "church."
92. Heb 12.23.

multitude and of the flock of the firstborn. "For through him we have access in the Spirit to God the Father."[93] We have become an offering that is good and acceptable, more so than a young calf with horns and hooves. For indeed, access through the blood of animals is base and earthy, and offers no pleasant aroma to God. Yet the worship that is in spirit[94] and through Christ is greatly pleasing to the Father. And so to the people of Israel who offer earthly things, God declares, "I will not receive calves from your home, nor goats from your flocks, for every wild animal is mine, and the cattle and oxen on the mountains. I know all the birds of the sky, and the beauty of the field is mine. If were hungry, I would not tell you; for the earth is mine and all it contains."[95] But to us who are justified in Christ and sanctified in the Spirit, he proclaims, "Offer to God a sacrifice of praise, and pay your vows to the Most High. Call upon me in the day of your affliction, and I will deliver you, and you will glorify me."[96] Surely then, spiritual offerings are better than those given from the earth, and the offering made through Christ is much more excellent than offerings made according to the law.

So God did not favor the offerings of Cain, but those of Abel. And for what reason? Israel did in fact rightly make offerings, for it was necessary to sacrifice to God. Yet they did not have the correct discernment, but were always attending to types, supposing that God rejoiced in those things that were in the form of shadows. Therefore, Israel sinned and were commanded to be still, that is, to cease from the old practices of the law and to receive Christ as their ruler. For it was said to Cain, *"You have sinned. Be still,"* and with regard to Abel, *"His attention will be on you, and you will rule over him."*[97]

If Israel had wanted access to God without recourse to earthly things, abandoning the unprofitable ministration according

---

93. Cf. Eph 2.18.
94. Cf. Jn 4.23–24. As noted in the introduction, Cyril devoted his first treatise on the Pentateuch, *De adoratione et cultu in spiritu et veritate,* to the idea that Christians, in contrast to the Jews, worship "in spirit and in truth."
95. Ps 50.9–12 (49.9–12 LXX).
96. Ps 50.14–15 (49.14–15 LXX).
97. See n. 66 above.

to the law, and if they had accepted Christ as their leader and guide for the way to something better, then they would have been made free along with us, and been entered in "the book of the living," as the Scriptures say.[98] Since, however, like Cain they considered the good character of our Savior as an occasion for envy and an incitement to murder, they fell under a curse and became liable to a sevenfold punishment.[99] For those wretched people became subject to many punishments and had to endure harsh penalties, perpetually *groaning and trembling*. For they were everywhere treated as strangers and outsiders, and they were fearful, lacking the self-determination which it is most proper for free people to possess.

Nevertheless, Cain received a sign that he would not be killed.[100] For Israel as a whole did not perish, but a remnant was saved, in accordance with [44] the words of the prophet who, having knowledge of this, declared it ahead of time, saying, "Unless the Lord of hosts had left us a seed, we would have become like Sodom, and we would have become the same as Gomorrah."[101] Also with regard to this, the divine singer beseeched the God of all that Israel should not totally be destroyed, saying, "Do not kill them, lest they forget your law."[102]

Yet Cain departed from the presence of God, for it is written that *Cain went out from the presence of God*. So the people of Israel experienced something such as this, concerning whom it is spoken through the mouth of the prophet, "When you stretch out your hands to me, I will turn my eyes away from you; and if you offer many prayers, I will not listen to you; for your hands are full of blood."[103] For they killed the Lord of all, and in their great profanity were so bold as to say, "His blood be upon us and upon our children."[104]

The blood of Abel cried out, one would suppose, only against his murderer, but the precious blood of Christ cried out against

98. Cf. Ps 69.28 (68.29 LXX); Phil 4.3; Rv 3.5; 13.8, etc.
99. See n. 67 above regarding the twofold sense of the word.
100. Var. add "that anybody who found him would not kill him."
101. Is 1.9.
102. Ps 59.11 (58.12 LXX).
103. Is 1.15.
104. Mt 27.25.

the cruelty and offensiveness of the Jews. Moreover, it delivered the world from sin,[105] since it was shed for it. That is why the divine Paul said that we who have been justified by faith have come near through "the sprinkled blood that speaks better things than that of Abel."[106] And it would be appropriate, I believe, to apply this to the things that have been stated.

Now after Abel had died, it says, *Adam knew his wife Eve, and she conceived and gave birth to a son, and called his name Seth, saying, "God has raised up for me another son*[107] *in the place of Abel, whom Cain killed."*[108] Then, after that it says, *Adam lived two hundred and thirty years, and he became the father of a son in his own form and in his own image, and he called his name Seth.*[109]

Note then, that after Abel's death, another son, Seth, was born, resembling him who was the image and likeness of God, that is, Adam. And so after Emmanuel died with respect to his flesh, he immediately brought forth another child for Adam, one who in himself possessed the surpassing beauty of the divine image in great abundance. For we who believe in Christ are formed anew through the Spirit. That the death of Christ was, as it were, the root and cause of this manner of people, he himself affirmed, saying, "Truly, truly, I say to you, unless a grain of wheat falls into the ground and dies, it remains alone; but if it dies, it bears much fruit."[110] So when like a grain he fell into the ground, he was like an ear of wheat, but later he bore fruit, and human nature was refashioned in him, brought back to the original image, to be just as the first man was.

4. It is also worthwhile for us to inquire into the progeny of both Cain and Seth, for to do so would certainly be of further profit to us.

It is written thus: *And Cain knew his wife, and she conceived and gave birth to Enoch,*[111] *and he was a builder of a city, and he named*

---

105. Var. "it presented to the world the forgiveness of sin."
106. Heb 12.24.
107. Lit. "seed," "offspring" (*sperma*).
108. Gn 4.25.
109. Gn 5.3.
110. Jn 12.24.
111. Cyril in fact here writes "Enos." Both the Hebrew text and the LXX

the city after the name of his son, Enoch. To Enoch was born Irad. Irad became the father of Mehujael, Mehujael the father of Methuselah, and Methuselah the father of Lamech. Now Lamech took for himself two wives. The name of one was Adah, and the name of the other was Zillah. [45] *He said to his wives, Adah and Zillah, "Hear my voice, you wives of Lamech; give ear to my words. For I have killed a man for wounding me, even a young man for injuring me. Since Cain is avenged seven times, Lamech shall be avenged seventy-seven times."*[112] In these words you have a plain account of the progeny descended from Cain. Let us now also look at the progeny of Seth.

It is further written: *Seth lived two hundred and five years and became the father of Enosh.*[113] Concerning Enosh the sacred Scripture says, *He hoped to call upon the name of the Lord God. And all the days of Seth were nine hundred and twelve years, and then he died. Enosh lived a hundred and ninety years and became the father of Kenan. And all the days of Enosh were nine hundred and five years, and then he died. Kenan lived a hundred and seventy years and became the father of Mahalalel. And all the days of Kenan were nine hundred and ten years, and then he died. Mahalalel lived a hundred and sixty-five years and became the father of Jared. And all the days of Mahalalel were eight hundred and ninety-five years, and then he died. Jared lived a hundred and sixty-two years, and became the father of Enoch.*[114] Then it says, *And Enoch pleased God, and he was not found, because God took him away.*[115]

We note, then, before anything else how those descended from Cain are named, and how the account of successive generations takes its course. The fact is, the length of the life of each one, in terms of the number of years, is not expressly presented, as is obviously the case with those born from Seth. For there the

---

read "Enoch" at this point. Evidently, Cyril confuses the first son of Cain (Gn 4.17) with Enosh, the first son of Seth (v. 26). In the list that follows in this section, the names are made to conform to the forms appearing in modern English versions, which for the most part consist of transliterations from the Hebrew.

112. Gn 4.17–19; 23–24. Again note the comment in n. 67.
113. Gn 5.6.
114. Gn 4.26; 5.8–9, 11–12, 14–15, 17–18.
115. Gn 5.24. The verb *metethēken* may also be rendered "translated," "transferred."

age of each one is precisely recorded, how long he lived, both before and after the birth of his children, that one might learn from the sacred Scriptures with more exactness and in greater detail. So how God did not suffer himself to know the life of those who loved sin is not an irrelevant piece of information for those who care to investigate such matters thoroughly. Accordingly, at the divine judgment seat those people will hear Christ saying, "Truly I tell you, I never knew you."[116] Now it is indeed the case that there is nothing that escapes the knowledge of the God of all things. Although in one sense, however, he knows those who love sin, in another sense he does not know them, since he is greatly indisposed towards them.

Therefore, in the case of those descended from Cain, the period of their life is passed over in silence. For they had surely done nothing worth remembering, but rather things that probably would be to the detriment of those who would read about them in this record. And so they are not mentioned by God, and quite rightly. He deems it pertinent to know the lives of the saints in detail, and nothing, it seems to me, of the lives of those who have forsaken a divine and undefiled mind. Our Lord Jesus Christ affirms the truth of this when he says, "Are not two sparrows sold for a penny? Yet not one of them falls to the ground apart from our Father in heaven. And even the hairs on your head are all numbered."[117] Now if even the number of their hairs is considered of interest to God, in that he clearly knows everything about them and does indeed care for them, how could it possibly [48] be that their very lifespans should be unknown? "For the eyes of the Lord," it says, "are upon the righteous."[118]

Also Enoch, the next in line immediately after Cain, had a city on earth named after him. Yet in the matter of the degree of glory that will belong to the saints, they should think and say, "Here we have no lasting city, but we are looking for the one that is to come, whose designer and maker is God."[119] They consider their life in this world to be a sojourning, and describe it as such.

116. Mt 7.23.
117. Mt 10.29–30.
118. Ps 34.15 (33.16 LXX).
119. Heb 13.14; 11.10.

So the divine David sings in a certain place, "Spare me, because I am a stranger in the land and a sojourner, as all my fathers were."[120] But with regard to those who mind earthly things, he says in the Forty-eighth Psalm, "They called their lands[121] after their own names."[122]

Now the divine Enosh came forth from Seth. About him it is written that *he hoped to be called by the name of the Lord his God.*[123] For in Christ the holy and sacred progeny live in the hope of a glory that transcends our human estate. Though being of the earth, we have been called to adoption as children of the Master of all and to be brothers of Christ, who for our sakes became one of us, so that thanks to him we may possess a better estate, transcending that which is human, and through his grace and love for humankind become "gods," and enjoy his glory. For he declares, "I said, 'You are gods, and you are all sons of the Most High.'"[124]

So Enosh hoped that others would call him by the name of the Lord his God, that is, "god." For since he was renowned as one who was admired for the splendor of his piety, some of the more refined sort of men who wished to bestow upon him the highest honor called him "god."

Let us, then, receive these words according to their proper intent. For the Jews, who are also representations of the offspring of Cain, because they exist, are known by the God of all. That they, however, are not registered in the book of life is evident from the fact that the lives of those descended from Cain are passed over in silence. That the progeny who are in Christ

---

120. Ps 39.12–13 (38.13–14 LXX); 119.19 (118.19 LXX).

121. Cyril mistakenly writes *genôn* ("generations," "families") for *gaiôn* ("lands"), possibly due to the presence of *genea* in the immediately preceding colon of the psalm.

122. Ps 49.11 (48.12 LXX).

123. Gn 4.26. Contrary to his first citation of these words earlier in this section, Cyril here alters the sense of the LXX, "to call upon the name," to the passive expression "to be called by the name." Indeed, it is not impossible that the text of the LXX itself may be rendered "to be called *the name of the Lord his God*," where the italicized words serve as a complement to the passive verb. By his change, therefore, Cyril may have believed he was bringing out a meaning inherent in the biblical text.

124. Ps 82.6 (81.6 LXX); cf. Jn 10.34.

are registered in the book, and also in God's memory, may be demonstrated, I believe, by the fact that the lives of the righteous, namely those descended from Seth, have been expressly recorded.

Now Enoch, being the second in line immediately after Cain, had a city named after him. Likewise, the wretched Jews are mindful only of the things of the earth, as they do not know the assembly[125] of the firstborn, nor do they strive to attain the heavenly city. But the son born to Seth, that is, Enosh, will be highly approved, for he is now called "god" by name. So through faith we who have run to Christ have been made rich with the same glory, being firmly established through our hope in him.

I would further add another important observation to the things I have said. If one cared to trace the genealogies from Cain and Seth beginning with Adam, who was, as it were, the root of each of them, he would in fact find that Lamech is the seventh in the line of descent through Cain, and that Enoch is the seventh in the line through Seth. The listing of the descendants in both lines is as follows: Adam, Cain, Enoch, Irad, Mehujael, Methuselah, Lamech; and Adam, Seth, Enosh, Kenan, Mahalalel, Jared, Enoch.

Let us note, then, what it says about each of these two—Lamech and Enoch. Lamech spoke to his wives [49], and said, *"Hear my voice, you wives of Lamech; give ear to my words. For I have killed a man for wounding me, even a young man for injuring me. Since Cain is avenged seven times, Lamech shall be avenged seventy-seven times."*[126] But by faith righteous Enoch was taken away so that he would not see death, as the blessed Paul declared, *and he was not found, because God took him away.*

For in the latter times when the Sabbath rest in Christ came into being, Israel was indeed fearful, appearing to have fallen under the dread of punishment, like someone who had killed a man, and who was being judged over the matter of shedding holy blood. Yet they were much more fearful than Cain was. For he who acted wrongfully against a man like us became liable to a sevenfold punishment, but those who treated Emmanuel him-

---

125. Or "church."
126. See n. 67. For "not see death," see Heb 11.5.

self so profanely have been held to account much more severely. For Cain was avenged seven times, and the offspring of Israel seventy-seven times. Indeed, punishment will follow profane deeds in due proportion.

Those, however, who, since the time of Christ's coming, have been approved through faith in him may no more be found when Satan seeks them. For they will be taken by God to an incomparably better and more wondrous life with him, removed from death and corruption to everlasting life, from concern with things of the flesh to desiring to do the things that please God, from dishonor to glory, from weakness to might, in Christ Jesus our Lord, through whom and with whom, be glory to the Father,[127] together with the Holy Spirit, for ever and ever. Amen.

---

127. Var. "to God the Father."

BOOK TWO: GENESIS 6–14

Concerning Noah and the Ark

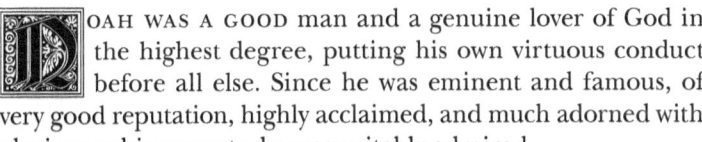OAH WAS A GOOD man and a genuine lover of God in the highest degree, putting his own virtuous conduct before all else. Since he was eminent and famous, of very good reputation, highly acclaimed, and much adorned with glorious achievements, he was suitably admired.

So the account proceeds with regard to Noah; and, since it establishes the course of events that happened as a picture and type, as it were, of the salvation through Christ, it would, in my opinion, be of immeasurable profit to the readers. Come then, and let us describe, as we are able, each detail concerning him, refining the earthiness[1] of the literal sense, and skillfully[2] transforming the things that occurred visibly into matter for spiritual contemplation.

2. Now Seth was born to Adam after the slaying of Abel. And from Seth there came Enosh, who hoped to be called by the name of the Lord his God.[3] [52] So Enosh was called "god" by his contemporaries. For admiring the great degree of righteousness that he possessed, they forthwith called him "god," it being especially fitting for them to assign a name to the man according to his virtue.

Descended from Enosh, the one named "god," there were others, after whom came Lamech, the father of Noah. At the birth of the child, he showed himself to be a prophet, just as Zechariah did at the birth of the blessed Baptist. For Lamech named his son Noah, which, when translated into our language,

---

1. *to pachos,* also "roughness," "coarseness."
2. *asteiôs,* "elegantly," "delicately," "subtly," "in a refined manner."
3. Cf. Gn 4.26 LXX. See the comment in Book 1, n. 123.

means "rest." Lamech gave the reason why he called him this, saying, *"This one will bring us rest from our labors, and from the earth that the Lord God has cursed."*[4] Thus it was with this radiant and most wonderful hope that the birth of Noah was announced to those of long ago.

Noah was the tenth from Adam in the genealogy through Seth. Leading up to him, those descended from Enosh, the one called "god," were duly called "gods" by all others. Then it says, *Noah was five hundred years old and he became the father of three sons, Shem, Ham, and Japheth.*[5] When translated from Hebrew into Greek, Shem means "perfection" or "plant,"[6] Ham means "heat," and Japheth "widening."[7]

Then the sacred Scripture says, *It happened that when there began to be many men upon the earth, and daughters were born to them, the sons*[8] *of God, seeing that the daughters of men were beautiful, took wives for themselves of all that they chose. Then the Lord God said, "My Spirit will not remain among these men for ever, because they are flesh. But their days will be a hundred and twenty years." Now there were giants upon the earth in those days, and also after that.*[9] *And when the sons of God went into the daughters of men, they bore children to them. Those were the giants of old, the men of renown.*[10]

So when the human race had greatly increased in number, the sons of God, it says, had an excessive and untoward desire for women, and they took wives for themselves of all that they chose. Now we are aware that certain manuscripts clearly contain *the angels of God, seeing the daughters of men.* And so some reject the view that men are being accused of the love of the flesh and fasten the blame upon fallen angels who did not keep to their own domain, according to what is written.[11] For my part,

4. Gn 5.29.
5. Gn 5.32.
6. In actual fact, Shem in Hebrew means "name." Cyril gives correct meanings for the other two names.
7. Or "enlarging."
8. Var. "angels." This reading for the text of Gn 6.2 is found in Codex Alexandrinus and several minuscules, and is also that adopted by Philo and Josephus.
9. Or, "and also after that when ..."
10. Gn 6.1–4.
11. Jude 6.

I would say, and indeed affirm, that all manner of disordered thinking would suit these beings, but to allow this as an explanation of this event would be to take things far beyond what is reasonable, and would, in my view, be quite out of place. For our aim is to be disposed to examine the truth of each thing that is written, and not at all to give undue consideration to the disorders of the horde of demons.

We should look especially to the lusts that always accompany the innate inclinations that are within us ourselves. The fact is, [53] we either love the passions of the flesh, or we tend to attach too much importance to those things which pertain to the flesh. Yet, it rightly seems to me, the desire for pleasure does not carry us beyond the bounds of natural laws. We could say that food and drink, or perhaps physical relations with women, are actions and passions of the flesh. Also, by the desire for riches and glory men serve the pleasures of the flesh. Indeed, almost every passion that is in the world comes through these things, as was stated by the wise disciple[12] with respect to "everything in the world, the lust of the flesh, the lust of the eyes, and the pride of life."[13] The intense and powerful lusts of this kind easily entangle us, so that our minds become fixed upon wanting and doing the things of the flesh. There is no argument, however, that could induce us to desire those things outside the body which are contrary to nature.

How then could it not amount to folly to say that spirits, which are distinct from and high above flesh, desire fleshly things? What manner of natural inclination could there be, or what kind of principle could provoke them to act as we ourselves most certainly do, that they should long after those things that arouse the passions? Indeed, we are not here removing any blame from the mass of demons, for they are unholy and profane, disposed towards anything whatsoever that is shameful. Moreover, it can seem that, together with these other things, they might even have a morbid craving for pleasures that are contrary to nature. When, however, the divine Scripture speaks of how the sons of God came together with women, they brought forth those called

---

12. Var. "as the wise disciple understood, saying ..."
13. 1 Jn 2.16.

giants, that is, extraordinary, wondrous beings, though they were rational humans nevertheless. What then ought one to think with regard to this? It was not, in fact, through spirits separated from flesh that the conception of humans in the women came about. Yet some do speak rashly about the matter and misrepresent it, and by means of what they imagine to be persuasive arguments they erroneously make it mean what is impossible. For they say that the evil demons came into men and conceived offspring through them. But we shall find their opinion to be extremely incongruous and full of ignorance. For how is it that we should accept what the divine Scripture has not stated and reckon it as being among those things that are true?

So let us read on: *The sons of God, seeing that the daughters of men were beautiful, took wives for themselves of all that they chose.* The explanation given by other interpreters further confirms that we have correctly read the Scripture in this matter. For Aquila in fact says, *The sons of the gods, seeing the daughters of men,* while Symmachus,[14] in the place of *sons of the gods,* has put *sons of the mighty.* So here it calls those descended from Seth and Enosh the sons of the gods and of the mighty on account of their piety and their love of God, and the ability to overcome, with God's help no doubt, all that opposes them. God showed forth that most sacred and holy race[15] to be illustrious, unmixed with the other race, that is, with those descended from Cain, and also from Lamech, who followed in the footsteps of his father and became a murderer, for he confessed, "I killed a man for wounding me, even a young man for injuring [56] me."[16] So long as the holy race continued in itself to be unmixed with that which was inferior, and while the uncontaminated beauty and radiant purity of godly piety were still theirs, they were to be commended. But when they fell into the love of the flesh, they were drawn away by the beauty of women into a state of rebellion,[17] for it says that they took wives from

---

14. The names of Aquila and Symmachus are associated with alternative Greek translations of the OT to that of the LXX. Both versions appeared during the second century of the Christian era.
15. Or "stock."
16. Gn 4.23.
17. Or "apostasy."

all that they chose of the daughters of men, that is, from the daughters of Cain. Though they were called gods, sons of gods, and sons of the mighty, they were then carried away to practice the habits of those others, being led into a shameful and profane conduct and lifestyle.

Furthermore, these women gave birth to extraordinary offspring. God in fact brought about a degradation in the beauty of their human bodies because of the women's lack of self-control in their appetite for loose sexual relations. So those who were born to them were *giants*, that is to say, men who were savage and of great strength, afflicted with an extremely ugly appearance and possessing bodies of greater size than others.

One should be aware that it is the custom of the language of inspired Scripture to call those who are extremely powerful "giants." So with regard to the Persians and Medes, for instance, it says through the mouth of the prophets, "Giants are coming to fulfill my wrath, rejoicing together and acting derisively."[18]

We will certainly not, however, give heed to the false accounts of the Greeks. For the chief men among them, especially the poets, according to what seemed good to them, were wont to make assertions and invent things about the kind of deeds the giants performed. They liked to make much of insignificant things and matters of no consequence, and by many false myths they thought they could make them great, as if the longer the tale the more appropriate it was. One claims that the whole of Sicily was thrown up into the sky by one of the giants, while another tells yet greater and more incongruous lies about some other giant.

So, as I was saying, the giants were fearful to behold, enormously strong, cruel and foreboding. With bodies of excessive stature, they were undoubtedly taller than other men, though not touching the clouds themselves, as those in the habit of inventing myths about them would claim.

3. So then, once the different races of men had become mixed with one another and all had become inclined towards unrestrained sin, it says, *The Lord God saw that the wickedness of men had increased upon the earth, and that everyone was intently contemplating evil in his heart all the time. God was greatly concerned* (or according to

---

18. Is 13.3 LXX.

another rendering, that of Aquila, *regretted*) *that he had made man upon the earth. He deliberated and said, "I will blot out man whom I have made from the face of the earth, both man and creatures, from the reptiles to the birds of the sky, because I am grieved that I made them." But Noah found favor before the Lord God.*[19]

Note that God determined to blot out every human being. But since Noah was adorned with a devout character, he had regard for him alone and would not destroy him with the rest, but would save all his family. And so God said to him, *"The end of all humankind has come before me, because the earth is filled with their iniquity. Now behold, I am going to destroy them, and the earth. Therefore, make for yourself an ark out of square timber; make the ark with compartments, and coat it with pitch inside and out. And you shall make the ark like this* [57]: *the length of the ark will be three hundred cubits, the width fifty cubits, and its height thirty cubits. You shall assemble the ark when you make it, and you shall complete it to a cubit at the top."*[20]

After other things it further says, *"You shall enter the ark, you, your sons, your wife, and your sons' wives with you, and also from all the wild animals, from all the cattle, and from every kind of flesh, two of each kind you shall bring into the ark so that you may preserve them with yourself. There shall be a male and a female from all of the birds according to their kind, and from all the cattle according to their kind, and from all the reptiles that creep upon the earth according to their kind. Two of each, a male and a female, shall come in to you to be preserved with you. From the clean animals you shall gather seven pairs,*[21] *but one pair from the unclean."*[22]

Subsequently, as the God of all decreed that all these things should come to pass, so all flesh drowned. The rains and hail under the entire heavens, the fury of the waters from the sky above, came flooding down. But the ark floated, with the souls of the righteous as its cargo.

---

19. Gn 6.5–8.
20. Gn 6.13–16. In the final sentence of the citation, the LXX, which Cyril reproduces here, makes little sense. The meaning of the Hebrew seems to be something like: "You shall make a window for the ark, and you shall finish it to a cubit from the top." This would appear to mean that there was the gap of a cubit all the way around immediately below the roof.
21. Or "seven of each."
22. Gn 6.18–20; 7.2.

After a short while, however, the waters began to abate. It says, *The ark came to rest upon the Ararat mountains. Then Noah opened the door of the ark, and he sent out a raven to see if the water had receded from the face of the earth, but it did not return. After that he released a dove, and not finding any resting place for its feet, the dove returned to him in the ark, for the water was still over all the surface of the earth. So Noah stretched out his hand and took it, and brought it back to himself in the ark. Then after seven days he sent it out a second time, and it came back in the evening with a twig of an olive tree in its mouth. After another seven days he sent it out a third time, and it did not return to him again. Thus Noah then knew that all the water had subsided from the earth.*[23] So the dry land appeared again, and everything upon it. When Noah, with his children and all those gathered together, saw that the earth was now rid of the waters, he straight away built an altar and promptly offered the clean and undefiled cattle and birds as burnt offerings. These, I believe, he dedicated as thank offerings to the God who had preserved them. When this took place, *The Lord God*, it says, *smelt the pleasing aroma. Then the Lord God took thought and said, "Never again will I curse the earth because of the deeds of men, for the mind of man is thoroughly inclined towards evil things from his youth. Therefore, I will not smite all living flesh again, as I have done. All the days of the earth, seed and harvest, cold and heat, summer and spring, day and night, shall not cease."*[24]

It further says, *The Lord God blessed Noah and his sons, and said to them, "Increase and multiply, and fill the earth, and have dominion over it. And the fear and dread of you will be upon all the wild animals of the earth, upon all the cattle, upon all the birds of the sky, upon all that moves upon the ground, and upon all the fish of the sea; I have placed them under your authority."*[25] [60]

4. The discussion has now brought us to this point, and viewing it as a narrative according to the letter and in its literal sense, nothing at all, it seems to me, has been left out. So let us now go over the things that have been said to bring out the hidden, inner, spiritual meaning, and let us trace out the mystery of Christ

---

23. Cf. Gn 8.4, 6–12. Here Cyril does not closely follow the LXX text but is quite paraphrastic, even to the extent of changing the order of some clauses.
24. Gn 8.21–22.
25. Gn 9.1–2.

and present Noah himself and the ingenious and mysterious[26] arrangement relating to the ark as a picture of the salvation that comes through Christ.

Now Noah was born to Lamech, not the one who had previously murdered a man and a youth, but the one with the same name in the line of Seth. So too our Lord Jesus Christ sprang up out of Israel, which was holy on account of the fathers, and yet he was of a people who were of the same kind as Lamech and of the same mind as a murderer, who shared the same name as the murderer. So in a certain place it is said to the Jews,[27] "Which of the prophets did your fathers not kill?"[28] And they are told by Christ, "Fill up, then, the measure of your fathers."[29] Again, through the mouth of Isaiah he says, "When you stretch out your hands to me, I will turn my eyes away from you; and if you offer many prayers, I will not listen to you; for your hands are full of blood."[30]

Noah was also the eleventh from Adam. Christ likewise was born according to the flesh in the eleventh and final season, as it were, and commenced the present economy for us. You can learn the truth of this—for you should make every possible inquiry—by being persuaded from the sacred Scriptures. For the one who hired workers for the vineyard at the eleventh hour called out to certain men, those who were from the Gentiles, saying, "Why do you stand here idle the whole day?" And when they openly stated, "No one has hired us," for before the coming of our Savior no one had called the Gentiles to the knowledge of God, he kindly and compassionately said, "You also go into the vineyard, and whatever is fair I will give you."[31]

Furthermore, the law given through Moses decreed that the slaying of the lamb should be carried out "between the evenings,"[32] that is, when the lamps were lit at eventide. Likewise,

26. *aporrētos*, "ineffable," "inexpressible," "esoteric."
27. Var. add "by Christ."
28. Cf. Acts 7.52.
29. Mt 23.32.
30. Is 1.15.
31. Cf. Mt 20.6–7.
32. This phrase, taken from the Passover instructions in Lv 23.5, is rendered by several modern English translations as "twilight" (e.g., NRSV, NIV, NJB).

when the time had come, as it were, for the sun to set, through the age that was then present being in effect shortened, the Only-Begotten Word of God became a man and endured being slain for all, freeing them from any penalty or punishment, removing those who believe far from all such fear. For he himself is the true Noah, that is, righteousness and rest, for that is what the name means.[33] For according to the Scriptures, we have been justified, not by works of righteousness that we ourselves have done, but according to his great mercy.[34] So now for us who believe, Christ has become our righteousness, and in truth our rest also.[35] For "he was bruised because of our iniquities, and was delivered up on account of our sins; and by his wounds we are healed," and also, "the Lord delivered him up for our sins," as the prophet says.[36]

So since Christ has suffered in the flesh for us, we are blessed and esteemed. [61] And why is that? Have we not been called to such things as this? Do we not delight in heavenly gifts, and are we not made rich through participation in these things? And casting off the grievous burden of sin, do we not enjoy spiritual well-being? For he himself called us to this very thing when he said, "Come to me, all who are weary and burdened, and I will give you rest. Take my yoke upon you, and learn from me, for I am gentle and humble in heart, and you shall find rest for your souls."[37] That Christ would give us rest, the[38] archangel Gabriel also declared to the holy Virgin, when he said, "Do not be afraid, Mary, for you have found favor with God. And behold, you will conceive in your womb, and you will bear a son. You will call his name Jesus, for he will save his people from their sins."[39] The divine prophets also eagerly foreannounced the rest that would come through him. One of them said, "Take courage, O Zion! Do not let your hands hang limp. The Lord your God is among you, the Mighty One will save you, and he will refresh you in his

33. Hebrew: *nōaḥ*, "rest."
34. Cf. Ti 3.5.
35. Or "and our rest also. For in truth ..."
36. Is 53.5–6.
37. Mt 11.28–29.
38. Var. add "blessed."
39. Lk 1.30–31; Mt 1.21.

love."[40] Similarly, Isaiah saw this, as it were, in a revelation and said, "Be strong, you weak hands and feeble knees. Comfort one another, you fainthearted; be strong, do not fear. Behold, our God! Behold, the Lord is coming with strength, and his arm with authority. Like a shepherd he will tend his flock; he will gather the lambs into his arms, and comfort those with young."[41]

Christ, then, has become our righteousness and rest, and has also saved us from the earth which the Lord God cursed. For this is what Lamech was saying when he prophesied to us in regard to Noah.[42] And there is no doubt that the charges brought against the transgression committed in Adam have been remitted in Christ. For he became a curse for us, as it is written,[43] so delivering the earth from the ancient curse. For we say that through him God the Father restores all things[44] to their pristine state. "The old things have passed away, but all things have become new," and "if anyone is in Christ, he is a new creation."[45]

Seeing that Christ is the second Adam, through his obedience he overturns the accusation against the first-formed man, by which I mean he brings about the pardon of the disobedience that occurred in the beginning. This is also what the divine Paul thought about the matter, since he wrote, "For as through the one man's disobedience many[46] were made sinners, so also through the one man's obedience many will be made righteous."[47] Christ was obedient to the Father to the point of death, the death on the cross.[48] So, as at the beginning the earth was put under a curse on account of the transgression committed in Adam, so it has been blessed on account of the obedience of Christ. Besides this, he has also redeemed us from the earth that was under a curse. For

---

40. Zep 3.16–17.
41. Is 35.3–4; 40.10–11.
42. Gn 5.29.
43. Cf. Gal 3.13.
44. *anakephalaiousthai*, "recapitulate, bring under one head"; cf. Eph 1.10.
45. 2 Cor 5.17.
46. The quantitative "many," which appears in the Harleian Codex, has been included. It is, of course, found in the text of Romans that Cyril is here citing.
47. Rom 5.19.
48. Cf. Phil 2.8.

we await new heavens and a new earth, according to his promises, just as the wise disciple of the Savior said.[49] So Christ made anew for us the way back into heaven above, [64] and he also entered as a forerunner on our behalf into the holy land,[50] which he said would be the inheritance of the meek,[51] that is, those who are instructed in the gospel teachings that lead to meekness. The law did indeed command those who had done wrong to be inflicted in return with the loss of "an eye for an eye, a tooth for a tooth, and a wound for a wound,"[52] yet Christ says to us, "To him who strikes you on the right cheek, turn to him the other also."[53]

So then, Noah was the eleventh from Adam through the line of Seth and Enosh, who hoped to be called by the name of the Lord his God on account of his devout behavior and love of God. Likewise, the holy evangelists record the lineage of our Lord Jesus Christ from Adam, and the account of the genealogy goes all the way up to Joseph himself, who was, one might say, a holy man.

5. We may say that the spread of the races into one another was like a mixed mass, a mass that was made up of the holy and that which was not so, namely the profane and abominable. For in the same manner in which those descended from Enosh, who bore the name of God, went madly after the daughters of men, and were of a very different character than he was, choosing to live according to the customs and laws of those men, so as to become afflicted with every extreme kind of corruption, so the same also happened to those descended from the race[54] of Israel. For while they were practicing a holy manner of life, and were noble imitators of the piety of their forefathers, shunning every kind of evil, and being in themselves wholly undefiled, they retained the glory of their commendable[55] behavior. But when they became entangled with the neighboring nations, even though the law spoke against it, they were easily seduced

---

49. 2 Pt 3.13.
50. Or "earth."
51. Cf. Mt 5.5.
52. Ex 21.24–25; Lv 24.20; Dt 19.21.
53. Mt 5.39; Lk 6.29.
54. Lit. "blood."
55. Var. add "and well-ordered."

and readily made unstable, and they soon became infected with the abominable behavior that was found among them. Indeed, by which of the most extreme forms of evil were they not infected and overcome?

Now this is most incredible. The nations, as they had come to serve the creature rather than the Creator and Maker, and had turned away to the error of polytheism besides, paid homage to the hordes of demons; and Israel, which was originally holy through its forefathers, reckoned total apostasy to be of little account. As a result, God said to them through a holy oracle, "Go to the isles of the Kittim and see; send to Kedar and take careful note, and see if such things have happened, whether nations will change their gods, though they are not gods. Yet my people have changed their glory for that which will not profit. Heaven is astonished at this, and the earth trembles exceedingly, says the Lord. For my people have committed two evils: they have forsaken me, the fount of living water, and they have hewn for themselves broken cisterns, which will not be able to hold water."[56] And again, "According to the number of your cities were your gods, O Judah; and according to the number of your streets, O Jerusalem, they sacrificed to Baal. Why will you speak to me? You have all become lawless, and you have all behaved in a godless way towards me, says the Lord."[57]

They fell into such perverse reasoning, and even more perverse deeds, since they were at that time having intercourse with erring women. When children were born, even though they were immediately marked with the sign of the Jewish ministration[58] [65], namely circumcision on the eighth day with the accompanying sacrifices, they were handed over to unclean demons as devoted offerings from a consecrated people. And this, I believe, is the meaning of what was spoken through the mouth of the prophet regarding these matters, "for strange children were born to them."[59]

Consequently, since the holy race had become corrupt through

56. Jer 2.10–13.
57. Cf. Jer 2.28; 11.13.
58. *latreia,* "worship," "service," "cultus," "ministration."
59. Hos 5.7.

their union with those who were inferior, as far as their character and their different disposition and customs are concerned, and since too the nations[60] had joined themselves to the one nation of Israel, the Maker of all justly pronounced the destruction of all the nations that were upon the earth. But being overcome by his innate goodness, he did not vent his wrath in equal proportion to their sins. That the race of men upon earth should not perish entirely, by means of Noah he foreshowed the justification that was by faith and the deliverance through water.

So, as it is written, the Only-Begotten became a man and lived among men, he being the true Noah. Furthermore, corresponding figuratively to that famed ark of ancient times, he constructed, as it were, the church, into which those rush who flee the destruction stored up for the world. Thus the divine Paul interpreted the mystery regarding the ark, saying, "By faith Noah, having been warned, prepared an ark for the salvation of his household,"[61] "in which," as Peter also says, "a few people, that is, eight souls, were saved through water. And baptism, which is prefigured by this,[62] now saves us—not as the removal of dirt from the body, but as the appeal of a good conscience towards God."[63]

Now then, in what manner was the ark constructed? *"You shall make the length of the ark,"* it says, *"three hundred cubits, the width fifty, and the height thirty. You shall assemble the ark when you make it, and you shall complete it to a cubit at the top."* That this construction signified the mystery of Christ, albeit very dimly, should be completely and utterly obvious, since when the divine Paul wrote to those justified by faith, he said how unceasingly he prayed for them, "that they may be able to comprehend with all the saints what is the breadth, and the length, and the height, and the depth, and to know the love of Christ that surpasses knowledge."[64]

---

60. Here reading "nations" (*ethnôn*) with the Harleian manuscript, rather than "customs" (*ethôn*).
61. Heb 11.7.
62. Or "which is the antitype of this."
63. 1 Pt 3.20–21.
64. Eph 3.18–19.

6. What, then, is the significance of the measurements of the ark? It is a true and proper indication of the holy and consubstantial Trinity, the one Deity who possesses perfection, indeed total perfection in absolutely everything. For when we give the matter our consideration, it is this that one might see hinted at in the numbers in question. As is customarily found in the inspired Scripture, those numbers which circle back on themselves constitute symbols of perfection.[65] What I mean is something such as this: a week begins with the first day and ends with a Sabbath on the seventh day, and then we count the sequence again beginning from the first up to the seventh. Similarly, when we come to the number ten, we once more begin with the first and continue until the tenth, and then the same thing happens again. The most perfect number of all, [68] namely one hundred, is the sum of ten times ten, at which point the cycle returns to a single unit again.

So what I am saying is that in the divine Scripture every number that goes back, as it were, once it has reached an end is a purposely designed and fitting symbol of perfection. See then how the perfection of the holy Trinity lies, after this fashion, in the three hundred cubits, which is the length of the ark.[66] And the fact that the Deity, who though being single[67] is a perfection of perfections, if we may put it thus, is especially well indicated by the width, which comes to fifty cubits, that is, seven times seven with a single unit added on account of the fact that the Deity is one being.[68] And then the height bears for us no other sense than this same, for while the height comes to completion in three decads of cubits, yet situated at the top was one single cubit that finished it off. For it says, *"its height will be thirty cubits, and you shall complete it to a cubit."*[69] For while the holy Trinity opens out, as it were, into three distinct subsistences, or separate Persons, it is as though it contracts into the one nature of Deity.

65. In what follows, the words "perfection" and "perfect" also bear the sense of "completion" and "complete."
66. Since 300 is three times the most perfect number, 100, as just described.
67. Or "though existing in a monad [*monas*]."
68. Or "the fact that the Deity has one nature [*phusin*]."
69. That is, a cubit from the top.

Whereas the Greeks erroneously follow the polytheistic way of worship, when we consider the Father and the Son and the Holy Spirit, though we do truly assign them their own distinct subsistences, it is our habit to adorn them with a unity of nature. It is as though by means of this identity of essence we were raising up together[70] the length, the width, and the height by that one cubit, so completing the ark.

So then, Christ preserves us by faith, and it is as though he brings the church to abide in the ark, in which we will sail over the fear of death and escape being condemned along with the world, for the righteous Noah, that is, Christ, will be with us.

7. I think it worthwhile to investigate in detail what interpretation might be given for those who flee with Noah into the ark, who enjoy the salvation that comes through faith and water. It is written that *Noah went into the ark, with his sons, his wife, and his sons' wives.*[71] Noah also took in with them some of every kind of animal and bird, seven pairs of those that were clean, and one pair of the unclean,[72] for God saw fit to issue a law regarding this matter. The names of Noah's sons were Shem, Ham, and Japheth. The meaning of Shem is "plant" or "perfection," Ham means "heat," and Japheth "widening."[73]

Now we have been saved in Christ through faith, having been brought out from the ineffectual manner of life according to the law into the perfection of the gospel teaching, having been bred,[74] as it were, like delicate young calves. The divine David therefore rebuked those of the Jewish people who did not accept the justification that is in Christ, and said, "You have loved wickedness more than goodness, unrighteousness more than speaking righteousness. You have loved all destructive words, and a deceitful tongue."[75] For they spoke ill of the Son without

---

70. Var. "we were closely connecting."

71. Gn 7.7.

72. Cf. Gn 7.8–9. As previously, rather than "seven pairs," the original intention may have been "seven of each." See n. 21 above.

73. On the meanings of the names, see p. 82 above. In the paragraphs that now follow, Cyril unpacks the meaning of each of the three names in turn.

74. *pephuteumenoi,* "engendered," "planted." Here it would seem that Cyril is playing on the supposed meaning of the name Shem, *phuteuma,* "plant."

75. Ps 52.3–4 (51.5–6 LXX).

restraint. "For this reason," it says, "God will destroy you for ever; may he pluck you up and remove you from your dwelling and your root from the land of the living."[76] But with regard to those who love the [69] justification and life that is in Christ, it says, "Those who are planted in the house of the Lord will flourish in the courts of our God."[77]

That Emmanuel wrought his grace in us, which is equivalent to a divine and spiritual fire, being like heat imparted through the Spirit, the divine Paul affirms, wishing those called in holiness to prove themselves "fervent in spirit."[78] The wise John also informs us of precisely this when he says, "I baptize you in water for repentance, but he who is coming after me is more powerful than I, he whose sandals I am not worthy to carry. He will baptize you in the Holy Spirit and fire."[79] For the love of the Jews grew cold because lawlessness abounded among them, as it is written.[80] We ourselves, however, are extremely hot in this respect. Therefore, we say, "What shall separate us from the love of Christ? Shall tribulation, or distress, or famine, or persecution, or nakedness, or danger, or the sword?"[81] Ham then, who is to be taken as meaning "heat," is an especially clear figure of those who are fervent in spirit.

That we, coming out of a straitened[82] life under the law, have been brought to an enlargement of heart, is suggested to us by the third son, Japheth, who bears a name meaning "widening."[83] For God declares to the Jews through the mouth of Isaiah, "Hear the word of the Lord, you straitened men, and you rulers of the people who are in Jerusalem."[84] And again, "Learn to hear, you

76. Ps 52.5 (51.7 LXX).
77. Ps 92.13 (91.14 LXX).
78. Rom 12.11. The verb *zeontas* includes the component of heat, thus "boiling," "seething."
79. Mt 3.11.
80. Cf. Mt 24.12.
81. Rom 8.35.
82. The Greek words rendered "straitened" in this paragraph also contain the idea of "narrowness," being the opposite of course to the meaning of "Japheth," the name presently under consideration.
83. Which might also be rendered as "enlarging" or "extending."
84. Is 28.14.

who are straitened."[85] So Paul, having come out from the narrow confines of the law, declared to certain of those who now believed, saying, "Our mouth has spoken openly to you, O Corinthians; our heart is wide open. You are not straitened by us, but you are straitened in your own affections. Now in return (I speak as to children), open wide your hearts also. Do not be yoked together with unbelievers."[86] For these were still following the commandments of the Jews and foolish and ill-conceived opinions. David too, as though assuming the role[87] of the new people of God in Christ, in a certain passage sings with regard to Christ the Savior of all: "I ran the way of your commandments, when you enlarged my heart."[88] For our mind was enlarged through wisdom when Emmanuel made his dwelling and habitation in the souls of all through the Spirit. These are they who are in Christ through faith.

8. That those who are justified by faith form the larger and purest multitude, and the Jews the lesser, one might readily learn here. For Noah brought seven[89] of the clean animals into the ark, but two of the unclean, that is, of the Jews who murdered the Lord. A remnant of them has in fact been saved, in accordance with the words of the prophet.[90] That some of the race of Israel, however, would later turn away and abandon the faith, is also here outlined. For it says, *he sent out a raven from the ark to see if the water had receded, but it did not return.* I suppose it was drowned in the waters, as it could not find any place to stop. Consequently, [72] to fall away from faith in Christ results in being completely lost.[91] So also to those who after coming to faith desired to be made perfect by the law, that is, those who thought they could so become perfect, the blessed Paul says, "You have been severed from Christ, you who seek to be justified by the

---

85. Is 28.19–20.
86. 2 Cor 6.11–14.
87. *prosôpon,* literally "person," "face." Here is meant the more technical sense of "persona," "character."
88. Ps 119.32 (118.32 LXX).
89. See nn. 21 and 72 above.
90. Cf. Is 10.22.
91. Var. add "and in death."

law; you have fallen from grace. For through the Spirit, by faith, we eagerly await the hope of righteousness."[92]

Note how among the unclean birds the raven is one that is uncontrollable. For after justification in Christ had come, some of the Jews went back to the shadows of the law. And it is concerning these, I would think, that the wise John writes, "They went out from us, but they were not of us. For if they were of us, they would have remained with us."[93] Now the Spirit plainly states, "In later times some will fall away from the faith, giving heed to deceiving spirits."[94] See how there is a clear figure of this also in what Noah did. For he sent out the first and second doves to view the earth, to see if the flood had subsided. But the doves settled into their nests in the ark, and one of them had[95] a twig in its mouth, a small branch from an olive tree, as it is written.[96] For the saints are sent by Christ to survey the world and those in it, yet they settle down, as it were, and speak peace. It is this, I believe, that is suggested by the branch of the olive tree placed crosswise in the mouth of the dove. For this tree is always a symbol of peace.

Now those lovers of God, who have been purified by faith and by the gentleness of the gospel way of life, are God's chosen ones. The type, however, indicates that in later times some of them will fall away, as I was just saying. For the third and final dove was sent out and had no thought of returning, since it stayed away. Then when the flood subsided, the ark came to rest upon the mountains of Ararat, the meaning of which is "witness of descent."[97] For in a way those in Christ through faith are as though they were high in the mountains on account of the exaltedness of their gospel way of life, and they proclaim to people everywhere God the Word, who descended from heaven above.

92. Gal 5.4–5.
93. 1 Jn 2.19.
94. 1 Tm 4.1.
95. Var. "held."
96. Cf. Gn 8.11.
97. This proposed meaning for Ararat is extremely doubtful. The latter part does bear some resemblance to the Hebrew verb *yārad*, "go down," "descend," but even this is far from precise. The Greek noun *katabasis*, "descent," is frequently used by the Church Fathers in incarnational contexts.

To them God himself declared through the prophet, "Be my witnesses, and I too am a witness, says the Lord God, and my servant whom I have chosen."[98] So then, the glory of those who are in Christ is higher than the low estate of the world.

9. Now, that Emmanuel has become a high priest for us, through whom also we have gained access to God the Father, and that we have been restored to our original state, having been set free from the curse, namely that placed upon the first-formed man, one can observe in those things that are written next.

For when the earth had dried up, it says that Noah and all those with him came out of the ark.[99] And then *he built an altar to God, and took some of every clean animal and every clean bird, and offered burnt offerings on the altar. And God smelled the pleasing aroma; and the Lord God considered this and said, "I will never again curse the [73] earth because of men's deeds."*[100] And later it says, *The Lord God blessed Noah and his sons, and said to them, "Increase and multiply, and fill the earth, and rule over it. And the fear and the dread of you will be upon all the wild animals, upon all the cattle of the earth, upon all the birds of the sky, upon all that moves upon the earth, and upon all the fish of the sea. I have placed them under your authority."*[101]

So then, when Christ became our high priest, and through him we were offered spiritually as a pleasing aroma to God the Father, we were then counted worthy of his abundant favor, and we have a sure foundation, that death would no longer have power over us. Also, that wrathful condition, even that which stems from the ancient curse, has been dissolved. For we have been blessed in Christ, through whom and with whom be glory to God the Father, together with the Holy Spirit, for ever and ever. Amen.

Concerning Noah's nakedness and Ham

1. Everything relating to the ark has been concluded, the flood is past, and Noah has now undertaken to till the ground.

---

98. Is 43.10.
99. Cf. Gn 8.19.
100. Gn 8.20–21.
101. Gn 9.1–2.

So we will next inquire into those things in the account that were done by Ham.

This passage urges those who would wish to live uprightly to count absolutely nothing as equal to having respect for one's parents, and distinctly to refrain, as something most perilous, from mocking them in any way whatsoever, even though it may be that they are carried away from proper conduct for a brief while by the weaknesses of their human nature.

That it is always necessary to be respectful to one's parents, the divine law itself also teaches us. For having previously commanded that one ought to love the one Being of God with the whole heart and soul, it says, "Honor your father and your mother, in order that it may go well with you, and you shall live long upon the earth."[102] Those who give us birth should be reckoned as though they were an image and representation of God, for it says, "Remember that it was through them that you were given birth."[103] Again it says, "The eye that mocks a father and dishonors the old age of a mother, let the ravens of the valleys peck it out."[104] Consequently, not to hold that one should honor one's parents and count them worthy of all respect results in a curse or a punishment, as one may readily learn through Ham.

The sons of Noah, it says, *who came out of the ark were Shem, Ham, and Japheth. Ham was the father of Canaan. These are the three sons of Noah. From these, people were scattered over the whole earth. Now Noah became a farmer and planted a vineyard. Then he drank some of the wine and became intoxicated and was naked in his home. And Ham the father of Canaan saw the nakedness of his father, and going out he told his brothers outside. Shem and Japheth took a garment, placed it upon their two shoulders and, walking backwards, covered their father's nakedness. Their faces were turned away, so* [76] *they did not see the nakedness of their father. When Noah became sober from the wine and learned what his younger son had done to him, he said, "Cursed be Canaan, he shall be a servant to his brothers." And he said, "Blessed be the Lord God of Shem; and let Canaan be his servant. May God enlarge*

---

102. Ex 20.12; Dt 5.16. Cyril is incorrect when he claims that the command to love God was given previously. This in fact comes later in Dt 6.5.
103. Sir 7.28.
104. Prv 30.17.

Japheth, and may he dwell in the tents of Shem; and let Canaan be his[105] *servant."*[106]

Now having planted a vineyard, and having labored much, Noah then drank more wine than was his custom. And so while he surprisingly fell under the charge of being a winebibber, suffering the unacceptable act of exposing himself, he remained unseen by most in the home. Yet the one who was unstable in mind, namely Ham, took occasion from the improper sight to engage in profane mockery. Though he might have covered him over, he did not in fact assist his father, who was overcome by drunkenness and led into committing a grave error through the wine. But, neglecting to do this, and showing little of the honor due to the one who had begotten him, Ham hastened to invite others to view the sight, and sought to subject the old man in his tent to the ridicule of his brothers. They, however, were above heeding such evil counsel. Rather, disapproving of what had occurred and wanting to cover the unseemly sight with garments, they walked in backwards. For they considered it a matter of piety not to feel shame at their father's private parts,[107] through which they had been begotten.

When the father woke up and learned of what had happened, he immediately cursed the one who without reason had taken no care to act properly and show him respect, and he justly placed a yoke of servitude upon Ham. In so doing, however, he uttered the name of Canaan, since the Canaanites, who would also share in his punishment, were descended from Ham, for the whole race was to be punished. But those who showed him honor he blessed.

2. Once again here in a figurative manner the mystery relating to the Jews is indicated. For the total number of peoples was three. There was that people which was there in the first instance, like Shem, then that which came in the middle, corresponding to the accursed Ham, and the third and final people, which is to be understood as Japheth coming at the end, whose name means "widening."

---

105. Var. "their."
106. Gn 9.18–27.
107. Lit. "thigh," a euphemism for the nearby genitals.

Now God the Father revealed his own Son to us, who is signified by the private parts of Noah, which is to say that besides the spiritual beauty of the Godhead he also related to what was shameful and unattractive on account of his being human, for "he had no form, nor comeliness," as the prophet said.[108] Then at that time, as the outcome of the events also bears witness, both the first and the last people, that is, those who were the first believers in the beginning, as well as those called in later times, treated Emmanuel with reverence, and so through him they were blessed by God the Father. But that people which came in the middle of the two, having mocked Christ for the uncomeliness of his human nature, and having greatly dishonored the Son who came forth[109] from God, remained in a state of bondage, having fallen away from the liberty of their forefathers.

That those among the Jews who came to believe in later times would be the first partakers and fellow residents, since they were brought together into a single city, or dwelling or home, which is the church, Noah indicated when he said, *"May God enlarge Japheth,"* that is [77], the third and final people, for Japheth was the third son, *"and may he dwell in the tents of Shem,"* that is, of the first son. *"And let Canaan be their servant."* This, I believe, is what Christ said to the people of the Jews: "Truly, truly, I say to you, that every one who commits sin is a slave of sin. The slave does not remain in the house for ever; the son does remain for ever. So if the Son sets you free, you will be free."[110] For the wretched Jews, who mocked the Incarnation[111] of our Savior and failed to honor the revelation of him, the revelation given to us from God the Father, have remained in a spirit of bondage.

---

108. Is 53.2.
109. Or "shone forth."
110. Jn 8.34–36. Cyril has omitted the adverb *ontôs,* "really," "indeed," from the final clause.
111. Lit. "economy."

Concerning the Tower and its Construction

Now nothing in human nature remained that was in a good or healthy state. For the Maker of all things had made it to be completely full of all manner of good. Yet that nature which had previously been great, which not long before had exceeding attractiveness, was now diminishing bit by bit, losing those things by means of which it reasonably ought to have appeared noble. It is as if to say that incorruption had been frittered away in Adam, for it was said to him, "Earth you are, and to the earth you shall return."[112] So after this he was deprived of the Spirit. For when God saw that those upon the earth wished only to give their minds to profanities of the flesh and to the foulest passions, he said, *"My Spirit shall certainly not remain among these men, because they are flesh."*[113]

Yet see what other matter awaits. Due to their impious scheming and senseless, rash actions, certain people were condemned and were caused to speak strange and discordant languages. For it says, *All the earth was of one language, and there was one speech for them all. And it happened that as they migrated from the east, they found a plain in the land of Sinar and they settled there. Then they said to one another, "Come, let us make bricks and bake them with fire." They had brick for stone and bitumen for mortar. And they said, "Come, let us build for ourselves a city and a tower, whose top will reach up to heaven, and let us make a name for ourselves before we are scattered over all the earth."*[114] Then God came down, for that is what the sacred Scripture says, and he confused their languages and also scattered them throughout all the earth.

While the God of all reproved their endeavors, he did not do so out of fear that they might complete their work. Rather, because they were planning something excessive, in his innate kindness, he brought their undertaking to an eventual end by making them speak many languages. In doing so he is showing that in his oversight of humankind, if they get carried away

---

112. Gn 3.19.
113. Gn 6.3. Cyril omits the temporal phrase *eis ton aiôna*, "for ever," which accompanies the verb "remain."
114. Gn 11.1–4.

somewhat by absurd undertakings, he does not let them go unreproved.

God confused their very languages, for the things that ought to be done only through the ability and authority of the Maker are not appropriate for any other to do, except for him alone. So the transformation of speech, and the increasing of the difference in the sound of words, one might justly and truly attribute to the One who alone is by nature the Maker.

Now what happened surely ought not to escape a great deal of ridicule, and fittingly so [80]. For those people supposed, though they did not know how, that they were entirely capable of building a tower out of brick and mud that would reach up even to heaven itself. So they serve as another figure, I believe, of the stupidity of the Jews, who supposed they could make for themselves a relationship with God.[115] In effect, they thought that the way up to heaven was not through choosing to do those things pleasing to God and esteemed by him, nor was it through faith in Christ, but by raising up some sort of tower, foolishly thinking that solely by the bare repute of their forefathers they could attain the highest things. For as they were constantly citing the name of Abraham, and by such earthly repute were building up, as it were, their own glory, they have ever stood condemned.

Yet God reproved those who planned to build the tower, and divided them into speakers of many languages. And we may say that in a certain way what then befell them was a declaration in advance of the things that happened to the Jews. For since they had minds set upon greatly exalted matters, through which things they were seeking the way to heaven above, he scattered them among those of many different languages, that is, among all the nations. For, being driven out of their homes, they were dispersed from their own lands and cities, and became "wanderers among the nations," as the prophet said.[116]

In Christ, however, the speaking of many languages was a good sign. For on the day of Pentecost, when the disciples were gathered together in one house, "suddenly there came," it says, "a sound from heaven, like the rushing of a violent wind, and

---

115. Or "establish for themselves a connection with God."
116. Hos 9.17.

it filled the whole house where they were sitting. Then there appeared to them what looked like tongues of fire that distributed themselves and settled upon each one of them. And they were all filled with the Holy Spirit and began to speak in other tongues, as the Spirit gave them utterance."[117] And what was it they were speaking? The Spirit was conveying the way upwards, the ascension into heaven through faith in Christ, in every language spoken upon the earth, by peoples and nations united into one gathering in the Spirit.[118] For every tongue among the people was confessing Christ and speaking of his mysteries.

So then, in connection with the tower the speaking in many languages was a sign of the scattering and the expulsion into all the nations. But in connection with Christ it was a sign of the gathering together into the unity of the Spirit and of the way up to heaven. For Christ has become our "strong tower," as the psalmist says,[119] which conveys us up to the heavenly city, and unites those upon the earth with the choirs of holy angels.

Concerning Abraham and Melchizedek

1. The God of all gave a law as an aid, for that is what is written.[120] That the law provides instruction[121] for children, however, while the mystery of Christ leads to maturity,[122] is not at all difficult for us to see from the sacred Scriptures, especially as we acquire a sure understanding and gather true teachings. Here, I believe, the divine Paul gives a sufficient explanation[123] regarding the two covenants when he says, "There is, on the one hand, an annulment of the former ordinance because of its weakness and ineffectiveness, for the law made nothing perfect; and on the other hand, the introduction of a better [81] hope, through

---

117. Acts 2.2–4.
118. Or "by the Spirit."
119. Ps 61.3 (60.4 LXX).
120. Cyril possibly has in mind Gal 3.24 ("the law was our instructor [*paidagôgos*] until Christ came").
121. Or "discipline."
122. Or "perfection."
123. Or "delivers an oracle."

which we draw near to God."[124] So one may indeed enter into a relationship with God extremely easily, not through the earlier Mosaic ordinance, but through the introduction of the hope that is here spoken of, which the interpreter of mysteries,[125] in considering the matter according to the truth, has it in mind to reckon as being the greater.

Paul plainly says that the matters contained in the law were to be annulled, and pronouncing the ordinance that came first to be unable to make anything perfect, he writes to the Hebrews, "For if the first covenant had been without fault, no occasion would have been sought for a second one. For he finds fault with it,[126] and says, 'Behold the days are coming, says the Lord, and I will establish a new covenant with the house of Israel and with the house of Judah, not like the covenant that I made with their fathers when I took them by the hand to bring them out of the land of Egypt, for they did not keep to my covenant, so I rejected them, says the Lord. For this will be the covenant that I will make with the house of Israel after those days, says the Lord: I will put my laws in their minds, and I will write them upon their hearts; I will be their God, and they will be my people. And each man will no more teach his fellow, and each one his brother, saying, "Know the Lord," because they will all know me, from the least of them to the greatest, for I will be merciful towards their sins, and I will not remember their lawlessness any more.'"[127] He then immediately adds, "When he says 'new' covenant, he has made the first obsolete; and what is obsolete and growing old will soon disappear."[128]

So then, the law is weak, and is also seen to have great impotence when it comes to being able to produce perfect sanctification. That justification in Christ and worship[129] in him are superior, however, you may hear God clearly proclaiming through the mouth of the prophets. To those who respected the minis-

124. Heb 7.18–19.
125. A designation for the author of Hebrews, which to Cyril's mind was Paul.
126. Cyril departs from the more common reading "with *them.*"
127. Heb 8.7–12; Jer 31.31–34.
128. Heb 8.13.
129. See n. 58 above.

tration under the law, and for whom it was as if they were tightly bound to the ordinance that has become obsolete, he at one time says, "Wash yourselves, be clean,"[130] then at another time, "I desire mercy and not sacrifice, the knowledge of God rather than burnt offerings."[131] We have indeed received mercy in Christ, and in him we have come to behold the Father spiritually and we have come to know the Being of God.

2. There is a countless number of relevant matters that could be accumulated to add to those that have been said, and the words of the holy prophets could be further adduced by means of which one might most plainly see that the ministration according to the law is unacceptable to God. But so that we do not drag out the discussion of the issue before us, and so that our discourse does not go too far, as though proceeding along some other path, we shall now move on to the divine Abraham.

When Abraham learned that his nephew Lot had unexpectedly been put in danger because he had been living in Sodom and was now among those taken to be slaves as the spoils of war, he called to arms the servants born in his household as well as certain other men, Eshcol, Aner, and Mamre, who were allied to him. Then he led them out, though not in some degenerate manner, against those who had been victorious, and he delivered Lot from the wrongdoing of those men. And with him he also rescued a great multitude [84] of people who had suffered wrong and been endangered.

When Abraham was returning home, bearing the illustrious tokens of the great courage he had shown against the enemy, those who were indebted to his efforts were obliged to come and meet him. For this is what is written: *The king of Sodom went out to meet him in the valley of Shaveh (which was the plain of the king) after he returned from the defeat of Chedorlaomer and the kings who were with him.* Then it adds: *And Melchizedek the king of Salem brought out to him bread and wine, and he was the priest of God Most High. Then he blessed Abraham and said, "Blessed be Abraham by God Most High, who created heaven and earth. And blessed be God Most High, who has*

---

130. Is 1.16.
131. Hos 6.6.

delivered your enemies into your hand." And Abraham gave him a tenth of everything.[132]

Observe, then, the types of the perfection in Christ that clearly shine forth in Melchizedek, and see also the inferior status of the ministration according to the law. There is absolutely no doubt that, as it is written, "the lesser is blessed by the greater."[133] Now the divine Abraham was the root, as it were, from which Israel came forth, and Levi, who in him was made preeminent and especially chosen to be appointed to the glories of the divine priesthood, was then still in his loins. For the blessed Abraham was the potential father of those who would later come forth from him. And this, I believe, is the meaning of that which was wisely spoken concerning Levi: "For he was still in the loins of his father when Melchizedek met him."[134] Therefore, the righteousness according to the law is blessed by the ministration that is in Christ, of which Melchizedek was a type.

So how could one doubt that this blessing is incomparably more excellent than that which lacks such an effect? We shall not, however, now spend more time contemplating such things in more detail.

3. Now he who wishes to contend with Christ will perhaps before all else want to inquire who this Melchizedek was. For certain people rave wildly in their different opinions about him, having foolishly fallen into meaningless nonsense, and giving little heed to the practices of the inspired Scripture. For there are those who say that it was specifically the Holy Spirit who took on a visible form like ours, and him alone who appeared to the victorious Abraham. But there are others who do not hold to this view, for they fear, I imagine, falling into excessive absurdity, and they assert that Melchizedek was a most special and eminent power among the multitude of angels.[135] So their weak and fool-

132. Gn 14.17–20.
133. Heb 7.7.
134. Heb 7.10.
135. It is not clear specifically whom Cyril is attacking here. There was a third-century Christian sect called the Melchizedekians, who understood Melchizedek to be a divine figure superior to Christ, but not specifically that he was the Holy Spirit. Epiphanius of Salamis (d. 403) claims that Hieracas of Leontopolis, a third-century Egyptian ascetic, identified the Holy Spirit with

ish minds lead them into this opinion of the matter. For since, some say, Salem means "peace," and Melchizedek is named the king of Salem, it should not be interpreted as a man, they say, but it is the Spirit that is signified. For in his own self the Spirit is the peace of God, and Melchizedek himself was the sole ruler of "peace." To this they add that if "he had neither beginning of days nor end of life,"[136] how can it not be open to a charge of foolishness to attribute this state without beginning or end to a man? So once again, this should be taken as meaning the Spirit. Also, if it says [85], "being like the Son of the Most High,[137] he remains a priest for ever,"[138] how can we think at all of Melchizedek as being human? Then, latching other arguments on to these, they suppose they are upholding the truth with reasons procured from I do not know where.

Now it is necessary for us to speak what thoughts come to mind, wishing to give a good and truthful answer to the dubious opinions of these people. For firstly, if they knew how to think reasonably, they themselves would acknowledge that Salem is a city over which Melchizedek was not the first nor the only one to reign as king, but there were doubtless many who came before him, and also others after him. If anyone should think we are not speaking truly, let him come and prove that Melchizedek is reigning over Salem even now, and further that it is one of the present cities in Judea, perhaps that one which is now called by the name of Jerusalem, which means "vision of peace."[139] Yet no one can prove this is so.

Melchizedek (*Panarion* 35.5.1–5; 67.3.1–5; 67.7.1–8). Interestingly, Jerome argues, in *Epistle* 73.1.1–2 and 73.2.1, that both Origen and Didymus also associate the Spirit with Melchizedek. While it is not clear whether Cyril read Epiphanius, we do know that Cyril was familiar with Jerome's commentaries. Whether, however, he is reliant on either of these figures for this section against those who claim Melchizedek to be the Holy Spirit is unknown. The length of Cyril's argument against this notion indicates its persistence, at least in Alexandria. (Thanks to Mark DelCogliano for allowing us to read an unpublished paper on the topic.)

136. Heb 7.3.
137. Var. add "God."
138. Heb 7.3.
139. The name of Jerusalem would appear to contain the element of "peace," but the remaining part remains obscure. Jerome likewise takes the

So then, to undertake to nullify those things which are obvious and widely accepted by giving heed to the meaning of names is something quite absurd. If we put our minds to it, we may see without any difficulty that the matter is foolish and that what they say about it abounds in stupidity. For Jerusalem means "vision of peace," as I just said, or "higher than death"; Israel is "a mind that sees God," while Judah means "praise" and "hymn-singing."[140] The sacred Scripture, however, clearly declares that those who were kings of Jerusalem ruling over Israel and Judah[141] in later times were unholy and profane. So "vision of peace," and "praise" and "hymn-singing," and "a mind that sees God" do not pertain to such earthly kings. Nor would it be applicable to a human being if they should say, in attending to the meaning of names, that those who later reigned as kings were shadows and images, and not men at all, but that it rather meant the Spirit, just as also in the matter of Melchizedek.[142]

One may learn from this that the import of names, that is, their meanings, in no way affects the actual nature of things. For should not one then think, or rather state it as being absolutely true, that if Jerusalem were a "vision of peace," Christ must be entirely overlooked? For "he himself is our peace," as the Scriptures say.[143] Yet it was not in visions of the mind that he was seen, through whom we have obtained access and are joined to the Father in the unity of the Spirit, who made the two into one, having created the two peoples into one new man.[144] How, then, is there a vision of peace unless one sees Christ? And if Jerusalem is "higher than death," that is to say, greater than and

---

meaning to be "vision of peace" (*Letter* 46.3 [PL 22.485]). Most commonly, however, the name is understood to mean "city of peace."

140. In Hebrew there does not in fact appear to be any connection between the name Jerusalem and "higher than death." Israel is variously understood as meaning "one who struggles with God," "a prince with God," or "let God contend." As regards the meaning of Judah, Cyril is correct.

141. That is, those places whose names were just explained.

142. Cyril here argues upon the assumption that the later kings of Jerusalem, from the way in which Scripture describes them, had to be nothing other than ordinary men.

143. Eph 2.14.

144. Cf. Eph 2.15, referring to the words that explain the "peace" of the previous verse.

above death, how is it that the wretched city utterly perished on account of their unbelief in Christ? For he himself declared to the Jews, "Truly I say to you, if you do not believe that I am he, you will die in your sins."[145] And if Israel is understood to mean "a mind that sees God," why did they not see the glory of Christ, through whom and in whom we know the Father himself? How could they have been overcome [88] by darkness? Or how was it said concerning those to whom it fell to lead others, "Leave them alone; they are blind guides of the blind"?[146] For what kind of blindness is it that may be interpreted as a mind that sees God?

It is therefore sheer folly to attribute wholly to qualities of actual things the significance of their names. So nothing at all prevents us, I believe, from rightly and properly supposing that Melchizedek was a man who at that time ruled as king in Salem, even though this name might perhaps be interpreted as indicating "peace."

4. One ought to give further consideration to these matters being discussed, for here we may see the divine mysteries faintly as in a mirror or in a figure. While among those things that have been created we have nothing at all with which to compare the divine, ineffable Being, yet from so many thousands of illustrations[147] we are in some measure able to gather something that can be understood or said concerning him to the degree that this is attainable. The mystery concerning Christ nonetheless remains extremely obscure, and the matter[148] of his becoming human is not easily comprehended by ordinary people.

The subject of the divine economy is, for sure, exceedingly deep. For the Only-Begotten, being God and also of God according to his nature, became a man and dwelt among us. Further, he is called our apostle and high priest,[149] and he has delivered us from the dull speech[150] of the law and has brought us to the har-

---

145. Jn 8.24.
146. Mt 15.14.
147. *paradeigmata,* "patterns," "examples," contained within Scripture.
148. Var. "manner."
149. Var. add "of our confession," as Heb 3.1.
150. The underlying Greek phrase can also be translated as "slow speech,"

monious voice of the gospel teachings. And this was not all, for he also set us free when we were held captive, having destroyed the ruler of this world, and rescued those who had died[151] from the depths of Hades. He likewise founded the church and was appointed ruler over us. By faith he crossed over the Jordan, he gave us the circumcision of the Spirit, and brought us into the kingdom of heaven.

Now the fact that he became one of us is sufficiently demonstrated, I believe, when the divine evangelist says, "And the Word became flesh, and dwelt among us."[152] And that he was anointed as a priest and apostle the induction of Aaron indicates very plainly. For Aaron was anointed with the consecrated oil, and was appointed the ruler and leader of the priests and people. Moreover, he received the golden ornament on the top of his forehead, that is, the metal plate upon which the name of the Lord was written. This item, like a radiant and impressive diadem, was a clear symbol of our Savior the King.[153]

That the ministration that came through Christ is superior to that under the law, one may perceive after a fashion in Aaron, just as was surely the case with Melchizedek. For according to the law the Levites received tithes from the people of Israel. God commanded, however, that a tithe from the Levites should be allotted to Aaron, as their leader, upon whom the highest honors were lavished on account of his particular priestly office. Note then how in the person of Aaron, Levi, the one receiving tithes, was tithed. This is because Aaron was appointed to a role corresponding to that of Christ. All the other Levites and priests performed the sacrifices according to the law, taking their places in the first compartment of the tabernacle. Yet of them all only the divine Aaron entered into the holy of holies once a year, as it is written, and not without blood, in accordance with the [89] law. And in this he was a type of Christ, who died once for our sins, according to the Scriptures, and who proceeded into the

---

as in the descriptions of Moses and of the law in the third paragraph below this one (on p. 113).

151. Lit. "fallen asleep."
152. Jn 1.14.
153. Var. "of the kingship of our Savior."

most sacred tabernacle above. So, in sanctifying the church by his own blood, he opened up a new way for us.[154]

Now the divine Moses, when he was appointed as God's messenger,[155] entreated God and said, "Please, Lord, I have never been eloquent, neither recently, nor in the past, nor since you began to speak to your servant. I stammer and am slow of speech."[156] And to this he added: "Appoint another person, someone capable, whom you can send."[157] Then the God of all answered him, "Is there not Aaron your brother, the Levite? I know that he will indeed speak for you, and behold, he himself is coming to meet you. When he sees you, he will be glad in his heart. And you shall speak to him and put my words in his mouth, and I will instruct you in what you should do. He will speak to the people for you, and he will be your mouth."[158] It must be admitted that the law of long ago was slow of speech and unable to speak distinctly, according to the letter that is, and only in a long and roundabout way did it stammer out, as it were, God's will to us. Christ, however, is the sweeter-sounding "mouth" of Moses,[159] who turns the types into reality, and who sets forth knowledge of those things that are necessary and makes them easily accessible everywhere. It says therefore in the Forty-eighth Psalm, "Hear these things, all you nations; listen, all you inhabitants of the earth."[160]

Christ then, for sure, is typified by Aaron, and this is beyond all expectation. Do not be amazed that among those who know him, and in their knowledge of his laws, the majesty of his own excellence is shadowed forth. This even includes how he came as a man of a foreign race, who set Israel free from captivity, who founded the holy and sacred city,[161] and who has irresistible power over all.

154. Cf. Heb 10.19–20.
155. Or "apostle."
156. Ex 4.10.
157. Ex 4.13.
158. Ex 4.14–15.
159. By which Cyril seems to mean "Aaron," who has just been described to Moses as "your mouth."
160. Ps 49.1 (48.2 LXX).
161. Var. "land."

These matters I will now explain clearly, and as briefly as possible.

5. Now Judah was at one time taken into captivity, and the people of Israel spent a lengthy period in Babylon, afflicted with a grievous and brutal servitude. But then Cyrus, son of Cambyses, king of both the Medes and the Persians, when he came to power, conducted a war against the neighboring Assyrians.[162] At that time he also forcibly seized Babylon itself and set free the Jews, who were bewailing the wrongdoing of the Assyrians and whose eyes were running with tears. They firmly believed it had been predicted by God through the mouth of his saints[163] that he would eventually come and that he himself would overwhelm their adversaries and undo the bonds of the oppressed, and that he himself would raise up his house again in Jerusalem, which the Assyrians had burnt down and so acted profanely against God.

If we examine the writings of the holy prophets, we shall find that the people of Israel were not speaking falsely in these matters. This is what God said through the mouth of Isaiah: "Thus says the Lord who redeems you, and who forms you from the womb: 'I am the Lord who performs these things; I alone stretched out the heavens and established the earth. Who else [92] will frustrate the omens of the soothsayers and diviners who speak from their own heart? He turns wise men backward and makes their counsel foolishness. He confirms the words of his servant and establishes the truth of the counsel of his messengers. He is the one who says to Jerusalem, "You shall be inhabited," and to the cities of Judah, "You shall be built," and he will raise up her desolated places. It is he who says to the deep, "Be dry, and I will dry up your rivers." It is he who tells Cyrus to be wise, and that he will perform all he desires. He says to Jerusalem, "You shall be built," and "I will lay the foundation of my holy house." Thus says the Lord God to my anointed one, Cyrus, whose right hand I have held, that the nations might be obedient to him; and I will break the might of kings. I will open gates before him and cities will not be shut up: "I will go before

---

162. Cyril here refers to the inhabitants of Babylonia as "Assyrians."
163. That is, the prophets.

you, and I will level mountains; I will shatter gates of bronze and break iron bars. I will give you the treasures of darkness, and I will open up to you hidden and unseen treasures, so that you may know that I, the Lord God, who calls you by name, am the God of Israel. For the sake of Jacob my servant and of Israel my chosen, I will call you by your name and will accept you. But you did not know that I am the Lord God, and there is 'no other God beside me, and you have not known me.'"[164]

Note how it distinctly says, "you have not known me." Not even among those who do know him did God deem one worthy to be appointed to such prominence, one whom he himself ordained to be superior to kings and lord of so many thousands of the Gentiles. Now those things relating to him were in fact figures of what was accomplished through Christ. For he foretold how he himself would frustrate the false divinations of the Babylonians and the omens of the soothsayers.[165] But the counsels, or predictions, of his own prophets, whom he also called his messengers,[166] he would show to be true. So he made it known before it happened that he would build the cities of Judah, and that he would make the deep become dry and would dry up all its rivers. By "the deep," I understand it to be speaking of Babylon, on account of the large number of people living in it. Its "rivers" are those of the nations who flowed into it from all over, seeking aid.

We shall now come to speak clearly of the things concerning Cyrus, skillfully[167] transforming those things accomplished by him into matters relating to the mystery of Christ.

6. Now Cyrus, whose mother was Mandane the daughter of Astyages, a ruler of the Medes, and whose father was Cambyses of the race of Persia, was extremely moderate[168] in his ways. Therefore, certain of the ancients called Cyrus a "mule," and also "one of a different nature." This was, I suppose, because his father and mother were of different races, for the Persians were of a nation different from the Medes.

164. Is 44.24–45.5.
165. Cf. Is 44.25.
166. Or "angels."
167. See n. 2 above on p. 81.
168. Or "fair," "reasonable."

You see then how this relates to Christ. For with respect to the flesh he was born of a mother, the holy Virgin, who was of human nature as we are. His father, however, was not at all like us, but, if we might express it so, he was of a completely different race, quite removed from us in nature, surpassing everything that was created. Accordingly, Christ said to the Jews who thought that he was like us and was born as we are, "You are from below, I am from above."[169]

Cyrus exercised power over many thousands of the Gentiles, and every city opened up to him.[170] He received treasures of darkness, hidden [93] and unseen treasures, and set Israel free from its long bondage. Emmanuel became king over everything under heaven, and every city receives him as the Savior and Redeemer of all. He now sets free every race that is bound by a devilish servitude and oppression, and that is compelled to act under the devil's control. Also, having descended into Hades he emptied the treasures of darkness, hidden and unseen treasures. He shattered gates of bronze and broke iron bars. For "he said to those in bonds, 'Come out,' and to those in darkness, 'Show yourselves.'"[171]

Furthermore, in times past God said to Job, that most longsuffering and invincible champion, "Have you been to the source of the sea, or have you walked in the paths of the deep? Did the gates of death open up to you out of fear, or did the portals of Hades quake when they saw you?"[172] From these questions we should understand that the words indicate those things accomplished through Christ, and those things done in the very depths of Hades.[173] "For to this end Christ died and came to life, that he might be Lord of both the dead and the living."[174]

Also, Cyrus long ago, having donated what was necessary, decreed that the temple in Jerusalem should be rebuilt. But Emmanuel founded the church, which is the real holy and re-

---

169. Jn 8.23.
170. Or "welcomed him."
171. Is 49.9.
172. Jb 38.16–17.
173. Var. "of death."
174. Rom 14.9.

nowned city, having wholly overthrown the most shameless and wanton idolatry, which was in a way like Babylon.

Further concerning Cyrus, God said, "He will perform all my will."[175] To the people of the Jews who rejected him, the Savior of us all declared in a certain place, "You judge according to the flesh,"[176] and elsewhere he said, "Even if I do judge, my judgment is true, for I do not seek my own will, but the will of the Father who sent me."[177]

To Cyrus, God also said, "I have called you by my name."[178] So Emmanuel, although he came as a man, is truly "the Lord."

Now, that the matters concerning Cyrus serve as a figure of the glory of Christ, the following words spoken by the prophet make perfectly clear: "It is I who made the earth and humankind upon it. With my own hands I established the heavens, and I commanded all the stars. I raised him up in righteousness, and all his ways are just. He is the one who will build my city and return the captives of my people, not for ransom or reward, says the Lord of hosts. Thus says the Lord: Egypt has labored, and the merchandise of the Ethiopians, and the Sabeans, men of stature, will pass over to you and will be your slaves. They will follow you with their hands bound in fetters, they will bow down to you and make supplication to you, because God is in you, and they will say, 'There is no God beside you.[179] For you are God, and we did not know it, the Savior, the God of Israel.' All those who oppose him will be ashamed and disgraced, and they will walk in shame."[180] For he who made the earth and humankind upon it, who adorned the heavens with the stars, raised up Jesus as our righteousness, who redeems us freely, for we have been

175. Is 44.28.
176. Jn 8.15.
177. Jn 8.16; 5.30. Cyril's argument here is that Christ, like Cyrus before him, acted according to the will of God, while the Jews acted according to the flesh.
178. Cf. Is 45.4. The Hebrew text and some Greek manuscripts read "by *your* name."
179. The text of the LXX is confused at this point in the matter of reference, and Cyril, or his editor, has made some necessary changes to render it more comprehensible.
180. Is 45.12–16.

justified by faith. It is Jesus who releases us from our bonds and captivity, who builds up the spiritual Jerusalem, and who founds the [96] church, which cannot be shaken even by the gates of Hades, nor be overcome by its enemies. It is he whom those in the past who were going astray recognized as being true God in nature, saying, "For you are our God, and we did not know it, and there is no God besides you." Him they shall worship, to him every knee shall bow, and every tongue shall confess that Jesus Christ is Lord to the glory of God the Father.[181] Some of the people of Israel dared to oppose him, but they were put to shame and cast down, and walked in the manner described by the prophet.

So then, Cyrus son of Cambyses founded the house of God in Jerusalem as a type of Christ. But that it would be Emmanuel himself who fulfilled the oracle spiritually, one may learn directly by means of another figure. For when Cyrus set Israel free from their bondage in Babylon, straight away leaders were appointed to rule over the people, namely Zerubbabel son of Shealtiel from the tribe of Judah, and Jeshua son of Jozadek, the high priest. And when they came to Jerusalem, God commanded them through the mouth of Haggai the prophet to attend to the work of building his house. This is what is written: "In the second year of Darius the king, in the sixth month, on the first day of the month, the word of the Lord came through Haggai the prophet, saying, 'Tell Zerubbabel the son of Shealtiel from the tribe of Judah and Jeshua the son of Jozadak, the high priest, saying, "Thus says the Lord Almighty: This people say, 'The time has not come to build the house of the Lord.' Then the word came through Haggai the prophet, saying, 'Is it time for you to live in paneled houses, while the house of the Lord lies in ruins?'"[182] After this it further says, "And the Lord stirred up the spirit of Zerubbabel son of Shealtiel from the tribe of Judah and the spirit of Jeshua the son of Jozadak, the high priest, and the spirit of all the rest of the people. And they went in and worked in the house of the Lord Almighty their God."[183]

181. Cf. Phil 2.10–11.
182. Hg 1.1–4.
183. Hg 1.14.

Note, then, how Emmanuel is present here in a twofold type and image, as a king in Zerubbabel, who was from the tribe of Judah, the tribe to whose lot it then fell to exercise authority in Israel, and also as a high priest in his namesake,[184] Jeshua the great high priest. Note him,[185] moreover, as the leader on the journey to the holy city from the land of foreigners, the Babylonians, that is, and as the craftsman and overseer of the work on the holy temple. For through faith we follow our leader Christ, as king and high priest, coming out of diabolical oppression, from the land of foreigners, so to speak, and out of worldly deceit, we enter into the holy city, the church of the firstborn, which Christ himself raises up, building it with spiritual stones, as it were. Paul also, writing to those who had been redeemed through faith, who sought to follow in the footsteps of Christ, would testify and say, "In him you also are being built together into a dwelling place of Christ in the Spirit."[186]

Furthermore, that the glory of the church would be greater than that which was there at first, in ancient times, that is to say, the [97] temple made of stones, God indicated when he further said through the mouth of Haggai, "Who is there among you that saw this house in its former glory? And how do you see it now? Is it not as nothing in your sight?"[187] Also after other matters it says, "The silver is mine, and the gold is mine, says the Lord Almighty. For the latter glory of this house shall be greater than the former, says the Lord Almighty. And in this place I will give peace, even peace of soul as a possession for everyone who works to raise up this temple."[188]

One could easily gather together those instances in which Christ is portrayed to us in the people of old. Yet, so that our discourse may not seem to be carried away by many more examples than would be appropriate, we declare that we shall allow ourselves to pass over the others for the time being.

---

184. The name Jesus is the Greek equivalent to the Hebrew "Jeshua" or "Joshua."
185. This would seem to refer back to Emmanuel.
186. Eph 2.22. The scriptural verse in today's Bibles reads "of God" rather than Cyril's "of Christ."
187. Hg 2.3.
188. Hg 2.8–9.

Surely then, we are altogether obliged to choose one of two options. We may completely set aside[189] those through whom these matters came to pass, censuring the great imperfection of the types, since they are understood to have been expressed through people like us, even though they were greatly worthy of God. Or else, claiming that it is always the Spirit that has taken on a form like our own, we will be obliged also to acknowledge that the Spirit once took on a form as Cyrus, who did not know God, for it was said to him, "you have not known me." Yet if those people who serve as types are done away with, this would equally apply to Aaron as a shadow, and to Zerubbabel the son of Shealtiel, as well as to Jeshua the son of Jozadak, the high priest, as they would have existed in mere name only.

7. I rather consider, however, that those who have been persuaded by reasonable arguments rightly consent to the view that Melchizedek was a man who reigned over the city of Salem, and that Paul, being of subtle mind, presented him as a type of Christ for our spiritual contemplation. Yet there are those who have subsequently opposed this view, and claim nothing other than that Melchizedek was not a man, but that he was the Holy Spirit, or at least another heavenly power from above that had some ministerial function.[190]

Since it pleases some to think thus, we are compelled to say that they err in two respects. They drag down the divine and ineffable Being of the Spirit in a manner that is quite improper for him, and they absurdly raise up to a sublime glory the creature that was begotten and made. In what way this is so I shall state.

With regard to Melchizedek it is written that he was priest of God Most High. But if Melchizedek was the Holy Spirit, then the Spirit is brought down into priestly service and takes on a ministerial duty. So he himself would in fact sing praises with the holy angels to God above, for it is written, "Bless the Lord, all his angels, his ministers who do his will."[191] For it is patently obvious that one who serves as priest does so entirely for another and does not serve himself, but he serves God, who is preeminent.

---

189. Or "reject," "do away with," "annul," "destroy."
190. See n. 135 above.
191. Ps 103.21 (102.21 LXX).

Therefore, if we say that the Spirit[192] became a priest, his divine nature is utterly abased. Rather, he too would be classed among creatures and worship along with us. He would not in any way consecrate[193] himself, since it is surely the case that what is consecrated is consecrated by what is wholly greater than its own nature. Yet he would be consecrated with us. So how could one who is consecrated still also be God in nature? [100] For is not every priest consecrated, and following this embarks upon his ministerial duties?

Now "no one takes to himself this honor," as it is written, "but he who is called by God, just as Aaron was."[194] Then Paul adds, "It was not Christ who gave himself the glory of being begotten as a high priest, but it was the one who said to him, 'You are my Son, today I have begotten you.' As he also says in another place, 'You are a priest for ever in the order of Melchizedek.'"[195]

It is necessary for one to know that the Son himself, the Word from God the Father, is not said to be a priest and to take up a ministerial function, unless he is considered to have become one of us. Thus, as he was called a prophet as well as an apostle, on account of his humanity, so also a priest. For a serving role was fitting for one in the form of a servant, and this is what the emptying was. For although he was in the form of the Father and equal to him before whom the seraphim stand in heaven and who is served by thousands and thousands of angels, when he emptied himself, he is then said to be shown forth as a minister of the saints and of the true tabernacle. The one who is over all creation was then also sanctified[196] along with us. For it says, "he who sanctifies and those who are sanctified are all of one origin.[197] For this reason he is not ashamed to call them brothers, saying, 'I will declare your name to my brothers.'"[198] So, while as

---

192. Var. add "Holy."
193. Or "sanctify."
194. Heb 5.4.
195. Heb 5.5–6; Ps 110.4 (109.4 LXX).
196. In the following discussion the verb "sanctify" may also be rendered "consecrate."
197. Or "from one Father" (as NASB). Greek: *ex henos*.
198. Heb 2.11–12; Ps 22.22 (21.23 LXX).

God he is one who sanctifies, when he became man and tabernacled among us, and was called our brother with respect to his humanity, then it is said that he was also sanctified with us.

So now, in the economy of his flesh he is behoved to perform a priestly duty and to be sanctified with us. And if we aim to think correctly and without error, we will attribute these things to the limitations imposed by the act of emptying himself. So if we say that the Spirit in no way underwent an emptying to become a priest, we would deprive him of the glory due to one who is divine, and reckon what is begotten to be among those beings that are below God, placing a limitation upon him. Or else, let them show us that the Spirit did indeed become a man, and underwent the subordination that pertains to this economy, just as the Son in fact did. For while the holy and adored Trinity is of the same substance, one would not for that reason ascribe the Incarnation to whatever Person one chose. For only the Son became man, and not the Father, nor the Holy Spirit. This is the mystery that the divine Scriptures have taught us.

What violence they do to the truth, in that the one who had no occasion to empty himself, namely the Holy Spirit, if he is actually to be counted among the number of those serving as priests, they bring him down into the limited state of having emptied himself! For Melchizedek was indeed a priest. Yet they claim that the Spirit himself took on form in this way to the honor of the Son in being a type of Christ's priesthood that was to come later. I would therefore ask, even though it would be foolish to think or say such a thing, whether the Holy Spirit has neglected the honor of the Son and love for him, and whether he would consider doing so to be of little worth. For the Paraclete, which is the Spirit, glorifies the Son [101], and concerning him the Son says, "He will glorify me."[199] This being so, why then did not he who wished to bestow honor in this perpetual manner rather become Aaron?[200] Why did he not also become

---

199. Jn 16.14.

200. In what follows, Cyril's argument is that if it was the intention of the Holy Spirit to honor the Son by typifying him through Melchizedek, then why did not the Spirit also do this with respect to other OT characters generally understood to be types of Christ? This would surely have been to bestow even greater honor upon the Son.

Cyrus who ruled over the Persians and the Medes? What of Jeshua son of Jozadak, and Zerubbabel son of Shealtiel from the tribe of Judah? And what of Moses, respecting whom it is said that he showed forth in himself the mediation of Christ—"I will raise up a prophet for them, like you, from among their brothers; and I will put my words in his mouth, and he will speak to them as I will command him"?[201] Or why did he not become Joshua son of Nun, the commander after Moses, who led the people of Israel across the Jordan, and circumcised them with stone knives, and brought them into the promised land? Were we not baptized in Christ and circumcised with the circumcision done without hands through the Spirit, and have we not become heirs of the kingdom of heaven? Yet is this not obvious? Or if we should grant that the Spirit has every time taken on the form of each of those named in order that he might honor the Son, that is, to assume for the moment that the matter is true, how little proper concern of the Spirit would be seen in this, for it would amount to saying that certain of the men of ancient times had been created only to be types and similitudes of the Son. Away with this absurd reasoning! Melchizedek therefore was a man, and not the Holy Spirit.

8. We shall now explain that Melchizedek cannot be understood to be a holy and ministering power, as some like to think, and we shall gather together appropriate arguments to demonstrate the truth of this. Now to these people the matter, as they themselves see it, seems to be so cleverly established. For since, they claim, it was written regarding Melchizedek that he was without father, without mother, and without genealogy, and that he even blessed such a one as Abraham, and there is no doubt that the lesser is blessed by the better and greater,[202] he should not be understood to be one of us, but to be by nature an angel, that is, one of those grand and glorious ministering powers of heaven.

I for my part, beloved, am greatly astonished that a kind of reverence for the divine Abraham has led them away from the pursuit of what is right and profitable, and has caused them to

201. Dt 18.18.
202. Cf. Heb 7.7.

stray from the arguments necessary for learning the truth. For when they portray to us Melchizedek as a similitude and type of Emmanuel, they do not consider the quality of his actions or discern the manner of his priesthood. Instead, they examine the natures of those present in the account. What trouble would be caused, one might appropriately ask them, were Abraham to have been blessed by Melchizedek as by a mere man, and not one who might be considered superior to him? For it is not their natures, but the meaning of the things being enacted, which is to be discerned—words of truth that portray in advance better things than the shadowy figures. For it is most improper, rather than to draw parallels between the events depicted and those things expressed in shadows, to pronounce instead upon the natures of those presented within the account, and thereby to know of such matters.

Aaron was a specially chosen person, one who presided over and governed the holy tabernacle, and who was adorned with the highest honors of priesthood. [104] How then was he sanctified?[203] Was not a ram slain, and the lobe of his right ear anointed with its blood, as well as the extremities of his right hand and foot?[204] When this had been performed he was ready to minister as priest. Dear friends, I would say, however, to these people that if the good element is associated with the natures of those sanctifying and of those sanctified, rather than arising out of their being a type and shadow relating to the excellent truth to come, how is it still the case that the lesser is blessed by the greater? What the greater in these things might be, let them declare. Shall we then put Aaron lower than a ram, seeing that what is rational is perfected by an irrational animal? If we should say that the one chosen for the priesthood was sanctified by the blood of sheep, and that the sprinkling of a heifer's blood sanctified the defiled, as regards the purification of the body, what would the point then be? Where is the depth of understanding?

The things enacted were types and images, and if we may put it thus, they were a foreshowing of the sanctification which is in

---

203. See n. 196 above.
204. Cf. Lv 8.22–23.

Christ. The type lies in what was done; it is not to be apprehended in the nature of those sanctifying, nor in the nature of those being sanctified. While it is so, as I said just now, that the greater is blessed by the lesser, the nature of a man is actually greater than that of a heifer or a ram. So one should not be embarrassed at this, that even though Abraham was much greater than Melchizedek, it says that he was blessed by him. For the type consisted in the one who was victorious, and not in the nature of the one blessing.

I marvel, then, that while they represent Melchizedek as a similitude and type of the Son, they say that it was as an angel that he was without mother or father, even though both these facts were in a certain way applicable to Christ also. For the holy Virgin was his mother upon earth, and God is his Father in heaven. I believe it then to be necessary for the figures to be portrayed as relating to such archetypal matters. Yet since the divine Paul said that Melchizedek had "neither beginning of days nor end of life,"[205] they thus contend that he was a ministering spiritual power, not realizing that something of crucial importance has escaped their notice. For none of those things that are created would be without a beginning with respect to time, but absolutely everything brought into existence also has a beginning of life and of days.

So what then was the blessed Paul's intention in these words? How did he depict Melchizedek as a type and similitude of Christ? Rejecting any interpretation arising out of careless reasoning, we shall now examine this matter and discuss it as we are able.

9. Paul, being very much learned in the law, does not offer an account to the Jews based on mere arguments, but on the Mosaic writings, which even those well acquainted with combating the truth would probably not be willing to disregard. So he takes Melchizedek as a similitude and pattern of Christ, in that he is called the king of righteousness and of peace. For according to its mystical sense this would be appropriate, it seems to me, solely for Emmanuel, the Lord of righteousness and peace who has been manifested to those upon the earth. And in him we

---

205. Heb 7.3.

have been justified, having rid ourselves of the burden of sin. [105] We also have peace with God the Father, having washed off the impurity of our ways that divided us and kept us apart, being united, as it were, to him through the Spirit, for "whoever is joined to the Lord," it says, "is one Spirit with him."[206]

So then, Melchi rendered into the Greek language is "king," and Zedek is "righteousness." One might see Melchizedek as abounding in the sense of his own name, according to the import of what is signified by "king of righteousness." And when he is said to be king of Salem, he is "king of peace." The divine Paul therefore applied these things to Christ, since he most plainly resembles Melchizedek. Moreover, Melchizedek took up the symbols of the priesthood that excels the law, offering Abraham both wine and bread when he blessed him. Likewise, we are not blessed in any other way except through Christ, the great and true priest. We are blessed like the divine Abraham, as we prevail mightily over the rulers of this age, showing that we are superior to the power of our enemies, and that we have no need of anything that is in the world. Rather, we count those things we have from God, the glorious and never-failing supply of heavenly gifts, as spiritual riches.

It is to be understood that Melchizedek blessed Abraham when he had won his victory and was returning from the defeat of the kings, as it is written, and when he did not deign to accept anything from the ruler of Sodom. For the one who ruled the people of Sodom spoke to Abraham as to one who was victorious, and said, *"Give me the men, and take the horses for yourself."*[207] Abraham, however, was determined to claim nothing that belonged to that man. *"I stretch out my hand,"* he said, *"to God Most High, who created heaven and earth, and swear that I will not take from all that is yours even a thread or a strap, so that you may not say, 'I made Abraham rich.'"*[208] For it is not the habit of the saints to rejoice over worldly riches.

---

206. 1 Cor 6.17.

207. Gn 14.21. Cyril follows the LXX in translating the Hebrew term *rᵉkûš* as "horses" rather than "goods." The original translators confused the former with *rekeš*, meaning "steeds" (cf. 1 Kgs 4.28 [5.8 MT]).

208. Gn 14.22–23.

So we, having prevailed over enemies visible and invisible, and accepting nothing from the world, but rather valuing heavenly riches, are blessed through Christ, the king of peace. We are blessed, as it were, with a heavenly gift, and we receive the mysteries as the provisions of life. These may for the present be left unmentioned, if it so pleases, yet we are blessed by Christ and by his entreaties on our behalf to the Father. Now when Melchizedek blessed Abraham, he said, *"Blessed be God Most High, who has delivered your enemies into your hand."* Whereas our Lord Jesus Christ, the atoning sacrifice[209] for us all, said, "Holy Father, keep them in your truth."[210]

From the interpretation of the names, then, Paul takes hold of what serves to prefigure Christ. He makes it clear also that the manner of priesthood itself shows the same thing, for Melchizedek brought out bread and wine. That Melchizedek, however, was without father and without mother, that is, without a genealogy, and that he had no beginning of days or end of life, the sacred Scripture nowhere expressly indicates. One might perhaps then say that [108] the divine Paul has uttered a lie. This is not what we say, not at all, for he is speaking the truth. Rather, the skilled instructor in mysteries holds to a spiritual interpretation, taking this as a figure of the glory of Emmanuel and as an account relating to the very matters of the divine economy. For the inspired Scripture reveals to us only the fact that Melchizedek was a priest. It does not identify his descent or the origins of his father or mother. Yet neither does it set a limit to how many years he lived, nor do we find that the kind of succession accompanying his priestly office is revealed. Consequently, the narrative of such things is outlined in figures for us, and this in a way resembles the perpetual nature of Christ that was without beginning, when he is considered as God. When it says "without beginning," evidently it is talking about quantity, quantity of time that is, for he himself is the Maker of the ages.[211] Besides this, it indicates the unceasing nature of his priesthood. Accordingly, the blessed Paul said with regard to Melchizedek that "he

---

209. *hilastêrion*, "propitiation," "propitiatory offering."
210. Cf. Jn 17.11, 17.
211. *aiônôn*, "ages," "eternity," "world."

had neither beginning of days nor end of life, but being like the Son of God, he remains a priest for ever."[212]

It appears that some other subtle matter is also intended. What this is, and the manner of it, I will now try to explain.

10. The Jews opposed what was proclaimed concerning Christ, and were so bold as to despise the zealous deeds of the apostles. They held to two courses of action. One of these was to nullify the command prescribed to the fathers through the mouth of the all-wise Moses as being something impossible to do, setting the law at naught, and so a different manner of living that was not recognized by those of ancient times was unexpectedly introduced. The other thing was that they did not insist upon restricting the glory of the priesthood to the tribe that was specially chosen, namely that of Levi. Yet God everywhere keeps away from the sanctuary those who were not of the priestly ministry, and instantly decrees the ultimate punishment for audacity in such a matter.

Now Paul, being an expert in the law, also endeavors to explain fully, both from reasonable arguments and from the inspired Scripture, that the coming of a new law heralds a change in the priesthood as well. And each of these is clearly indicated beforehand by means of types.

Paul accepts that Melchizedek was not from the tribe of Levi, and then shows that he was a priest of God Most High, who brought forth bread and wine. This is what he says about him: "See how great this man was, to whom even Abraham the patriarch gave a tenth of the spoils. And those of the Levites who received the priestly office had the commandment to tithe the people, that is, their kinsmen, according to the law, even though they had come forth from the loins of Abraham. But this man, whose genealogy is not derived from them, received tithes from Abraham, and blessed the one who had the promises. Now without any dispute, the lesser is blessed by the greater."[213] Nevertheless, we say that the excellence of Melchizedek lay not in his nature, but in the manner of his priesthood. As our forefather Abraham did not hold back, but set apart a portion to present to

212. Heb 7.3.
213. Heb 7.4–7.

him, in this way, through the presentation of tithes, he thought to honor him.

Now [109] those of the line of Levi received tithes from the people, even though they were their kinsmen, but this man Melchizedek, who was not of their genealogy (as he was not of the tribe of Levi), took tithes from Abraham and blessed him. Now there is a figure present in these things. Once again being portrayed here by means of shadows is Christ, who was likewise without genealogy with respect to those appointed to serve as priests under the law (for he was descended from the tribe of Judah, in connection with which Moses said nothing regarding priests),[214] and who received tithes from the Levites, that is, from the priesthood under the law. So Christ long ago received tithes in Melchizedek, and later in Aaron too. For Aaron himself also obtained tithes from the Levites, so presenting a type of the priesthood of Christ, as we said above.

11. So through Melchizedek it has been demonstrated that at some time there would be a change in the manner of the priesthood, of the tribe serving as priests under the law, as indeed was so, and that another kind of priesthood and law would arise. For it was necessary that when the priestly ministries were changed, there was at the same time also a change in the law itself. Accordingly, the divine Paul speaks of these matters wisely when he says, "Now if perfection were through the Levitical priesthood (for under it the people received the law), what further need was there to speak of another priest arising in the order of Melchizedek, and not in the order of Aaron? For when there is a change in the priesthood, of necessity there is also a change in the law."[215] And again, "And this is far more apparent if another priest arises in the order[216] of Melchizedek, who has become a priest, not through a law of physical descent, but through the power of an indestructible life. For it is attested of him, 'You are a priest for ever in the order of Melchizedek.'"[217]

---

214. Cf. Heb 7.14.
215. Heb 7.11–12.
216. The text of Hebrews here actually says, "according to the likeness [*homoiotês*] of Melchizedek."
217. Heb 7.15–17.

See how he affirms that nothing could bring about perfection through the priesthood under the law, and so he declares that a better and more beneficial ordinance would be brought in instead. For if what was needful existed in that former priesthood, why not rather, he says, indicate that there would be another priest in the order of Aaron, and not in the order of Melchizedek, a similitude and type of Christ, who did not at all further serve as a priest in a fleshly manner, but through the power of an indestructible life? For through his mystical priestly ministrations he sustains[218] us for a life that is unending, even as Aaron was serving as a priest in a fleshly manner. For through the latter there were sacrifices of oxen and the slaying of sheep, and the sprinkling of those who were defiled with the ashes of a heifer for the purification of the flesh, and other things besides these, which did not perfect the consciences of the worshipers, since it is not possible for the blood of bulls to take away sins.[219] Therefore, when another kind of priestly ministry was brought in for us, having deposed the first and more ancient practices, there was also a completely different priest. God promised a new covenant when the first had become old, this being the priest in the order of Melchizedek, with regard to whom it was proper to understand that he would live for ever. This was none other than our Lord Jesus Christ, through whom and with whom be glory to God the Father, together with the Holy Spirit, for ever and ever. Amen.

218. *trephei,* "nourishes."
219. Cf. Heb 10.4.

BOOK THREE: GENESIS 15–27

[112] *Concerning Abraham, the promise regarding Isaac, and how through them the mystery of the faith was prefigured*

HE DIVINE PAUL writes that Christ became the high priest and apostle of our confession.[1] And further, he plainly affirmed that Christ became the guarantor of a better covenant which he inaugurated for us,[2] namely that of the gospel, a covenant which is incomparably superior to and which far surpasses the ancient ordinance given through Moses. And this word is true. For the law in fact produces wrath,[3] and serves to expose sin, but the grace administered through the goodness of our Savior justifies us. He himself says in a certain place that he did not come to judge the world, but that the world might be saved through him.[4]

So, even though he did not come from the tribe of Levi with respect to the flesh, he is called and actually is a high priest for ever in the priestly order of Melchizedek, as the word has now made abundantly plain to us.[5] Also, because the mystery of righteousness by faith is foreannounced earlier in the law of circumcision, and because it is portrayed beforehand in type to the people of Israel, there can never be any other way to be saved except through Christ alone, who justifies the ungodly and forgives the charges against them.

Besides this, we may now say that those related to the promise made in Isaac to the blessed Abraham are heirs of God and

---

1. Heb 3.1.
2. Cf. Heb 7.22.
3. Cf. Rom 4.15.
4. Jn 12.47.
5. Cf. Heb 5.6; 7.17; Ps 110.4 (109.4 LXX).

have been allocated a place among those who are most certainly his true children, since we[6] obtain this from the sacred Scriptures themselves, and consider them to be absolutely trustworthy in each and every detail.

2. Now the most holy Paul writes to the Romans, "What shall we say, then, that Abraham, our forefather according to the flesh, found? For if Abraham was justified by works, he has something to boast about, but not before God. What in fact does the Scripture say? 'Abraham believed God, and it was reckoned to him as righteousness.'[7] To the one who works, wages are not reckoned as a gift, but as something due. But to the one who does not work, but believes in him who justifies the ungodly, his faith is reckoned as righteousness. So also David speaks of the blessedness of the man to whom God reckons righteousness apart from works: 'Blessed are those whose iniquities are forgiven, and whose sins are covered. Blessed is the man whose sin the Lord will not reckon against him.'[8] Is this blessedness, then, for the circumcised, or for [113] the uncircumcised also? For we say that faith was reckoned to Abraham as righteousness. So how was it reckoned? When he was circumcised or uncircumcised? It was not when he was circumcised, it says, but when uncircumcised. He received the sign of circumcision as a seal of the righteousness he had by faith when uncircumcised, so that he would be the father of all who believe without being circumcised, in order that righteousness might be reckoned to them. And he is also the father of the circumcised who are not only circumcised but who follow in the footsteps of the faith which our father Abraham had when he was uncircumcised."[9]

In addition to this, Paul gives a yet stronger affirmation of the mystery. This is what he says: "For the promise to Abraham and his offspring that he would be heir of the world was not through law, but through the righteousness of faith. For if those who are of the law are heirs," he says, "faith is made void and the promise is of no effect, because the law produces wrath. Where

---

6. Or "they."
7. Gn 15.6.
8. Ps 32.1–2 (31.1–2 LXX).
9. Rom 4.1–12.

there is no law, there is no transgression. For this reason, the promise is of faith, so that by grace it may be made sure to all the offspring, not only to those who are of the law, but also to those who are of the faith of Abraham. He is the father of us all (as it is written, 'I have made you the father of many nations'),[10] our father in the sight of God in whom he believed, who gives life to the dead and calls into being things that do not exist."[11]

Note that it is stated and maintained throughout, and that not in a short space, how it was not when he was circumcised, but rather while still uncircumcised, that the grace was given to Abraham that justified him through faith. It is also stated that those wishing to follow in the footsteps of the faith that our forefather Abraham had when uncircumcised are made heirs of the gifts given by God, while they do not at all make it their habit to vaunt over the shadow ministered through Moses and boast in Abraham as a fleshly father. The latter was called "father of many nations," and though Israel was then just one nation, it would expand into an innumerable multitude. For Abraham became the father of those with faith, who are from all parts, that is to say, gathered out of every land and city. They have been made fellow members of the body of Christ and have been called into a spiritual brotherhood.

The Jews are indeed descended from Abraham. "Not all those of Israel," however, "are Israel, neither are the offspring of Abraham all his children."[12] Rather, the faith that he had resides in those who have come to believe while uncircumcised. For the promise was made and the grace that justifies was given, not when Abraham was circumcised, but when he was uncircumcised, according to the faith of the sacred Scriptures.

3. Though the promise came through Abraham, that the gift of righteousness by faith did not pertain solely to him but also spread to all others who have come to believe, the most-wise Paul also affirms to us. To what I said just now he adds, "It was not written for his sake alone that 'it was reckoned to him as righteousness,' but for our sakes also, for those who believe in

10. Gn 17.5.
11. Rom 4.13–17.
12. Rom 9.6–7.

him who raised our Lord Jesus from the dead, who was delivered up [116] for our transgressions, and was raised for our righteousness."[13]

So then, the grace that justifies us on the basis of faith is a provision from heaven and a gift coming down from the divine beneficence. And those are counted among the children of Abraham who are not merely descended from him with respect to the flesh, but those who have been richly blessed in the same way as he was, and who believe in our Lord Jesus Christ, considering themselves to be brothers. It is these, who disdain the unbelief of Israel according to the flesh, that will be heirs of the gifts from God. This is represented in an especially clear[14] way in the mystery regarding Isaac.

Let us now speak of this as we are able, setting forth what Moses wrote so as to make it known.[15] There it reads as follows: *After these things the word of the Lord came to Abraham in a vision, saying, "Do not fear, Abraham; I myself will protect you. Your reward will be exceedingly great." Abraham said, "Master, what will you give me, since I go childless, and this Eliezer of Damascus, the son of Masek*[16] *my maidservant, will be my heir?" He further said, "Seeing that you have not given me any offspring, my household servant will receive my inheritance." And immediately the voice of the Lord came to him, saying, "This man will not receive your inheritance, but one who shall come forth from you will be your heir." Then he took him outside and said to him, "Look up at the sky and count the stars, if you are able to number them." And he said, "So shall your offspring be." Then Abraham believed God, and it was reckoned to him as righteousness.*[17]

Living together with Abraham was his spouse, the blessed Sarah (which means "princess"), an eminently beautiful and fine-looking woman, as the sacred Scripture testifies. Yet the homeborn servant was persuaded to render service by entering into a second, unlawful union; this was Hagar (which means "wanderer").[18] Sarah, not yet having experienced the pangs of giving

13. Rom 4.24.
14. Var. "detailed."
15. Var. add "accurately."
16. Var. "my son by my maidservant."
17. Gn 15.1–6.
18. The name Hagar is, in fact, of uncertain meaning.

birth to her own children, lamented her childlessness. Hagar, on the other hand, gave birth to Ishmael.

These, then, are the matters contained in the literal sense of the account. God addressed Abraham, saying, *"I myself will protect you. Your reward will be exceedingly great."* What did he say in answer to this? *"Master, what will you give me, since I go childless, and this Eliezer of Damascus, the son of Masek*[19] *my maidservant, will be my heir?"* Observe the words carefully. *"What will you give me, O Master?"* he says. You note how he asks for absolutely nothing in the way of earthly possessions, nor that he might become the owner of yet more things. He would consider nothing more pleasing, he says, than that he should have a proper heir, one who was truly a son, born of his marriage to the free woman.

Take note then, for a clear understanding of what is profitable, that human nature acts on its own instincts and without written laws. Although there was a son, Ishmael, the divine Abraham called himself childless.[20] So human nature very obviously recognized that it was not at all suitable to call him a son who had been brought forth from a fraudulent and illegitimate marriage. For, according to what is written, "he will not put down deep roots."[21] Though there [117] might have been a child for them from the maidservant at that time, it was a completely lifeless and vain affair, nor was it described with the joy appropriate to a marriage with a free woman. This is demonstrated when Abraham says, *"this Eliezer of Damascus, the son of Masek my maidservant, will be my heir."* That is, the son of the home-born servant would henceforth be a "kiss of blood" to him, for that is the meaning of "Damascus."[22] He would also be reckoned as a "help" and "succor" from God, for that is the meaning of "Eliezer."[23] So it is as though he expressly said, "The son of my home-born servant will, of necessity, be a kiss of blood and a help from God instead of the blood of a real son and of

19. Var. omit "of Masek."
20. The sequence of events here is inaccurate; see n. 33 below.
21. Cf. Wis 4.3.
22. Elements within the name "Damascus" bear some resemblance to the Hebrew words for "blood" and "kiss." The order, however, prohibits the meaning "kiss of blood."
23. Here the meaning of the name is correctly given.

the love ...[24] and he will also be my heir. What, then, will you give me? Unless I have a real son to succeed me, O Master, this Abraham of yours will be utterly reproached on all sides, for the man who is destitute of true children will be abandoned even by the free woman."

God, however, does not leave the righteous grieving for long. Immediately the offspring was promised in Isaac, an offspring that he also says would be equal in number to the uncountable host of stars. And it was affirmed that Abraham would be called the father of such a great multitude of nations, even though he was greatly dismayed by his childlessness. Then it says, *Abraham believed God, and it was reckoned to him as righteousness.* So the one who by faith honors the Master of all has righteousness as a reward. This bore witness to the fact that it was possible for everything to go well for him. But the one who disbelieves and who is indifferent will be boastful and insolent. Thus he will be called to account and incur punishment.

So Abraham believed God and was justified by him. Now it requires a sign to confirm the truth of those things previously promised, that they would come to pass. God, therefore, by way of accommodation[25] provided confirmation by binding himself with an oath, not letting him who believed be troubled in any way by a doubting mind. For this is what is written: *He said to him, "I am the God who brought you out of the land of the Chaldeans, to give you this land as an inheritance." And Abraham asked, "Lord and Master, how shall I know that I will inherit it?" God said to him, "Bring me a three-year-old heifer,*[26] *a three-year-old ram, a turtledove, and a dove." So he brought all these to him, and he cut them in two halves and placed them opposite each other. The birds, however, he did not cut in two. Then birds of prey came down upon the divided carcasses, so Abraham sat down with the pieces. Around the time the sun was setting, a trance came upon Abraham, and behold, a great, dark dread fell upon him. Then Abraham was told, "Know of a certainty that your*

24. The Greek text appears corrupted at this point.

25. *oikonomikôs.*

26. Although Cyril omits the "three-year-old goat" from the list of animals here, he makes mention of it below in sections 124 and 128, interpreting its spiritual significance in the latter.

offspring will be aliens in a land that is not their own, and they will serve its people, who will afflict them for four hundred years. But that nation which they serve I will judge, and afterwards they will come forth to this place with many possessions. As for you, you will go to your fathers in peace and be buried at a good old age. In the fourth generation they will come back here, for the sins of the Amorites have not yet reached their full measure, even till now." When the sun was about to set, there was a flame, and behold, a smoking furnace and fiery torches, which passed between those [120] *divided pieces.*[27]

What this event is all about, the one who is keen to learn will examine, and will take pains to investigate the manner in which the oath was made. What are the divided pieces meant to indicate? What of the flight of the birds and their gathering upon them? What about Abraham sitting with the pieces? What of the flame passing between them? So now we will offer an explanation.

4. For the Chaldeans, passing through the middle of animals that were cut in two was a necessary requirement for making an oath. It was as if to declare through what was being enacted: "May I not become like these." Since Abraham was of the Chaldean race, and had only recently come out from that place, the Master of all instructed him by way of accommodation to perform these customs pertaining to the oath, at the same time finely weaving in the mystery of Christ through the animals that were sacrificed.

When Abraham spread out the pieces upon the ground, it was as though God were about to proceed in between them. *Many birds,* it says, *gathered upon them, so Abraham sat down with the pieces.* This means that he prepared himself and kept guard in order that no harm might be done, and that those things arranged for making the oath might not become food for unclean birds. Then it says, *Around the time the sun was setting, a trance and dread fell upon Abraham.* Again, how this might be understood, I shall explain as far as is possible. It is helpful and wholly unobjectionable to assume that it was also a custom for the Chaldeans to observe closely the flight of birds. And so by way of accommodation the God of all permitted some things which he knew to be a custom for certain people, in order to give instruc-

27. Gn 15.7–17.

tion about what was coming in the future. Now when the birds had gathered upon the pieces, the divine Abraham was fearful,[28] having perhaps some notion of what this sign pointed to. For those most loathsome birds flying down upon the sacrifices seemed to be something bad, a cause of some concern, as it is always the habit of unclean things to devour flesh. Now since he was afraid for his own sake, lest the matter should somehow befall himself, he is freed from any anguish over these things, for it says, *"The birds swooping down will not come upon you.*[29] *But know of a certainty that your offspring will be aliens in a strange land."* And those wanting to afflict them would be very many, of whom the birds coming down upon the sacrifices were a figure.[30] Once they have caused a little distress, however, their punishment will be exacted. So it continues, *"As for you, you will go to your fathers in peace and be buried at a good old age."*

Then it says, *When the sun was about to set, there was a flame of fire, a furnace, and torches, which passed between those divided pieces.* The Deity here, who brings the oath into effect, is perceived in the form of fire, according to the usage of the Chaldeans. The divine Paul also speaks about the force of the oath, and says, "When God made the promise to Abraham, since he could swear by no one greater, he swore by himself, saying, 'I will surely bless you, and I will surely multiply you.'[31] And having waited patiently, he obtained the promise. For men swear by one greater than themselves, and with them an oath given as confirmation puts an end to all dispute. In the same way God, desiring even more to show to the heirs of the promise the unchangeableness of his purpose, guaranteed it with an oath, so that by two unchangeable things in which it is impossible for God to lie, we who have taken refuge might have strong encouragement to take hold of the hope set before us."[32] [121]

5. It was most especially by way of accommodation that God

28. Var. add "extremely."
29. This first sentence is not taken, of course, directly from the text of Genesis, but is part of Cyril's interpretation, understanding the birds to represent the nation that would later oppress Abraham's descendants.
30. Or "type."
31. Gn 22.17.
32. Heb 6.13–18.

made the promise and, even though he did not know how to tell a lie, bound himself by oath. This was, as the divine Paul writes, in order that we might have "strong encouragement," one which totally surpasses all limitations so that we no longer have any doubts.

Now turning our discussion for a moment to what happened earlier,[33] while Hagar was bearing Ishmael, Sarah was troubled, not being able, one would suppose, to endure the boasting and unrestrained haughtiness of the home-born servant over the fact that she was pregnant. Sarah therefore drove her out of the home, and commanded her to go wherever she might wish, while her legal spouse, Abraham, permitted her to do this. Yet, as the sacred Scripture says, *An angel of the Lord God found her by the spring of water in the wilderness on the way to Shur. And the angel of the Lord said to her, "Hagar, maidservant of Sarah, where have you come from, and where are you going?" She replied, "I am running away from my mistress, Sarah." Then the angel of the Lord said to her, "Go back to your mistress, and submit to her authority."*[34] So Hagar went back and submitted to a yoke of servitude.

God then gave Abraham the law of circumcision, saying, *"As for you, you shall keep my covenant, you and your offspring after you throughout their generations. And this is the covenant that you shall keep between me and you, and your offspring after you throughout their generations. Every male among you shall be circumcised. You shall be circumcised in the flesh of your foreskin, and it will be a sign of the covenant between me and you. Throughout your generations every male child among you shall be circumcised when he is eight days old, including the one who is home-born and the one who has been bought with money from any son of a foreigner who is not of your offspring. Whether born in your house or bought with money, he must be circumcised. My covenant will be upon your flesh as an everlasting covenant. But an uncircumcised male, who has not been circumcised in the flesh of his foreskin on the eighth day, that person shall be utterly destroyed from among his people because he has rejected my covenant."*[35] As it was

---

33. Cyril is mistaken. The events he here refers to in fact happened later than the passage he has been discussing (Gn 15).
34. Gn 16.7–9.
35. Gn 17.9–14.

necessary to submit to the laws of God, the divine Abraham was circumcised with all his household. He circumcised the others also, including Ishmael.

Then the son of the free woman was eventually born, that is, Isaac. And what happened after this? It was intolerable that the illegitimate son, Ishmael, should be mocking Isaac around the home when he ought, one might suppose, to have shown him exceptional honor. For it says, *Sarah saw the son of Hagar the Egyptian, who was born to Abraham, making fun of Isaac her son.*[36] Then she came to Abraham, in tears no doubt, and said, *"Drive out this maidservant and her son, for the son of this maidservant shall not receive an inheritance along with my son, Isaac."*[37]

This matter regarding his son, it says, was the cause of considerable distress to Abraham: *Then God said to Abraham, "Let not this matter concerning the son and the maidservant distress you. Whatever Sarah tells you, listen* [124] *to her, because it is in Isaac that your offspring will be named. And the son of this maidservant I will make into a great nation, because he is your offspring." So Abraham arose early in the morning, took some loaves of bread and a skin of water, and gave them to Hagar. Then he put the child upon her shoulder and sent her away. Going off, she wandered about in the wilderness near the Well of the Oath.*[38] *When the water from the skin was all gone, she placed the child under a fir tree, then went and sat down opposite him about the distance of a bowshot away. She said, "I cannot watch my child die," and so she sat opposite him. The child cried out and wept. God heard the voice of the child coming from the place where he was, and an angel of God called to Hagar from heaven and said to her, "What is the matter, Hagar? Do not be afraid, for God has heard the voice of your child coming from the place where he is. Get up, take the child, and hold him in your hands." Then God opened her eyes, and she saw a well of fresh water.*[39] *So she went and filled up the skin with water and gave the child a drink. And God was with the child as he grew up.*[40]

The divine Abraham, being overcome by the natural law of

36. Gn 21.9.
37. Gn 21.10.
38. That is, Beersheba.
39. Lit. "living water."
40. Gn 21.12–20.

fatherly love, changed his mind about Ishmael. But when the Deity addressed him in an oracle, telling him to devote himself to Isaac alone as the one to whom the promise pertained, Abraham dismissed Hagar and ordered her, together with the child, to leave the home of her mistress. In this the law was foreshowing a type of the mystery regarding Christ.

6. It is necessary that we should return to our original discussion. For in these matters one may see most readily that what comes through Christ is older than what appears in the law. Justification by faith is revealed even earlier than the circumcision of the flesh. For circumcision, according to what the most-wise Paul says, was given to Abraham as a sign of the faith he had when uncircumcised.

Now the blessed Abraham was troubled, because he had not become the father of a free child. Though he had a son from the Egyptian woman, Hagar, he remained disheartened, reckoning that to have an illegitimate offspring rather than one that was free was the same as being childless. But when he received the promises concerning a genuine child, namely Isaac, he plainly heard that he would be the father of a countless number of nations, and believing this he was justified. Besides this, Abraham would take possession of the land that God had shown him. *"For to you,"* he said, *"I will give this land."*[41] To be sure of this, he entreated God and asked, *"Master, how shall I know that I will inherit it?"*[42] Then God commanded him to prepare the pieces, the three-year-old heifer, with the goat and the ram, and the turtledove and the dove. Abraham cut the four-legged animals into two, and placed them opposite one another, that is, in a row. The birds, however, he did not cut in two. He also drove away the birds of prey wanting to consume them. And late in the evening, when the sun was setting, in a form of fire God passed through the pieces. What kind of spiritual meaning we might assign to these things, we shall speak of as we are able.

7. Now Israel according to the flesh was a first son, as it were, to the God of all, for it says, "Israel is [125] my firstborn son,"[43]

---

41. Cf. Gn 13.15; 15.7; 17.8; 24.7.
42. Gn 15.8.
43. Ex 4.22.

though one that was redeemed from slavery and from Egypt. But God did not think Israel fit to be counted among his children (for it is his nature to love what is free and genuine). Rather, he looked for a pleasing people, that is, a people that come into being through faith in Christ according to the promise, in whom they have also become, in the wake of the divine Abraham, fathers of many nations. For they have inherited that glory such as was not found in Israel according to the flesh, but in those who have been saved through faith from among the nations. Paul also bears witness to this when he writes, "For the promise to Abraham, that he would be heir of the world, was not through law, but through the righteousness of faith."[44] We who came to believe when uncircumcised lay claim to Abraham as our father, and we are justified by God in the same way as he was.

Paul, an expert in the law, makes the divine mystery especially clear to us. For he writes to the Galatians, rebuking them for going back to the law after the perfection in Christ had come, saying, "Tell me, you who wish to be under the law, do you not listen to the law? For it is written that Abraham had two sons, one from a maidservant, and the other from a free woman. The one from the maidservant was born according to the flesh, while the one from the free woman was born through the promise. These things are an allegory. The two women are the two covenants. One is from Mount Sinai, who gives birth to children for slavery; this is Hagar. Now Sinai is a mountain in Arabia. This corresponds to the present Jerusalem, for she is in slavery with her children. The Jerusalem from above is free, and she is our mother. For it is written, 'Rejoice, O barren one, who bears no children. Cry out and shout, you who are not in labor; for the children of the desolate women are more than those of the woman who has a husband.'[45] Now we, brothers, are children of the promise, as Isaac was. But just as at that time the one who was born according to the flesh persecuted the one born according to the Spirit, so it is now also. But what does the Scripture say? 'Drive out the maidservant and her son, for the

44. Rom 4.13.
45. Is 54.1.

son of the maidservant shall not receive an inheritance along with the son of the free woman.'[46] Now we, brothers, are not children of the maidservant, but of the free woman. For freedom Christ has set us free. Stand firm, therefore, and do not submit again to a yoke of slavery."[47]

You see, then, how he plainly says that Hagar and Sarah are representations of two covenants. The maidservant represents the mother of the Jews, that is, the Jerusalem upon earth, since she is in subjection to the law of bondage and is not endowed with a free spirit. As for the first and free woman, Sarah, the one whose name may be translated as "princess," he says she is a figure that applies to the Jerusalem on high. He also clearly affirms that she has become the mother of those justified by faith, who have been called through the promises of God so as to be children of Abraham. "For we," it says, "are children of the promise, as Isaac was." We were set free in Christ, through whom and in whom we are richly blessed with the divine Spirit from above. We have been assigned a place among the children of God, and "we cry out Abba, Father."[48] We have also become heirs [128] of the good things promised to the saints, God having bound himself, so to speak, in swearing an oath "by himself." For the Son, whom the mystery concerns, was introduced with the oath of the Father. It is the custom of the Father to swear, as it were, according to his own power, which is the Son. This is what it means to swear by himself, seeing that the Son is not another beside the Father, that is, as far as the question of essence[49] and the identity of their deity is concerned.

So too the divine Moses, when he portrayed to us God swearing an oath, very plainly represented him as saying, "I will raise my hand up to heaven, and swear by my right hand."[50] Now the right hand of God the Father is the Son, by means of whom he prevails over all things and, as it were, has a hold on everything. Moreover, as is fitting for one who is God, the Son performs

46. Gn 21.10.
47. Gal 4.21–5.1.
48. Rom 8.15.
49. Or "being."
50. Dt 32.40.

the task of calling things that do not exist into being, and keeps things that already exist well-ordered.

Surely then, in the matter of the oath for confirming the faith of those who would inherit the promises, the mystery of our Savior was presented. Christ was further pictured in the heifer, the goat, and the ram, and in the two birds, the turtledove and the dove. And how this matter might be understood, I will now explain as much as the opportunity allows.

8. It is evident that, owing to its great strength and invincibility in a fight, a young bull serves on occasion as a fitting likeness to Christ's deity. At other times, with respect to his human nature, and because he is under law, he is termed a heifer. It is always the case that the female is the lesser and secondary, while the male is the ruler and preeminent. For the Son is far above all creation, and he bears a nature and a glory of such incomparable excellence that far surpasses those of created things, coming from the highest possible source,[51] namely the Father and God of all. When he came as one of us, he was reckoned as being under the authority of the law. He therefore said, "I have not come to abolish the law, but to fulfill it."[52] And we shall refer this, if we wish to understand correctly, to the matter of his emptying himself.[53] For this reason, Christ is a heifer, fulfilling the figure of the law of Moses, as the law defines with regard to him.

He is also compared to a goat. For what reason?[54] Because he offered himself for our sins, according to the Scriptures. The he-goat was a sacrifice for sin according to the law.[55]

He is also likened to a ram, on account of his leading the spiritual sheep. For Christ is the one leader over us, and "we are the people of his pasture and the sheep of his hand," as it is written.[56] When, having emptied himself, he was made in all respects like his brothers, that is, like us, he is described as a

51. Lit. "root."
52. Mt 5.17.
53. *kenôsis*.
54. Var. "For what sin?"
55. Cf. Lv 4.28.
56. Ps 95.7 (94.7 LXX).

ram, meaning one who leads, for rams are always the leaders of the flock.

So then, Christ is a heifer, since he was under the law; he is also a goat, as being a sacrifice for sin; and he is a ram, since he is one who leads.

Now we should want to follow in his footsteps, and do so eagerly. We will then be in good pasture, and in a fertile place, as the prophet says,[57] and we will dine in sacred courts. For he will cause us to inhabit the heavenly dwellings, he himself being, as it were, both a ram and chief shepherd. As [129] one of us he is under the law and yet also over the law, being himself God, our whole justification, although "he was counted with the transgressors,"[58] and endured being slain for our sakes.

He is also pictured as a turtledove and a dove. For he is the unique spiritual turtledove that sings out, the truly eloquent bird who is from heaven above, who has summoned everyone under heaven through the proclamation of the gospel, to whom also the bride, that is, the church of the nations, called out, "Show me your face and let me hear your voice, because your voice is pleasant and your face is beautiful."[59] He is the pure, innocent[60] dove, which is without deceit, for as it is written, "no deceit was found in his mouth."[61]

He is likewise the three-year-old heifer as well as the other animals, for he is the all-perfect Lord, the age of the animals beautifully showing forth the perfection in deity of the Only-Begotten.

The animals were separated, for they were cut into two pieces. Yet the two birds, remember, were not cut up. And what does this mean? The Only-Begotten Word of God became flesh, as if he were divided in two, and the matter we have to consider concerning him extends into two parts. For on the one hand we perceive his divine and ineffable generation from the Father, while on the other we speak also of the mystery of his Incar-

---

57. Probably alluding to Ezek 34.14; cf. also Is 5.1.
58. Is 53.12.
59. Song 2.14.
60. Var. add "truly."
61. Is 53.9.

nation. This is the profundity of the divine economy—we both make separate and take as one, thereby imparting knowledge to those who do not understand this mystery. Although our consideration of him has become twofold, however, he himself is wholly one, not capable of being divided into two following his union with flesh.[62] Nor can he be separated into two sons, for Christ is one and undivided. The fact that the birds were not divided would also be a distinct figure of this very thing, for it says, *"Do not cut the birds in two."* That he is from the earth on account of his humanity was in a way signified by means of the young cow, the goat, and the ram. That he is also from heaven above on account of his being God is understood by means of the birds. Though Christ willingly endured being slain for us, his flesh, as it is written, "did not see corruption,"[63] and according to what the psalmist says, "The enemy will have no advantage over him, and the son of lawlessness will not harm him any more."[64] Again, the divine Abraham very plainly indicates this in a figure, when he drives away the birds of prey wanting to consume[65] the divided pieces.

The harsh treatment later to be experienced in Egypt by those descended from Abraham,[66] that is, Israel, was announced to him ahead of time, as was their incredible deliverance. It says, *Around the time the sun was setting, a smoking fiery furnace, and fiery torches, passed between the divided pieces.* For the law of Moses[67] brought to light matters relating to the promise before they happened, that is, the slavery of the Israelites and their deliverance, presenting far-off events to those who heard the account.

Now it was in the latter times of the world, which was as though it were towards evening, that "the Word became flesh."[68] For I believe that it was he, and none other, who was [132] that

62. Var. add "With regard to the hypostasis, he cannot be separated..."
63. Ps 16.10 (15.10 LXX).
64. Ps 89.22 (88.23 LXX).
65. Here Cyril uses the verb cognate to the noun translated "corruption" in the foregoing citation from Ps 16.
66. Lit. "those of his blood."
67. By this phrase Cyril here means the Pentateuch rather than the Mosaic law given at Sinai.
68. Jn 1.14.

divine and ineffable Being[69] that passed between the pieces in the form of fire. *There was*, it says, *a flame of fire, a fiery furnace, and fiery torches*. For the sacred mystery of the Incarnation has truly occurred, which, for those choosing to disobey and who turn aside to unrestrained behavior, is like a furnace and a flame, and the unendurable last judgment of all. So with regard to the Israelites who ignorantly inveighed against the mystery of Christ, who were inclined to be antagonistic and boastful, David said to him who is Father and God of all, "You will make them like a fiery furnace at the time of your presence, Lord; in your wrath you will trouble them, and fire will consume them."[70] The time of the Father's presence is reasonably understood as the time of the Incarnation, seeing that the Son is both the presence and image of God the Father. He is a fierce flame and a furnace to those who wish to reject the mystery of the Incarnation of the Only-Begotten. Yet to those who acknowledge his appearing, he is, as it is written, "a lamp shining in the darkness,"[71] which makes the earthy, devilish gloom[72] recede and does not permit the many who worship him to stumble by falling into sin.

Thus God the Father put forward[73] the Son for us, saying through the mouth of Isaiah, "For Zion's sake, I will not be silent, and for the sake of Jerusalem I will not rest, until my righteousness goes forth like light, and my salvation burns like torches."[74] For the Son has become both our salvation and righteousness from God the Father. Since it is true that we are justified in him, overcoming also the death that long ago subjected us to its dominion, we are again restored to incorruption and transformed into that very nature which we had in the beginning.

9. That it was necessary, once Emmanuel had appeared and his mystery had been manifested in the world, for the types of the Mosaic ministration to be removed and to give way to the

---

69. *phusis*.
70. Ps 21.9 (20.10 LXX).
71. Cf. Jn 1.5.
72. Lit. "mist."
73. Or "dedicated."
74. Is 62.1.

teachings of the gospel, the better and more perfect ordinance, is again foreshadowed in an earthy type. And what is this type I will speak of? As Sarah had not borne any children, while Hagar was pregnant with Ishmael she was seen to hold the free woman in contempt. Sarah could not bear this haughtiness and began to mistreat the Egyptian woman. So Hagar ran away from home and wandered about in the wilderness. An angel from heaven asked her where she was going and where she had come from. *She answered, "I am running away from my mistress, Sarah."* Then what did the divine angel say? *"Go back to your mistress, and submit to her authority."*[75]

Foreshown here is the ministration of the law laboring to give birth to Israel.[76] This was a servant, for in it there was no spirit of freedom. Before the new teaching of the gospel, it conceived, as it were, the people who had come out of Egypt. It therefore became high-minded and persecuted those in Christ, and greatly exalting itself against the divine oracles of the gospel, in numerous ways it stood condemned. For the synagogue of the Jews censured the holy apostles, expressly saying, "We strictly commanded you not [133] to teach in this name, and look, you have filled Jerusalem with your teaching!"[77]

You see how the Egyptian woman exalted herself against Sarah, how the serving girl was emboldened against the free woman. Yet in time she was overcome and she ran away, receiving after a fashion the penalty of her unrestrained behavior.[78] She was then commanded, through what the angel said, not to reject the free woman, that is, the teaching that leads to the dignity of freedom, but rather to submit to her authority.

The ministration of the law, conducted through figures and types, is in a way a servant of the gospel teachings, dimly portraying in itself the beauty of the truth. The law that was appointed long ago by Moses through angels, also through the voice of an

75. Gn 16.8–9.
76. Since the noun *latreia* ("service," "worship," "ministration," "cultus") is feminine, Cyril is able at one and the same time to talk about both the servant woman Hagar and the ministration of the Mosaic law. In the following sentences, therefore, "it" could equally well be read as "she."
77. Acts 5.28.
78. Or "in a way incurring the penalty of banishment."

angel is ordered to submit to the oracles given through Christ, and to bow,[79] even if unwillingly, to the free woman. This, I believe, is how we are to understand Hagar's submission to Sarah. It ought also to be remembered that the divine Paul takes these women as two covenants, one bearing children for slavery, corresponding to the present Jerusalem,[80] and the other bearing children for the dignity of freedom, which is Sarah.

The blessed Abraham was evidently taught that when Christ came, the time of circumcision in the Spirit[81] would assuredly come with him. God gave the law that circumcision should be carried out, foreshowing, I believe, spiritual things through fleshly figures. Now it says, *"every male shall be circumcised."*[82] And for this reason he metes out ruin and destruction as the punishment for neglecting to obey, for it said that *"an uncircumcised male, who has not been circumcised in the flesh of his foreskin on the eighth day, that person shall be utterly destroyed from among his people*[83] *because he has rejected my covenant."*[84]

You see that circumcision in the flesh is a type that foreshows circumcision in spirit and truth. It was performed on the eighth day, the same as when Christ came back to life from the dead. And it was the occasion of partaking of the Holy Spirit and receiving circumcision in him, not one that causes pain to the flesh, but which purifies the spirit, not removing the filth of the body, but freeing us from diseases of the soul.

When Christ came back to life, having annulled the power of death, then he also put within the holy disciples the firstfruits, as it were, of the Holy Spirit. It says that he breathed upon them and said to them, "Receive the Holy Spirit."[85] The meaning of this the most-wise John also understands, saying, "For the Holy Spirit was not yet given, because Jesus had not yet been glorified."[86] Christ was indeed glorified when he rose from the dead,

---

79. Var. "and to submit, even if unwillingly, to the call of the free woman."
80. Var. add "with her children" (cf. Gal 4.25).
81. Or "in spirit."
82. Gn 17.10.
83. Var. "from that place."
84. Gn 17.14.
85. Jn 20.22.
86. Jn 7.39.

which was on the eighth day. Consequently, the Spirit was also conveyed to us, and in him we have been circumcised with a spiritual circumcision performed without hands. This, in fact, is the kind of circumcision that is pleasing to God. Therefore, the divine Paul says in a certain place, "For he is not a Jew who is one outwardly, nor is circumcision that which is outward in the flesh. Rather, he is a Jew who is one inwardly, and circumcision is that of the heart, by the Spirit, not by the letter. Such a person's praise is not from men, but from God."[87]

10. The ministration under the law being of no more effect, and the new ministration in Christ now being in force, those [136] who are a people through faith have now been displayed. They have been incorporated among the children of the free woman, who do not have a servile spirit (for they cry out, "Abba, Father"). Accordingly, the time came for the congregation and synagogue of the Jews to be sent away, and to be disinherited as the people of the promise. It is, however, also the case that in due course they will repent and be accepted. They will obtain mercy from the Father above, as they acknowledge the Savior and Redeemer of all. This too the sacred Scripture reveals.

Now the two boys, Isaac and Ishmael, were playing about, leaping after one another. Chasing is, I suppose, a kind of childish amusement. Ishmael is said to be the one who was chasing, and Isaac is depicted as the one running away. The free woman, Sarah, however, felt indignant at this. So she said to the divine Abraham, *"Drive out this maidservant and her son, for the son of this maidservant shall not receive an inheritance along with my son, Isaac."*[88] The situation indeed sounded troublesome[89] to Abraham. Yet he heard from God that he should be persuaded by the words of Sarah. So, having supplied Hagar with loaves of bread and water, he commanded her to take the child and leave the home of her mistress. Hagar went off distraught and in tears, and wandered about in the wilderness. But when the life of the child was in danger and he was crying out, it says that

---

87. Rom 2.28–29.
88. Gn 21.10.
89. Var. "harsh."

God opened Hagar's eyes, and she saw a well of fresh water and gave the boy a drink.[90]

Note, then, how even the playing of children can be valuable to some degree for understanding the mystery, for Ishmael pursued Isaac.[91] The fact that Ishmael, the son of the maidservant, would persecute the son of the free woman, namely the people which is in Christ through faith, the blessed Paul explained with reference to Ishmael and Isaac. He said, "But just as at that time the one who was born according to the flesh persecuted the one born according to the Spirit, so it is now also."[92] Since Ishmael was hostile towards the children of the free woman, the synagogue of the Jews has now been sent away, with bread and water as its paltry sustenance. This latter indicates, as it were, that knowledge and piety were given in measure, by means of which it was not at all possible that the Jews should go off and die out completely. For God in a certain place said that he had left a remnant in Israel, a few offspring who showed some virtue with respect to the law: "And I will be a little sanctuary for them in the countries where they go."[93] He says he would become "a little sanctuary" for the people of Israel after their dispersion among the nations. On account of the lack of strength on the part of the Jews which made them unable fully to obey the law given through Moses, they observed only a very few things, like circumcision in the flesh perhaps, and resting on the Sabbath. So then, by water and loaves of bread she who was born for slavery, that is, the synagogue of the Jews, was just barely sustained.

Abraham took it very hard when Hagar ran away, though he had dismissed her at God's command. In a similar way, when Israel fell away it was a cause of sorrow to [137] the holy apostles and evangelists. These were separated from Israel, not willingly, but because of God's purpose and for the love of Christ. The divine Paul therefore writes, "It is the cause of great sorrow to me and of unceasing pain in my heart. For I could wish that

---

90. Gn 21.19.
91. The verb here translated as "pursue" is identical to that translated "chase" a few sentences earlier and "persecute" in the following sentence.
92. Gal 4.29.
93. Ezek 11.16.

I myself were accursed and cut off from Christ for the sake of my brothers, my countrymen according to the flesh, who are Israelites."[94]

When the mother of the Jews was sent away, she wandered for a long time, and she was even in danger of perishing completely. If, however, her offspring were eventually to cry out earnestly to God, they will be shown complete and utter mercy.[95] For he will open the eyes of their understanding, and they too will see the fountain of living water,[96] that is, Christ. And so drinking, they will live through him. Being washed, they too will be made clean, as the prophet says.[97] That Christ is the fountain of life, the psalmist makes very clear when he says to God the Father in heaven, "How you have multiplied your mercy, O God! The sons of men will have hope in the shadow of your wings. They will drink from the abundance of your house, and you will give them drink from the river of your delights, for with you is the fountain of life."[98] This is none other than Christ, through whom and with whom be glory and power to God the Father, together with the holy, consubstantial, life-giving Spirit, for ever and ever without end. Amen.

Concerning Abraham and Isaac

1. *Now after these things God tested Abraham and said to him, "Abraham, Abraham," and he said, "Here I am." God said, "Take your beloved son, Isaac, whom you love, and go to the hill country, and offer him as a burnt offering on one of the mountains, which I will tell you about."* Such were the instructions given by God. So without delay, that righteous man saddled his donkey, as it is written, and choosing just two of his household servants to accompany him, he took his beloved son and set off to perform the sacrifice.[99]

---

94. Rom 9.2–3.
95. Here Cyril switches from the feminine singular, speaking of Israel's mother, to the masculine plural, "they," meaning the Israelites descended from her.
96. "of living water": *zôntos hudatos,* the same words translated as "fresh water" above, pp. 140 and 151.
97. Cf. Is 1.16.
98. Ps 36.7–9 (35.8–10 LXX).
99. Cf. Gn 22.1–3.

When he arrived at the sacred place on the third day, he said to the servants, *"Stay here with the donkey, while the boy and I go over there. We will worship, then come back to you."* Placing the wood for the burnt offering upon his son, he told him to go ahead while he followed.[100]

When the boy asked his father, *"Here is the fire and the wood, but where is the lamb for the burnt offering?"* Abraham answered, *"God will provide for himself a lamb for the burnt offering, my child."* Having constructed the divine altar, he piled up the wood. Then, after binding the boy upon it and taking up the knife, the voice of an angel stopped him, telling him that he should not slay the boy, as God knew that he had the right intention.[101]

Then that righteous man, seeing a ram with horns caught in a thornbush,[102] completed the sacrifice and offered it up instead of the boy. He then went down [140] to the servants, bringing his son safely back to them.[103]

Cutting short the full extent of the literal sense, we shall bring together in a few words what is most useful for showing that the mystery regarding our Savior is prefigured through these matters. Again we do not hesitate to explain this as it lies within our power to do so. If one does not give an account of everything present in the literal sense of the narratives, he ought not be blamed, for the spiritual meaning is often hidden within a large amount of literal. This can be likened to the most fragrant flowers in the meadows, which are wrapped around with ordinary leaves on the outside. If one cuts them open, he will find and lay bare what is good and profitable. So we now come to the figurative[104] meaning.

2. When the blessed Abraham was tested and commanded to sacrifice his beloved son, it was doubtless the cause of some distress, since he was the one who fathered him. Though it was as if his natural affection had been pierced by a hot sting, he nevertheless gave priority to the good that would come from

---

100. Cf. Gn 22.4–6.
101. Cf. Gn 22.7–12.
102. Cyril follows the LXX in calling this bush a *sabek,* a transliteration of the Hebrew term appearing in Gn 22.13 meaning "thicket."
103. Cf. Gn 22.13, 19.
104. Or "allegorical."

the matter. The same thing is revealed to us very clearly in those words spoken by the Savior, "For God so loved the world that he gave his Only-Begotten Son, so that everyone who believes in him might not perish, but have eternal life."[105] For if one needs to say something in human terms to show distinctly what this means, God the Father was in a way greatly troubled in sending the Son to die on our account, even though he knew he[106] would suffer none of the pains, since as God he was impassible. Intending, however, something advantageous to come from his death, namely the salvation and life of all, the affection appropriate to a father was set aside.

Paul also marveled at him, saying, "who did not spare his own Son, but gave him up on behalf of us all."[107] In what exactly does the wonder of the love of God the Father for us consist, except that he was pleased to bear the giving up of his own Son for us who were unwilling? For in such a way Paul persuades us to understand the words "he did not spare." Therefore, such words were never spoken with reference to just anybody, but only to those endeavoring to accomplish some great task, as in "Extend your cords, and strengthen your stakes; spread out further to the right and to the left," and "Fix your stakes, do not spare."[108] And again, "Deliver those who are being led away to death, and rescue those who are to be slain; do not hold back."[109] And such a thing, in the words *"Take your beloved son,"* would also be said to us.

As for the two servants accompanying the old man on the three-day journey, these are a figure of the two peoples called to servitude through the law, that is to say, the people of Israel and the people of Judah. These were meant to follow only the decrees of God the Father, as those servants followed Abraham. Yet they did not at all perceive the Son through whom all things exist, nor did they recognize the Father's heir, whose most beau-

---

105. Jn 3.16.
106. "he": By this pronoun Cyril clearly means the Father.
107. Rom 8.32.
108. Is 54.2–3. In this and the following citation, "do not spare" has, of course, the sense of "do not exercise restraint."
109. Prv 24.11.

tiful image was presented to us by the little Isaac lying in the bosom of his own father, not yet bearing the authority appropriate to the master of the house. For the all-perfect Son in fact was and is [141] eternally Lord and God.

What was not evident to all, and especially to the profane Jews, who only see fleshly things, was that the little child was to be considered as a certain somebody. In a way knowledge concerning him exists in a measure proportionate to the understanding that people have. This knowledge is found to be little among the little, but great among the great. At any rate, the prophets indeed do say, "He is great and awesome to all those that are around him,"[110] that is, those who have come near to him by means of considerable mental application.[111] Paul also labored with certain people "until Christ be formed in them,"[112] which is to say, until his great and remarkable divine characteristics were gradually molded into their minds.

The fact that the servants followed until the third day and were not permitted to go up to the high and sacred land, but were rather instructed to stay with the donkey, suggests the two peoples following God through the law, which they continue to do until the third age, that is, the last, when Christ was manifested to us. For the whole age is divided into three epochs, namely that which is passed, that which is present, and that which is to come. The end, therefore, comes in the third. The divine Scripture says that Christ came in the final age of the world. So Israel, having followed after God through the law until the time of the coming of our Savior, did not wish to follow Christ through faith, to follow him who went up to his death on behalf of all, but rather they were prevented on account of their many sins. In fact, "a hardening has come upon part of Israel,"[113] which is signified through the donkey that was then present with the servants. For the donkey is a symbol of their final irrationality, hardening being the offspring of irrationality.

The separation of the servants and the departure of the fa-

110. Ps 89.7 (88.8 LXX).
111. Or "prudence."
112. Gal 4.19.
113. Rom 11.25.

ther with the son, to speak of it once again (for it says, *"The boy and I will go over there. We will worship, then come back to you"*), signifies the temporary withdrawal of God from the people of Israel and his future return to them at the completion of the age, which is accomplished through their coming to faith in Christ. For it says, "when the fullness of the Gentiles has come in, then all Israel will be saved."[114]

Now the blessed Abraham did not openly say that he would go and sacrifice his son, but stated his intention with the words *"We will go over there."* This may be taken as a clear indication that the mystery of Christ would not be believed by the Jewish people. This explanation concerning the matter seems true to us. For when we see Jesus speaking to the Jews, it is in parables and figures, yet when speaking to his own disciples, he says, "To you it has been given to know the mysteries of the kingdom of God, but to the rest it is given in parables."[115]

As for the boy, Isaac, the wood for the burnt offering was laid upon him by his father, and he carried it until he came to the place where the sacrifice would be made. So Christ, carrying[116] his own cross upon his shoulder, suffered outside the gate [144]. It was not by human strength that he was forced to suffer, but it was of his own will and the will of God the Father, as he said to Pontius Pilate, "You would have no authority over me unless it had been given you from above."[117]

Isaac, having the wood placed upon him, is led away to suffering and death. Yet it is the ram given by God that is offered up as the sacrifice. For the Word was in reality of the substance of God the Father, shining radiantly in his own temple, that which was supplied through the Virgin, and which was nailed to the tree. Although as God he was impassible and immortal, he took himself away to suffering and death, and through his own body he offered up a pleasing aroma to God the Father. He himself, therefore, is said to have been accepted by the Father, in accordance with what is written in the Psalms, as though it were spo-

---

114. Cf. Rom 11.25b–26a.
115. Lk 8.10.
116. Var. "having."
117. Jn 19.11.

ken by him: "Sacrifice and offering you did not desire, but you have prepared a body for me; burnt offerings and sin offerings did not please you. Then I said, 'Behold, I come; in the scroll[118] of the book it is written concerning me. I desired to do[119] your will.'"[120] That the matters arising out of the literal sense presented to us here make a most beautiful[121] reference to Christ he himself testifies when he says, "in the scroll of the book it is written concerning me." Now the book is the whole of that eminently wise, five-part writing of Moses. The head and beginning of the whole book is that which is called Genesis, in which these things are written concerning Christ. The word "head" in the divine Scriptures also indicates the beginning. That you might be fully convinced of this, take note of what Paul says: "the head of every man is Christ, the head of woman is man, and the head of Christ is God."[122] Christ is the beginning of man as the one who brings him into being out of non-being. Then man is the beginning of woman on account of what was said and what was actually done—"She shall be called woman, because she was taken out of her husband."[123] God is said to be the beginning of Christ since the Son is from him with regard to his nature. So he who is without beginning has the one who has begotten him as his beginning, while at the same time he coexists eternally with him.

3. In my opinion, therefore, it is best to take the words of the literal account as applying to the mystery of Christ. Yet it is necessary, I believe, that we hold the divine Abraham in great wonder and with the highest praise, and that we declare his manifest glory to one and all. Furthermore, we ought to give careful attention to the depth of God's wisdom. For the divine Abraham was tested, though God was not ignorant of what

---

118. The word *kephalis*, here translated "scroll," is a diminutive form of *kephalê*, "head," and so may also have the sense of "little head." In what follows Cyril plays upon the relationship between these two terms.
119. Var. add "O God."
120. Ps 40.6–8 (39.7–9 LXX).
121. Or "most excellent."
122. 1 Cor 11.3.
123. Gn 2.22.

would happen.[124] Indeed, nothing is beyond the notice of the mind that knows everything. Therefore, he said, "Who is this that hides counsel from me, and confines words in his heart, thinking to conceal them from me?"[125] And through the mouth of Isaiah he said, "For I am God, and there is no other beside me, who declares the latter things before they come to pass, and they are completely fulfilled."[126] Consequently, it would be absolutely astounding and most improper if we should fail to understand the matter correctly by supposing that the God of all did not know what would happen, and that this was his reason for testing Abraham. It was necessary, however, [145] for that righteous man to have such splendid repute not in the knowledge of God only, but also for his most excellent glory to be magnified and for all to know that through this act of testing, his glory is attested as being above all virtues. It was necessary, then, for the extent of his obedience also to be proclaimed through the sacred Scriptures, and so the account given in the divine oracles is lengthy, lacking nothing.

Abraham came to this event with determination and willingness, as though regarding the son he loved as of no account, nor did he fear the charge of being a child-murderer. Even more remarkable is the fact that by means of this child he expected to become the father of many nations. Yet he knew that God had not lied in saying this. So he took the child away to be sacrificed, not doubting the promises but committing them into the hand[127] of the Master, believing that he knew how to fulfill the oath he had sworn.[128]

Furthermore, this matter was not without profit for Abraham, even though the trial brought him so much grief. For by what was about to happen he was being taught the astounding wonder of the resurrection of the dead, which surpasses all reason, and, in addition to this, the great and noble mystery of the Incarnation of the Only-Begotten. The divine Paul states,

124. Var. "of the mystery."
125. Jb 38.2.
126. Is 46.9–10.
127. Lit. "power."
128. Var. "how to fulfill the things mentioned."

"By faith Abraham, when he was tested, offered up Isaac, and he who had received the promises offered his only-begotten son, though he had been told, 'In Isaac your offspring will be named.'[129] He reckoned that God was able even to raise someone from the dead, and figuratively speaking, he did receive him back from death."[130] And so God the Father would in due course show forth Abraham to be the root and origin of many thousands of Gentiles, when Emmanuel died for the world.

So by means of this testing, that righteous man was profitably taught the extraordinary and ineffable love for us of God the Father, "who did not spare his own Son," as we said earlier, "but gave him up on behalf of us all," who have been justified by faith and are reckoned as children of our forefather Abraham.

If one must describe things on a human level, I would say that the command of God for Abraham to sacrifice Isaac was burdensome and intolerable to that blessed man. For how do you suppose he was affected when ordered to do this thing? Here was a man who had reached considerable old age, endowed with a single, late-born son, deprived by age of the ability to become the father of any other children, having also a very elderly spouse (for Sarah herself was an old woman), who was commanded to slay without hesitation his much-longed-for son, his only-begotten and much-prayed-for son. How did the old man expect his hand to be able to bring the knife down upon the boy, and thus undertake to commit the pitiable slaughter of his own offspring? Is it not reasonable to suppose that an extremely bitter and turbulent throng of thoughts unbearably ravaged the soul of that righteous man? At one time his natural affection was impelling him, while at another the divine oracle was persuading him, and it was most probably necessary for him to summon forth the unwished-for readiness[131] to obey.

Great indeed, then, is the marvel of that righteous man, and [148] his love of God is beyond all praise. For having bade farewell to the laws of nature, and having trodden down the pangs of the affection he inevitably felt, allowing no earthly

---

129. Gn 21.12.
130. Heb 11.17–19.
131. Var. "desire."

thing to oppose his love for God, he offered up the spiritual sacrifice. Therefore, he was glorified and was called "the friend of God."[132] Also, the things he hoped for turned out to be far beyond what was expected. He became, in fact, the father of a countless multitude of nations in Christ, through whom and with whom be glory to God the Father, together with the Holy Spirit, for ever and ever. Amen.

Concerning Isaac and Rebekah

1. To those who have been justified in Christ, and who enjoy abundant union with him through partaking of the Holy Spirit by the goodwill of the Father, the wise Paul writes, "I betrothed you to one husband, to present you as a pure virgin to Christ."[133] For the blessed disciples became, as it were, those who summon to the wedding banquet and who lead forth the bride, bringing near those yet far off and joining them to Christ, binding them together in the unity of the Spirit. Though it was God the Father who had raised her up, introduced her, and pledged her to his own Son, Christ will in fact present the church to himself. That the saints,[134] however, act as go-betweens none would doubt. The divine David foreannounced the mystery to us, when in one passage he said to the church, "Listen, O daughter, consider and incline your ear. Forget your people and your father's house, because the king has desired your beauty. He is your lord, and you will bow down to him."[135] Paul also agrees, as I just said, that in a way believers are like a bride presented[136] to Christ.

Yet someone, no less than we do, might further observe the exceedingly sublime and truly remarkable mystery in what follows. It is written that *Abraham was old and advanced in years; and the Lord blessed Abraham in everything. Now Abraham said to the old-*

---

132. Jas 2.23; see also 2 Chr 20.7, Is 41.8.
133. 2 Cor 11.2.
134. Here "saints" refers, as the context demands, not to the people of God in general, but to the apostles and prophets.
135. Ps 45.10–11 (44.11–12 LXX).
136. Var. "betrothed."

est servant of his household, who had the charge of all his possessions, "Put your hand under my thigh. I adjure you by the Lord, the God of heaven and the God of the earth, that you do not take a wife for my son Isaac from the daughters of the Canaanites, among whom I dwell. But you shall go to the land where I was born, and to my kindred. From there you shall take a wife for my son Isaac."[137] So, when Abraham had given these instructions, the servant immediately swore the oath, placing his hand under the thigh of his master. From this it is understood that the oath was made with respect to the entire offspring that would come from Abraham.

Then, loading ten camels with all kinds of choice goods from Abraham, the servant went swiftly to Mesopotamia. Coming to a halt at the city of Nahor, he made the camels rest outside the city beside the well of water; it was towards evening time when women go out to draw water.

On arriving in that place, the servant beseeched God to make the way ahead clear and to show him a healthy and hospitable maiden,[138] one whose demeanor would show her to be eager for love. *He said,* [149] *"The young woman to whom I say, 'Dip your waterpot that I may drink,' and who says, 'Drink, and I will also water your camels until they have finished drinking,' let this be the one whom you have prepared for your servant Isaac."*[139]

After a short while there came a beautiful-looking and comely young woman, namely Rebekah. When the servant asked for a drink, she gave it willingly. She also offered to water the camels, and what she offered to do was promptly done. From this the servant concluded that this young woman, and no other, was the one. So, taking bracelets and earrings, he presented them to her. She then made to go home and enjoined him to follow her immediately.

When he came to the house, he was received hospitably. There he gave them a dazzling account of his own master's wealth, adding that he also had a single, beloved son, Isaac, to whom he had given everything, and that the young man was master over it all.

---

137. Gn 24.1–4.
138. In what follows, "maiden" and "young woman" might also be translated "virgin."
139. Gn 24.14.

When the servant who came for a bride wished to depart together with the young woman, they asked Rebekah if she would go along with the man who had invited her. She welcomed the departure, consenting to it willingly.

Now when Rebekah arrived, Isaac desired to bring her immediately into his home. Thus, although his mother had recently died, he was greatly comforted.

The literal account, then, is of considerable length. Yet we have shortened it as much as possible, and what we have said will suffice. So now let the force of the spiritual meaning come forth in its own ingenious way, and let it once again display the mystery of Christ in a type, which, though yet lying in obscure shadows, nonetheless bears the reality.

2. Abraham did not think it fit to betroth any of the daughters of Canaan to his beloved son, Isaac. Rather, he commanded the servant who belonged to him to set out for the land of idol-worshipers in order to obtain a woman who would be especially suitable for him. For God the Father did not want the synagogue of the Jews to be joined to Christ, who is signified by Isaac.

Isaac was born late in Abraham's life and was beloved. And so in the latter times Christ appeared, and he too is beloved. He is also the cause of delight and rejoicing, which is what the name "Isaac" means.[140]

That the Canaanites may be considered a type of Israel should be clear and readily understood from the interpretation of the name, seeing that "Canaanites" means "prepared for humbling."[141] For which people was it appropriate that they should experience humbling, or rather that they should have experienced it already, except for the Jews? They have been humbled since they have fallen away from the glory that is in Christ, and have sunk into a whole range of excessive deeds. Accordingly, it was not from Canaan but from Mesopotamia that Isaac's bride came. For, as I said, it was not from the Jews, but

---

140. The Hebrew name Isaac means "laughter."
141. Cyril here relates the term "Canaanites" to the Hebrew verb *kāna'*, meaning "to humble," "subdue," "bring down."

from the nations that the church is spiritually joined to Christ the Savior.

Moreover, through the will of the Father there are servants, being especially faithful and true, who act as go-betweens. These we understand to be the disciples, who became keepers and stewards of the mysteries concerning Christ as God,[142] having in their hands, so to speak, everything in their master's house. Leaving Judea behind, just as Abraham's servant did Canaan, they went down into a country of idol-worshipers, loaded up, in a sense, with good things from God the Father, having minds full of heavenly wisdom, [152] and gifts given in full measure through the Spirit.

Also observe that the servant of Abraham is unnamed. This is so that the figure representing servanthood might be extended to every faithful and approved disciple.

That servant stopped at a well of water towards evening time. He then entreated God in prayer to grant assistance, wishing to give approval to[143] the young woman in the matter of drawing water. The divine disciples, as I said, also came to the lands of the nations towards evening, that is, in the latter times of the world, and approved a spiritual maiden by the side of water. This is the church, which is deemed most suitable, which is to say, having the ability to draw forth the life-giving word from the wells of salvation, as it is written.[144] She also does not lack the right ability of mind to be able to supply others too with the things leading to life. For Rebekah gave water to the servant and the camels. The servant, on one hand, may be understood as a type of the people of Israel. For those people who had the law already had a tutor, and though the mystery of Christ may still have been in shadows, they were nevertheless not completely without a guide in this matter. The people of the Gentile nations, on the other hand, were no different from irrational beasts, and so are suitably represented here by the camels. According to the law these animals are impure.[145] Such, then, are

---

142. Cf. 1 Cor 4.1.
143. Or "test."
144. Cf. Is 12.3.
145. Lit. "unholy." Cf. Lv 11.4.

people who do not yet know God at all[146] or his true nature. The church, therefore, is very capable of watering with the sacred and divine streams[147] both those from among the Jews who come to receive the love that is in Christ and those called out from the Gentiles.

When the disciples saw what kind of young woman the church was, they immediately adorned her with bracelets and placed ornaments in her ears. This means they glorified her wonderful and most splendid obedience, for the adorning of her ears points to her readiness to obey. They undertook for her to be conspicuous by her deeds also, that is, the virtuous actions done by her hands. This, I believe, is what is meant by putting bracelets on her arms.

Abraham's servant related to those in Haran the riches of his master and that he had a single, beloved son as his heir. So the divine disciples instructed the Gentiles in the mysteries, declaring the riches of God the Father, which are hope, life, and sanctification, and they clearly proclaimed that Christ is his one and only true Son with respect to his nature, who has been appointed heir of all things.

The young woman was asked if she was willing to go with the servant, and she immediately indicated that she was. Now the church taken out of the nations is most willing, quite fervent in fact for the love of Christ. The divine David testifies concerning the congregation taken from among the nations when he says, "Your ear is inclined to the willingness of their hearts."[148]

When Isaac was united with Rebekah, it says, *he was comforted with regard to his mother.*[149] From this we are to understand that Christ was grieved when the synagogue of the Jews, from which he had been born with respect to his flesh, died, as it were, through unbelief. [153] Yet when he became the bridegroom of the church taken out of the Gentiles, it was as though he ceased that mourning for her. In a certain passage it was said to the church through the mouth of the prophets, "It shall come

---

146. Var. "are all the people who do not yet know God."
147. Var. "commands."
148. Ps 10.17 (9.38 LXX).
149. Gn 24.67.

to pass that as the bridegroom rejoices over the bride, so shall the Lord rejoice over you,"[150] through whom and with whom be glory to God the Father, together with the Holy Spirit, for ever and ever. Amen.

Concerning Esau and Jacob, that they stand as a type of two peoples, the people of Israel and those who are a people through faith in Christ

1. *These are the generations of Isaac, the son of Abraham. Now Abraham became the father of Isaac, and Isaac was forty years old when he took as his wife Rebekah, the daughter of Bethuel the Syrian of Mesopotamia, the sister of Laban the Syrian. Isaac prayed to the Lord concerning Rebekah his wife because she was barren. And God heard him, and Rebekah his wife conceived. Now the babies were jumping around within her, and she said, "Why is this happening to me?" So she went to inquire of the Lord. The Lord said to her, "Two nations are within you, and two peoples will be separated from your womb. One people will have preeminence over the other, and the elder will serve the younger." Then the time came for Rebekah to give birth, and there were twins in her womb. When the firstborn son emerged, he was red and hairy all over, like an animal skin, so she called his name Esau. After this, his brother came out with his hand holding on to Esau's heel, so she called his name Jacob. Isaac was sixty years old when Rebekah gave birth to them. So the boys grew up. Esau was a man skilled at hunting, and lived in the open country. Jacob was a simple man, who liked to stay at home. Now Isaac loved Esau, because he liked to eat wild game, but Rebekah loved Jacob. Once Jacob cooked some stew. Esau came in from the field exhausted, and he said to Jacob, "Give me some of that red stew to eat, because I am exhausted." For this reason his name was called Edom. Jacob said to him, "Sell me your birthright this very day." Then Esau said, "Behold, I am about to die; what use is this birthright to me?" Jacob said to him, "Swear an oath to me today." So he swore to him, and Esau sold his birthright to Jacob. Then Jacob gave Esau some bread and some lentil stew, and he ate and drank, got up, and went. So Esau despised his birthright.*[151]

150. Is 62.5.
151. Gn 25.19–34.

God, who does not know how to lie, promised that the divine Abraham would indeed be the father of many nations. He also affirmed that the multitude that would come from him would in all be of a vast quantity, for he says, *"They will be as uncountable as sand and like the stars of the heavens in number."*[152] Yet such remarkable glory was not limited to Israel only, but extended also to the congregation of the Gentiles. For these latter were invited on the basis of faith, and such are all the more in Isaac, that is to say, of the promise.

The most-wise Paul testifies to this when he writes, "The Scripture, foreseeing that God would justify the Gentiles by faith, announced the gospel to Abraham beforehand, saying, 'In you all the nations will be blessed.'[153] [156] So those who are of faith are blessed along with believing Abraham, while all who are of the law of works are under a curse, as it is written, 'Cursed is everybody who does not continue to do everything written in the book of the law.'[154] That nobody is justified before God by the law is evident, for 'the righteous will live by faith.'[155] Yet the law is not of faith, but 'he who does them shall live by them.'"[156] He includes here the fact that the things that were promised came to fulfillment, by no means through those instructed in the law, but through those justified by faith.

So when the ordinance given through Moses was introduced as part of the divine economy, the promise was not set aside. Rather, the law gave instruction concerning it, pointing in a certain measure to the calling that was through faith. Further, in exposing the weaknesses of those who had come beforehand, it shows forth how grace through faith and justification in Christ are most needful and indispensable for all.

This is what the divine Paul further said: "Brothers, I speak in human terms: even when a covenant is a human one, once it has been ratified, no one can annul it or add to it. Now the promises were spoken to Abraham and to his seed.[157] It does

---

152. Cf. Gn 22.17; 26.4.
153. Cf. Gn 12.3; 18.18; 22.18.
154. Dt 27.26.
155. Hab 2.4.
156. Gal 3.8–12; Lv 18.5.
157. Or "offspring."

not say, 'and to seeds,' referring to many, but 'and to your seed,' referring to one, who is Christ. What I am saying is this: the law, which came four hundred and thirty years later, does not abolish a covenant previously ratified by God and so nullify the promise. For if the inheritance is based upon the law, it is no longer based upon a promise, yet God freely granted it to Abraham through a promise."[158]

To these things Paul immediately adds the cause for which the law was introduced,[159] saying this: "Why, then, the law? It was added on account of transgressions, until the seed should come to whom the promise had been made, and was ordained through angels by the hand of a mediator. Now a mediator does not act for one party; but God is one. Is the law then opposed to the promise of God? Certainly not! For if a law had been given that was able to impart life, then righteousness would indeed have been on the basis of law. But the Scripture has confined all under sin, so that what was promised through faith in Jesus Christ might be given to those who believe. Yet before faith came, we were in the custody of the law, being kept for the glory that would later be revealed. So the law was our tutor to bring us to Christ, that we might be justified by faith. But now that faith has come, we are no longer under a tutor, for you are all sons of God through faith in Christ Jesus."[160]

One may not in the least bit doubt that the law reproved the weaknesses of those being instructed, and made their faults and sins all the more obvious. For "where there is no law," Paul says, "neither is there transgression."[161] And again, "I would not have known sin, except through the law."[162] And "when the commandment came," he says, "sin came to life, and I died."[163] Yet again, "Before the law, sin was in the world, but sin is not reckoned where there is no law,"[164] for "the law produces wrath."[165]

---

158. Gal 3.15–18.
159. Var. "the law was added, as it were, to faith."
160. Gal 3.19–26.
161. Rom 4.15.
162. Rom 7.7.
163. Rom 7.9.
164. Rom 5.13.
165. Rom 4.15.

So the law served as our tutor with regard to Christ, at one and the same time reproving transgressors and instructing people upon the earth through their very experiences, [157] teaching how humankind, being afflicted with the proneness to sin, is incapable of escaping the indictment of the law, and so must wholly look to the salvation that comes through Christ, who justifies us by faith and in mercy.

2. It is evident, then, that the words of the divine economy before us presented through the ordinance of Moses a most useful[166] portrayal ahead of time of the grace in Christ that was to follow on directly after, which would bring forth the offspring foreannounced in the promise of God, that is, those who are in Christ through faith. For it was in this way that the divine Abraham became the father of an uncountable number of offspring.

Observe, therefore, the form of the divine economy, finely fashioned once again by means of a type involving the two brothers originating from Isaac, namely, Esau and Jacob. So it was said by God to the divine Abraham, *"In Isaac will your offspring be named."*[167] Paul, one who was learned in the law, when interpreting this oracle, said, "The promises were spoken to Abraham and to his seed. It does not say, 'and to seeds,' referring to many, but 'and to your seed,' referring to one, who is Christ." It is in Christ, then, that the things promised were brought to fulfillment, and in some manner Isaac was ordained as a representation and type of him.

Now the designation "Isaac" means delight and joy. The divine David speaks of Christ as "joy" when, as if in the presence of those longing for the salvation that comes through him, he says, "You are my joy, to deliver me from those who have surrounded me."[168] For in Christ we have escaped the attacks of murderers; in him we have trampled upon snakes and scorpions; we who believe in him have trodden upon the asp and the basilisk.[169]

The prophetic word also convinces us that Christ is termed

---

166. Or "most forceful."
167. Gn 21.12. For the Pauline quotation following, see n. 158.
168. Ps 32.7 (31.7 LXX).
169. An unidentifiable venomous snake; cf. Ps 91.13 LXX. See also Lk 10.19.

"joy" by the divine Scriptures, as is found here: "And the Lord will cause righteousness and joy to spring up before all the nations."[170] Emmanuel in fact became righteousness and joy not only to those of Israel, but also to the nations and peoples of all the earth. For we have been justified in him, and have been removed from under that ancient and ignominious curse. Having been set free from sin and death, we have been clothed with gladness and joy; and why not, seeing that we have been made rich with good things from God above?

Accordingly, we have been taught to give praise, saying, "May my soul rejoice in the Lord; for he has clothed me with the garment of salvation, and the robe of gladness."[171] And what is this robe of gladness? The most venerable Paul explains, saying, "For as many of you who have been baptized into Christ have been clothed with Christ."[172] And again, "Clothe yourselves with the Lord Jesus Christ, and make no provision for the flesh, to gratify its lusts."[173]

So then, in these most useful objects of contemplation set before us, Isaac, through his being a type of Christ, may be taken as this "joy."

Now this man's wife was Rebekah, whose name may be interpreted as "abundant and holy perseverance."[174] Yet, if we understand the person of this woman correctly, we shall also take her as indicating the church, whose glory lies in its perseverance. At all events, for those who are her children, meaning her children by faith and by the Spirit, [160] perseverance shows itself to be the way of salvation.[175] For at one time the sacred words addressed them saying, "By your perseverance you will gain your souls,"[176] and at another time saying, "For you have need

---

170. Is 61.11.
171. Is 61.10.
172. Gal 3.27.
173. Rom 13.14.
174. Or "patience." How Cyril, or his source, arrives at this meaning of "Rebekah" is something of a mystery. The cognate Hebrew verb *rābaq* means "bind" or "join."
175. Or "for those who are her children, patience shows itself to be the way of salvation, so to speak, by faith and by the Spirit."
176. Lk 21.19.

of perseverance, so that when you have done the will of God, you will obtain what was promised."[177]

Observe, then, that Rebekah, being in labor after some time and with some difficulty (for she had been barren), through both the beneficence of God and the affection[178] of Isaac, brought to the birth her firstborn son Esau, and also Jacob who came out immediately after. In these we see most excellently portrayed once again two peoples, namely, Israel and of course the people taken out of the Gentiles. The firstborn is Israel, the one who is summoned forth first through the law. After that comes the second, that which is a people through Christ by faith.

One might see the difference between the two peoples as being in disposition and habit, and also, I believe, in the names that each of the two had, and in the form of their bodies or their constitution. On one hand, the name "Esau" actually means "oak tree,"[179] that is to say, hard and unbending. In one passage God said to Israel, "I know that you are hard, and your neck is an iron sinew and your forehead bronze."[180] Jacob, on the other hand, means "supplanter,"[181] that is trickster, or one who knows how to prevail. Now one supplants him who is inferior. It is not at all the people under the law but those who are a people through faith in Christ who so prevail, thwarting the accusations of sin and debilitating the very power of death.

Furthermore, it is written here that Esau was *red and hairy all over, like an animal skin,* while Jacob was *a smooth-skinned man.*[182] Redness is a figure of anger and wrath, since it is indeed always the case that one's complexion reddens in a state of anger. And how could one doubt that hairiness and roughness are characteristics relating to beastliness? Everybody, I believe, can

177. Heb 10.36.
178. Var. "petition."
179. This is another questionable derivation. More probably the name relates to the idea of "hairy"; cf. Gn 25.25.
180. Is 48.4.
181. In both Greek and Hebrew the word is related to "heel," and may mean "one who grasps the heel"; cf. Gn 25.26. This may indeed be an idiom for "supplant" or "take advantage of."
182. Gn 27.11.

perceive that Israel lived in bestial habits, controlled more by wrath[183] than by proper reason, being much inclined towards audacious and wild behavior. Accordingly, they slew the holy prophets, and also in later times treated Emmanuel in an ungodly fashion. As for smoothness, however, this is manifestly something that pertains to humanity. The new people of faith are exceedingly gentle and extremely mild. Politeness of speech is in fact a clear indication of inner spiritual beauty,[184] just as we have taken the hairiness and redness of Esau to signify wildness.

Yet these two sons both had the same mother, Rebekah. And so our Lord Jesus Christ presented to himself the church as a pure virgin, who in a way served to produce the spiritual regeneration[185] of the two peoples. As far as the aim of Christ's advent is concerned, he created these into one new man, making peace and reconciling them both in one Spirit, as it is written.[186] Yet Israel, being the firstborn in time, was antagonistic and unrestrained in their conduct towards the younger people of God. For it is apparent, as I consider it, that the jostling about of the babies in the womb in a way signified the coming hostility between them. But that the younger would be the greater and would exceed [161] Israel, the firstborn, in glory, the one who knows all things straight away indicated, saying, *"One people will have preeminence over the other, and the elder will serve the younger."*

The mystery concerning these two was proclaimed ahead of time through the mouth of the saints,[187] and that the "Israel of the nations" would follow later was earlier promised to us in diverse ways. The oracle of God was showing forth the matter in the birth itself. Esau indeed came out of the womb first, yet when it said that Jacob took hold of Esau's heel, it demonstrated that he would supplant and prevail over his brother,

3. The foregoing are, for the moment, the things that may be said which arise out of the form of their bodies and the manner of their birth. Nonetheless, by means of other considerations

---

183. Var. "... habits, rather than by proper reason."
184. Or "beauty of mind."
185. Or "new spiritual birth."
186. Cf. Eph 2.15–16.
187. That is, the prophets.

we may, as we are able, speak further concerning these two sons. Information is in fact given about the disposition of each one and each one's way of life. The young men were indeed the same age as one another, yet they were not equal in discernment nor similar in their purposes. For Esau loved to spend his time in the countryside hunting, while Jacob was fond of home life; evidently he was affable and sociable, a man who naturally preferred to stay at home. Esau was uncontrollable with respect to his carnal lusts, disregarding the most excellent of his own endowments, as if they were something most mean, exchanging them for the most basic necessities. Jacob, on the other hand, was a ceaseless admirer of noble things,[188] seeking out everywhere the things by means of which he might become eminent. For he purchased the right of the firstborn when Esau cast it aside, counting the fullness of his stomach to be more important than his own dignity, for which he cared nothing. His name from then on was therefore called Edom, that is, "earthy."[189] The fact that he had no regard for the glory that was laid up for him and no concern whatsoever for the privileges of being the elder is clear proof of his truly earthly and most base mind. Rather, he preferred temporal pleasure as being something better and of greater value, accounting momentary enjoyment as more excellent, even though it might mean much loss to himself.

The divine Paul, therefore, suitably called one who had chosen to live in such a shameful manner "immoral and profane." In a way he puts forward Esau as a type of those who sink down into this kind of despicable conduct. At any rate, he brings an accusation and indictment against unrestrained desires, which are manifestly carnal and more earthy, saying, "See that no one becomes immoral or profane like Esau, who sold his birthright for a single meal."[190]

Surely, then, it is appropriate that we should closely compare the conduct of these young men with the dark behavior of the Jews and the pure and free assembly of those taken from among

---

188. Or "noble men."
189. In Hebrew the name "Edom" is etymologically related to *'ădāmâ*, "earth," "soil."
190. Heb 12.16.

the Gentiles. For Israel was indeed wild and earthy, having a mental disposition that was both haughty and aggressive, terrible in their bloodthirstiness, corresponding to the wild killer of beasts, Esau. Indeed, even the prophetic word accuses them, saying that "they have laid snares to destroy men."[191] Christ himself is roused against them, saying, "Without cause they have hidden their snare of destruction for me; without reason they have reproached my soul. May a snare come upon them unawares; and may the trap which they have hidden catch [164] them."[192] For they sent certain of the Pharisees along with those called Herodians (these were exactors of tax), who tested him, saying, "Is it lawful to pay taxes to Caesar, or not?"[193] Israel then was a hunter.[194]

The new people of God, however, those who are so by faith, who correspond to the divine Jacob, are urbane and lovers of home life, gentle and calm, sincere and without guile, staying at home, according to what is written. It is true to say that the peaceable congregation of those justified by faith, which constitutes the church,[195] is like a certain splendid, well-ordered city, and a house firmly established, immovable when tested, whose conduct and life are wrought in Christ. Their minds are sincere, free from all perversity. They consider that false thinking and feigned behavior should be greatly shunned. It is concerning these, I believe, that the divine David somewhere said, "The Lord gives the single a home to dwell in."[196] For those who are single-minded[197] are the sincere in Christ, who are given a home to dwell in. Indeed, one of the holy prophets declared to Israel, saying, "You have become weary in your many wanderings."[198]

---

191. Jer 5.26.
192. Ps 35.7–8 (34.7–8 LXX).
193. Lk 20.22.
194. That is, one who traps or snares.
195. Lit. "registered as the church."
196. Ps 68.6 (67.7 LXX).
197. In the psalm citation the adjective *monotropos* has the physical sense of being "alone," while Cyril follows this with the spiritual sense, that is, "single-minded," which in Greek belongs to the same domain as "sincere" (*haplous*).
198. Is 57.10.

Those in Christ, then, take up their dwelling, as it were, in a house of reverent conduct and sanctified living. In attaining this they are, in a manner, weaving garlands[199] for their heads, counting it also as a happy way of life. Therefore, on one occasion they say, "I was glad when they said to me, 'Let us go into the house of the Lord,'"[200] and on another, "One thing I have asked from the Lord; this I will seek." And what was the request? What did this one favor consist of? "That I may dwell in the house of the Lord," it says, "all the days of my life, to behold the beauty of the Lord and look upon his holy temple."[201] Do you hear how dwelling in the house of God and spending time in the divine courts is reckoned to be such a wonderful and exquisite form of grace? This state of dwelling, however, is not physical, but is rather to be interpreted as steadfastness of mind and virtuous living.[202]

It further says that *Isaac loved Esau, because he liked to eat wild game.* Israel the firstborn was in fact worthy of heavenly love, because the people brought to God, as it were, a manner of food, in the form of a correct legal way of life and labors performed on the basis of the law. For even in Israel there were saints who loved God and observed the law. And so when the prophet Isaiah denounced the Jerusalem that played the harlot, he said that at one time "righteousness lodged in her,"[203] that is, rested and stayed there, in that there were many within her who adopted the glorious way of life set down in the law.

Israel then, being the firstborn, had glory with God, yet he did not permanently preserve the honor that had been bestowed upon him of being the elder son. But, in that he was greatly inclined towards the things of the flesh and of the world, he handed over the right of the firstborn to the new people of God that followed, that is, those taken from among the Gentiles. In the gospel parables we read how, "The king gave a wed-

---

199. The term *stephanos* is usually translated "crown." The sense here is that of a victor's "wreath."
200. Ps 122.1 (121.1 LXX).
201. Ps 27.4 (26.4 LXX).
202. Var. "a life showing love of virtue."
203. Is 1.21.

ding feast [165] for his son."[204] Then those sent to invite the guests to the feast went and announced to them the message from God, which was: "Behold, I have prepared my banquet; my bulls and fattened calves have been slain, and everything is ready. Come to the wedding feast." It says, however, that they did not want to come. Rather, each one seemed to have an excuse. One said, "I have married a wife. Please excuse me." Another said, "I have bought a field and am not able to come." You see, then, in what way they resemble Esau, counting temporal, fleshly pleasures as being of greater value than glory from God, and so in effect they hold out the right of the firstborn for others to take. For those of the Gentiles who believed were immediately invited in their place on account of their readiness to obey, their great virtue, and their being moved to perform those things that are pleasing to God. And so they benefited from the glory and blessing that ought to have been Israel's. We have here also the testimony of the divine David, who says this about them: "You have heard the desire of the needy, Lord; your ear is inclined to the willingness of their hearts."[205] For those who are the people of God through faith are always most ready to obey, even though the people of Israel had previously received greater instruction through the law. Although the multitude of the Gentiles suffered from a lack of divine teaching, they had much better things by faith that endowed them with an ear attentive to the oracles of Christ. To this the latter utters his own testimony. For through the singing of the psalmist he said, "A people I did not know served me; as soon as they heard, they obeyed me."[206]

With regard to Israel, however, once they had fallen into a state of estrangement and no longer considered it worthwhile to live uprightly, it says that their faculty of thinking was incapacitated: "Sons of strangers dealt falsely with me, sons of strangers grew weary and stumbled lamely off their paths."[207] The straight and true paths, being the instruction given through the law and

204. For these parables, see Mt 22.1–14 and Lk 14.15–24.
205. Ps 10.17 (9.38 LXX).
206. Ps 18.43–44 (17.44–45 LXX).
207. Ps 18.44–45 (17.45–46 LXX).

the predictions of the holy prophets, lead to Christ. But when they reached the end indicated by the law and the prophets, that end being Christ, they were lame through their lack of understanding. So it was not due to sound thinking that they raged against him and were bold enough even to put to death the Author of life.[208]

That the new people of faith, having a more excellent disposition for submitting to the divine commands, took hold of the blessing due to Israel, we may also understand from this. For it is written here: *When Isaac was old, his eyes became so dim that he could not see. He called Esau, his firstborn son, and said to him, "My son." And he said, "Here I am." Isaac said, "Behold, I have grown old, and I do not know the day of my death. So now take your weapons, your quiver and your bow, and go out into the country, and hunt game for me. Prepare the meat for me the way I like it, and bring it for me to eat, that my soul may bless you before I die."*[209] This is what the father said to Esau.

Esau immediately succeeded in hunting down an animal [168], and, bringing it home, he freshly prepared it. And what happened next? Rebekah persuaded Jacob to do the same thing before Esau did, and to take hold of the blessing as well. At first Jacob was afraid to do it. But as his mother urged him, he brought in two goats from the fields, fine and tender, and cooked them nicely. Placing their skins on his shoulders, covering the exposed part of his neck, he managed to reproduce the hairiness and shagginess of Esau, so that if he happened to be touched, he would deceive his father's hands.[210]

Then taking the meal in his hands, *Jacob went in to his father, and said, "Father." Isaac said, "Here I am. Who are you, child?" Jacob said to his father, "I am Esau, your firstborn son. I have done what you told me. Come and sit down, and eat my game, so that your soul may bless me." When the old man had eaten what was set before him, he said to the lad, "Come here and kiss me, child." Jacob went and kissed him. When Isaac caught the smell of his clothes, he blessed him and said to him, "Behold, the smell of my son is like the smell of a full-grown field,*

---

208. Cf. Acts 3.15.
209. Gn 27.1–4.
210. Cf. Gn 27.5–16.

which the Lord has blessed. Now may the Lord give you of the dew of heaven, and of the richness of the earth, an abundance of grain and wine. May the nations serve you, and the rulers bow down to you. Be lord over your brother; the sons of your father will bow to you. He who curses you shall be cursed, and he who blesses you shall be blessed."[211]

So Jacob obtained the blessing of his father first. Later Esau brought in his game from the fields and, setting it before his father, he found it not to be required. He then learned what had happened, for he immediately heard from Isaac, *"Your brother came deceitfully and took away your blessing."*[212] With tears Esau said, *"Do you have only one blessing, father? Bless me too."* But Isaac further said, *"Behold, your dwelling will be away from the richness of the earth and away from the dew of heaven above. By your sword you will live, and you will serve your brother. But the time will come when you break free and loosen his yoke from your neck."*[213]

So then, having brought together the broad span of the literal account into just a few words, we have suitably set it before the readers. I take it to be necessary, by means of those physical events that happened, to make application to spiritual things.

4. We are saying, therefore, that even before those others, namely, those called in Christ, became the people of God through faith, the Master and Father of all gave commandments to Israel. These related to wonderful rewards, so to speak, to the fruits of virtuous behavior, and to the profit of good works, that the people of Israel should be moved to offer to God a pleasing manner of life. This way of life was described long ago in the law, though to a large extent it lay hidden in types, and certain matters could be overlooked on account of the many words used. It was not unattainable, however, to those desiring to go hunting for it through careful spiritual contemplation. This latter is, I believe, the meaning of Isaac's desire for the game meat of Esau.

Yet Israel, as I said, was instated first as the people of God, and, what is more, they undertook to perform these duties correctly. For at Horeb, when the congregation was gathered

211. Cf. Gn 27.18–19, 26–29.
212. Gn 27.35.
213. Cf. Gn 27.38–40.

together and God descended in the form of fire upon Mount Sinai, Israel said, "Everything that the Lord God says, we will do and obey."[214] But, even though they were set to receive the promise, events showed their extreme negligence. That is why they would have to lose their place, and so it was that the supplanter Jacob, [169] that is, the new people of God through faith, then took precedence. Rising up as the people who would be the firstborn, they presented to God the things required, bearing the fruit of faith, which is a form of food that divine nature produces.[215] And so when the Savior pointed out to the holy apostles the conversion of the Samaritans, he said, "I have food to eat, which you do not know about."[216] Then he explained plainly what he meant: "My food," he says, "is to do the will of him who sent me, and to complete his work."[217]

Moreover, Christ taught us by means of a parable that Israel's readiness to undertake their duties was in fact worthless to them, since it was not followed up with actions. The parable also taught that the lateness with which the Gentiles came to faith in no way hindered them from coming to know the Redeemer and honoring him henceforth with their ready obedience in all kinds of good works. He said, "A certain man had two sons, and going to the first, he said, 'Son, today go and work in my vineyard.' But he answered, 'I don't want to.' Yet later he changed his mind and went. The father went to the other son and said the same thing. That one answered, 'Yes, sir,' but he did not go. Which of the two[218] did the will of his father?"[219] Evidently it was the one who went into the vineyard, even though there was a short period of weakness that caused him to delay doing so.

We see here Esau very ready to be sent forth to hunt game and undertaking to do so, but he is preceded in this by Jacob, who, although he at first refused to do it, nevertheless received his father's blessing. So too the new people of God take hold

---

214. Cf. Ex 19.8; 24.7; Dt 5.27.
215. Cyril here means the "divine nature" that is created within his people (cf. 2 Pt 1.4).
216. Jn 4.32.
217. Jn 4.34.
218. Var. add "does it say."
219. Cf. Mt 21.28–31.

of the blessing, having in effect an outward form of the Jewish manner of life, just as Jacob skillfully reproduced the hairiness of Esau by means of the goatskins. Yet he immediately heard his father exclaim, *"The voice is the voice of Jacob, but the hands are the hands of Esau."*[220]

In what way can this becoming similar in outward form be applied to those who are the people of God through faith? And what about their copying the Jewish manner of life while having a voice that is different from theirs? We affirm, as is always the case with respect to the divine Scriptures, that the hand symbolizes work, deeds, or practical activity. As far as the similarity of their activity and the extent of their deeds are concerned, those in Christ fulfill the law by performing a spiritual priestly ministry, offering themselves as a pleasing aroma to God the Father. In fact, Christ plainly set before us laws in connection with the gospel also. "Do not think," he says, "that I have come to abolish the law or the prophets. I have not come to abolish the law but to fulfill it. For truly I say to you, until heaven and earth pass away, not one jot or one tittle will pass away from the law, until all is accomplished."[221]

So you see that those who are in Christ fulfill the law by receiving circumcision in the Spirit, rather than the circumcision of the flesh. Also, when they enter into the rest given by Christ, they are keeping the Sabbath in Christ. And so they show that they are Jews inwardly in a hidden manner. This, I believe, is what it means to have the hands of Esau [172] while having a voice different from his. For we have no use for the unbridled speech of the Jews, neither is it our practice to blaspheme by denying the Master who redeemed us. Rather, we glorify, alongside God the Father, the Son, whom we name Lord, Savior, and Redeemer.

5. I think it worthwhile also to examine the import of the blessing with regard to both sons and to speak of what comes to mind, for such matters might be of benefit to the readers.

The blessed Isaac said in the presence of Jacob, *"Behold, the smell of my son is like the smell of a full-grown field, which the Lord*

---

220. Gn 27.22.
221. Mt 5.17–18.

has blessed. Now may the Lord give you of the dew of heaven, and of the richness of the earth, an abundance of grain and wine. May the nations serve you, and the rulers bow down to you. Be lord over your brother; the sons of your father will bow to you. He who curses you shall be cursed, and he who blesses you shall be blessed." In these words the literal sense has in a way mixed things together and through two persons arrives at one truth, to which witness is also given by their actions.

These matters were not in fact wholly fulfilled in Jacob but in Christ and in those who have been justified by faith, who have also become children according to the promise in Isaac. Therefore, the sense of the prophecy will also apply to the new people of God and to Christ himself, the one who comes first and takes the lead. He is also considered to be a second Adam, and he was born as a second root of humanity. For what is in Christ is a new creation, and we are renewed in him for sanctification, incorruption, and life. The words of the blessing, I believe, denote the spiritual aroma in Christ, like that of a field or a meadow blooming abundantly, spreading a beautiful and pleasant fragrance from its spring flowers. So Christ described himself to us in the Song of Songs, saying, "I am a flower of the plain, a lily of the valleys."[222] He was, indeed, a lily and a rose sprung up from the earth, for the sake of humankind. Since he knew no sin, he was the most Godlike of those inhabiting the whole world, bringing forth a pleasing aroma through the perfection of his deeds. Therefore, it likens Christ to a field blessed by God, and rightly so, as he is the fragrance of the knowledge of God the Father. Again the divine Paul says, "Thanks be to God, who always leads us triumphantly in Christ, and reveals the fragrance of his knowledge in every place through us."[223] Our Lord Jesus Christ is revealed through the holy apostles as the fragrance of the knowledge of God the Father. "For if anyone knows the Son, he also fully knows the Father,"[224] because he shares in the very same nature, and because in absolutely everything he holds equal and identical possession.

222. Song 2.1.
223. 2 Cor 2.14.
224. This inexact citation is reminiscent of Jn 14.9 and Mt 11.27.

These things, then, apply to Christ, and may also be suitably applied to the new people of God: *"May the Lord give you of the dew of heaven, and of the richness of the earth, an abundance of grain and wine."*[225] For the dew of heaven and the richness of the earth, that is, the Word coming forth from God the Father, has surely been given to us according to our participation in him through the Spirit, and through him we have "become partakers of divine nature."[226] We have also obtained an abundance [173] of grain and wine, that is, strength and gladness. Indeed, the word is true that says, "Bread strengthens the heart of man, and wine makes it glad."[227] Bread is the symbol of spiritual strength, and wine of gladness. These are given to those in Christ through him. How else, then, were we made firm and immovable in piety, knowing how to think aright, and to stand unshakeable? For we have received authority to tread upon snakes and scorpions and upon all the power of the enemy.[228] This I believe to be the abundance of grain. But we have also received wine. "In hope we rejoice,"[229] and "We have been made glad,"[230] as it is written. For we look forward to dwellings above, life incorruptible and everlasting, and to reigning with Christ. These things, therefore, may be said about us. The words are reasonably taken as indicating this.

The content of the blessing would later be transferred upon Emmanuel himself. *"Let nations serve you,"* it says, *"and let rulers bow down to you, and be lord of your brother."*[231] Emmanuel was named "firstborn" when he became one like ourselves, one who was "among many brothers."[232] But not on this account should we forget that he is also God and Lord of all. We worship him as Master, and he has dominion as God over those called to be his brothers through grace. "For who in the heavens," it says, "can be compared to the Lord? And who among the sons of God

---

225. Gn 27.28.
226. 2 Pt 1.4.
227. Ps 104.15 (103.15 LXX).
228. Cf. Lk 10.19.
229. Rom 12.12.
230. Ps 126.3 (125.3 LXX).
231. Gn 27.29.
232. Rom 8.29.

can be likened to him?"²³³ Therefore, Emmanuel has dominion as God over those brought into his brotherhood, and to him "every knee shall bow in heaven and on earth, and under the earth, and every tongue shall confess that Jesus Christ is Lord, to the glory of God the Father."²³⁴ And cursed is he who curses, and blessed is he who blesses.²³⁵ This saying is clear. Those who slander him are accursed and hateful to God; those who bless,²³⁶ that is, those proclaiming his divine glory, are filled with heavenly gifts from God.

6. That, then, is the blessing of Jacob, the import of which has reference to Emmanuel himself and to those justified by faith. Let us look also at the other blessing, that is, the one given to the firstborn, evidently indicating that blessing given to Israel, of which Esau was a type. Now it says, *"Behold, your dwelling will be away from the richness of the earth and away from the dew of heaven above. By your sword you will live, and you will serve your brother. But the time will come when you break free and loosen his yoke from your neck."*

The blessing granted to Israel was in fact the law given through Moses, for it was the word of Christ administered through angels. That it was Christ himself who was speaking to those of old the most-wise Paul proves when he writes, "At many times and in many ways God spoke long ago to the fathers by the prophets, but in these last days he has spoken to us by his Son."²³⁷ The Savior himself also showed the law to be his own words when he said,

233. Ps 89.6 (88.7 LXX).
234. Phil 2.10–11.
235. Cf. Gn 27.29.
236. Var. "those eager to bless."
237. Heb 1.1–2. In this argument, occurring several times elsewhere in his writings (e.g., PG 68: 489; 70: 893), Cyril expresses his belief that it was the Son of God who spoke in the OT revelations as much as in the New. His understanding of the Hebrews citation does not seem to be that "long ago" and "in these last days" there were two distinct sources of revelation, but rather that the Son is source of both, and that only in the case of the latter is that revelation unmediated. In the older dispensation it had been mediated through the prophets and through angels. For this reason, the latter revelation, directly from the Son, may be regarded as the superior. For further discussion of this issue, see Matthew R. Crawford, *Cyril of Alexandria's Trinitarian Theology of Scripture* (Oxford: Oxford University Press, 2014), 116–18, 126–27.

"Truly I say to you, until heaven and [176] earth pass away, not one jot or one tittle will pass away from the law until all is accomplished. Heaven and earth shall pass away, but my words will never pass away."[238] Therefore, since it is true that even the law given through angels was the word of Christ, it was a form of blessing to Israel, and we may consider *"the dew of heaven"* and *"the richness of the earth"* to be Christ. For as the multitude of the angels is abundantly watered by the spiritual dew of heaven, so too the earth delights in giving its riches through the spiritual rains that cause it to produce spiritual fruit.

We, however, who are in Christ through faith, have been made rich in bread and wine. Israel does not share in these things, for such were not conferred by the blessings given to Esau. The poor Jews likewise do not share in the mystical blessing, since neither was this given under the ministration of the law. Rather, it was reserved for the people who are in Christ by faith. We, moreover, are at peace through Christ, while Israel is at war. We have inherited the land promised literally,[239] which was a type of that which is spiritual and heavenly. This the Savior himself spoke of, saying, "Blessed are the meek, for they will inherit the earth."[240] Also, we are included among the children of God through the Spirit of freedom. We are admitted to Christ as to one who is like us, a brother, and we perform a noble and willing obedience.

Israel, on the other hand, was placed under a yoke, weighed down by the laws of Moses, suffering death as the punishment for transgressions. For Esau heard the words, *"and you will serve your brother,"* that is, "you shall be made subject, unwillingly, to one whose nature is like yours." Now Moses too was a man like us, there being nothing extraordinary about him as far as his humanity was concerned.[241] For this reason the Master of all called Israel the people of Moses. For when they made the calf in the wilderness, God said to Moses, "Go down quickly from

---

238. Mt 5.18; 24.35.
239. Meaning "the land promised at the literal level of meaning."
240. Mt 5.5. The Greek word for "earth" here is the same as the one for "land" in the previous sentence.
241. Or "as far as a human evaluation is concerned."

here, for your people, whom you brought out of Egypt, have acted lawlessly."[242] So also the divine Paul attributes the written law to the blessed Moses, when he said, "Anyone who disregarded the law of Moses dies without mercy on the testimony of two or three witnesses."[243]

Yet Israel will lay aside the yoke placed upon them through the all-wise Moses when Christ calls them to the grace that comes through faith. This was indicated in advance by the words, *"But the time will come when you break free and loosen his yoke from your neck."* For those of Israel who have come to believe have loosened the exceedingly heavy yoke of the law from their necks, in that they have been called to the dignity of freedom through faith in Christ, through whom and with whom be glory to God the Father, together with the Holy Spirit, for ever and ever. Amen.

242. Ex 32.7.
243. Heb 10.28.

BOOK FOUR: GENESIS 27–30

[177] *Concerning the patriarch Jacob*

IT IS TRUE that "all who desire to live a godly life in Christ Jesus will be persecuted."[1] For the sons of iniquity pounce upon them like wild animals, reckoning the excellence of those whose practice it is to live respectably as a reason to denounce them and to accuse them of a kind of depravity. For in some way those things that are worse are always exposed[2] when placed alongside those things that are better, and the ugly nature of that which is inferior serves to outline that which is of greater value.

What, then, do we learn from this? The arrows of envy and the smoldering fire caused by the jealousy of those shown to be inferior are the beginning of madness and the origin of wickedness against those who have chosen to live most nobly. Yet these latter, although they may encounter trials and suffering, are by no means easily overcome by those who war against them. For he who governs the affairs of the saints certainly does not overlook those who expose themselves to danger for his sake. Rather, he will all the more readily deliver them and, having ordained these struggles as an exercise in hardship for them, he will show them to be of a more excellent character.

The divine Paul also affirms this when he writes, "God is faithful, who shall not let you be tested beyond what you are able to bear, but with the trial he will also provide the way out, so that you can endure it."[3] Further, those acquainted with trials, who have nobly borne with the pain of persecutions, cry out

---

1. 2 Tm 3.12.
2. Or "reproved."
3. 1 Cor 10.13.

in the book of Psalms: "You have tested us, O God; you have refined us with fire as silver is refined. You brought us into the snare; you laid afflictions upon our backs; you set men upon our heads. We went through fire and water, but you brought us to a place of respite."[4] You understand that it is not at all a matter of them having learned how to endure the things by which they are tested. Rather, they rejoice in the fact that they are being shown to be better people. What they are is made known by means of the trial itself, and through their suffering testimony is given to the extent of their piety. For they said that they indeed went through fire. In the same way, I believe, the finest incense, when it comes into contact with fire, then brings forth the demonstration[5] of the fragrance that it is endowed with. Thus also the pious soul, when burnt in the fire, as it were, through testing and suffering, brings forth a most distinct manifestation of the manifold virtues present within it.

Besides this, with regard to every saint the divine David in one place also sings out, "The angel of the Lord encamps around those who fear him [180], and he will deliver them."[6] Again, the one who provides succor himself expressly says, "Because he has put his hope in me, I will deliver him. He will cry out to me, and I will hear him. I am with him in affliction; I will deliver him and glorify him. With long life I will satisfy him and will show him my salvation."[7]

So what manner of salvation is this salvation of God the Father? From him comes God the Word, who in the economy of his Incarnation became like us for our sakes and took on the form of a servant. It was concerning him that the Father spoke through Isaiah, saying, "And the nations will see my righteousness, and kings my glory. My salvation shall burn like a lamp."[8] He, the Son, has in fact become our righteousness and glory from God the Father, and indeed our salvation also. For in him we have been justified and been brought into the glory of adop-

---

4. Ps 66.10–12 (65.10–12 LXX).
5. Or "proof."
6. Ps 34.7 (33.8 LXX).
7. Ps 91.14–16 (90.14–16 LXX).
8. Cf. Is 62.1–2.

tion as sons. So how could there be any doubt that we have been saved also, escaping the bonds of death and being translated into immortality? For the Son appeared to us like a lamp in the night and in the darkness, the divine light which penetrates the souls of those who believe. Therefore, he said, "I am the light of the world."[9] Moreover, as the Savior also said, "Blessed are those who are persecuted for the sake of righteousness,"[10] for through the aid of the God and Savior of all they will have a portion in heaven. Furthermore, they will come to see the very mystery pertaining to Christ, and certain of them might learn nothing less than those matters concerning the blessed Jacob. So I consider it appropriate to set forth those things written about him, that the readers may have a more accurate knowledge.

The account reads as follows: *Now Esau was indignant at Jacob over the matter of the blessing which his father gave him. So Esau said to himself, "Let the days of mourning for my father draw near so that I may kill Jacob my brother." And the words of Esau her elder son were reported to Rebekah. Then she sent and called for Jacob her younger son and said to him, "Behold, Esau your brother is threatening to kill you. So now, my son, obey my voice; rise up and flee to Mesopotamia, to Laban my brother in Haran. Stay with him for a while until the wrath and anger of your brother subside, and he forgets what you have done to him. Then I will send and fetch you back from there. I do not want to be bereaved of both of you in a single day."*[11]

Then Rebekah provided her son with a suitable occasion to make the journey. Going to Isaac she said, *"I am weary of my life because of the daughters of the Hittites. If Jacob should take a wife from the daughters of this land, what reason would I have to live?"*[12] In order that the blessed Jacob might not run away without the consent of his father and so be seen as one who causes grief and anger, the woman cleverly persuaded the old man to allow their son to make the journey. It says, *Isaac called Jacob and blessed him, and then commanded him, saying, "You shall not take a wife from the daughters of* [181] *Canaan. Rise up and go to Mesopotamia, to the*

9. Jn 8.12.
10. Mt 5.10.
11. Gn 27.41–45.
12. Gn 27.46.

house of Bethuel, your mother's father, and take a wife for yourself from there from the daughters of Laban, your mother's brother. May my God bless you and cause you to grow and multiply, that you may become a multitude of nations. May he give you the blessing of Abraham your father, that you and your offspring after you should inherit the land where you have been living, which God gave to Abraham."[13]

2. As far as the letter is concerned, that is, those matters revealed at the literal level, it is appropriate that both Rebekah and the blessed Jacob should be the cause of considerable astonishment. For when she brought to Isaac, the man who was chief, her request concerning their son, he, as the rightful decision-maker, immediately handled the matter according to the law of nature and instructed the son to avoid the marriage that his mother did not wish. It was with some tenderness that he directed his child, who had been brought up piously, to follow in the footsteps of his father's virtue. The divine Jacob is in fact everywhere seen to comply with the commands of his parents, giving a clear and indisputable indication of his devotion towards God.

As far as the contemplation of spiritual matters is concerned, I intend to go over the course of events again, looking at the inner meaning, undertaking to bring to mind that which is profitable. The subject here to be contemplated is in fact quite readily made manifest.

Now Rebekah, before the labor pangs came upon her, while she was still pregnant with the two boys to whom she would give birth, had an overwhelming sense of evil foreboding and was in fear of dying as the babies within her were leaping about to an excessive degree. The cause of the matter eluding her,[14] she wished to consult God, and asked, "Why are things happening to me this way?"[15] And how does God respond to this? "Two nations and two peoples will be separated from your womb. One people will have preeminence over the other, and the elder will serve the younger."[16] We shall then represent Esau and Jacob

---

13. Gn 28.1–4.
14. Var. "Inquiring into the cause of the matter."
15. Gn 25.22. The Greek of the LXX here literally reads: "If it is going to be this way with me, why is this to me?"
16. Gn 25.23.

as types of two peoples—the people of Israel and the people of faith.

Now it says, *Esau was indignant at Jacob,* because he had been deprived of the privileges of being the elder son, having sold the right of the firstborn and having passed his prerogatives over to another. Also, in bringing in the meal of game meat second, he failed to obtain the blessing. And so he gave himself to violent schemes, and out of malice he thought to murder the one who was his companion and brother. So Israel, the firstborn, was likewise indignant and exceedingly angry with those who succeeded him, that is, the new people of God through faith. This was because the latter became the first in order before God, counted as having the portion of the firstborn, and was filled with heavenly blessing, having been made rich through the Spirit with the grace that is in Christ. So Israel rose up against those in Christ through faith, and forcefully laid hands upon them, as much as he wished. He became a bitter murderer, a bringer of persecution, and one who inflicts wounds with the arrows of murder[17] and maliciousness.

Rebekah, however, persuaded Jacob to forsake his own home in order to escape his brother and to go to Laban, who was an idol-worshiper. Also, the divine Isaac, the father of Jacob,[18] himself insisted that a marriage with a woman of Canaan should be avoided, bidding Jacob to obtain a spouse [184] from among the daughters of Laban instead.

Now the church, of which Rebekah was a type, wisely counseled the new people of God, being threatened and persecuted, to escape the wrath of those wishing to murder them. Similarly, the husband of Rebekah, that is, Christ, also gave instructions himself regarding such a thing, that a spiritual relationship should have precedence over one with those stirred up to godless passions, who think to commit cruel murder. The marriage signifies that relationship, in which the daughters of the house of Laban, that is, of the Gentiles, were to be preferred.

We find that the holy apostles, who were in fact the firstfruits of the new people of faith, were eager to fulfill the commands

17. Var. "malice."
18. Var. "of the young man Jacob."

given to Jacob. For they distanced themselves from the company of the Jews, seeing that these were threatening to murder them. Moving to another country and town, they were sensibly quick to get away from the wrath of those persecuting them. These latter are spoken of by Christ when he denounces them, saying, "When they drive[19] you out of this city, flee to another."[20] The apostles also addressed those of the race of Israel, those who had chosen to disobey and who were causing injury without mercy. They said, "It was necessary to speak the word of God to you first; but since you reject it and judge yourselves to be unworthy of eternal life, behold, we turn to the Gentiles, for thus the Lord commanded us."[21] You note that Christ, the bridegroom of the church, has commanded his apostles[22] to go off to the multitudes of the Greeks, and there to give birth to children, and to show themselves to be, as it were, fathers of the peoples. In keeping with this, the most-wise Paul writes to those Gentiles who had come to believe through him, saying, "For though you might have ten thousand instructors in Christ, you do not have many fathers, for in Christ Jesus I myself became your father through the gospel."[23]

That God will be united with those who are a people through faith and will richly bless them, the divine Isaac demonstrated most readily. When Jacob was about to flee from his father's home, Isaac crowned him with heavenly blessings, saying, *"May my God bless you and cause you to grow and multiply, that you may become a multitude of nations. May he give you the blessing of Abraham your father."* Now those in Christ have indeed been blessed and have grown exceedingly. They have become numerous, a multitude of nations, and have been instated as fellow heirs with the holy fathers, for "they will recline at table with Abraham, Isaac, and Jacob in the kingdom of heaven," as the Savior him-

---

19. The verb may also mean "persecute," yet since Cyril changes the Matthean "in this city" to "from this city," its manner of rendering in English has necessarily been changed.
20. Mt 10.23.
21. Acts 13.46–47.
22. The Greek phrase lacks a noun, merely saying "his own."
23. 1 Cor 4.15.

self says.[24] And we shall be further blessed by him, for he said concerning us, "Holy Father, keep them in your truth."[25]

Now if Rebekah is understood also as the mother of Esau, the spiritual contemplation of what she represents is by no means undone. For we have portrayed Esau as a type of the people of Israel, while we have assigned to Rebekah the part of the church. There are, however, those of Israel who are also sons of the church through faith in Christ. These are no longer reckoned as being that old and ancient people, but rather they have been transformed into the new people of God, being mixed together with those of the nations. Indeed, "If anyone is in Christ, he is a new creation."[26] He also "created the two into one new man, making peace," as the Scriptures say, "reconciling both in one Spirit [185] to the Father,"[27] for "he has broken down the dividing wall and abolished the law with its commandments and decrees."[28]

3. So then, having been granted the blessings of his father, Jacob started out[29] on the journey that was set before him. What manner of things happened on the way we learn from the sacred Scriptures. The account reads as follows: *Now Jacob departed from the Well of the Oath*[30] *and set out for Haran. And he arrived at a certain place and lay down to sleep there, because the sun had set. He took one of the stones of that place and put it under his head, and he went to sleep there. Then he had a dream, and behold, a ladder was set up on the earth, the top of which was in heaven, and the angels of God were going up and down on it. And the Lord stood upon it*[31] *and said, "I am the God of Abraham, your father, and the God of Isaac. Do not be afraid. The land on which you are lying I will give to you and to your offspring. Your offspring will be like the sand of the sea. They will spread out to the west,*[32] *to the south, to the north, and to the*

---

24. Mt 8.11.
25. Cf. Jn 17.11, 17.
26. 2 Cor 5.17.
27. Eph 2.15–16, 18.
28. Eph 2.14–15.
29. Lit. "his feet carried him off."
30. That is, Beersheba (cf. Gn 21.31).
31. Or "above it."
32. Lit. "to the sea," that is, the Mediterranean in the west; var. "on the earth."

east. And in you and your offspring all the families of the earth will be blessed. Now behold, I am with you and will watch over you wherever you go. I will bring you back to this land, for I will not leave you until I have done everything that I have spoken to you."Then Jacob woke up from his sleep and said, "The Lord is in this place, and I did not know it." He was afraid and said, "What an awesome place this is! This is nothing other than the house of God and the gate of heaven." In the morning Jacob rose up and took the stone that he had placed under his head. He set it up as a pillar and poured oil on top of it. He called the name of that place House of God.[33] We say the name of that town is Well of the Oath because this is written concerning it: "It happened on the same day that Isaac's servants came and informed him about the well that they had dug, saying, 'We have not found water.'[34] So he called it Oath.[35] For this reason he called the town Well of the Oath to this day."[36] We speak further of the matter since one might wish to learn about the Well of the Oath. This was the place where the leaders of the Gerarites, namely Abimelech and those with him, had enacted an oath of peace with Isaac.

The divine Jacob, then, removed himself from his father's home and town and was separated from his family. And so he went wandering off in fear. He gave some thought to the possibility of being a vagabond and a refugee, and that he should live among foreigners. Maybe he should be under the authority of others and take on a yoke of slavery to which he was unaccustomed, for it is necessary even for those of noble birth to submit to those who rule. Yet the God who knows hearts and minds soon intervened and did not allow the soul of that righteous man to be overwhelmed by such severe apprehensions. He showed him that a multitude of angels, traversing up and down, takes care of those who depend on him. It was [188] precisely this, I believe, that Jacob was taught through the dream. Now from a literal point of view, Jacob beheld the ladder extending upwards, yet the symbol of descending and ascending

---

33. Gn 28.10–19.
34. The LXX adds the negative. The Hebrew reads, "We have found water."
35. Hebrew: *Sheba*.
36. Gn 26.32–33.

was describing matters, as it were, in earthly types. Jacob also heard God's voice speaking to the angels, instructing them that he himself would be the object of the blessing given to Jacob by his father, that is, *"your offspring will spread out to the east and to the west, to the north and to the south."* The voice said that Jacob would have God himself as the one who helped him and watched over him everywhere. When he woke up, the divine Jacob was not a little astonished, and he said moreover, *"The Lord is in this place, and I did not know it."*

How can it not be worthwhile considering what this account might wish to reveal? Among those of ancient times we find quite feeble notions with regard to God. For they supposed that the Deity was unconcerned with every other land, and was restricted to that land only,[37] to which they had also been called by him, having left their home and departed from the land of the Chaldeans. For since those who worship idols are afflicted with the error of polytheism, assigning to each of the divinities its own country, as it were, and making those gods worshiped to be in effect supreme rulers in each locality, they did not believe that all gods had power everywhere and ought to be honored. So too the blessed patriarchs, even after being delivered from the practice of idolatry[38] and the error of polytheism, and being moved to worship the one who is the true God by nature, supposed that he was not present with them in every land nor able to help them in every place, since they still retained quite defective views of God.

The blessed Jacob, therefore, was enriched through his journey, being instructed in what was lacking in his faith. For he learned that the Deity is in every place and in every country. He dwells in heaven, yet has dealings with the whole world and fills the earth. All the spirits in heaven, who are directed to traverse up and down, are subject to him, having God as their head presiding over them. It is for this reason that Jacob was amazed and said, *"The Lord is in this place, and I did not know it."* Supposing the stone to have been the cause of the dreams, Jacob honored it with those things at hand, smearing it with oil. Moreover, he

---

37. Here meaning the promised land of Canaan.
38. Var. "idolatrous nations."

called that place the House of God and the Gate of Heaven, and set up the stone as a pillar.

4. Let it be said once again that these things are presented to us in very earthy narratives. So it has first been necessary to explain those matters considered difficult at the literal level. But now, moving on to the spiritual contemplation of what is set before us, we again say this—that the new people of God through faith, considered as firstfruits by the holy apostles, were in fact forced to flee to escape the wrath of those intent on murder, by which I mean the Jews. Moving from town to town, they won over[39] multitudes of the Gentiles, very much desiring to gather them to themselves through the fellowship formed by the Spirit. Jacob, of course, was urged to act similarly with regard to the daughters of Laban, when Esau showed that he was intending to commit savage murder.

Now once the people of God through faith have come to rest upon Christ, who is "a choice stone, a precious cornerstone,"[40] for this, I believe, [189] is what is indicated by the act of sleeping upon the stone, we then learn that they will not be alone upon the earth, but they will have the holy angels, traversing up and down, as their assistants and helpers. For in one place Christ said, "Truly, truly, I say to you, from now on you will see heaven opened and the angels of God ascending and descending on the Son of Man."[41] This is, I believe, the ladder—the passing up and down of the holy spirits, "sent to serve for the sake of those who shall inherit the kingdom."[42] Christ is stood firm on the top of the ladder, while those holy spirits come up to him, having him as their overseer, not that he is one of their kind, but is God and Lord. David in one place says to every person wanting to live with the help of the Most High, "He will command his angels concerning you, to guard you in all your ways. They will take you up in their hands, so that you do not strike your foot against a stone. You will tread upon the asp and

---

39. Or "courted."
40. Is 28.16; cf. 1 Pt 2.6.
41. Jn 1.51.
42. Cf. Heb 1.14; var. "inherit salvation."

the basilisk, and trample upon the lion and the serpent."[43] We indeed have trodden upon snakes and scorpions and upon every power of the enemy, Christ giving us the authority. Those, then, who are in Christ are indeed worthy also of divine oversight and ought to be disposed boldly, because he will stand by them and succor them, everywhere he will save them and make them fruitful. "I am with you always," he says, "even till the end of the world."[44]

That the blessed disciples were richly blessed in becoming the fathers of innumerable nations by faith in Christ and by spiritual generation is everywhere evident. Paul plainly says to those who came to faith through him, "Though you might have ten thousand instructors in Christ, you do not have many fathers, for in Christ Jesus I myself became your father through the gospel."[45] Therefore, their seed became as countless as grains of sand, and it spread to the east and to the west, to the right and to the left, to the south and to the north.

Yet the stone was set up as well, smeared with oil, and honored as a type of Christ. For Emmanuel was anointed by God the Father "with the oil of gladness above his fellows."[46] He was also raised up from the dead, and yet he had gone down to death willingly. And this, I believe, is what the setting up of the stone means. Our Lord Jesus Christ is proclaimed through the holy apostles as the one anointed with the Holy Spirit by the Father and risen from the dead, through whom and with whom be glory[47] to God the Father, together with the Holy Spirit, for ever and ever. Amen.

More concerning the patriarch Jacob

1. One cannot doubt that it is especially needful for us to learn how to long for and to thirst after the divine oracles, as this is the most noble thing of all and that which is accounted

---

43. Ps 91.11–13 (90.11–13 LXX). Cf. Lk 10.19 for next sentence.
44. Mt 28.20.
45. 1 Cor 4.15.
46. Heb 1.9.
47. Var. add "and power."

by God to be worthy of the highest honor. That the significance of every word is important and should fulfill its object for our benefit, the Savior himself assures us [192] when he says, "The kingdom of heaven is like a merchant looking for fine pearls. When he found one pearl of great value, he went and sold everything he had and bought it."[48] So it is necessary that we seek for fine pearls, for we shall find that one pearl of great value, which is Christ. Whatever the fine pearls might be, the task of seeking to possess them is worthwhile and brings one particular pearl to the fore, and so I say that all of them are holy. Concerning these the prophet says, "Holy stones are rolled upon the ground."[49]

So then, those things that the people of old both said and did are matters well deserving of our inquiry. For through these things we shall look into the depths of the mystery of godliness, which is Christ, foreshadowed in types with much wisdom and skillfulness. We shall further find that the economy of the Incarnation is also to be perceived in such matters, portrayed by means of certain vague shadows, yet not so obscurely as to be completely indiscernible.

So now, those things regarding the divine Jacob will be expounded, and the way in which he lived his life will be discussed. Also, by means of Jacob we will set forth clearly the form of the whole economy, that is, the gospel economy, flying around the most colorful elements of the literal account in the manner of bees, gathering from each what is profitable for interpreting the word. If every matter written about Jacob is not included among the spiritual interpretations, let no one be troubled. One should realize that some things that happened at the literal level are just as they are in themselves. Yet other things indeed allow also for reflection upon inner meanings and figuratively present the import of the mystery.

2. It is further written here: *And Jacob set out and went to the land of the east, to Laban the son of Bethuel the Syrian, the brother of Rebekeh, the mother of Jacob and Esau. And he looked, and behold, there was a well in the field. There were three flocks of sheep resting by it,*

48. Mt 13.45–46.
49. Zec 9.16 LXX.

for out of that well the flocks were watered, and there was a large stone over the mouth of the well. All the flocks would be gathered there, and they would roll away the stone from the mouth of the well and water the flocks. Then they would put back the stone in its place over the mouth of the well. Jacob said to the shepherds, "Brothers, where are you from?" They replied, "We are from Haran." He asked them, "Do you know Laban the son of Nahor?" They answered, "We know him." Jacob asked, "Is he well?" And they said, "He is well." Now Rachel his daughter was coming with the sheep.[50] *Jacob said, "The sun is still high; it is not yet time for the animals to be gathered. Water the sheep, then go and let them graze." The shepherds said, "We cannot do this until all the shepherds are gathered here. Then they will roll the stone away from the mouth of the well, and we will water them." While they were still speaking, Rachel the daughter of Laban came with her father's sheep, for she tended his flocks. And it happened that when Jacob saw* [193] *Rachel the daughter of Laban his mother's brother, he came and rolled the stone away from the mouth of the well and watered the sheep of Laban, his mother's brother. Then Jacob kissed Rachel and lifted up his voice and wept. He told Rachel that he was her father's nephew and Rebekah's son. Rachel ran and told these things to her father. When Laban heard the name of Jacob, the son of his sister, he ran to meet him. He embraced him and kissed him, and brought him to his house. Then Jacob told Laban everything. Laban said to him, "You are indeed my bone and my flesh!"*[51]

Following that remarkable vision and divine revelation in which Jacob beheld a ladder reaching up into heaven,[52] with the Lord standing upon it and the angels traversing up and down, he was expressly told that God would be with him and that his offspring would increase so as to become an innumerable multitude of peoples.

After he had set up the stone as a type of Christ, being then encouraged and having a firm hope in God for the future, Jacob

---

50. This sentence might, as in Hebrew, be a continuation of the speech of the shepherds, "... and behold, Rachel his daughter is coming with the sheep." The change of tense, however, in the LXX to "*was* coming" makes this reading difficult in Greek.
51. Gn 29.1–14.
52. Var. add "from the earth."

urged himself on towards the goal of his journey and came to the land lying in the east. He immediately made himself known to many shepherds as someone who was himself also thoroughly experienced in shepherding. That this was a familiar business for him is made evident when he says, *"The sun is still high; so now water the sheep, then go and let them graze."*

Jacob also made himself known to Laban's daughter, bestowing upon her the firstfruits,[53] as it were, of his noble character, in that he considered it worthwhile to attend to the sheep she was herding and to water them. For this signified[54] in a way that he was most probably one brought up in a noble manner, that it was quite improper for Rachel, being a virgin and ripe for marriage, to wait for the gathering of the shepherds so that once the stone had been moved she might water the sheep, and also that submitting to others on account of being the weaker was modest behavior becoming to a young woman. Moreover, it was the law of natural affection that was calling him to perform his duty to those of the same blood and to show himself useful to his relatives. Therefore, he watered Rachel's sheep, rolling away the stone by himself.

One ought to remember that the divine Moses when fleeing from the land of Egypt came to the region of the Midianites, where he too soon set about the work of shepherding. When he saw the daughters of Jethro being ill-treated, he likewise showed a similar zeal. This is what was written about him: "Moses departed from the presence of Pharaoh, and dwelt in the land of Midian. When he came to the land of Midian, he sat down by a well. Now there were seven daughters of the priest of Midian, who were tending the sheep of their father Jethro. They came to draw water and filled the troughs in order to water their father's sheep. Then some shepherds came and chased them away. So Moses got up and rescued them. He also watered [196] their father's sheep. The daughters went to Jethro their father. He said to them, 'Why have you come back so soon today?' They replied, 'An Egyptian man rescued us from the shepherds. He

---

53. Cyril here uses a doublet, literally "first-spoils and first-fruits."
54. The subject of the main verb is here left unspecified, whether "it" or "he." It might also mean, "She understood perhaps …"

also drew water for us and watered the sheep.' He said to his daughters, 'So where is he? Why did you leave the man behind? Invite him to have something to eat.' So Moses lived with the man."[55]

You see, then, how the meanings of both passages are in a way sisters, and how those things revealed in them are very much related. The divine Moses, disdaining the excessive behavior of the other shepherds, both drew water and watered the flocks of Jethro. And so Jacob rolled the stone away by himself, although even those accustomed to doing this could not manage it without considerable effort, and he likewise watered the animals of Laban. Furthermore, as Moses took up residence with a man who was an idolater, so did the divine Jacob. For Laban was then a worshiper and servant of idols.

As the word confers upon Jacob a role in which he represents those who are the people of God through faith, let us now speak of inner meanings and discover those things hidden within the earthiness of the literal sense.

3. The "people yet to be created,"[56] of which the psalmist speaks, I do not suppose to be anything other than the new people of God in Christ, that is, those who through faith have been brought into the glory of the firstborn, having superseded the first people, Israel, who fell away. For the one who was the head has become the tail, that is, the one who took the first position, who was also known first, is now said to be the one that follows the calling of others. They have been made the back, and come behind the people of the Gentiles.

So then, the people of God in Christ through faith have supplanted those who were first, and their position is now reckoned with respect to that of the divine Jacob. The band[57] of the holy apostles, who were from the race and stock of Israel,[58] are to be understood as a kind of firstfruits of such a group. When they had been richly blessed through faith in Christ and crowned themselves, so to speak, with the grace given by the Holy Spir-

---

55. Ex 2.15–21.
56. Ps 102.18 (101.19 LXX).
57. Lit. "choir," "chorus."
58. Var. "of Jerusalem."

it, they clashed with those of their own race. Therefore, they had to leave them, as they were threatening murder and raging wildly. Departing from what was in effect their paternal home, the land in which they lived, namely the land of Jerusalem, the country of the Jews, they turned their attention to the regions of the Gentiles. They had Christ as their helper, assisting them in all manner of good things, and the angels also as their companions. Sustained by a heavenly hope and looking to become the fathers of many nations, to the east and west, the north and south, from them the seed spread forth, that is to say, those who were born again in the Spirit through faith and justified in Christ. These they addressed, saying, "You are a chosen race, a royal priesthood, a holy nation, a people for his own special possession, that you might proclaim the excellencies[59] of him who called you out of darkness into his marvelous light. Once you were not a people, but now you are the people of God in Christ."[60] That those appointed to teach them should be called "fathers of the peoples" by the divine Scripture, how could one question? So they forsook the land of the Jews. Leaving that arrogant and unruly people, they turned to the Gentiles, in accordance with the commandment of our Savior.

Yet [197] the apostles demonstrated forthwith that they were also spiritual shepherds, skilled in divine instruction. In this task, which was most proper for them to perform, they allowed themselves no slackness. For they earnestly conveyed the word of instruction in Christ; bringing forth what was needful, they persuaded others to comply. This is, of course, similar to what the divine Jacob did with respect to the shepherds of Haran. That he himself was a shepherd, he made plain when he said, *"The sun is still high; it is not yet time for the animals to be gathered. Water the sheep, then go and let them graze."* Do you hear how he instructed the shepherds to tend the sheep? Peter, that most-wise disciple, also commanded the elders of the people, namely the bishops, to do this same thing. "Therefore, I exhort the elders among you," he says, "as a fellow elder and witness of the suf-

---

59. Or "praises."
60. 1 Pt 2.9–10.

ferings of Christ, and one who will also share in the glory to be revealed. Shepherd the flock of Christ which is among you."[61]

So passing through each land and town, they appointed countless other shepherds[62] to lead the people and to care for the spiritual sheep, to feed them, as it were, in good pasture, in a fertile place, and to bring them to the most wonderful grass, namely, the inspired Scripture. For the word of God is life-giving food for the soul. Therefore, let it be said to these spiritual shepherds: "Tend to the fresh vegetation in the field, cut down the grass, and gather ripe fodder, so that your sheep may provide you with clothing." Yet the divine disciples, in presenting to their hearers the most true teaching, showed themselves to be instructors in a way quite different from those who were shepherds among the Gentiles, that is, their wise men and teachers. And that the disciples were much more able and superior to those others, one who considers the matter might discern with no great difficulty.

Now a very heavy stone was placed over the well, and a gathering[63] of a great many shepherds could just about move it. Yet Jacob managed to do this alone. So what the well stands for, and what the stone also signifies, we will now speak of as we are able. In this way we will come to know the difference between the strength of the shepherds and the preeminent and surpassing strength of understanding as possessed by the disciples of the Savior.

4. Now it is the custom of Scripture to liken knowledge concerning God to water. That this knowledge was life-giving the Savior testified when he said to the Father in heaven, "This is eternal life, that they may know you, the only true God, and Jesus Christ whom you have sent."[64] Also, when he was speaking with the woman of Samaria, he said, "If you knew the gift of God, and who it is that is saying to you, 'Give me a drink,' you would have asked him, and he would have given you living

---

61. 1 Pt 5.1–2.
62. Here and in what follows, the same word could be translated "pastors."
63. Var. "pushing."
64. Jn 17.3.

water."[65] I believe that the words and instruction he spoke were in a sense life-giving. So too the Master proclaimed, "If any one thirsts, let him come to me and drink."[66]

Furthermore, speaking through the prophet, God accuses certain people who, after the instruction given in the law, had ignorantly turned aside and resorted to other teachers, inclining to the teachings and commandments of men.[67] This is what he said: "Heaven is astonished at this and [200] exceedingly horrified, says the Lord. For my people have committed two evils: they have forsaken me, the fountain of living water, and they have dug for themselves broken cisterns, that can hold no water."[68]

So then, the life-giving water is the divine word. Yet it lies at a great depth, and I do not suppose one would ever be able to get to it without considerable effort. For it is not willing to be obtained by those who simply wish to have it. Being covered, as it were, with a heavy stone that is difficult to move, its obscurity defeats the feebleness of our mental abilities. So much labor and sweat are necessary on the part of those tending the spiritual flocks in order to take the word out from its obscurity, to draw it from the depths, as it were, and bring it up into the open, and so to set it forth clearly for the life-giving benefit of their listeners.

Regarding, however, those shepherds among the Greeks, that is, the many wise and leading men[69] among them, the majority of whom agree together in the doctrines relating to God, these in effect subvert the truth, for they do not hold correct views concerning him. While they confess the being of God, they apportion the glory of the Godhead to whatsoever they might choose.[70]

Now, just one of those shepherds in Christ is enough to take the stone off the well, despite the fact that it is extremely dif-

---

65. Jn 4.10.
66. Jn 7.37.
67. Cf. Is 29.13.
68. Jer 2.12–13.
69. Here Cyril means the Greek philosophers and teachers.
70. Cyril is here referring to the widespread practice of polytheism.

ficult to move. This indicates the removal of the covering and obscurity that lay over those notions concerning God. Accordingly, these shepherds make the truth clear to the Gentiles and they do not hesitate to show forth the one true being of God. The blessed Paul, for example, when he came to Athens, set the living water before the leading men, saying, "Men of Athens, I see that in every respect you are very religious. For as I was passing through, looking at your objects of worship, I even found an altar on which was inscribed, 'To the unknown god.' Therefore, the one you worship as unknown, him I proclaim to you."[71]

You see how those who were leaders of the people, who were their shepherds and instructors, could scarcely move the heavy stone away from the well. Considering themselves to be godly through their reverence for the divine, they erred greatly regarding the truth. For they had dedicated an altar on which the words were inscribed, "To the unknown god," that is, to the deity who was not known. Yet they maintained that they held noble views concerning God. Now the divine Paul put this inscription to good use, and with great skill he led them to what was needful, namely that the God who was unknown to them was Christ. "The one you worship as unknown," he tells them, "him I proclaim to you." You see how he opened up the well, having rolled away the stone, and how he pointed them to life-giving knowledge. So the wisdom displayed by the shepherds is incomparably different. Those Greeks, though being very many, pursued the true notion of God, and yet, overcome by the obscurity of the doctrines, they erred in their opinions. Paul, however, though alone, set forth the truth.

Jacob rolled away the stone alone, and watered the sheep under Rachel's care. Yet he also considered the girl to be lovable, for it says that he kissed [201] Rachel. He soon made himself known to Laban, who welcomed him into his home. Laban reckoned his sister's son as being worthy of love and acceptance, and considered him as one of his close relatives, for he said, *"You are indeed my bone and my flesh!"*

Now "Rachel" means "sheep of God."[72] So one might most

---

71. Acts 17.22–23.
72. More precisely the Hebrew name Rachel means "ewe."

reasonably take her as being a figure of the church taken out from among the Gentiles. For she is the sheep of Christ that is now joined to the earlier flocks, and enclosed within the sheepfolds of the Savior. This is why he said, "I have other sheep which are not of this fold. I must lead them also, and they will hear my voice; and there will be one flock and one shepherd."[73]

So the divine disciples also shepherded the church of Christ, by which is meant the spiritual sheep, and they became her friends and marriage negotiators, "presenting her to God as a pure virgin,"[74] "without spot, or wrinkle, or any such thing, but rather holy and blameless."[75]

5. From the words of Laban we also understand that the Israelites originated from among the Gentiles, like the sprouting forth of the first shoots from the root. For a man who was an idolater embraced Jacob, and said that he was born to one of his close relatives, evidently meaning Rebekah, and he called him his own flesh and bone. The divine Abraham was, in fact, called when he was uncircumcised, having been brought up in the land of Chaldea according to pagan customs and laws. "He received circumcision as a sign, a seal of the faith he had while uncircumcised," as it is written.[76]

Israel the firstborn, then, was a kinsman to those Gentiles, and yet they were set apart by the law, so as to be considered different. In Christ, however, the two have become one. For he removed the dividing wall, having annulled the law with all its writings and the distinguishing mark of circumcision. We have been made into one new man,[77] the Gentiles sharing in the same body and soul as the people of Israel.

It can also be seen that we have surely been brought together in such a way through communion in the Spirit, for Christ said to God the Father in heaven, "I desire that as you and I are one, they also might be one in us."[78] He is our peace, having broken

73. Jn 10.16.
74. 2 Cor 11.2.
75. Eph 5.27.
76. Rom 4.11.
77. Cf. Eph 2.14–15.
78. Cf. Jn 17.21.

down the dividing wall, as I just said, and having removed what separated us, joining us together in unity through the Spirit. So then, the fact that Laban embraced Jacob and acknowledged him to be his own bone and flesh is an especially clear representation of the spiritual oneness of the two peoples by means of faith.

In addition to the foregoing, let us now speak of another matter that we derive from the sacred Scriptures. It says, *Laban said to Jacob, "Just because you are my relative, you will not serve me for nothing. Tell me what your pay will be." Now Laban had two daughters. The name of the elder was Leah, and the name of the younger was Rachel. Leah's eyes were weak,*[79] *but Rachel was fine-looking with an extremely beautiful face. Jacob loved Rachel and said to Laban, "I will serve you seven years for Rachel your younger daughter." Laban said to him, "It is better that I give her to you than to some other man.* [204] *Stay with me." So Jacob served seven years for Rachel. Yet they seemed to him to be just a few days because of his love for her. Then Jacob said to Laban, "Give me my wife that I may go into her, for my time is completed." So Laban gathered all the men of that place and made a marriage feast. When it was evening, Laban took his daughter Leah and brought her to Jacob, and Jacob went in to her. Laban also gave Zilpah his servant girl to Leah his daughter to be her maidservant. Now when it was morning, behold there was Leah! So Jacob said to Laban, "What is this you have done to me? Did I not serve you for Rachel? Why, then, have you deceived me?" Laban said, "It is not done in our country, to give the younger before the elder. Finish the marriage-week*[80] *for this daughter, and I will give you the other also in return for another seven years of service for me." Jacob did so, and completed that marriage-week; then Laban gave him his daughter Rachel as his wife. Laban gave Bilhah his servant girl to Rachel his daughter to be her maidservant. Then Jacob went into Rachel, and he loved Rachel more than Leah. Then he served Laban for another seven years.*[81]

---

79. The original significance of this is uncertain. It might indicate that she was unattractive. Alternatively, some modern English Bible versions interpret this as a positive feature (e.g., NRSV, "Leah's eyes were lovely"; NJB, "Leah had lovely eyes").

80. Lit. "her sevens." This might alternatively refer to the period of seven years.

81. Gn 29.15–30.

6. The matters arising out of the literal account ought not to require any explanation for there is nothing at all difficult among them, except that someone might say they would like to learn more precisely about the customs found there. We do not in fact consider it too irrelevant to first attend to the issue of being married to two people and of living with two wives, who were sisters at that! In response to these matters we say that for those of long ago the whole purpose of life was to produce many children, and what is more, the most important thing of all was reckoned to be prosperity. So one was free from all blame if one slept with not just two wives but even with many more, so as to expand one's posterity into an innumerable multitude. Accordingly, they took the birth of children to be in the highest order of blessing from God. Furthermore, the Master of all himself promised both the saints of old who lived before Moses and those who were under the tutelage of the law that he would grant them the gift of offspring. For he said, "There shall not be any one childless nor a widow[82] among the people of Israel."[83] We do not receive this saying as belonging to the category of law, but rather we say that it is a promise. There are certain things, as presented in these laws, which relate to us, and properly so. There are matters, however, that do not relate to us, but they are that sort of laws which have come to a complete end, in which case the law has no authority. It is evident, then, and not in the least bit obscure, that the Maker did not issue it by way of a command that there should be no barrenness or childlessness among the people of Israel. But rather, if they were observant of the law, they would prove to be fruitful, as God had promised. Surely then, for those of ancient times, to have many children was considered to be a matter of honor and one of great seriousness.

As for us, however, we are transformed in Christ, so that we should rather be fruitful in the Spirit. Without dishonoring marriage, we choose that life which greatly exceeds this, and which, in the judgment of the inspired Scripture, bears a much more excellent crown. [205] This, I say, is to live without distrac-

---

82. Var. "nor barren" (as LXX).
83. Cf. Ex 23.26; Dt 7.14.

tion, to wait upon God, and not to be concerned about worldly things. "For the unmarried man," Paul says, "is concerned about the things of the Lord, but the married man about the things of the world, how to please his wife, and so he is divided."[84]

7. This discussion of these matters will suffice us. Let us now come, through applying our minds to spiritual contemplations, to something that is very appropriate for us to consider. Let us take a look at how the labor of the holy apostles in preaching was not without reward, nor was their effort unrecompensed. For Laban said to Jacob, *"You will not serve me for nothing."* The divine disciples in fact deemed the multitude of believers in former times to be the cause of the most wondrous rejoicing.[85] Paul, for instance, addressed them as "My joy and crown."[86]

Now I judge it to be necessary to make mention of the most useful matters that we have received from those early times. I said that the figure of Jacob, considered spiritually, sometimes stands for the band of the holy apostles, who were the firstfruits of those sanctified in the Spirit and justified by faith. He also stands for Christ himself, who was the firstfruits of a renewed humanity destined for incorruption, the firstborn among many brothers, a second Adam, a second root of the human race coming after the first. So then, the discourse always turns to the object to be considered spiritually, as it is appropriate to do. Indeed, the failure to apply the proper reasoning leads to a much less refined explanation of these spiritual considerations.

So what was figured by the person of Jacob is now taken up by Emmanuel. He is the heavenly bridegroom, who not without considerable effort has taken the daughters of Laban. It especially pertains to the most supreme Being of all to succeed in a matter without any effort at all. And this he might choose to do. In one place the blessed prophet Isaiah said concerning him, "He will not become hungry, nor grow weary, and his understanding is unsearchable."[87] For the Deity has no need with respect to anything, but he has full perfection in himself. He does

---

84. Cf. 1 Cor 7.34.
85. Lit. "glorying," "boasting."
86. Phil 4.1.
87. Is 40.28.

not receive power from anything outside of himself, nor does he get energy by means of physical food or drink. Rather, by his very nature he himself is power. Therefore, he establishes the heavens, and with authority he distributes the exercise of power to whomever he might choose.

Yet, while the Deity is not disposed by nature to experience pain, he is spoken of as if he did feel pain.[88] For he says in a certain place to the mother of the Jews, evidently meaning the synagogue, "You have caused me pain in all these things."[89] The divine Paul also writes in a certain passage, "And do not grieve the Holy Spirit of God who dwells within you."[90] Although he is said to suffer in this way, we claim with regard to this that it is not the case that he feels pain.[91] It is rather that, when he accomplishes the most exalted and remarkable things, he undertakes these as though he were wont to suffer. These are things that would evidently entail the enduring of terrible and bitter pain, if it were any one of us.[92]

Moving on from such human notions to loftier considerations, we shall examine the attention that the pure Being gives to us, which is performed, one could almost say, with great exertion and sweat.[93] At all events, we shall of necessity set aside[94] [208] the question of his experiencing pain, since it is not the same as it is with us, but rather he is over all creation, dwelling in his own excellencies and being in full possession of them.

So then, it was not without reward, yet neither without effort, that Christ gathered first the synagogue of the Jews, which we take as being represented by the figure of Leah. She is under-

---

88. In this sentence and in what follows, the verb *lupein* may have the sense of either "cause pain" or "grieve."

89. Ezek 16.43.

90. Eph 4.30. Cf. Rom 8.9; 1 Cor 3.16.

91. Here and in what follows Cyril uses terms (*ponos*, *ponein*) that bear the sense of both "pain" and "labor." According to his understanding, for God to exert himself in labor would be, in a sense, for him to experience pain, which is not possible.

92. Or "if he were somebody like us."

93. In a clause that does not allow literal translation, Cyril compares the exertions with "drunken raving."

94. Or "dismiss."

stood as toiling, and then as being made new. She toiled when she was harshly oppressed by the Egyptians, bearing a heavy yoke of slavery. And she was made new with respect to the worship conducted by the forefathers. For she was reformed when she was brought out from idol-mad worship to know him who is truly God by nature. For he declared to the Israelites through Moses: "Hear, O Israel, the Lord your God is one Lord," and, "You shall have no other gods besides me."

Yet in the beginning Christ in fact desired Rachel, that is, the church gathered out from the Gentiles. Therefore, with regard to the synagogue of the Jews, he said to that teacher of spiritual truths, Moses, "I have spoken to you once and again, saying, 'I have seen this people, and indeed, they are a stiff-necked people. Let me alone that I may destroy them and blot out their name from under the expanse of heaven. And I will make you a great and mighty nation, more numerous than they.'"[95] It was, however, necessary for those who still had inconstant and easily moved minds not to be brought hastily to perfection and to the teaching that exceeded the mind and discernment of Moses, by which I mean that of the gospel. Rather, they first needed to be instructed through lesser things, and for the instruction under the law to be in effect a preparatory training for life in Christ.

In the beginning, therefore, the heavenly bridegroom desired the younger woman, that is, the church gathered from the Gentiles. He, however, first took to himself the elder, and that not without effort, since Jacob had to serve for Leah. That by many great exertions Israel was delivered from the toil of slavery under the Egyptians is obvious. The whole of creation in fact fought against them.[96] So then, the service of Jacob, which was in no way performed without toil, signified the fact that Israel would not be redeemed without considerable effort, and also the subsequent ministration set out in the law.

When the marriage-week[97] for the elder woman was fulfilled, Jacob took to himself Rachel, the younger woman, the one who was desired in the beginning. For the second woman, the Gen-

---

95. Dt 9.13–14.
96. Cyril here means the series of plagues that fell upon the Egyptians.
97. See n. 80 above.

tile church, the flock of God, was called in after the first. This is how Rachel is to be interpreted, as I said before. That Christ in a way also worked for her, the divine Jacob again demonstrated to us when he endured another seven years of labor for Rachel. For if it is admitted that he, the Son, experienced hard toil, although he was by nature God, how much more was this so in the persecution he suffered from Herod at the beginning, the plots of the Pharisees, the false accusations of the leaders, the spitting, the blows, the strikes upon his back, the drunken behavior of the soldiers, and finally his death upon the cross?

Laban's daughters, Leah and Rachel, were daughters of a man who was still an idolater. They were then called out [209] from the nations. The first was the synagogue of the Jews, even the divine Abraham[98] himself being of Gentile origins, and the second, younger one, following on after the first, is the church.

Now Leah's eyes were weak and feeble, while Rachel was fine-looking with an extremely beautiful face. Christ also said to the holy apostles with regard to the Jews, "Leave them alone; they are blind guides of the blind,"[99] but "Blessed are your eyes because they see, and your ears because they hear."[100] And so the feebleness of the Jewish synagogue with respect to beholding the divine is suitably signified by means of Leah's eyes. Yet wisdom and prudence, and the wonderful abundance of understanding of those who are in Christ through faith, and also indeed the conspicuousness of their works, are all depicted beforehand by the beauty of Rachel. In one case, let the prophetic word proclaim to the mother of the Jews, "Behold, your eyes and your heart are no good."[101] But in the other, let Christ call the church out from the Gentiles and let him say about her, "Your eyes are doves."[102] For "he desired her beauty," as the psalmist says.[103]

So then, Christ first took to wife the synagogue of the Jews,

---

98. Var. "Jacob."
99. Mt 15.14.
100. Mt 13.16.
101. Jer 22.17.
102. Song 1.15.
103. Ps 45.11 (44.12 LXX).

with Moses as the marriage negotiator and the angels as mediators. In the matter of the second wife, the Gentile church, the blessed Baptist was employed as a kind of mediator with regard to her. Accordingly, signifying to us this spiritual and divine marriage, he said, "He who has the bride is the bridegroom. The friend of the bridegroom, who stands and hears him, rejoices greatly on account of the voice of the bridegroom. Therefore, my joy has been made full. He must increase, but I must decrease."[104]

Mercy and faithfulness were wedding gifts for the bride. For the one coming from above, the heavenly bridegroom, said through the mouth of the prophets to the church taken from the Gentiles, "I will betroth you to myself for ever; indeed, I will betroth you to myself in righteousness and justice, in mercy and compassion. I will betroth you to myself in faithfulness, and you will know the Lord."[105] As I said just now, he took to himself the elder woman before the Gentile church. The manner, however, of the betrothal and the strength of the union were not to be everlasting. For he also said elsewhere concerning her, "She is not my wife, and I am not her husband,"[106] and again, "I put into her hands a certificate of divorce."[107] She was cast off as one who had committed sexual immorality and who stands condemned of the grossest indecency. For he said in one place concerning her, "If a man divorces his wife, and she leaves him and becomes another man's wife, will she indeed return to him once more? Will not that woman be utterly defiled? You played the harlot with many shepherds,[108] yet you return to me, says the Lord. Raise your eyes, look before you, and see where you have been defiled. You sat for them by the wayside like a crow in the wilderness.[109] [212] You polluted the land with your immorality and wickedness. You had many shepherds who were a

---

104. Jn 3.29–30.
105. Hos 2.19–20 (2.21–22 LXX).
106. Hos 2.2.
107. Jer 3.8.
108. The Hebrew word underlying this rendering by the LXX may be read as "companions" (*rēʿîm*) or "shepherds" (*rōʿîm*).
109. Lit. "like a desolated crow." The Hebrew noun here could be understood as "crow" (*ʿōrēb*) or "Arab" (*ʿărāb*).

stumbling block to you. You had the countenance of a harlot, you acted shamelessly towards them all. Have you not called me your family, your father and the guide of your maidenhood? Will he be angry for ever?"[110] These matters concern the elder sister. The younger Rachel, however, that is, the Gentile church, was betrothed to him permanently.

In saying "to myself,"[111] this may be understood in the following way. When he betrothed to himself the synagogue of the Jews, it was through Moses acting as a mediator. But when he was united with the church of the Gentiles, he invited her into this union with his own voice, appearing as a man, as one who lives upon the earth. He in fact granted what the bride asked for when she cried out, "Show me your face, and let me hear your voice."[112] For the people of old heard him speaking only through Moses or the prophets. In these last days of the world, however, the Son has spoken to us himself, as the wise Paul also testified.[113]

8. In addition to these matters, it is also worth examining the births of the sons of Jacob, to see how many there were and which women gave birth to which sons.

Leah, the first wife, gave birth to four sons: Reuben, Simeon, Levi, and Judah. Since Rachel was still barren and without child, being at a loss and extremely distraught, she used her wit to try to overcome the problem of her childlessness. She persuaded Jacob, saying, *"Here is my maidservant Bilhah. Go into her, and she will give birth upon my knees, so that I also may have children through her."*[114] When this had been carried out, two sons were brought forth to Jacob: Dan and Naphtali. Then Leah gave her own housemaid Zilpah to sleep with Jacob, so making him the father of two other sons: Gad and Asher.

What happened after this? It says, *Reuben went in the days of the wheat harvest and found mandrakes in the field which he brought to his*

110. Jer 3.1–5.

111. Cyril is referring back to the phrase in Hos 2.19 (2.21 LXX) cited above.

112. Song 2.14. Cyril has mistaken the speaker in the passage. Here, in fact, it is the man who addresses the woman.

113. Cf. Heb 1.2.

114. Gn 30.3.

mother Leah. Rachel said to Leah her sister, "Give me some of your son's mandrakes." But Leah said, "Was it not enough for you to take away my husband that you want to take my son's mandrakes as well?" Rachel said, "That's not the way it is. He can sleep with you tonight for your son's mandrakes." So when Jacob came in from the field in the evening, Leah went out to meet him and said, "You will come to me tonight, because I have hired you with my son's mandrakes."[115] Then when this happened, Leah further gave birth to Issachar, and after that to Zebulun.

To these were then added the remaining number of sons coming from Israel. It says, *God remembered Rachel. The Lord heard her and opened her womb. She conceived and gave birth to a son for Jacob. Rachel said, "God has taken away my reproach." She called his name Joseph, saying, "God has added*[116] *to me another son."*[117] Then she gave birth to Benjamin. This is what is also written about Rachel: *It happened that as he was nearing Chabratha to go into the land of Ephratha, Rachel began to give birth, and it was a very hard labor. As she was giving birth with much difficulty, the midwife said to her, "Take courage; for you will have another son." Then as her soul was departing (for she was dying), she called the child's name "Son of my pain."*[118] *But his father called him Benjamin.*[119] So when Rachel was dying through difficulty in childbirth, she wished to be delivered from that pain which is the common experience of us all.

This, then, was the birth of the sons of Jacob. What, however, the inner meaning of the things recorded might be, he himself knows who knows everything, as it is written, "in whom are hidden all the treasures of wisdom and knowledge."[120] So let us ourselves make careful investigation[121] and, as we are able, overcome the obscure earthiness present in these matters, and in attempting to do so, let us say to him who gives wisdom to the

---

115. Gn 30.14–16.
116. The name Joseph is derived from the Hebrew word "add."
117. Gn 30.22–24.
118. Hebrew: *Benoni*.
119. Gn 35.16–18.
120. Col 2.3.
121. Lit. "investigate with fine eyes."

blind, "Open my eyes, that I may behold wonderful things in your law."[122]

Therefore (reminding you of the things I said earlier), Leah, the elder wife, can most suitably be likened to the synagogue of the Jews, while Rachel, we may take to be the church of the Gentiles. Having first laid down a foundation for faith by these words, we shall now build further upon this.

9. So Leah, the first wife, gave birth to four sons; then there were subsequently four other sons from the two maidservants Bilhah and Zilpah. Then Leah and Rachel divided between them the mandrakes found in the field by Reuben, and both of them became mothers. In addition to her first four sons, Leah gave birth to Issachar, the "reward," then Zebulun, which means "blessing" or "prosperity." Rachel gave birth to Joseph, the one "added" by God. Then after him, as she was dying, she bore Benoni, "the son of pain."

The first wife, who was older in age, produced for God the congregation of the Jews, that is, the synagogue. That God called sons those who were born from her, you can readily see when he says to Moses, "Israel is my firstborn son,"[123] and again speaking through Isaiah, "Hear, O heaven, and listen, O earth, for the Lord has spoken. I fathered sons and reared them, but they have rejected me."[124] Yet, through their forefathers, they were born from those who were free, upon whom God did not cast the yoke of the law. Even the divine Paul himself showed us the freedom of their forefathers when he said, "I was once alive without the law."[125] When he says "I," he is referring to the root of the race, tracing his origin back to the forefathers. Even though the Jews were born from those who were free, the fact that they would be placed under a yoke of bondage through the law is figuratively portrayed in the birth of the four sons from the maidservants.

Now also in these things there is a mystery. Those sons born from Bilhah, Dan and Naphtali, were ascribed to Rachel, while

122. Ps 119.18.
123. Ex 4.22.
124. Is 1.2.
125. Rom 7.9.

those born from Zilpah, Gad and Asher, were ascribed to Leah, and were born later than the sons of Bilhah. I suppose one might strongly question, and it would be very reasonable to do so, how it is that the sons born to a slave, namely those from Bilhah, should be ascribed to Rachel, and yet also serve as a type of the church of the Gentiles. What can we say about this? We note that in ancient times the blessed prophets were, on the one hand, reckoned to be among [216] the children of the Jerusalem that was in servitude, yet, on the other hand, were in a way sons of the Gentile church. For they understood those things that pertained to the church, saying that it would be revealed and that in due course the mystery of Christ would shine forth. This they prefigured in countless different ways, bringing it, in effect, right before the eyes of the people of old.

Those who came after the prophets, still being born in bondage, did not accept Christ, the one who would grant them freedom. That those who lived earlier were better than those who came after them requires no effort to see. God says through the mouth of Isaiah, "How the faithful city of Zion, once full of justice, has become a harlot! Righteousness lodged in her—but now murderers!"[126] You see how she was once actually full of justice, that is to say, uprightness, and it says that Jerusalem, namely Zion, was the dwelling place of the righteous, yet in later times she was full of murderers.

10. One can very plainly see, if so desired, from the names of the sons that those born through Bilhah were in fact the church's foster children, while those from Zilpah were its enemies. For the meaning of Dan is "judgment," [127] and that of Naphtali "enlargement."[128]

This was the message given through the prophets—that Christ would judge the world in righteousness, and would bring about the condemnation of Satan, who gained the advantage over us and destroyed us, that he would save us and bring our hearts out from so much distress into a broad place, as it were,

126. Is 1.21.
127. Or "justice," "vindication." The Hebrew name "Dan" is correctly related to the idea of judgment.
128. Naphtali in fact means "wrestling" (cf. Gn 30.8).

and to show us no such grievousness ever again. For the blessed psalmist, as though assuming the role[129] of those in Christ sanctified by the Spirit, exclaimed, "I ran the way of your commandments, when you enlarged my heart."[130] And the most-wise Paul, writing to those believers of Corinth wishing to be unequally yoked, said, "We have spoken openly to you, O Corinthians; our heart is enlarged.[131] You are not restricted by us, but you are restricted by your own affections.[132] Now as a fair exchange—I speak as though to children—you also enlarge your hearts. Do not be unequally yoked with unbelievers."[133]

That the judgment given by Christ was right and just the blessed David himself, assuming the role of those who are maltreated, further makes clear, saying to Christ the Savior of all, "Rise up, O Lord, and attend to my judgment, to my cause, O my God and my Lord."[134] For the Savior himself makes this plain when he says, "Now is the judgment of this world; now the ruler of this world will be cast out. And I, if I am lifted up from the earth, will draw all people to myself."[135] Do you see, then, that the prophets, when speaking of the mystery pertaining to Christ, proclaimed ahead of time a future righteous judgment for us and an enlarging of our hearts?

So the sons of Bilhah were Dan and Naphtali, that is, "judgment" and "enlargement." The sons of Zilpah were Gad and Asher. The meaning of Gad is "testing," and that of Asher is "riches."[136] Were not the later people of the Jews, who came af-

---

129. *prosôpon*, literally "person," "face." Here is meant the more technical sense of "persona," "character."

130. Ps 119.32 (118.32 LXX). Here the verb "enlarge" (*platunein*) relates to "broad place" (*plateia*) shortly before.

131. Or "opened wide," as in most modern translations. Here the translation "enlarged" is retained to make clear the connection with Cyril's understanding of the name Naphtali as "enlargement."

132. These words admit of different translations. Other alternatives include: "There is no restriction in our affections, but only in yours" (NRSV), and "Any distress you feel is not on our side; the distress is in your own selves" (NJB).

133. 2 Cor 6.11–14.

134. Ps 35.23 (34.23 LXX).

135. Jn 12.31–32.

136. Asher in Hebrew relates to a word meaning "happiness" or "blessed-

ter the first, of such a kind? How could there be any doubt? One might in fact perceive this from those things that happened with regard to Christ. For the Jews, together with those called Herodians, tested him, saying, "Teacher, we know that you are truthful and show no preference for anybody. For you do not regard people with partiality, but you teach the way of God in truth. Is it lawful to pay tax to Caesar, or not?"[137] They were there testing him, in order that they might trap him. Such is the testimony of the divine evangelist.

It was on account of profit and greed that these people did not accept the Son. For we are told that they said among themselves, "This is the heir. Come, let us kill him so that the inheritance might be ours."[138] That the Pharisees, as well as that profane mass of scribes, were lovers of wealth and extremely greedy, one can very easily see by considering the things written about them. Our Lord Jesus Christ said that those who have chosen to set their minds on things above ought to sell their earthly riches and to distribute their possessions to the poor, that they might gain heavenly treasure. As the evangelist says, however, "The scribes and Pharisees, who were lovers of money, heard these things and mocked him."[139] These were eager to engage in subtle arguments with great attention to minute details, even going into the most insignificant of matters. Nor were they lenient with respect to those who did not bring the tithes prescribed by the law, and yet they themselves had little regard for the law. The Lord made this abundantly clear when he said to them, "Woe to you, scribes and Pharisees, hypocrites! For you

---

ness" (cf. Gn 30.13). Gad has been interpreted by modern scholars as meaning either "good fortune" (cf. Gn 30.11 NRSV) or a "band" or "troop" of men (NKJV), either of soldiers or outlaws. It is perhaps significant that the Greek term here employed by Cyril, *peiratêrion*, has two distinct senses. Firstly, it may mean "testing," as Cyril uses it. Secondly, however, it may indicate a "band of robbers." Since this latter is in fact one of the actual meanings present in the Hebrew, it seems evident that Cyril obtained his interpretation of the names from a Greek source in which he found Gad interpreted as *peiratêrion*. In this his source was in all probability correct, yet Cyril mistakenly took the word in its other sense of "testing."

137. Mk 12.14.
138. Mt 21.38; Mk 12.7; Lk 20.14.
139. Lk 16.14.

tithe mint, dill, and cumin, and have neglected the weightier matters of the law: justice, mercy, and faith."[140]

So then, Gad indicates "testing," and Asher "riches." Both of these were born from the maidservant Zilpah after Dan and Naphtali, who were born from Bilhah. In these matters, however, the time before the coming of our Savior is described for us, during which Rachel, the Gentile church, was still barren. That she would give birth to many and would rear a countless number of children, Isaiah had in fact earlier proclaimed when he said, "Rejoice, O barren one, who bears no children. Cry out and shout, you who are not in labor; for the children of the desolate woman are more than those of the woman who has a husband."[141] The divine David himself also said plainly with regard to God, "He settles the barren woman in a home, a mother rejoicing over her children."[142] Also, the Master and God of all said to this barren woman in one place, "Lift up your eyes, look around and see them all,"[143] and again, "Behold, they come from afar, some from the north, and some from the west, and others from the land of the Persians."[144]

Let us examine, as seems appropriate, at what point in time the barren woman gave birth to children in this way. Now after those sons were born to the maidservants, Reuben, the firstborn of Jacob, found the mandrakes in the field and brought them to Leah his mother. When Rachel asked for some, she gave them to her. Leah, having taken the mandrakes, gave birth to two more sons, Issachar and, of course, Zebulun. Then God remembered Rachel; her womb was opened, and she gave birth to Joseph and, last of all, to Benjamin.

So then, that Leah prefigures the Jewish synagogue [220] and Rachel the Gentile church, the word indicates to us many times. Since it is not profitable to go on repeating this fact, let us leave this matter, and let us now state what figurative meaning the mandrakes found by Reuben the firstborn might have. And

---

140. Mt 23.23.
141. Is 54.1.
142. Ps 113.9 (112.9 LXX).
143. Is 49.18.
144. Is 49.12.

what should we suppose is the meaning intended by the distribution to both women equally? For Leah gave some to Rachel. And what about the matter of the births of the children and the mystery this brings forth in the meanings of their names?

11. Mandrakes grow out in the fields and have the appearance of apples. That they induce drowsiness and bring a deep drunken-like stupor upon those who partake of them, I think there is no need to demonstrate with many words. It is in fact sometimes the practice of doctors to use mandrakes as a natural remedy in treating those suffering from insomnia.

Mandrakes also give us in a figure a hint at the mystery of Christ, who in a certain manner fell asleep for us.[145] Coming down, he emptied himself even to the point of death, though he came to life again. For he was by nature God and became flesh. Where death is taken as actually being in the order of a sleep, it requires also a coming back to life. So it is as though the whole mystery of Christ were present in these things.

So too, the divine Paul lays it upon those who were taken away from what is easy to understand to a strange way of thinking, saying, "I delivered to you as of first importance what I also received, that Christ died for our sins according to the Scriptures, and that he was buried, and that he was raised on the third day according to the Scriptures."[146] And later, "If Christ is proclaimed as raised from the dead, how do certain people among you say that there is no resurrection of the dead?"[147] Since Christ was the first among men to show forth death as sleep (for he was by nature life), he henceforth became a door or path, as it were, being born in the nature of man in order to triumph over death. Accordingly, the most-wise Paul in various places speaks of those taken in death as having fallen asleep, as though they will presently also come back to life through Christ. Again he says, "For if we believe that Christ died and rose again, even so God will raise up with Jesus those who have fallen asleep, and will present them with us."[148]

---

145. Sleep may have connotations of death (cf. Dn 12.2; 1 Cor 15.20).
146. 1 Cor 15.3–4; var. omit "according to the Scriptures."
147. 1 Cor 15.12.
148. 1 Thes 4.14; 2 Cor 4.14.

The mandrakes, then, signify sleep. These were found by Reuben the firstborn who brought them to his mother, and she shared them with her sister. Those of firstborn Israel, who came first in time, had a rich understanding of the mystery pertaining to Christ. When they brought to their own mother, Jerusalem, the wonderful discovery they had made through the discernment of their minds, they gave her reason to rejoice. For before the call of the Gentiles, the divine disciples instructed the Jews throughout all Judea in the mystery of Christ. Though it may be that not all of them believed, they[149] had the first contact with the message about Christ. Yet a remnant was in fact saved, as the Scriptures say.[150]

That the Jews preceded the Gentiles in the matter of faith is absolutely clear and not in the least bit obscure. Having taken the mandrakes, Leah gave birth to two sons, Issachar and Zebulun. Issachar means "reward," while the other name, Zebulun, means "prosperity" or "blessing." [221] As I have already stated, through the holy apostles the synagogue of the Jews was, in effect, receiving the mystery of Christ from its own children. The mother was shown through the prospering of her children what it means to have a reward and blessing before God. For the forgiveness of our offenses directly proves that faith toward Christ is not without its reward. Our Lord Jesus Christ himself also confirmed this when he said, "Truly, truly, I tell you, he who believes in me has eternal life."[151] The blessed Paul, too, says nothing less: "The word is near you, in your mouth and in your heart, that is, the word of faith which we proclaim. If you say with your mouth that Jesus is Lord, and you believe in your heart that God raised him from the dead, you will be saved. For with the heart a person believes, resulting in righteousness, and with the mouth he confesses, resulting in salvation."[152] What, then, could be a greater or more precious reward than the preserving of one's soul? That this matter is more important and more excellent than every other thing, the Savior himself per-

---

149. Var. add "all."
150. E.g., Is 10.21; Rom 11.5.
151. Jn 6.47.
152. Rom 10.8–10.

suades us when he says, "What profit is it to a man if he gains the whole world yet loses his soul? Or what will a man give in exchange for his soul?"[153] The reward, then, is glorious salvation for those who believe.

That the blessing granted to those justified in Christ ought to be valued greatly cannot be doubted. We have indeed been sanctified by the Spirit. The blessed David says, "The blessing of the Lord be upon you. May you be blessed by the Lord, who made heaven and earth."[154] Through Isaiah God also said to the mother of those who believe, namely the church, "I will put my Spirit upon your offspring, and my blessing upon your children."[155] The most-wise Paul also wrote to those justified by faith, saying, "Blessed be the God and Father of our Lord Jesus Christ, who has blessed us with every spiritual blessing."[156] Those who partake richly of heavenly blessings, how can they not prosper in every good work? For "the way of the godly," it says, "has been made straight, and the way of the godly has been prepared; for the way of the Lord is justice."[157]

Now concerning the synagogue of the Jews, God said in one place, "Behold, I will hedge up her ways, and she will not find her path."[158] You, however, he brings into the heavenly places along a level path, like a road that has been cleared, and he instructs his holy ministers, "Open the gates, let the people that observes righteousness and proclaims truth enter, maintaining truth and keeping peace."[159] And again he says, "Prepare a way for my people, and cast the stones out of the road,"[160] lest falling over stumbling blocks in the way they should shrink back from those good things they eagerly pursue.

So then, Leah gave birth to those made prosperous through a reward and blessings from God. Rachel likewise received the

---

153. Mt 15.26.
154. Ps 129.8 (128.8 LXX); 115.15 (113.23 LXX).
155. Is 44.3.
156. Eph 1.3.
157. Is 26.7–8.
158. Hos 2.6 (2.8 LXX).
159. Is 26.2–3.
160. Is 62.10.

mandrakes[161] and gave birth to Joseph. The church, having received the [224] mystery of Christ through the holy apostles in a similar way to her sister, the Jewish synagogue, has shown herself to be the mother of a people always being added to, and so becoming an immeasurable multitude (for Joseph means "added by God"). The church of the Gentiles, then, is added to the flock of Israel. Accordingly, Christ also said, "I have other sheep, which are not of this fold. I must lead them also, and they will hear my voice; and there will be one flock and one shepherd."[162]

So to the former sheep, the flock taken out from the Gentiles has been added, as I just said, and they enjoy continual and unending bountiful increase, until in later times Benjamin himself is born, that is, the people who are the "son of pain."

12. Who, then, is this that ceases to bear any further children and who has, as it were, passed into another life? For Rachel died in the pangs of giving birth to Benjamin. To ascertain this precisely, we shall again refer ourselves to God, and also to those who have more understanding than we do. It then does no harm to speak what comes to mind.

I think, then, that the people who are the "son of pain" might suitably be interpreted as the multitude of believers at the end times of the world. For at that time there will be the son of lawlessness, "who opposes and exalts himself against all that is called God or that is worshiped, so that he takes his seat like God[163] in the temple of God, declaring himself to be God."[164] Who, then, is this? He will oppose the saints and will be no different from wild animals. For as the Savior himself said, "There will be great tribulation, such as has not been from the beginning of the world[165] and never will be."[166] That the perversity and inhumanity of that one will fall upon no others but the saints, Christ himself clearly indicated when he added, "Unless

161. Var. add "from her."
162. Jn 10.16.
163. Var. omit "like God."
164. 2 Thes 2.4.
165. Var. "of creation."
166. Mt 24.21.

those days were shortened, no human being would be saved. Yet for the sake of the elect those days will be shortened."[167]

For when persecution shall come against the faith of all who are elect and genuine believers, how terrible and unbearable will the violence be, and how lamentable the torments. That time, when the strength of those undergoing suffering is put to the test, will therefore, I believe, be greatly contracted and limited by the compassionate God. This is what the most-wise Paul encourages us to think when he says, "God is faithful, who shall not let you be tested beyond what you are able to bear, but with the trial he will also provide the way out, so that you can endure it."[168]

So when Benjamin was born, that is, the people accompanied by pain and death, Rachel ceased to be.[169] For, as I said just now, the church passed into another life, meaning that we ourselves through faith in Christ have been richly blessed in our union with God through the Spirit. Do not be amazed that death brought about a change in Rachel with respect to the things of this world. For this matter at times confuses some when they are applying the spiritual meaning of what happened long ago. The church in fact will eventually cease to be and will in a certain manner be extinguished by death, this being the transference of the church to better things.

Concerning this we say the following. When you hear the word "church" [225], it means the holy company of believers. Dying may have respect to the fleshly way of life in the world. Such is the way to progress in one's conduct and life in Christ and the manner in which to be transported to better and more transcendent things. For this reason the blessed Paul fiercely rebukes some, saying, "If you have died to the basic principles[170] of the world, why do you submit to regulations as though you were still living in the world?"[171] He further writes to those who have cast off the fleshly and pleasure-seeking life, "For you have

167. Mt 24.22.
168. 1 Cor 10.13.
169. Or "she rested."
170. Or "elemental spirits."
171. Var. omit "in the world"; Col 2.20.

died, and your life is hidden with Christ in God. When Christ, your life, appears, then you will also appear with him in glory."[172] So, he plainly says, we must put to death our earthly members, meaning immorality and uncleanness, and things of that kind.

Surely then, the death of Rachel signifies that of the whole company of believers, namely the church. It is understood as dying in Christ and being transported, as it were, to another life, since it is indeed the case that our condition will be transformed from corruption to incorruption, from death to life, from weakness to power, from dishonor to glory, from finite time to endless life. It is in this state also that we shall continually be with Christ, through whom and with whom be glory and might to God the Father, together with the Holy Spirit, for ever and ever. Amen.

172. Col 3.3–4.

BOOK FIVE: GENESIS 30–35

Concerning Jacob

T MANY TIMES and in many ways[1] the inspired Scripture set forth in advance figures of the salvation to come through Christ, thereby bringing considerable benefit to those reading it. Very much as those thoroughly trained in the skill of drawing make use of various forms involving many colors, bringing the shadows into clearer vision and much enhancing the elegance of what is drawn, so also God, the wise Artificer of all things, through many diverse glorious things foreshowed in a subtle manner[2] the beauty of the mystery. As a result, by perceiving the mystery in figures and by applying their understanding to this initial and introductory instruction, those being taught these things might be better prepared to receive the truth.

Now we spend our lives in this world differing little from, or perhaps even being inferior to, the irrational animals. For God directed a just rebuke [228] against the people of Israel when he said, "An ox knows its owner, and a donkey its master's manger; but Israel does not know me, and my people do not understand."[3] If the Jewish people, who had the law as a tutor, were condemned for such dreadful ignorance, how much more accountable will the Gentiles be, upon whom the great darkness of the error of polytheism has fallen? Ever inclined towards what is base, and being caught up in fleshly desires, they hasten only after thoughts of earthly things. It cannot so much as be

---

1. Cf. Heb 1.1.
2. Or "in fine detail."
3. Is 1.3.

said that they are capable of raising their minds[4] to consider the wonders of love for God.

For this reason the blessed prophets, lamenting and weeping over us men, expended many thousands of words. For indeed the blessed Isaiah said, "The grave[5] has enlarged its appetite, and opened its mouth without ceasing."[6] For men did not turn away from evil, but Satan exercised his tyrannical power against us with unbearable harshness, and we wretched ones have descended into Hades, from which we need to be delivered. There death, finding us to be sinners, greedily devours and feeds upon us, so to speak.

Therefore, as I said earlier, it was not without tears that the divine David himself spoke of this plight. He once said this concerning us: "Like sheep they are placed in Hades; death will feed upon them."[7] Then again he said, "Give heed, O Shepherd of Israel, you who lead Joseph like a sheep; you who sit upon the cherubim, manifest yourself. Stir up your might, and come to save us."[8] Consequently, not all of us remain under the hand of death. For God the Father sent to us from heaven the good shepherd, our Lord Jesus Christ, who does not feed in Hades upon those placed under his care, but rather leads them to life and incorruption. For he grazes his sheep among the lilies, in good pasture and in a fertile place, according to what is written.[9] He sets before us spiritual fodder, making us intoxicated upon the springs of heaven and filling us with abundant fruit. He multiplies us, moreover, into an immeasurable multitude of peoples.

One may again observe how the divine Jacob portrays matters by means of shadows, which is the very thing I said. So the events written about him as presented in the word and those elements that seem obscure in the literal account we will make as clear as we are able.

---

4. Lit. "the eye of the mind"; var. "opening their eyes."
5. LXX has "Hades."
6. Is 5.14.
7. Ps 49.14 (48.15 LXX).
8. Ps 80.1–2 (79.2–3 LXX).
9. Cf. Ezek 34.14.

Now it is written here: *It happened that when Rachel had given birth to Joseph, Jacob said to Laban, "Send me away that I may go to my own place and my own land. Give me my wives and my children, for whom I have served you, so that I may leave. You know the service I have rendered you, and how your animals have fared under my care. For before I came you had little, and it has increased abundantly, and the Lord has blessed you since I arrived.*[10] *So now, when shall I also make a house*[11] *for myself?" Laban said to him, "What shall I give you?" And Jacob said, "You shall not give me anything. If you will do* [229] *this one thing for me, I will still tend your sheep today and look after them. Let all your sheep pass by today,*[12] *and separate from among them every sheep that is spotted or dark, and every grey animal from among the rams, and also every one that is white and speckled from among the goats. These will be my reward. So my righteousness will answer for me in the future, when those animals which are my reward come before you. Whatever is with me that is not speckled or white among the goats, and whatever is not grey among the rams, will be considered stolen by me." Then Laban said to him, "Let it be as you say." But that same day he separated the male goats that were speckled and white and all the female goats that were speckled and white, every animal that had white in it, and every grey animal from among the rams, and he put them in the care of his sons. Then he put a three-day journey between them and Jacob, while Jacob continued to tend the sheep of Laban that remained.*[13]

We must again bring together into a short space the breadth of material found in the literal account, and further, we must discuss what appropriate meaning might be found in the spiritual contemplation of these things.

2. So the blessed Jacob served Laban for his two daughters, Leah and Rachel. Then after a long time had passed, Joseph was born to him from Rachel, the wife who was especially beloved. Following this, Jacob felt restless, and understandably so, as he wished to return to his own home as soon as possible. The

---

10. Lit. "at my foot" (see further below). See n. 14 below.
11. Here meaning "household" or "family." Since Cyril is presently to relate this term to the "house" of God in the sense of a temple, a literal rendering has been retained.
12. Var. omit "today."
13. Gn 30.25–26, 29–36.

reason given for his departure is not implausible. Jacob said, "For if I were going to tend your animals continually for no reward, when could I ever make a house for myself also?" That is to say, "When could I ever provide the necessities of life for my own children, and be called the master of my own house?" This is how it was with Jacob. Laban, on the other hand, wanted to hold on to Jacob, seeing that he was a good shepherd, and he said he had been blessed since Jacob's arrival. He would never let him go, therefore, even though the prescribed period of service for his daughters had come to an end.

So Laban promised to provide him with a pleasing reward. He openly affirmed that Jacob had been useful, capable, and most hard-working, and had moreover brought him a blessing from God, since Jacob said, *"God has blessed you since I arrived."*[14] Laban said these things anticipating what he would do. Then Jacob claimed his reward and promised to tend Laban's flocks. But Laban picked out and separated animals for himself from those that were marked, which were white and dark-colored. Jacob and his own children were some distance away with the flock allotted to him, yet he also continued to shepherd the rest of Laban's flock.

So what the plain meaning of these matters might be for us, and how the spiritual subtleties are to be made clear, it is now necessary to state.

3. First of all, we can say without any doubt that Jacob stands for Christ himself,[15] for Christ is the true "one who overcomes,"[16] in that he utterly trampled upon sin. And as it is understood, he appeared as a man, being younger and born later than those who came before him, by which I mean the holy prophets and Moses. Nevertheless, he possesses the privileges of the elder and is the firstborn on account of his being the Only-Begotten among many brothers. He is himself the one blessed by the [232] Fa-

---

14. Cyril here includes a brief explanation of the Hebraic idiom, which is literally "at my foot." He adds: "Instead of 'arrival,' 'foot' has been put."

15. Lit. "clothed with the face of Christ."

16. Cyril uses the Greek term (*pternistēs*) that relates to the name of Jacob, meaning "one who grasps the heel [*pterna*]," that is, one who supplants or gets the better of another (cf. Gn 25.26).

ther through an abundance of wheat and wine.[17] The nations serve him, and the rulers bow down to him. He who curses him is accursed, but he who blesses him is blessed, according to the blessing of Isaac.[18]

Christ is the one who left heaven, just as Jacob left his father's home. And he came to Laban, who may be likened to the world, to one who never knew the true nature of God, to one very much plagued with the error of polytheism, for Laban was an idolater. The world was indeed Christ's own, since he is also understood to be in very nature God and the Lord and Maker of all. Yet the world is not any more his own because of man's apostasy and it seems now to belong to another on account of sin. It is Satan who is in fact upheld as king.

So the Word came down from heaven, having left, as it were, his Father's home, as I just said. He was like a stranger in his own world. To this, the wise John bears witness when he says, "He was in the world, and the world was made through him, but the world did not know him."[19] While this may perhaps be well applied to the time when he resided among us, even before his Incarnation among his own creation, while he was God, he was unknown to the world. Yet he still enacted for us his providential care out of his natural goodness and divine kindness. This the divine Jacob, being himself a type, directly showed forth. For Jacob tended Laban's sheep, even though he had absolutely nothing from him as a reward. Yet, having been led to be joined in marriage to Laban's two daughters, Leah and Rachel, and having become the father of his own rightful children, the one thing he had was hope.

Now the Son, being by nature God, was in the world, which is represented by Laban. And, being God, he was, in a certain manner, tending[20] to humankind and administering the necessities of life, giving produce from the earth, sending forth streams of water and flowing rivers, making the sun to rise, and

17. Cf. Gn 27.28.
18. Cf. Gn 27.29.
19. Jn 1.10.
20. Cyril here uses a verb (*katepoimaine*), probably of his own invention, related to shepherding.

sending down the rains, according to what is written.[21] He places within human nature an innate understanding, for he himself is "the true light which gives light to every man coming into the world."[22] He carried out these things, as I said, only on account of his natural kindness, and he received at that time nothing by way of a reward from those in the world—no praise, no worship, no right notions or any sure understanding of himself. He foreknew, however, that he would in time have two wives who would be mothers of his own rightful children, to whom in a spiritual sense they would give birth. And who were these women? The first was Leah, the elder, who is a type of the synagogue of the Jews. A short while later came the second, the much-longed-for Rachel, the younger, who is the church of the Gentiles. And Rachel gave birth to Joseph, meaning "added by God," for the company of the Gentiles has been added to those of Israel. In other words, the interpretation relates to the eventual adding of others to the immeasurable multitude of believers.

Take note of this, for the detail present in these matters is extremely profitable. Leah gave birth before Rachel, and then the two maidservants Bilhah and Zilpah did so. [233] During this time Jacob kept quiet,[23] and as yet had no plans for making his own house. Then Rachel gave birth to Joseph, following which Jacob desired his own house. He asked, *"When, then, shall I make a house for myself?"* For indeed the synagogue of the Jews had given birth to those who were in bondage under the law.

Evidently, Christ allowed that he would not at that time have his own house, since he did not in fact greatly approve of the stone temple that Solomon built. On that account the Lord once severely rebuked the insolent Jews over this temple, saying, "Heaven is my throne, and earth is the footstool under my feet. What kind of house will you build for me? What will the place of my rest be?"[24] Neither, however, was Israel the spiritual house of God, for he did not dwell among them. Yet once the Gentile church had given birth to the new people of God, that is, those

---

21. Cf. Mt 5.45.
22. Jn 1.9.
23. Or "remained inactive."
24. Is 66.1.

who were "added," the Savior then prepared his own house for himself. And what house is this? It is we who have come to believe, about whom he says through the prophet, "I will put my law in their minds, and I will write it upon their hearts. I will be their God, and they will be my people."[25] So he dwells within us through the Spirit, as I just said, and not in Israel. That the Jews who lived before Christ's advent did not partake of the Spirit the most-wise John, speaking in a manner corresponding to the type, would make clear in saying, "For the Spirit was not yet given, because Jesus had not yet been glorified."[26]

After Christ had been raised from the dead and set about reforming the nature of humankind in the divine image, he breathed upon the holy apostles first, saying, "Receive the Holy Spirit."[27] The divine Paul also said in one place, "For you did not receive a spirit of bondage leading again to fear, but you received the Spirit of adoption as sons, by whom we cry out, 'Abba, Father.'"[28] Within Israel, then, there was a spirit of bondage. Yet within us who come forth from Rachel, from the church taken out of the Gentiles, there is the Spirit of God, which brings us to adoption as sons, making us into a spiritual house. So the offspring of Rachel are free.

Now Rachel's eyes were fine and beautiful. Leah, however, did not have such good eyes, since the synagogue of the Jews does not see well. The most-wise Paul also bears witness to this when he says, "For until this very day the same veil remains over the reading of the old covenant. It has not been removed, because only in Christ is it done away with. Even to this day, when Moses is read, a veil lies upon their hearts. But when anyone turns to the Lord, the veil is taken away. Now the Lord is the Spirit, and where the Spirit of the Lord is, there is freedom. Yet we all," he continues to say, "with unveiled faces, beholding[29] the glory of the Lord, are being transformed into the same image from one degree of glory to another, which comes from the

25. Jer 31.33.
26. Jn 7.39.
27. Jn 20.22.
28. Rom 8.15.
29. Or "reflecting."

Lord, who is the Spirit."[30] Do you understand that we behold the glory of the Lord with good eyes and unveiled faces? For, as I just said, Rachel's eyes were bright.

When Rachel, the younger woman, had given birth to Joseph, the divine Jacob was then eager to go home. Laban, however, sought to keep him and [236] said he had been blessed through an enormous increase in his flocks. So the world is greatly in need of God. Even though perhaps it does not say this, it does know and concede that all the necessities of life and all good things are from God.

Now the blessed Jacob, no longer being able to stay for nothing, requested a reward. And the reward, namely the spotted and dark-colored animals, was not displeasing to him. Accordingly, even though right from the beginning he had been caring for the world out of his natural and divine kindness, the Word of God, through whom all things exist, allowed those in the world to walk in their own ways, as is written.[31] Since the church has given birth to the new people of God, which is ever increasing, that is, those who have now received spiritual rebirth through faith in him, in return for his providence he is asking the world for the reward, as it were, of those who are most willing to believe, of whom the dark and spotted animals are figures.

What does this mean, then? Always among flocks of sheep and goats there are single-colored animals which are more valued by those who tend them. Those which are spotted and marked are of lesser worth and are not reckoned equal to the others. Their wool is not of a single color, but occurs in small alternate markings or is of different colors all mixed up. And so Christ receives from the world, not by any means those who are honored by it or valued among men, but rather he receives as many that are considered of low estate among them and those of less repute. The divine Paul also affirms this fact when he writes to the believers, "Consider your calling, brothers, that not many of you were wise according to human standards, and not many mighty, not many of noble birth. Rather, God chose the foolish things of the world to shame the wise, and God chose the weak things of

30. 2 Cor 3.14–18.
31. Acts 14.16.

the world to shame the strong."[32] Looking at it in another way, should one wish to be more precise about such things, these are the dark and spotted ones. For those who are in Christ have a varied manner of attractiveness in both works and speech.

The grey and the black may in fact be reckoned as a figure and shadow of the mystery pertaining to Christ, and which many take as depicting some dark and obscure teaching[33] concerning him. For the divine David said somewhere in the book of Psalms, "He made darkness his covering, his tabernacle around him, dark water in the clouds of the air."[34] It is as though it were likening the difficult nature of the doctrines about God to a tabernacle, specifically mentioning also the darkness and dark water in the clouds of the air. Yet Wisdom also promises to grant freely to certain people the ability to interpret parables and dark words, sayings of the wise, and obscure figures. So then, the depth and darkness of the doctrines relating to Christ are presented figuratively to us in the grey color. The other color, that is, the white, applies to what is manifest and, as it were, conspicuous, by which I mean godly deeds. Accordingly, the Master of all indicates ahead of time the cleansing by faith in Christ, saying through the prophet, "Learn to do good, seek justice, deliver the one who is wronged, [237] plead for the orphan, and obtain justice for the widow. Come now, and let us reason together, says the Lord. And though your sins be as crimson, I will make them as white as snow; and though they be as scarlet, I will make them as white as wool."[35]

So then, those of lower status in the world are special and highly valued in the sight of Christ the Savior of all. While being in a way inferior to others, and surpassed in glory, the spotted and those of different colors are to be interpreted spiritually as indicating the deep matters of the doctrines about God. These are rich with respect to dark meanings, and also especially bright and conspicuous in godliness.

Jacob's reward, then, was the spotted animals. Now let us

32. 1 Cor 1.26–27.
33. *logon*, "word," "account," "message."
34. Ps 18.11 (17.12 LXX).
35. Is 1.17–18.

carefully examine, if it so please, the way in which he managed to outwit Laban, and how he increased the number of the animals he obtained, and let us learn from the sacred Scriptures themselves. The account reads as follows: *Jacob took for himself fresh rods from the styrax tree, the almond, and the plane tree. And Jacob peeled them to make white stripes. As he tore away the green bark, the white stripes that he peeled became distinctly visible on the rods. Then he placed the rods that he had peeled among the channels of the watering troughs, so that whenever the sheep came to drink, coming before the rods to drink, the sheep would mate by the rods. The sheep gave birth to white, multicolored, dark, and spotted young. Jacob separated the lambs, and he set a white ram before the sheep, and every multicolored one among the lambs. He set flocks aside for himself and did not mix them with the sheep of Laban. So at the time when the sheep mated, conceiving in the womb, Jacob put the rods before the sheep at the water channels, so that they would mate by the rods. But he did not bring them indiscriminately whenever the sheep gave birth.*[36] *So the insignificant sheep were Laban's, while the notable ones were Jacob's. In this way the man became exceedingly rich.*[37]

We know with respect to the profession of shepherding that sheep and goats give birth to young that resemble themselves in every way, and also that the colors which their offspring end up having are the same as what is being looked at in the act of conceiving. It appears that in some way this happens according to the operation of natural laws. Yet words cannot at all explain such things, and our minds are not able to grasp them.

Now the divine Jacob considered the dark and the spotted animals as valuable according to a divine revelation. For he said to Leah and Rachel, *"It happened that when the sheep were breeding and were pregnant, I saw with my eyes in a dream, and behold, the he-goats and the rams, those that were white, multicolored, dark, and spotted, were mounting the she-goats and the sheep. And the angel of God said to me in a dream, 'Jacob.' And I said, 'What is it?' And he said, 'Lift up your eyes and see the he-goats and the rams mounting the sheep*

---

36. The meaning of the LXX version of this sentence, which Cyril quotes precisely, is difficult to determine.

37. Gn 30.37–43.

and the she-goats, those male animals which are white, multicolored, dark, and spotted."[38] Thus says the sacred Scripture.

Leaving the lower sense of the literal interpretation, let us come now to spiritual matters.

4. A rod figuratively portrays to us Emmanuel once again, for he is specifically so named by the [240] inspired Scripture. The divine Isaiah says, "And a rod will come forth from the root of Jesse, and a blossom will come up from his root."[39] Indeed, the divine David, assuming the role[40] of those who believe, declared to God the Father in heaven, "Your rod and your staff, they have comforted me."[41] We have now in fact received comfort in Christ, and we have made him our support. For it is written, "The Lord will uphold the righteous."[42]

For us spiritual sheep and goats throughout the whole of the inhabited world, Christ presents himself in a certain fashion as a rod—indeed, not merely a rod, but one from *the styrax tree, the almond, and the plane tree.* A tree stands for the uprightness of those things to which testimony is being given. The styrax tree is a symbol of death, for the body which has died is treated with aromatic spices, and the styrax is the most pleasant of spices. So it was that Christ died for us and was buried according to the Scriptures.[43] The almond is a symbol of waking[44] and watchfulness, for by nature it has such an effect upon us. So it was that Christ was raised up for us. For he was not restrained by the gates of Hades, neither was he wholly overcome by the bonds of death. The wood of the plane tree further indicates the passageway upwards, that is to say, the ascension of Christ into heaven, since the plane grows higher than the tallest of trees. So the Son was exalted into the presence of the Father, for Peter said

---

38. Cf. Gn 31.10–12.

39. Is 11.1.

40. *prosôpon,* literally "person," "face." Here is meant the more technical sense of "persona," "character."

41. Ps 23.4 (22.4 LXX).

42. Ps 37.17 (36.17 LXX).

43. Cf. 1 Cor 15.3–4.

44. The word used here (*egrêgorsis*) is a close cognate of terms denoting the idea of resurrection.

that he has been "exalted to the right hand of God."[45] Paul, too, said he has been greatly exalted and has received "the name that is above every name," and receives worship from all.[46]

If one wishes, he may interpret the plane tree in another way. And what way is that? Those who concern themselves with the etymologies of words say that it is because the leaf is extremely wide that the plane tree is so called. Now we too, growing up out of Christ, are in effect made wide[47] through faith and love. Yet the law of the Jews is extremely narrow. The thinking also of those who practice idolatry is greatly limited. Accordingly, through the mouth of the prophet God declares to those of the flocks taken from among the Gentiles, "Learn to hear, you who are straitened."[48] And to the Corinthians, who chose to sink back into the ancient error[49] after experiencing the wideness of the faith, Paul writes and says, "Our mouth has spoken openly to you, O Corinthians; our heart is wide open. You are not straitened by us, but you are straitened in your own affections. Now in return (I speak as to children), open wide your hearts also. Do not be yoked together with unbelievers. For what partnership is there between righteousness and lawlessness? Or what fellowship is there between light and darkness? Or what agreement does Christ have with Belial?"[50] The psalmist also does away with the narrowness of the law when in the Spirit he says to Emmanuel, "Your commandment is exceedingly broad."[51] Again he says, "I ran the way of your commandments, when you enlarged my heart."[52] Further still, he says, "I walked in a wide place, because I sought your commandments."[53] Also, that the

45. Acts 2.33.
46. Cf. Phil 2.9–11.
47. The verb "we are made wide" (*platunometha*) is related to the noun for plane tree (*platanos*).
48. Is 28.19–20. The verb "straitened" (*stenochôroumenoi*) contains an element related to the adjective "narrow" (*stenos*).
49. That is, polytheism.
50. 2 Cor 6.11–15.
51. Ps 119.96 (118.96 LXX).
52. Ps 119.32 (118.32 LXX); "enlarged" may equally be translated "widened."
53. Ps 119.45 (118.45 LXX).

almond rod is [241] a natural cause of wakefulness,[54] as I said just now, God says to the prophet Jeremiah: "What do you see, Jeremiah?" And he said, "A rod of an almond tree." Then the Lord said to him, "You have seen well, for I am watching over my words to perform them."[55]

So then, Christ presents himself to us in the form of a rod which is to be interpreted as one who died and rose again, as one exalted into heaven, and as one who through the Spirit makes wide in a spiritual sense the hearts of those who receive him.

But where did Jacob place the rods? Among the watering troughs. And these troughs and watering places of the spiritual[56] herd—us, that is—may be understood as the writings of Moses and the prophetic declarations, as the word that all but bursts forth to us from God above. For it is written, "And you shall draw water with joy from the wells of salvation."[57] There we will find Emmanuel, the rod of power, who by his death for us is also the firstborn from the dead and is exalted in glory, and who increases the number of believers, as I just said. All the words of the holy prophets and of Moses hint at the mystery of Christ. Therefore, the wise Paul also says, "Christ is the end of the law and the prophets."[58]

Furthermore, Jacob peeled white stripes in the rods by pulling off the green. And so the animals next to them conceived a multicolored offspring. Christ in a way pulls off the shadow from the law, and the veil from the prophetic writings. Thus, revealing to us the pure[59] and quite striking doctrine contained within them, he imparts to it a spiritual fragrance. Moreover, he leads people to conceive virtue, those who wish to be multicolored, that is to say, to practice a double virtue in both word and deed. And so the divine prophets of those justified by faith,

---

54. Or "watchfulness."

55. Jer 1.11–12. The Hebrew contains a verbal pun on "almond" (*šāqēd*) and "watching over" (*šōqēd*).

56. Although the adjective *logikos* has the basic meaning of "rational," it may also convey the more specialized sense of "spiritual," as in Rom 12.1 ("spiritual service") and 1 Pt 2.2 ("spiritual milk").

57. Is 12.3.

58. Rom 10.4.

59. Lit. "whitened."

delving beneath the surface,[60] clearly proclaim, "Because of the fear of you, O Lord, we have conceived and been in labor, and we have brought forth the breath of your salvation."[61] The blessed Isaiah in another passage characteristically says, "Be strong, you weak hands and feeble knees. Comfort one another, you faint-hearted; be strong, do not fear. Behold, our God renders judgment, and he will render it."[62] And again, "Behold, the Lord is coming with strength, and his arm with authority. Like a shepherd he will tend his flock; he will gather the lambs in his arms, and comfort those with young."[63] That is to say, he will be a spiritual comfort for those already laboring with the divine word, that they should be fruitful, and for those about to bring forth the glories of a gospel life. For this is the fruit of a holy and undefiled soul.

It says that Jacob set apart flocks for himself and did not mix them with the sheep of Laban. For what is profane is liable to affect that which is holy, and what is dirty that which is clean. Now those who belong to Christ are set apart and refuse to mix together with those of the world, having been set free from all love of the flesh. They are not insignificant [244] with respect to this life, but are most noteworthy on account of their virtue. For it says, *the insignificant sheep were Laban's, while the notable ones were Jacob's.*

Yet Jacob was envied. Once they saw that he was rich and successful, Laban's sons were consumed with jealousy. Jacob therefore planned to take his leave and to go back again to his father's home. For it is written: *The man became exceedingly rich, and had many flocks, oxen, male and female servants, camels, donkeys, and mules.*[64] *Now Jacob heard the words of Laban's sons, saying, "Jacob has taken everything belonging to our father and has gained all this splendor from what was our father's."*[65] And Jacob noticed Laban's atti-

---

60. Lit. "running under the face." Cf. the rendering in Migne's Latin column: *figuram prae se ferentes aperte* ("openly bringing the image before themselves").

61. Is 26.18.

62. Is 35.3–4; var. add "which we have performed upon the earth" (as LXX).

63. Is 40.10–11.

64. Var. omit "mules."

65. Gn 30.43–31.1.

tude, and indeed it was not the same towards him as it had been before. Then the Lord said to Jacob, *"Return to the land of your father and to your relatives, and I will be with you."*[66] So Jacob sent and called Rachel and Leah to the field where his flocks were. He said to them, *"I can see that your father's attitude towards me is not as it was before, but the God of my Father has been with me. You yourselves know that I have served your father with all my strength. But your father deceived me and changed my wages for the ten lambs."*[67] Then he said, *"God has taken away all the livestock of your father and given them to me."*[68] For indeed our Lord Jesus Christ has truly become rich, gathering his own worshipers together in the world as an immeasurable multitude, who are also a wonderful offering of good hearts[69] that are subject to him and who confess, "We are the people of his pasture and the sheep of his hand."[70]

At these things, however, the sons of the world are not content to remain silent. Seeing their own father being robbed, as it were, and the hand of the good shepherd extending to the more notable among the sheep, which being brought to the birth by Christ also vary with regard to many different kinds of virtues, these sons of the world grumble and say, *"Jacob has taken everything belonging to our father and has gained all this splendor from what was our father's."* And they were by no means speaking falsely, for their words are true. Christ has in fact gathered to himself all those in the world; having enclosed in his own folds the flocks of those who have come to believe, he has riches befitting God and the most excellent glory. For in one place he himself said to God the Father in heaven, "All that is mine is yours, and all that is yours is mine, and I am glorified in them."[71]

So we also note Jacob's reward.[72] *He had,* it says, *many flocks, oxen, male and female servants, camels, and donkeys.* You see Christ, too, gathering people from every race, according to what is writ-

---

66. Gn 31.3.
67. Contextually, the LXX reading "for the ten lambs" makes little sense. The Hebrew here reads "ten times."
68. Gn 30.43–31.9.
69. Lit. "mind" or "thinking" (*dianoia*).
70. Ps 95.7 (94.7 LXX).
71. Jn 17.10.
72. Var. "wealth."

ten: "The kingdom of heaven[73] is like a net which is cast into the sea, and which gathers in some of every kind."[74] He takes in the slave in order that he might make manifest glorious freedom. He takes in those under the law who in a way are already holy [245] and suitable for becoming a spiritual sacrifice, having as it were the place of an ox, in order that, having brought them into the brilliance of the gospel way of life, he might make them holier still. Moreover, he takes in the unholy and unclean, who have the place of a camel or a donkey, so to speak, in order that, having refined them from the impurity of the error of polytheism, he might join them cleansed and sanctified to the assembly[75] of the saints.

Therefore, since Laban's sons were moved to envy, and since Laban himself also began to look downcast and sullen, and his countenance was filled with jealousy—*"his attitude," it says, "was not the same as it had been before"*—God commanded Jacob to return to his own family. So he sent for his wives, Leah and Rachel, and openly told them of the wrong done by their father. *Then he further said, "God has taken away all the livestock of your father and given them to me."*[76] *Rachel and Leah answered and said to him, "Is there still any portion or inheritance for us in our father's house? Are we not considered strangers by him? For he has sold us and completely consumed our money. All the wealth and glory which God has taken away from our father will be ours and our children's; now, then, do whatever God has said to you."*[77]

Now while the world and its children show a sad countenance because of Christ, comfort from heaven above, that is, from the Father, is given to the brides of the Savior, namely to the churches. Yet this comfort comes through the Son, conveying to us, as it were, words from the Father, for "he whom God has sent speaks the words of God," as John states.[78]

Note how God spoke to Jacob and then Jacob in turn spoke to his brides, Leah and Rachel. The word of comfort was that

---

73. Var. "of God."
74. Mt 13.47.
75. Lit. "choirs."
76. Gn 31.9.
77. Gn 31.14–16.
78. Jn 3.34.

they should depart from their father's household together with their own bridegroom. So the blessed psalmist says to the church in the Spirit, "Listen, O daughter, consider and incline your ear. Forget your people and your father's house, because the king has desired your beauty. He is your lord, and you will bow down to him."[79]

Jacob, therefore, spoke to his brides of the matters he had heard from God. And what were Jacob's words? They were an indictment of Laban—how he had been unjust and wicked, and how when a reward was owed he had been slow to pay it. Christ himself also indicts the world of exceedingly great dullness of heart, since it refuses to render thank offerings to him who is Master, and has no desire to bring spiritual offerings, namely faith and love, by way of a debt and repayment for the care he gives it. All things, however, have come into his possession, God the Father drawing them to him. For in a certain place the Son said to him, "Those you have given me out of the world were yours, and you gave them to me."[80] This, then, is what *"God has taken away all the livestock of your father and given them to me"* was referring to.

So the chaste brides of the Savior are commanded to follow him willingly, and he says they had been sold to him, as it were, out of [248] the world. For with his own blood Emmanuel has bought the churches, and they have long since been separated from their father. There is no share or portion for them in the world, out of which they have been called. Rather, they and their children have riches that surpass all reason and understanding. They are granted a portion and lot, glory and praise, and everything whatsoever that leads to splendor and prosperity.

Therefore, the world and its children are downcast over Christ. When they see the extent of his glory, and how he makes everything under heaven subject to himself, and how he has dominion over the earth, they are consumed with burning jealousy. As they grumble about these things and denounce them, their frenzy against him increases. They even commit acts of persecution and murder; such is the force of their endeavors with

79. Ps 45.10–11 (44.11–12 LXX).
80. Jn 17.6.

which they oppose the glory of the Savior, and of the hostility that they show towards the churches under his authority, and towards his children, that is, the multitude of believers. Such a thing is not hard to see for those who care to learn from the events that follow.

It says, *Then Jacob arose, put his wives and his children upon camels, took all his possessions and all the household baggage that he had acquired in Mesopotamia, and everything that belonged to him, and left to go to Isaac his father in the land of Canaan. Now when Laban had gone to shear his sheep, Rachel stole her father's idols. Then Jacob set out secretly from Laban the Syrian, and did not tell him that he was running away. So he fled with all that belonged to him. He crossed the river and hurried to Mount Gilead. On the third day Laban the Syrian was told that Jacob had fled. So taking all his kinsmen with him, he pursued Jacob for a seven-day journey and caught up with him at Mount Gilead. But God came to Laban the Syrian in a dream at night, and said to him, "Be careful that you do not say anything evil to Jacob." So Laban caught up with Jacob. Jacob pitched his tent on the mountain, and Laban placed his kinsmen on Mount Gilead.*[81]

When Laban met up with the divine Jacob, he greatly criticized him for having fled secretly, and for having, in effect, stolen his daughters and also his household gods. Laban said to him, *"Now you have gone away because you so desired to leave for your father's house, but why did you steal my gods?"*[82] *Yet Jacob did not know,* it says, *that Rachel his wife had stolen them.*[83] Then Laban looked for his gods, but he did not find them with Leah, nor in the tents of the maidservants Bilhah and Zilpah. When Rachel knew that she would be searched by her father, she outwitted him in a most elegant way. For it says that *she took the idols and put them inside the saddle of a camel and sat upon them.*[84] She said to her father, *"Do not be displeased, sir, that I am not able to stand up before you, because the way of women is upon me."* So Laban searched the whole of Jacob's household, but he did not find the idols.[85]

81. Gn 31.17–25.
82. Gn 31.30.
83. Gn 31.32.
84. Gn 31.34.
85. Gn 31.35.

Now while Laban was feeling perplexed and in all probability [249] mourning the loss of his gods, the blessed Jacob not unreasonably complained at how Laban had pursued him for no good reason and had made completely unfounded accusations against him. Then the matter of an agreement between them was proposed, and a pact to unite the two of them in peace was transacted. It says, *Laban answered and said to Jacob, "Your daughters are my daughters, and your sons are my sons, and your animals are my animals, and everything that you see here belongs to me and my daughters. But what can I do to them today and to the children they have borne? So now come, let us make a covenant, me and you, and it shall be a witness between me and you." Laban also said to him, "Behold, although no one is with us, understand that God is witness between me and you." Then Jacob took a stone and set it up as a pillar. He said to his kinsmen, "Gather stones." So they gathered stones and made them into a heap, and they ate there by the heap. Laban then said to Jacob, "This heap shall testify between me and you this day." So Laban called it "Heap of Testimony," while Jacob called it "Witness Heap."*[86]

5. So in these things above we have related the account in a flowing and brief manner, giving our attention to the literal events. It is now necessary to explain their inner meaning.

It does not require many words to demonstrate clearly the fact that the world became mad at Christ, and was incited by rage, because he was made rich with the flocks of believers. For see how, when Jacob departed together with his children, Laban pursued him and called after him. In a way, Christ also departs from the world, together with his brides, that is, the churches. It is as though he removes himself with his entire household, calling out to those who belong to him, "Rise up, let us go from here,"[87] speaking spiritually that is. The manner of departure is not physical, nor does it involve any bodily move from one place to another. It would be quite strange to think or say such. Rather, it is the moving away from the mind set upon worldly things to the desire to do things approved by God that is profitably attained. As the blessed Paul writes, "Here we have no lasting city, but we are looking for the one that is to come, whose designer

---

86. Gn 31.43–44, 50, 45–48.
87. Jn 14.31.

and maker is God."[88] Another of the holy apostles writes, "I urge you as strangers and aliens to abstain from fleshly lusts, which wage war against the soul."[89] Though we walk upon the earth, our manner of life is heavenly, and we are indeed eager not to live carnally any more but rather in a holy and spiritual way. Paul urges us to do this when he writes, "Do not be conformed to this world, but be transformed by the renewing of your mind, so that you may discern what is the good, acceptable, and perfect will of God."[90] When we are not conformed to the world and have come out from worldly error, we shall be imitators of Christ. And knowing this to be so, the Savior said, "If you were of the world, the world would love its own. But since you are not of the world, for this reason the world hates you."[91] Surely then, as it hates you, so it persecutes you.

God, however, restrains him who is murderous and wild with uncontrolled rage, and he does not so much as permit him to cause distress through harsh words. For God had said to Laban, *"Be careful that you do not say anything evil to Jacob."* But the world in fact accuses him of having committed robbery, and of destroying its gods. Now it was Rachel who had stolen them. Yet note Laban's attempt to find them. Laban, it says, searched Leah for his gods, and then the two maidservants also, but [252][92] did not find them. Rachel was sitting upon them, giving the excuse that she was suffering from the way of women. So what does this mean? It means that the overthrow of idols was not accomplished by the synagogue of the Jews, neither by the reformation of those born to bondage. Rather, it was accomplished by Rachel, that is, the church, who covered those man-made objects in disgust. Not only this, but with regard to the idols she also fulfilled what was spoken through the prophet: "And you will cast away the idols overlaid with silver, and you will grind to powder the idols overlaid with gold, and you will

---

88. Heb 13.14; 11.10.
89. 1 Pt 2.11.
90. Rom 12.2.
91. Jn 15.19.
92. The numbering of the Migne columns has omitted 250 and 251, although no text is missing.

throw them away[93] like the discharge of an unclean woman, and be rid of them like dung."[94]

When Laban's gods were not found, he then made a peace agreement with the divine Jacob. For the world, when it no longer has any falsely called gods, will make friends. It has now come even into a bond of peace with Christ. He is that most esteemed and precious stone, the honored cornerstone, which has become the head of the corner and the foundation of Zion.[95] For it says, "Jacob set up a pillar," as a type of Christ. Other stones of the holy apostles are heaped up with it, namely of those who are justified by faith and sanctified in the Spirit, beautifully prefiguring the multitude gathered in Christ. Indeed, concerning the holy apostles, the prophetic word said, "Holy stones are rolled upon the ground."[96] For the divine disciples ran about all over the earth, conveying the gospel message to the nations. And the wise Paul writes to those justified by faith, "In him you also are being built together into a dwelling place of God in the Holy Spirit."[97]

Furthermore, the collection of stones is called *"Heap of Testimony"* by Laban, while the divine Jacob, calling the thing that had been made *"Witness Heap,"* assigns to it a greater and incomparably surpassing meaning, that is, with regard to Christ. For Christ himself is the head of those who believe.

Now that the multitude of angels minister to Christ the Savior of all, who saves his own people, delivering them from the evil in the world; and that it is also evident that they carry out the service prescribed for them, one might readily learn by studying these things further. For when Laban was returning, going peacefully back down to his home, it says, *Jacob looked up and saw an army encamped, and the angels of God met him. When he saw them, Jacob said, "This is the army of God," and he called the name of the place "Camps."*[98] It is written, "The angel of the Lord en-

---

93. Following the LXX, the text reads "you will crush" (*likmêseis*). The Hebrew reading, however, is "you will scatter."
94. Is 30.22.
95. Cf. Is 28.16; also Ps 118.22 (117.22 LXX, *eis kephalên gônias*).
96. Zec 9.16 LXX.
97. Eph 2.22.
98. Gn 32.1–2 (32.2–3 LXX).

camps around those who fear him, and he will deliver them."⁹⁹ And again, "He commands his angels concerning you, to guard you in all your ways."¹⁰⁰ Our Lord Jesus Christ does indeed save all those who love him, through whom and with whom be glory to God the Father, together with the Holy Spirit, for ever and ever. Amen.

More concerning Jacob

1. For those who have chosen to live a most excellent life, the conduct of the saints[101] is wonderful indeed, and the splendor of their behavior transcends all words. [253] It is a good example to those who wish to live devoutly, showing clearly and in various ways how one should conduct oneself correctly so as to be like God and to please him.[102] For I myself (though in actual fact it is the word of inspired Scripture) consider it necessary that we ought to examine carefully what the saints of old accomplished through their manner of life and to imitate their faith. And not only this, but that we should also follow in the footsteps of their virtuousness. For it would be absurd to imagine that those with knowledge of the craft of kingship should put themselves forward as instructors in this matter to those who came before them, and that those who had an especially thorough understanding of these things should take pains to emulate them! It would also be absurd to think that we ourselves, to whom progress in virtue is set forth as a goal, should not apply our minds[103] to the virtuousness of those in ancient times, in order that in a certain manner we may acquire from them the means by which we might be more approved by God, and that we ourselves might cultivate our own sense of how to behave chastely.

Therefore, let the divine Jacob, who is in no way inferior in

---

99. Ps 34.7 (33.8 LXX).
100. Ps 91.11 (90.11 LXX).
101. Here Cyril is speaking of those "saints" found in Scripture, as is later made clear.
102. Or "so as to please God reasonably."
103. Lit. "the eye of our understanding."

this respect, be set before us as one who was above reproach, I mean one who at that time followed an appropriate way of life with respect to his behavior, having the God of all as his helper and guide, though indeed he sometimes allowed him to suffer difficulties to good purpose. For nobody can attain the glories of virtuousness without pains. Yet after the struggles God bestows upon him a crown of joy and, just like the strongest competitors in the games, makes him rich with a prize.

Do not say to yourself, "Why has not God granted that the saints may rejoice without going through pain?" For this would be to make concessions to those who have not exerted themselves and, worse still, to make it possible that the reward of virtuousness be imparted to them. Instead, the divine benevolence towards them should cause the will of those who have not been tried to produce fruit and to have the wonderful and worthy desire for the gifts of his grace.

Rather, it was first necessary that those of old should be seen as having been approved, and by their deeds to be shown as worthy of the divine blessings, and also that they should be set forth to those coming after them as distinct examples and models of how one should choose to be extremely hardworking and active. So they indicate that for those living a slothful and reprehensible life there will be no reward, whereas the most remarkable blessings of all will follow those who are especially hardworking and who prefer to spend their efforts in life on doing the most pleasing good works.

Thus a certain wise man said, "Child, when you come to serve the Lord, prepare your soul for testing. Set your heart aright and persevere."[104] For perseverance gives birth to a tested character, and a tested character gives birth to hope; and "hope does not disappoint," as it is written.[105]

So we shall now come to the subject matter lying before us.

2. After Laban had departed from Mount Gilead, the divine Jacob was eager to get to his homeland and wished to hasten on with his journey. Having barely escaped the onslaught of Laban, and having had only a brief respite, he straightaway encoun-

---

104. Sir 2.1–2.
105. Rom 5.5.

tered the most fearful difficulties. Upon leaving Mesopotamia and running away to the land of Canaan, it was necessary to pass through Seir, where Esau lived, and so Jacob was greatly afraid. [256] For Esau had not forgotten that he had been aggrieved over the matter of the blessing and the right of the firstborn. Yet how could it not be appropriate to marvel at the way in which he set aside his grief over these matters and treated his brother with love and kindness?

Now it is written: *Jacob sent messengers ahead of him to Esau his brother in the land of Seir, the country of Edom, and he commanded them, saying, "This is what you will say to my lord Esau: 'Your servant Jacob says this: I have been staying with Laban and remained there until now. I have oxen, donkeys, sheep, and male and female servants; and I have sent to tell my lord Esau so that your servant may find favor in your sight.'" The messengers returned to Jacob and said, "We came to your brother Esau. He is coming to meet you, and there are four hundred men with him." Jacob was exceedingly afraid and distressed. He divided up the people who were with him, and the oxen and sheep, into two companies. Then Jacob said, "If Esau comes upon one company and attacks it, then the second company will be safe." Jacob also said, "O Lord God of my father Abraham, and the God of my father Isaac, who said to me, 'Return quickly to the land of your birth, and I will do good to you,' let me have sufficient of all the righteousness and truth that you have shown your servant. For with this staff of mine I crossed over the Jordan, and now I have become two companies. Deliver me from the hand of my brother Esau, because I am afraid of him, lest he should come and attack me, and the mothers with their children. But you said, 'I will do good to you, and I will make your offspring like the sand of the sea, so that they cannot be counted for number.'"*[106]

You see how Jacob coaxes his way into favor with Esau. Not only does he flatter him who had been aggrieved, but he also tries to remove the possibility of uncontrolled anger through speaking appropriate words. Even though better things were allotted him on account of his father's blessing, and he was privileged to possess the right of the firstborn, and even though he had God as his helper, he was submissive in a manner befitting a saint, altogether preferring to prevail by that means.

106. Gn 2.3–12.

"If possible, so far as it depends on you, live at peace with all men."[107] For at times some people do indeed find a particular statement extremely difficult to oppose and cannot in any way treat it with contempt. As the wise composer of proverbs wrote, "A submissive answer turns away wrath."[108] And see how the cleverness of the righteous leads to godliness. For Jacob sent messengers to plead for peace, who conveyed to Esau the gentlest of words. He instructed them to say expressly, *"Your servant Jacob says this."* Furthermore, he himself turned to prayer, and did not cease seeking the help and deliverance it could afford. Jacob affirmed that trial clearly manifested the hope that could be obtained from things now past. He said, *"With this staff of mine I crossed over the Jordan, and now I have become two companies."* He meant, "Having only the staff brought from my own home, I passed over the Jordan, and through your goodness, O Master, I have become the master of many."

So from this [257] we too learn that it is necessary to be meek and peaceable, and that we ought always strive to get through situations without being contentious. For "the Lord's servant," it says, "must not be quarrelsome, but should be gentle with everyone," as it is written.[109] I consider it to be most commendable that nothing should keep us from making use of human artifice to good ends. Yet if this situation happens to befall us, it is necessary to request God's involvement and help from above, not being high-minded, but rather it is written, "As much as you are great, humble yourself that much, and you will find favor with the Lord."[110]

If we choose both to think and to act in this way, we will obtain the good things that come from peace, and we will turn the fierceness we face into gentleness. "For the wild animals," it says, "will be at peace with you."[111] This is what Jacob managed to do. For he did not appease his brother by means of artful speech and tender words only, but he also gave him a share of

---

107. Rom 12.18.
108. Prv 15.1.
109. 2 Tm 2.24.
110. Cf. Jas 4.10; 1 Pt 4.5–6.
111. Jb 5.23.

his possessions as a gift, setting apart for him a rich portion—sheep, oxen, goats, donkeys, camels, and calves. For peace is better than material wealth, and the attainment of brotherly love ought to come before temporal blessings.

And so the divine Jacob was indeed fearful of his brother Esau, as I said, and as he was expecting soon to suffer severely from his brother's anger, he was fainthearted. Yet having overcome his former malice, Esau clung to Jacob and greeted him with tears, and by the laws of nature he was able to put an end to his previous attitude and offer him love. For it is written that *Esau ran to meet him, and, embracing him, he kissed him and fell upon his neck, and they both wept.*[112]

Now all these virtuous acts of meekness are the fruit of a submissive and humble mind, and a gift of God's benevolence to those who love him. It levels the steep and smooths the rough, and it satisfies the desires of those who earnestly seek to be devoted to him.

I now think it necessary, however, for us to change the form of our exposition to spiritual contemplation. Come then, let us go back and return to the beginning of the whole matter, for the mystery of Christ will become clear to those who care to learn it.

3. So then, fearing the murderous and savage intent of his brother, and reasonably so, the divine Jacob had set out on his journey to Haran and to Laban, his father Isaac agreeing to his flight. For in this way Jacob thought it necessary to evade the onslaught of the aggrieved Esau.

When he came to Laban, he was wed to the man's two daughters, Leah and Rachel. He was enriched through the birth of children and through herds of animals, and other possessions besides these. But when he came into such prosperity, he undertook to have his own household. So he departed from Haran and from the home of Laban with those things he had acquired, and with his wives and children.

When Laban pursued him and caught up with him, Jacob made a covenant of peace with him. Christ also confirmed the bond of love, for the stone that was set up was a type of Christ.

Then, following this, [260] once he had left Laban and was

---

112. Gn 33.4.

heading for home, he also made peace with the one who had previously had savage and murderous intentions against him, namely Esau. For they embraced one another, their love for one another in a way combining so as to overcome the former ill-will.

While it is with these matters that the whole of the literal account concludes, we are nevertheless mindful that we assign to Jacob the role[113] of representing Christ himself, as well as of those who are justified by faith. We also say that Esau prefigures in himself the people of the law and circumcision. Further, it is especially noteworthy that God the Master of all, while the labor pains were still upon her who was having twin boys, said to Rebekah, "Two nations and two peoples will be separated from your womb. One people will have preeminence over the other, and the elder will serve the younger."[114] This, too, was fulfilled in Christ. For although first in order of time came the people of Israel, who were for this reason named the firstborn, they were in fact second in rank and have been placed behind those who have become a people through faith in Christ. It is these who have inherited the glory of the Firstborn, even though he is Only-Begotten, into whose likeness they have also been formed, having received the regeneration through the Spirit that leads to incorruption and holiness.

So, as he was inflamed with jealousy, Esau, representing Israel, persecuted Jacob, by whom we mean Christ. And as I said, in these matters we find that no distinction is made in the account, which always follows what is appropriate—at one time referring to Jacob as Christ, and at another to the new people of God through faith.

Christ, then, having been persecuted, after a certain fashion departed into the land of the Gentiles, though not willingly. He then cried out these words: "I have forsaken my house, I have abandoned my inheritance; I have given the one beloved of my soul into the hands of her enemies. My inheritance has become to me like a lion in a thicket. She has roared out against me;

---

113. See n. 40 above.
114. Gn 25.23.

therefore I have hated her."[115] In his kindness and love, however, Christ manifested himself to the women in the garden after his resurrection from the dead, and said, "Go, tell my brothers that they should go to Galilee, and they will see me there."[116] He came into Galilee just as the divine Jacob came into Haran and tended the sheep belonging to Laban, that is, to the world, which serves the creature and is deceived, just like Laban.

While Christ was there among the Gentiles, like a bridegroom he spiritually took to wife a pure virgin, namely the Gentile church, represented by Rachel. He also brought in with her the one who had already been yoked to him through the law, that is, the synagogue of the Jews, of which Leah was a type. For "the remnant of Israel has been saved," in accordance with what the prophet said,[117] even though perhaps the whole mass of them did not value the grace that comes through faith in Christ.

Christ, therefore, is shown to be the bridegroom for the Gentiles. And since by grace he brought to the new birth a great many appointed for adoption as sons in the Spirit, and gathered together a truly numerous flock of spiritual sheep, he was persecuted by the world. For certain of those in the world, being devoted to receiving the highest honors and [261] having supreme power on earth, were hostile to the glory of Christ. Yet his divine grace put them to shame, and the world made a peace agreement with Christ, just as Laban did with Jacob.

Moreover, in later times our Lord Jesus Christ will be reconciled with Israel, his persecutor of old, just as Jacob embraced Esau after his return from Haran. That Israel itself after some time will be received into the love of Christ through faith, we who submit to the words of the inspired Scripture may not in the least doubt. There is a passage where the Master of all says through one of the holy prophets, "For the people of Israel will abide many days without a king or a ruler, without sacrifice or an altar, without a priesthood or revelations.[118] And after these

---

115. Jer 12.7–8.
116. Mt 28.10.
117. Cf. Is 10.22.
118. Or "manifestations."

things the people of Israel will return and seek the Lord their God and David their king, and they shall hope in the Lord and in his goodness in the latter days."[119]

While, however, Christ, the Savior of us all, is still gathering out of the nations those who believe, how is Israel desolated! They have no law for appointing their rulers, nor can they offer at the divine altar the sacrifices prescribed by the law. So they wait for Christ to return from calling the Gentiles, that he may also receive Israel through faith and unite them to the others by the law of his love. Observe how Jacob, who rejoiced over the birth of his children and over his numerous herds of animals, returned from Haran and received Esau back into his affection. In time, then, after the calling of the Gentiles, Israel will be converted and will marvel at these riches in Christ.

This very thing, for those who care to examine it, is also readily to be found in the literal events that happened. Jacob sent gifts to Esau, and so, by honoring him with these things, changed his attitude to one of love. He also sent ahead messengers to speak to him words of peace. Christ also plainly revealed at times that those things that establish friendship with Israel will eventually come to pass. For in a certain passage he said to the Jews through the mouth of the prophet, "And behold, I will send to you Elijah the Tishbite before the great and glorious day of the Lord comes. He will restore the heart of the father to the son, and the heart of a man to his neighbor, lest I come and severely afflict the land."[120] That one will come and, as would be reasonable,[121] he will turn back unruly Israel and bring them out from the state of wrath in which they have been for so long. He will restore them to peace and friendship with Christ, showing in effect the precious gifts he has to offer, that is, the hope given to those who believe. For the matters relating to the promise will not further be delayed for those who then believe, but the free gift will be near, and grace will be close at hand. Indeed, once the "son of sin" has been overthrown,[122]

---

119. Hos 3.4–5.
120. Mal 4.5–6 (3.22–23 LXX).
121. Or "in all probability."
122. Here Cyril makes possible allusion to 2 Thes 2.3, where there are the

Christ the Savior of us all will come down from heaven with the holy angels. Through him and with him be glory to the Father, together with the Holy Spirit, for ever and ever. Amen. [264]

More concerning Jacob

1. Now through sin human nature fell into a state of death. And since he was totally separated from him that knew how to save, the one fashioned in the divine image was all but a slave, weighed down with the burden of servitude. For he did not willingly submit[123] to the tyranny of Satan, who through his exceedingly great arrogance (for that evil spirit was haughty) acted defiantly, so to speak, against all those upon the earth, and said, "With my hand I will seize the whole world like a bird's nest, and I will take them like eggs that have been abandoned; and there is none who will escape me or oppose me."[124] He has exercised his rule arrogantly, as I said, and is even named "the god of this world."[125] For the world worshiped him and served the creature rather than the Creator.[126]

Since, however, in such a situation God had mercy upon those brought into this state of wretchedness, he promised to send us his Son from heaven to restore human nature to how it was in the beginning. Those in Christ are a new creation, as the Scriptures say.[127] And the blessed prophets were the bearers of good tidings for us, "who prophesied of the grace that would come to us, seeking to know what person or time the Spirit of Christ within them was indicating when he bore witness in advance to those things Christ was destined to suffer and to the glories that would follow. It was revealed to them that it was not themselves they were serving but us."[128] For this is what the disciple of the Savior wrote.

---

variant readings "man of sin" and "man of lawlessness," and to Jn 17.12, "the son of perdition."

123. Lit. "place his neck under."
124. Is 10.14.
125. 2 Cor 4.4.
126. Cf. Rom 1.25.
127. Cf. 2 Cor 5.17.
128. 1 Pt 1.10–12.

These prophets also had a good deal to say about our Savior becoming man, and the fact that he would eventually come as a redeemer. It would do no harm to say a few words about this for the better instruction of the readers. This matter suitably serves to establish a charge against the people of the Jews, as can be seen from the events themselves. For even though they could discern the advent of the Savior out of the prophetic oracles, as well as understand it, one might suppose, from the shadows present in the law, those wretches perversely set themselves against the divine revelations and against Christ himself. This is in fact what the wise Paul said to us: "A hardening has come upon part of Israel,"[129] so that "seeing they may not see, and hearing they may not hear, nor understand."[130] The Savior himself also said the same thing.[131]

So too, the divine Isaiah presented to us Emmanuel in his own writings, when he plainly said, "The Spirit of the Lord is upon me, because he has anointed me; he has sent me to preach good news to the poor, to heal the broken-hearted, to proclaim release to captives, and recovery of sight to the blind; to declare an acceptable year of the Lord, and a day of recompense."[132] For these were the marvelous deeds he would perform at his coming.

In another place Hosea also said concerning him, "The people of Judah and the people of Israel will be gathered together, and they will appoint for themselves one ruler; and they will come up out of the land,[133] for great will be the day of Jezreel."[134] For most teachers among the Jews at that time [265] persuaded them to honor the God of all with their lips only, teaching the people in their charge the commandments of men as their doctrine.[135] But now Christ has been appointed as the one ruler over everybody and everything; and we have come up

---

129. Rom 11.25.
130. Is 6.9.
131. Mt 13.13; Lk 8.10.
132. Is 61.1–2; var. omit "and a day of recompense."
133. Or "earth."
134. Hos 1.11 (2.2 LXX).
135. Cf. Is 29.13.

out of the land;[136] that is, we have been taught to set our minds upon the things above.[137] For the day of Jezreel, which means "sowing the seed of God," will truly be great, that seed which is sown being the Son.[138]

The divine David also spoke to us of this day when he said, "This is the day that the Lord has made, let us rejoice and be glad in it."[139] The most-wise Paul further adds, "Behold, now is the acceptable day; behold, now is the day of salvation,"[140] evidently meaning that day on which we were saved, since it is to this very thing that Christ calls us. For as the wise disciple said, "There is no other name under heaven given among men by which we must be saved."[141]

Hear, too, what Jeremiah plainly says, "Behold, the days are coming, says the Lord, when I will raise up for David a righteous branch,[142] and a king will reign and understand; he will execute judgment and righteousness upon the earth. In his days Judah will be saved, and Israel will dwell safely. And this is his name, which the Lord will call him among the prophets—Josedek."[143] For Christ the righteous king has taken up his reign over us; he has executed judgment and righteousness, having delivered those going astray in their sins, and having condemned that tyrannical enemy,[144] Satan. And his name is Josedek, that is, "the righteousness of God." For we have been justified[145] in him, not through works of righteousness that we ourselves have done, but through his great mercy.[146]

Accordingly, God the Father also stated, "My righteousness draws near speedily," and "My mercy will be revealed."[147] For

136. Or "earth."
137. Cf. Col 3.2; var. add "having the mind that rejects earthly things, and we have been ordained to a better death."
138. By this Cyril probably means the Incarnation.
139. Ps 118.24 (117.24 LXX).
140. 2 Cor 6.2.
141. Acts 4.12.
142. Lit. "a righteous dawn [*anatolê*]." Cf. Zec 6.12 LXX.
143. Jer 23.5–6.
144. Var. "destroyer."
145. That is, "made righteous, declared righteous."
146. Cf. Ti 3.5.
147. Is 51.5; 56.1.

Christ has become the mercy and righteousness that comes to us from God the Father. It is by this very name Christ, "the anointed," that he is called by the glorious band of the saints. For indeed the blessed Samuel, notable among the prophets, declared to the people of Israel, saying, "And behold, I have walked before you from my youth until today. Here I am; testify against me before the Lord and before his anointed."[148] And again, "The Lord is witness among you, and his anointed is witness this day, that you found nothing in my hand."[149]

Furthermore, the blessed David most clearly accuses the Jews of rebellion, of unrestrained insolence against Christ, of futile scheming and puerile arguments, when he says, "Why did the nations rage, and the peoples plot vain things? The kings of the earth took their stand, and the rulers gathered together, against the Lord and against his anointed."[150] Truly the foolish plots of the Jews against Christ were in vain. For he who is the Life did not die, he who said to the spirits below, "Come forth," and to those in darkness, "Show yourselves," nor was he overpowered by the gates of Hades.

Again, [268] the prophet Jeremiah lamented over Jerusalem, as being unholy, profane, ill-disposed, and the murderer of the Lord. For he said, "The breath of our nostrils, the anointed Lord,[151] was caught in their destructive snares, of whom we said, 'In his shadow we will live among the nations.'"[152] For when they ought to have taken hold of the grace that comes through faith as the way of salvation, they contended against God and were condemned.

Therefore, the Author of all things, the Only-Begotten Word of God, condescending to empty himself, was anointed by the Father and became one of us. And the goal of this emptying was to save those upon the earth. The prophet Zephaniah, for example, proclaimed the good news, saying, "Rejoice greatly, O

---

148. 1 Sm 12.2–3. "Anointed" in the LXX, here cited by Cyril is, of course, the term *christos*.

149. 1 Sm 12.5.

150. Ps 2.1–2.

151. *christos kurios*. The Hebrew text, as well as some copies of the LXX, in fact state "the Anointed of the Lord."

152. Lam 4.20.

daughter of Zion, shout out, O daughter of Jerusalem, rejoice and be glad with all your heart, O daughter of Jerusalem. The Lord has taken away your iniquities, he has redeemed you from the hand of your enemies. The Lord will reign over Israel in your midst, and you will see disaster no more."[153]

The disobedient and hard-hearted, however, and those who were insolent beyond measure, abused him most shamefully, acting rashly and scheming most recklessly. And so they brought forth the just deserts of their transgressions. For the evil perish in an evil way. Yet this does not apply to all of them. For the remnant was shown mercy and saved, as the prophet says.[154]

2. Now the divine Jacob was taught that these things would eventually happen this way, since God wonderfully portrayed the matter to him. And how this was so, I will state, making necessary reference to those things found in the sacred Scriptures.

The account reads as follows: *Rising up that night, he took his two wives, his two maidservants, and his eleven children, and crossed the ford of the Jabbok. He took them and sent them across the river, and he also sent over all his possessions. Then Jacob was left alone, and a man wrestled with him until daybreak. When the man saw that he could not overpower him, he touched the broad part of his thigh, and this part of Jacob's thigh became numb*[155] *as he wrestled with him. And the man said, "Let me go, for the day has dawned." But Jacob said, "I will not let you go unless you bless me." The man asked him, "What is your name?" And he answered, "Jacob." Then he said to him, "No longer will your name be called Jacob, but your name will be Israel, because you have prevailed with God and you are mighty with men." Jacob asked him and said, "Tell me your name." The man said, "Why is it that you ask me my name?" He then blessed him there. Jacob called the name of that place "Appearance of God,"*[156] *for he said, "I have seen God face-to-face, and my life has been spared." The sun rose upon him when the appearance of God passed on, and Jacob limped upon his thigh.*[157]

153. Zep 3.14–15.
154. See n. 117.
155. Or "stiff."
156. Or "Form [*eidos*] of God." The Hebrew name, Peniel, literally means "face of God."
157. Gn 32.23–31.

So the divine Jacob sent all his possessions over the River Jabbok, while he himself stayed behind alone. How can it not be worthwhile looking into what this means? Come then, and let us investigate the reason for it all. For this account will directly lead us on to spiritual concerns.

3. Esau lived in Edom and Seir, and he had dominion over the land and over those regions which were not under the control of Jacob. But when the latter left Mesopotamia [269] and the home of Laban, and was eager to return to the land of his father, it was absolutely necessary for him to make his journey through Edom. With great diplomacy he sought to greet his brother in a peaceful manner, and told messengers to go ahead bearing wonderful gifts, for he himself would come on more cautiously. Jacob also instructed the messengers to inform him in advance, so that he would know if by the gifts and through their message he had managed to placate Esau's former raging and murderous hostility.

When those sent ahead returned and said, *"We came to your brother Esau, and behold, he is coming to meet you, and four hundred men are with him,"* the divine Jacob was very fearful. For he had no way of knowing for sure whether he would meet with one who was friendly and peaceable, or with one who would show nothing but the usual fearsome brazenness and who would choose to act maliciously.

Now Jacob sent all that belonged to him across the river, while he stayed behind alone. He did this, I suppose, having thoroughly considered the situation. Esau might perhaps appear propitious and gentle, causing no problem nor saying anything harsh, in which case his wives and children would be sent back again. On the other hand, Esau might come still feeling bitter and contentious, wanting nothing more than to commit murder, in which case he would spare the children, and show mercy at the tears of the women. He would seize Jacob only and execute his wrath on him, the death of the one who grieved him being enough to satisfy him. Yet what in fact happened to Jacob, through the power of God, far exceeded his hopes, for, as we previously said, they embraced one another.

So then, from these things that occurred, the import[158] of the mystery is taught. How and in what manner, I will now tell. It is indeed the case that *he sent across the river all that belonged to him*, and that *when he stayed behind alone, a man wrestled with him until daybreak*. We say that the one wrestling with him was a holy angel, a type of Christ who, on account of his humanity, was just like us. So because Jacob himself did not also cross over the river with the others, the river being the Jabbok, which means "wrestling," he and the other man engaged in what seems to be a fight.

What might the interpretation of this matter be? That is, what is its inner meaning? Now Christ does not wrestle with those who cross over the Jordan, of which the Jabbok was a type, nor does he count among his opponents or adversaries those who honor his mysteries. Rather, he preserves those who have overcome the world as in a spiritual fight, so to speak; he crowns them and decorates them with heavenly honors.

The name of the river was "wrestling," for "the kingdom of heaven suffers violence, and the violent seize it by force."[159] Also, "Narrow is the gate, and difficult is the way leading to life, and there are few that find it."[160]

The things that happened here foreshadow the fact that those descended from Jacob at a later time would not cross over the Jordan, that is, receive the grace that comes through holy baptism, and that they would impiously dishonor Emmanuel and have him henceforth as their adversary. For those who do not honor him by having faith will be reckoned as though they are totally opposed to him. This the Savior himself affirms when he says, "The one who is not with me is against me."[161] As those who are with him are those who have come to faith, that the [272] converse is also true how could one doubt?

Now it says, *The man wrestled with Jacob until daybreak, and saw that he was not able to overpower him*. Note how the fight happened during the night. In falling and being overpowered, Jacob re-

---

158. Lit. "power," "force."
159. Cf. Mt 11.12.
160. Mt 7.14.
161. Mt 12.30.

ceived a reproof, because he was seeking what was unattainable, choosing to fight against God, and to get the better of him who is stronger than all. It is this, I believe, that the divine David also spoke of in the Psalms concerning the people of Israel, saying that terrible things would be visited upon their heads, not to mention that against Christ "they devised a plot in which they would never be able to succeed."[162]

Israel, then, fought against Christ, since they were in darkness, that is, they did not have the divine mind to enlighten them, nor, speaking spiritually, did they have the dawning day or the morning star that rises in the hearts of believers.[163] They have in fact continued in their unbelieving state, as the prophet says, "While they were waiting for light, darkness came upon them; while they were waiting for brightness, they walked in gloom."[164]

Contrariwise, the divine Paul, writing to those justified by faith, who have been richly blessed through the Spirit, says, "We are not of the night, nor of the darkness, but we are sons of light and of the day."[165] That these are in a better state than the ignorance of the Jews and have escaped the darkness that manifestly covers them,[166] Paul makes evident when he further says, "The night is far gone, and the day is near. So let us lay aside the works of darkness, and let us put on the armor of light. Let us walk decently, as in the day."[167]

So then, those who believe are of the day, while those who disbelieve, since they are of the night and the darkness, fight against Christ. This is what the people descended from Jacob did. Yet they were weak and defeated, unable to stand. For it says that *the man wrestling with Jacob touched the broad part of his thigh, and this part of Jacob's thigh became numb as he wrestled with him.* What we should understand, then, from this, we will now declare. In inspired Scripture the thigh mostly stands for those

162. Ps 21.11 (20.11 LXX).
163. Cf. 2 Pt 1.19.
164. Is 59.9.
165. 1 Thes 5.5.
166. That is, the Jews.
167. Rom 13.12.

parts of the body necessary to procreate children, and also for the offspring themselves, which are procreated from these. This is because the reproductive organs of all creatures are located in the area of the thighs. And so the blessed Abraham, when he sent his servant to Mesopotamia to take a wife for Isaac, ordered him to swear an oath, and said to him, "Put your hand under my thigh,"[168] which means, "Swear by God, and by those who shall come forth from me, the offspring of your master." The thigh, then, signifies those who come forth from the loins.

Now Jacob's thigh became numb, indicating that those coming from his loins, namely the people of Israel, would become lame. The Savior himself thus says through the mouth of David, "Sons of strangers dealt falsely with me; sons of strangers grew weary and stumbled lamely off their paths."[169] And that Israel has continued to be spiritually lame the wise Paul also understood, for he writes, "Therefore, strengthen your feeble hands and your weak knees, and make straight paths for your feet, so that [273] what is lame may not stumble,[170] but rather be healed."[171] The healing of such lameness may not happen in any other way except through faith and love toward Christ. According to the words of the blessed Paul, those who have not come to faith continue in their lameness and hurtful stumbling. So then, the injury that happened to Jacob's thigh while he was wrestling was a figure of the spiritual lameness of Israel.

That we are not saying anything false when we affirm that Christ opposes and, in a certain manner, wrestles against those who are of the night, who have a darkened mind, and inflicts them with spiritual lameness, one might readily learn from what follows. For the man wrestling with Jacob said to him, *"Let me go, for the day has dawned."* See how he does not persist in wrestling once the day has dawned. For there is no fight for those who have come into the light. It would be fitting for those who have passed into such brightness to say, "O God, my God, I come to you at dawn."[172] Further to this, "In the morning you shall hear

168. Gn 24.2.
169. Ps 18.44–45 (17.45–46 LXX).
170. Or "be dislocated."
171. Heb 12.12–13.
172. Ps 63.1 (62.2 LXX).

my voice, in the morning I shall stand before you, and you shall look upon me."[173] When the light of righteousness, which is Christ, arises in our minds and brings spiritual radiance into our hearts, then, through his manifold goodness, we shall stand before him in brilliant splendor, and we will show ourselves worthy to be looked upon from above. For it says, "The eyes of the Lord are upon the righteous."[174] So once the dawn has come, it brings an end to the fight.

Observe how cleverly and skillfully he teaches Jacob when he wants to leave, and how he is greatly desirous of imparting to him those things necessary for his salvation. For even though the one who was defeated might not wish to release him, he who was utterly victorious and able to withdraw placed the authority in the other's hands, as it were, for what he himself wanted to do, and, perhaps because he was held tightly, he said, *"Let me go."*

We find that this is similar to what was most wisely and cleverly spoken by God to Moses. For God intended to exact the punishment due to senseless Israel when they committed idolatry in the wilderness (for they had made a calf). Yet he allowed the blessed Moses to prevent his wrath, if he so wished, and to make entreaty on behalf of those who had sinned. "I have spoken to you," the Lord said, "once and again, saying, 'I have seen this people, and behold, they are a stiff-necked people. Leave me alone that I may destroy them and blot out their name from under heaven; and I will make you into a great nation.'"[175] But when Moses perceived the divine disposition to show mercy, he sought to prevent the punishment, and said, "If you will indeed forgive their sin, then forgive it; but if not, blot me out also from the book which you have written."[176]

So in a manner much like this, the words *"Let me go"* were spoken to Jacob by the one who was wrestling with him. Quickly learning who it was with whom he was wrestling, and coming to an understanding of the whole affair, Jacob strived exceedingly,

---

173. Ps 5.3 (5.4 LXX).
174. Ps 34.15 (33.16 LXX).
175. Dt 9.13–14.
176. Ex 32.32.

and said, *"I will not let you go, unless you bless me."* And he was blessed, [276] and the way in which the blessing was given was that his first name was changed to another. For he was told, *"No longer will your name be called Jacob, but your name will be Israel."* Jacob means "one who overcomes," that is, one who employs great effort and vigilance to enable him to succeed in what must be done. The name Israel, on the other hand, means "one who sees God."[177]

We shall now go back a little way in the narrative and offer an explanation of these matters.

4. So Jacob, having wrestled and been defeated, and having suffered the benumbing of his thigh in the darkness, as it was getting light and the morning was beginning to dawn, still held on, though not in an aggressive way, to the one he had wrestled. He insisted that he give him a blessing, and indeed he was blessed, as his name was changed to Israel. For disobedient and stubborn Israel opposed Emmanuel, yet they did so in ignorance and darkness, that is, on account of their lack of understanding, since they were hardened. They were almost completely unaware that the divine light had risen upon them, spiritually speaking.

Israel was blessed by Christ, though not fully, but only through a certain portion of them who believed. "There is a remnant of Israel, chosen by grace," as it is written,[178] and those of the Jews who came to believe were not a few in number. Even before these, there were the divine disciples, who represented Jacob. Though under the law they were weak, they acted as such who overcome, exerting themselves vigorously, because they sought especially to have an encounter with God. For they were blameless with respect to the righteousness which is according to the law.[179]

After this, Israel was further blessed, that is, they were transformed in their minds so as to see God. Now, to know Christ,

---

177. Cyril here is referring to the meaning present in the place name "Peniel" (Gn 32.30), that is, "face of God." The name Israel itself most probably means "one who strives with God."
178. Rom 11.5.
179. Cf. Phil 3.6.

who he is, how he became one of us, and what his manner of life was like subsequent to his Incarnation,[180] this, I say, is to receive into one's mind the light of the true divine vision. That the knowledge of God is greater, more profitable, and incomparably better than the way of life under the law, he himself affirms, saying through one of the prophets, "I desire mercy and not sacrifice, the knowledge of God rather than burnt offerings."[181]

Paul too, though he was outstanding and blameless with respect to righteousness according to the law, "counted all things as loss because of the surpassing worth of knowing Christ."[182] That genuine knowledge of Christ is superior to the glory that comes from performing works, Paul again makes clear when he writes to Timothy, telling him to "train himself in godliness, for bodily exercise profits a little, but godliness is profitable in every way, since it holds promises for the present life and for the life to come."[183] As the Savior himself said to the Father in heaven, "This is eternal life: that they might know you, the only true God, and Jesus Christ, whom you have sent."[184]

So then, though someone may perhaps be a Jacob, that is, he may be able to overcome, and by his strength and cleverness be able to escape everything that induces weakness and leads to sin, it is through Christ that he will succeed and come to an understanding that befits the saints. So he will be called Israel—"one who sees God." Then, being mighty with God, he will also be mighty with men.

Accordingly, to know God and to appropriate knowledge of him does not come from the feeble effort of the frail, though [277] he might see dimly as in a mirror.[185] But it is achieved by the one who is brought to such a state of weakness, who reckons carnal and worldly things of no account, and who with a vigorous and active mind is able to strive for what is pleasing to God. This is the one who will be mighty among men, and mighty with God.

180. Lit. "after the economy of flesh."
181. Hos 6.6.
182. Phil 3.8.
183. Cf. 1 Tm 4.7–8.
184. Jn 17.3.
185. Cf. 1 Cor 13.12.

So then, the divine Jacob was indeed blessed, and he further said, *"Tell me your name."* The other replied, *"Why is it that you ask me my name?"* God did not tell him his name, because revealing it in such a manner would have been the natural way[186] to do it. For the way in which a man has a name is not at all how it is with God. He, however, is named in manifold ways from the things that he has brought into being. For he is Light, Life, Power, and Truth. He is the Only-Begotten, Radiance, and the Image of the One who begot him. He is Mercy, Wisdom, Righteousness, and Redemption. Perceiving him to be God, to whom no name may properly be applied, the blessed Jacob called the name of that place "Appearance of God."[187] For he said, *"I have seen God face-to-face, and my life has been spared."* Note, then, how Jacob became Israel, namely "one who sees God." When the man wrestled with him, Jacob said that he saw God face-to-face, and yet his life was preserved.[188] For knowledge concerning Christ is something that leads to preservation.[189]

The Word, therefore, is God in human flesh, for the patriarch Jacob said that he had seen God face-to-face. *When the sun rose,* it says, *the appearance of God passed on, and Jacob limped upon his thigh.* Similarly, as I have already stated, when the light shone upon the Jews, the fight came to an end. Also, the appearance of God moved on, that is to say, Christ ascended into heaven. Yet lame Israel was not delivered. For not all were saved. Israel continues to suffer, so to speak, through those who disbelieve, with the result that it is not at all able to walk correctly. So then, since Israel had seen the appearance of God, it was called by a new name—"the one who overcomes" was altered to "the one who sees God spiritually."

Now what happened after this? *Jacob journeyed on,* it says, *to Tabernacles, and he made a home for himself and tabernacles for his livestock. For this reason he called the name of that place "Tabernacles."*[190] You see here how Jacob lived in tabernacles. This was a

---

186. Lit. "according to nature" (*kata phusin*).
187. See n. 177 above.
188. Or "saved."
189. Or "salvation."
190. Gn 33.17; the Hebrew term, rendered as "Succoth" in English versions, means "tabernacles," "tents," "shelters."

clear sign of the pursuit of something better, which was in the mind of Israel. For having made these tabernacles, he lived in them.

For the mind that now sees and has been worthy of a divine vision, that has been nurtured and reared by various endowments to progress towards a state of perfection, is a most valuable gift[191] from God. It no more reckons the things of this world to be of any account, but rather deems life in the body to be a temporary residence. For this mind is divine[192] in character and is a genuine indication of a distinguished and transformed way of life. Give heed to the important words of the blessed David in the Psalms: "Spare me, because I am a stranger in the land and a sojourner, as all my fathers were."[193] Paul, too, writes to those who have come to the stature of the fullness of Christ and who have reached mature manhood [280], saying, "Here we have no lasting city, but we are looking for the one that is to come, whose designer and maker is God."[194] So the fact that the divine Jacob, namely Israel, chose to live in tabernacles is symbolic, the significance of which is not, one may suppose, at all obscure for those rightly disposed. For those whose eyes are upon God, and whose minds have been enlightened, the things of the present world are reckoned to be like a temporary residence.

Then Jacob came to Salem, a city of Shechem, which was in the land of Canaan.[195] Here once again that righteous man was tried, suffering wrong in the affair involving Dinah his daughter. This girl, though still quite young and a virgin, went out from her father's tent to take a look at the local girls.[196] It is in fact the case that the female of the species is always desirous of friendship with those of the same age. So the young woman went off.

Shechem the son of Hamor shamefully seized Dinah and, being carried away on a wave of unrestrained lust, he raped her. He then thought to make the girl his wife. At this, Sime-

191. Lit. "fruit."
192. Or "holy."
193. Ps 39.12–13 (38.13–14 LXX).
194. Heb 13.14; 11.10.
195. Gn 33.18. Cyril follows the LXX in interpreting the Hebrew term "safely" (*šālēm*) as a place name (Salem).
196. Cf. Gn 34.1.

on and Levi, the young woman's brothers, were provoked to wrath, and, not being able to tolerate the outrage, they planned to carry out godless acts against the offenders. They persuaded the men of Shechem to join with them in their ancestral law of circumcision. But then they killed them all without any mercy or compassion. The divine Jacob, however, was extremely indignant at this, and rebuked his sons, saying, *"You have made me hateful, so that I am evil to the inhabitants of the land."*[197] Indeed, those murderers did not restrain their wrath and, though they had been brought up by a righteous father, they did not consider anything of what they did to be the slightest bit depraved. For they wrought destruction, and killed those who trusted them and intended to become one with them.

So then, the profit we can get from this (for the inspired Scripture never says anything without purpose), we shall explain as we are able.

5. Now, we have been born by means of a spiritual generation, and through Christ we have been granted a place among the children of God. Perhaps a soul, once reborn through holy baptism and ordained a daughter of God,[198] may become defiled by those wont to do things of such a kind, or may be led away by carnal desires, or may go astray in her thinking with regard to God (for the contemptible opinions of the profane heretics are truly of such a nature). Then those who in respect of their faith are brothers to the injured party, if they belong to the priestly order—as in fact Levi did, and as may perhaps be supposed also of Simeon, being among the ranks of the obedient (for Simeon means "obedience")—become indignant when one of their household of faith is wronged. They should not, however, proceed to demand blood, nor should they exact a heavy penalty from those who have wrought harm. This would be to pay no heed to Christ, who says to them, *"You have made me hateful, so that I am evil to the inhabitants of the land."* It must also be remembered that the Savior himself once rebuked the di-

---

197. Gn 34.30.
198. Since the Greek noun for "soul" (*psuchê*) is feminine, Cyril here speaks of it as God's "daughter," thus making an apt parallel with Jacob's daughter Dinah.

vine Peter when he drew his sword, saying, "Put your sword back in its sheath. For all [281] those who take up the sword shall perish by the sword."[199] Indeed, it is not fitting for us, who have been chosen to contend earnestly for piety toward God, to arm ourselves with swords against our enemies. Rather, we should be longsuffering. And though some people may wish to persecute us, when reviled we bless,[200] when suffering we do not grumble;[201] instead we give ourselves over to him who judges justly.

Those wishing to avoid destruction, however, ought to be careful not to go off somewhere out of their father's tent, that is, the house of God, nor to attend to the gatherings of foreigners or of those with strange ideas. For when Dinah went out from her father's tent, she was brought into the house of Shechem. Yet she would never have been abused if she had stayed[202] in the dwellings of her father and resided among the tents of the saints. That such a thing is good and not without profit, the blessed David declares in the Psalms, "One thing I have asked from the Lord, this I will seek, that I should dwell in the house of the Lord all the days of my life, and that I should behold the delightfulness of the Lord and survey his holy temple. For he hid me in his tent on the day of my troubles, he sheltered me in the secret place of his tabernacle."[203]

So then, as Jacob was altogether fearful and fainthearted, God commanded him to move away. The account reads as follows: *God said to Jacob, "Arise, go up to Bethel, and live there. Make an altar there to the God who appeared to you when you were fleeing from Esau your brother." So Jacob said to those of his household and to all those with him, "Remove the foreign gods from your midst, and purify yourselves and change your clothes.[204] Then arise, let us go up to Bethel, and let us make there an altar to God, who heard me on the day of my distress and who has been with me and preserved me wherever I have gone." So they gave Jacob the foreign gods which they had and the*

---

199. Mt 26.52.
200. Cf. 1 Cor 4.12.
201. Var. "threaten."
202. Var. "chosen to stay."
203. Ps 27.4–5 (26.4–5 LXX).
204. Var. omit "and purify yourselves and change your clothes."

rings that were in their ears. Then Jacob buried them under the terebinth tree that was at Shechem, and thus he destroyed them to this day.[205]

The God of all summoned that righteous man from Shechem to Bethel, and he was not disobedient. Then while he was in Luz,[206] Jacob was deemed worthy of beholding a divine vision, and the promise that he would be the father of many nations was confirmed. When he went up to Bethel, it says, *Jacob set up there a pillar in the place where God had spoken with him, a pillar of stone, and he offered a drink offering on it and poured oil upon it. And Jacob called the name of the place where God had spoken to him Bethel.*[207]

Many such things happened which give a clear portrayal of Jacob's return to the land of Israel, and of his choosing to move to an incomparably better situation. Jacob did indeed live in tabernacles and by this means he in effect demonstrates the people of the saints to be sojourners in the world. Then, having suffered those things that happened to his daughter, and being exceedingly grieved at the base deeds shamefully enacted by Simeon and Levi in their fury, he severely rebuked them [284], showing us through his actions the patience and longsuffering under trials that befits the saints.

When called by God, Jacob went up to Bethel, that is, to the house of God (for that is what "Bethel" means). He performed sacrifices to God and showed himself to be learned in the mysteries. He plainly sets out for those coming after him the proper manner of coming to the house of God, for he commands them to cast off the foreign gods like garbage and filth, and to change their clothes. This practice is also fitting for us when we are called into the presence of God or brought into his divine temple, especially at the time of holy baptism. For it is necessary, by way of casting the foreign gods from our midst and abandoning such falsehood, that we should say, "I renounce you, Satan, with all your pomp and all your worship." Furthermore, we must all change our clothes by stripping off the old man that is corrupt through deceitful lusts, and putting on the new that is being re-

---

205. Gn 35.1–4.

206. According to the Hebrew text of Gn 35.6, Luz was another name for Bethel (cf. Gn 28.19).

207. Gn 35.14–15.

newed according to the image of its Creator.[208] Also the women with Jacob got rid of the ornaments in their ears. So women who enter the house of God without any carnal adornment and who leave their hair loose avoid being accused, one may suppose, of beautifying their heads. This I believe is the significance of the women removing the ornaments in their ears.

Whenever, therefore, we go up to Bethel, that is, to the house of God, we shall there acknowledge the stone, the elect stone that has become the head of the corner, which is Christ. We shall see the one anointed by the Father with all the gladness and joy under heaven. For the Son, as I said, has been anointed by God the Father with "the gladness of us all, with universal[209] joy," as the psalmist says.[210] So you see that this also is prefigured in the things just stated to us about Jacob setting up the stone and sprinkling it with oil and wine. What was done was indeed a type of the mystery regarding Christ, through whom and with whom be glory to God the Father, together with the Holy Spirit, for ever and ever. Amen.

208. Cf. Eph 4.22; Col 3.10.
209. Lit. "worldwide."
210. Cf. Ps 45.7 (44.8 LXX).

BOOK SIX: GENESIS 36-48

Concerning Joseph

WITHOUT ANY DOUBT the mystery of godliness, which is Christ, is great,[1] and what is said about him is exceedingly deep, as is the purpose for which he took on flesh. Yet with some effort its meaning becomes apparent, not so much to those who merely have the desire, but to those who are right-minded, [285] since they are illuminated by divine grace, are wise and perceptive, and are knowledgeable in the writings of the law and the prophets. Take the divine Peter, for instance, who was chief among the disciples, being placed over the others; he gave a correct confession of faith, and was told by Christ, "Blessed are you, Simon son of Jonah, because flesh and blood did not reveal this to you, but my Father, who is in heaven."[2] So God the Father instructs us in the mystery concerning the Son, and also delivers us by bringing us to him as our Savior and Redeemer, for Christ said, "No one comes to me unless the Father who sent me draws him."[3]

Accordingly, if we understand, let us say, what is said about him throughout all the holy Scripture, and if we acquire an unerring comprehension of the faith, this will prevent us from having a heart that is, as it were, stirred up by confounded double-mindedness, or that raves drunkenly, or that falls afoul of agitations arising from ignorance. Let us further hear what God says through the mouth of the prophet: "They have loved to wander, and have not held back; therefore, God has not been pleased with them."[4]

1. Cf. 1 Tm 3.16.
2. Mt 16.17.
3. Jn 6.44.
4. Jer 14.10.

For this reason, through numerous images[5] God informs us of the truth, and has helpfully laid down the things that happened at that former time as a foundation for faith in Christ, setting forth distinct representations, as it were, that give knowledge concerning him. Let us see, therefore, whether what I have just said is true also in those matters relating to the divine Joseph.

The account about him reads as follows: *These are the generations of Jacob. Joseph, a young man of seventeen, was tending to the sheep with his brothers, the sons of Bilhah and of Zilpah, his father's wives, and Joseph accused them of bad conduct before Israel his father. Now Jacob loved Joseph more than all his other sons, because he was the son of his old age, and he made a coat of many colors for him. When his brothers saw that his father loved him more than all his other sons, they hated him and were not able to speak peaceably to him.*[6]

2. The writer of the book has composed an accurate enumeration of those descended from Esau.[7] The sacred Scripture here instructs us concerning who was born from whom, which land each of them inhabited, and which of them attained to rulership. There is nothing, however, as regards noble character, nor mention of worthy deeds done by any of them. The passage, in effect, consists entirely of a list of those named, and is little in comparison with what is related concerning the divine Joseph. For those in the lineage of Jacob distinct narratives have been composed.

Now Joseph was younger than the others (he was seventeen years old), yet he did not shy away from the hard work of shepherding, but took part unreservedly in the same pursuits as the other brothers. He did not attach any value to an easy life, which those in their youth generally find pleasing and agreeable. He did not shun the unwelcome cares of life, nor did he prefer to leave things undone, as if he were still just a boy. Rather, he already had the reasoning powers of an older person, possessing a well-advanced mind, and employing the speech of

---

5. Or "similitudes," "representations." Cyril is of course referring to the many types and figures of the OT.

6. Gn 37.2–4.

7. Referring to Gn 36.

the mature,[8] so giving an anticipation of the wonderful nature of his future brilliance. [288] Indeed, he suitably amazed his blessed and loving father, and was counted especially worthy of his love and care. For Joseph was, it says, *the son of Jacob's old age*. And what is the significance of this? Our account here delves into our human dispositions. There is not anything at all equal to, or greater than, the affections that parents have for their children. Nature, in fact, frequently gets the better of the mind and overpowers it, and I reckon that nature is able to persuade us that a child is somewhat needier than others, as though it actually required greater care and attention. On occasion, with regard to many of those born, the situation is different. Somehow the excessive love of the parent fades and finally reaches an end, the earlier affection in some way later being overcome. For the human mind has a tendency to love what is new. While it does not completely rid itself of its former excesses over previous things, nor the things it presently has, it sets great store by what has recently been procured, and has a much stronger desire for things that are new.

Therefore, the divine Jacob loved Joseph more than the others, because he was the son of his old age. Yet, I suppose someone might say about this—how can the divine Joseph be understood as the son of his old age when Benjamin was born after him?[9] One can surely see that, even though it was Leah that Jacob married first in Haran, he actually loved Rachel, who gave birth to Joseph, and who died giving birth to Benjamin. In this regard, we may say that both of these were in fact sons of his old age.

Now the natural cleverness of Joseph with respect to absolutely everything was unequalled among all others. The maturity granted to him, and which he manifested, was completely unique. Most probably he thought that he would be someone famous and important. Since he gave no thought to the boisterousness of youth, and was already acting like a man, how can he not be considered a marvel?

---

8. Lit. "of the grey-haired."

9. The Harleian Codex includes this addition of this sentence, which the flow of thought seems to require.

So the blessed Jacob made new things for Joseph, more so than for his other sons. He wove him a coat of many colors, honoring him with garments fit for the most eminent of people. What happened as a result of this? The sons of Zilpah and Bilhah were provoked to anger, and at these things they were caused the most extraordinary vexation. The sons of the free woman, Leah, were also envious of the young man. Yet the lad had in fact done them no wrong. But it was the father's affection and the natural genius of the boy that kindled within them the burning fire of unrighteous malice. In the first instance, they assailed him with their words, railing furiously at him and tearing him apart in the same way that the lad would be taunted by his enemies. It is to this, I believe, that it refers when it says, *Joseph accused them of bad conduct before Israel their father.* These onslaughts were then but the beginnings[10] of their godless scheming, the castigations and mockery by an unbridled tongue deployed to serve their jealousy.

The reason this most vehement hostility was kindled within them was that God foreshowed to the young man that he would one day be famous and admired, superior to his brothers, and crowned with the utmost glory. This challenge befell him, I suppose, so as to spur on the youth to pursue virtue. In a way this is like trainers preparing young athletes. They stir them up to more daring enterprises,[11] and persuade them [289] to endure hardship by telling them beforehand what the prizes will be which those organizing the games will liberally confer upon those who win. They tell them of the acclamations of the spectators, the praises, and the applause. Similarly the God of all, when he sees a well-disposed person,[12] who stands out as having a genuine and excellent heart, and who gives careful attention to all that is noble, he then calls that person to take hold of that which is good. He reveals to him beforehand the things that are to come, and so deliberately stirs him up to a ready willingness, that is, a willingness for what is virtuous.

So then, on one occasion a vision and heavenly message was

10. Lit. "firstfruits."
11. Var. "thinking" or "mind."
12. Lit. "soul."

delivered to the young man Joseph, and I would imagine that he caused some astonishment to his brothers when he communicated it to them. *He said, "Listen to this dream that I dreamed: I saw that we were binding sheaves out in the field, and my sheaf arose and stood upright, and your sheaves turned and bowed down to my sheaf." The brothers said to him, "Will you indeed reign over us, or have dominion over us?" So they hated him even more because of his dreams and his words.*[13]

See, then, how their maliciousness arises and grows, and in a way the matters revealed in the dreams provided some sort of fuel for their jealousy. Since they were wholly and utterly given over to vexation to begin with, especially over the fact Joseph should be honored, how unbearable would it be for them to be brought to bow down, and to treat him as being of the highest and most noble rank?

It is worth observing that jealousy always proceeds in an ungodly fashion, and in every instance leads to evil. We find that it is blind and extremely wild, as well as being opposed to God. For note that when God announced to Joseph his future glory and fame—and it is necessary here to understand clearly that God does not decide to do things like this for those not worthy to take hold of heavenly honors—then the others should have rejoiced over such a distinguished brother, who now possessed such a hope and was privileged with divine favor. Yet they did not do this. Rather, they were provoked to extreme envy, and raged like wild animals. Further, they found fault, in effect, with God, who promised to give him this glory and who foretold that he would be a person of some importance.

This same thing, we find, is what happened in the case of Cain and Abel. For while the God of all found Abel's sacrifice worthy of approval, and fire came down from heaven and received the offering, he had no regard for that of Cain. Immediately Cain was filled with murderous envy, and, directing his wrath at the one who enjoyed the favor of heaven, he deceived his brother, and, what is more, he utterly destroyed him. In such instances jealousy always takes matters to an extreme.

Yet what was the interpretation of the visions? We take the

13. Gn 37.6–8.

sheaf as a sign of a future time. The rising up of one sheaf in reality indicates something eminent in glory. So then, that the time would come when the divine Joseph would indeed be glorious, and the rest of the brothers would also fall down before him, as it were, and be subject to him, Joseph's sheaf figuratively portrayed when the sheaves of the others bowed to it.

The revelations given to Joseph in his dream, however, were not limited to these things, but [292] he saw another dream, and again he told it to his blessed father and his brothers. *He saw another dream*, it says, *and he related it to his father and his brothers. He said, "Behold, I dreamed another dream: the sun, moon, and eleven stars were bowing down to me." Then his father rebuked him and said to him, "What is this dream you have dreamed? Shall I and your mother and your brothers actually come and bow down to the ground before you?" So his brothers were jealous of him, but his father kept the matter in mind.*[14]

The old man was clever and eminently endowed with wisdom from above. For he did in fact understand the implications[15] of the visions, and he rebuked the boy, saying, *"Shall I and your mother and your brothers actually come and bow down to the ground before you?"* What can this mean, but that this manner of rebuke was both necessary and wise? For with innate cleverness he restrained the jealousy of those who had heard the dreams, and in a certain way he also curbed the insufferable and excessive boldness which the young man exuded in abundance, and called him to a milder manner of conduct. But he did not let the hope that the dreams had given the lad be depreciated by his brothers. Yet neither did he lightly esteem the respect due to himself as a father, as though Joseph should seize his future preeminence before the time came. See, then, how skillfully Jacob softens the unwelcome effect of the visions.

Now Rachel, who had given birth to Joseph, had already died. Yet Jacob said, *"Shall I and your mother bow down to you?"* But he did this, as I just said, to bring down the high-mindedness of the young man, and to ease the jealousy of the brothers that had been stirred up against him.

14. Gn 37.9–11.
15. Lit. "force."

Jacob himself actually expected the dreams to come to pass. For he had not been listening inattentively, nor did he overlook the importance of the words, as though he had taken them to be meaningless. But *he kept the matter in mind*, because he was confident perhaps that these things would be fulfilled in due course.

After the account of the dreams, the brothers set off together to graze the flocks in Shechem. Then, when a short space of time had passed, the father urged young Joseph to go and visit his brothers. *He said, "Are not your brothers tending the flocks in Shechem? Come, I will send you to them." And Joseph answered him, "Here I am." Israel then said to him, "Go and see if your brothers and the sheep are well, and bring me word."*[16] Then Joseph agreed to go most willingly, and so he set out and left the valley of Hebron.

When Joseph was wandering around the wilderness, he happened to meet someone who asked him why he was there, and where and to whom he was going. In response to this Joseph immediately replied, *"I am looking for my brothers. Can you tell me where they are grazing the flocks?" The man said to him, "They have moved on from here, for I heard them saying, 'Let us go to Dothan.'"*[17]

As Joseph was approaching that place, there was an unexpected plot against him. For the earlier jealousy seemed to be still active at that time. So the sons of Bilhah and Zilpah, the maidservants, were eager to kill him. [293] *They said, "Behold, that dreamer is coming. Come now, and let us kill him and throw him into one of the pits; and we shall say, 'A wild animal has devoured him.' Then we shall see what will become of his dreams!" Reuben heard this, and he tried to deliver him from their hands, saying, "Let us not take his life." Reuben said to them, "Do not shed blood. Throw him into one of these pits in the wilderness, but do not raise a hand against him." He said this in order to deliver him from their hands and return him to his father.*[18] So removing the coat of many colors, they put Joseph down into a pit alive, though he would soon die.[19]

Then some Ishmaelites, traders in spices, were making their

16. Gn 37.13–14.
17. Cf. Gn 37.15–17.
18. Gn 37.19–22.
19. Cf. Gn 37.23–24.

way to Egypt. Judah made the decision (for he had evidently appealed for them not to kill their brother), and they sold the boy to the traders, who were willing to pay twenty pieces of gold for him. And so Joseph was carried off to Egypt.[20]

Reuben, however, did not see what had happened. He came to the pit, and when he did not see the boy, he supposed him to have suffered some kind of danger. So he tore his garments, and blamed his brothers for what had happened to Joseph. *He said, "The boy is no more. And as for me, where shall I go now?"*[21] In effect this meant, "How can I return to our father, or how will he welcome us back without the son he so loved? What shall we say when our father asks about the boy?"

So they dipped the coat of many colors in goat's blood and brought it to their father. They fabricated a story full of guile and deceit, *and they said, "We found this. See now if it is your son's coat or not."*[22] The father began to lament, perhaps also to some degree crying out against his sons' jealousy and ungodly scheming, *and he said, "A wild animal has devoured Joseph."*[23] It was impossible for him to be consoled, and he paid no heed at all to their attempts. He responded to the fate of the boy with despair, for it says, *He did not wish to be comforted, and said, "I will go down to the grave[24] to my son, mourning."*[25]

Moving now beyond the bounds of the literal sense, inquiry will be further made into the interpretation of inner meanings. By filling in the shadows, which are things perceived by the senses, with the colors of the truth, the extraordinary beauty of the spiritual contemplation will be unfolded, as we are able.

3. Now the wife who had given birth to Joseph was the younger Rachel, the one beautiful in appearance, with bright eyes that radiated beams of charm. Yet Leah did not have such an attraction. How do we know this? Because it is written, "Leah's eyes were weak, but Rachel was fine-looking, with an extremely beau-

20. Cf. Gn 37.25–28.
21. Cf. Gn 37.29–30.
22. Gn 37.32.
23. Gn 37.33.
24. Or "Hades."
25. Cf. Gn 37.35.

tiful face."[26] Leah, we say, is the mother of the Jews, that is, the synagogue. We obtain proof of this both from the description of her eyes, and from the meaning of her name. For the inner, spiritual sight of the Jewish synagogue is in actual fact devoid of beauty and greatly infirm, since "they have eyes, but do not see," as the prophet says.[27] For they were not acquainted with the writings of Moses, nor were they inclined to examine the mysteries present in them, through which Emmanuel is portrayed in many different ways. Also, as we have stated elsewhere, Leah means "laboring."[28] For the Jewish synagogue labored under the heavy and intolerable burden of the law given through Moses. Accordingly, Christ [296] calls those who are laboring and burdened to the liberty that comes through faith, saying, "Come to me, all you who labor and are burdened, and I will give you rest."[29]

Whereas Leah was of such a nature, the eyes of Rachel were very pure. For the church of the Gentiles saw the glory of Christ, and beheld the Father in him. The church was called to communion with Christ as his spiritual bride, following the first bride. For this younger bride has no defect,[30] while the first has aged[31] and become old, and is ready to disappear.[32]

Now the name Rachel means "flock of God."[33] For the church is the flock of the Savior, who spoke to the Jews through one of the holy prophets and said, "I will not be your shepherd. What is to die, let it die, and what is to perish, let it perish. Let those that remain eat one another's flesh."[34] But concerning us he says, "My sheep hear my voice and follow me, and I will give them eternal life." He is therefore a good shepherd, and he is preeminent in all things.[35]

---

26. Gn 29.17.
27. Jer 5.21.
28. The Hebrew verb $lā'āh$, with which the name Leah seems to be cognate, indicates a state of weariness.
29. Mt 11.28.
30. Lit. "wrinkle"; cf. Eph 5.27.
31. Var. "turned grey."
32. Cf. Heb 8.13.
33. The Hebrew term $rāḥēl$ means "ewe."
34. Zec 11.9.
35. Cf. Jn 10.14; Col 1.18.

Yet, since he became one of us, he is also called a sheep. And so the wise John pointed him out to the people of the Jews, saying, "Behold, the Lamb of God who takes away the sin of the world."[36] Many thousands of animals were sacrificed as types under the law, but not one of them wiped away the sin of the world, for "it is impossible for the blood of bulls and goats to take away sin."[37] But it is the Lamb without blemish, the true and perfect sacrifice, who has taken away the sin of the world. So then, he too is reckoned to be a sheep along with us. And for this reason he is also called a son of the church, being the firstborn among brothers.[38]

One ought to know also that Joseph means "added by God" or "growth of God." For the holy assembly of the children of the church is always growing. Therefore, she was told, "Lift your eyes, look around, O Zion, and see them all. Behold, they have gathered together and have come to you."[39] And again, "Behold, they come from afar, some from the north, and some from the west, and others from the land of the Persians."[40] Further, it is written somewhere in the Acts of the Apostles that "the Lord added to their number daily those who were being saved."[41] And also, "More and more people believed and were added to the Lord, multitudes of both men and women."[42] In the spiritual sense then, Joseph, as I have already said before, is suitably interpreted as those in Christ, namely those added by God.

So it would be quite accurate for us to say that Joseph indicates Christ under the present economy and those who believe in him. For he himself is indeed the head, and we are the body and individually members of it.[43] Also, he is the vine, and we are like the branches that grow upon it,[44] joined together in the unity of the Spirit through sanctification.

36. Jn 1.29.
37. Heb 10.4.
38. Rom 8.29.
39. Is 49.18.
40. Is 49.12.
41. Acts 2.47.
42. Acts 5.14.
43. Cf. 1 Cor 12.27.
44. Cf. Jn 15.5.

It says that Joseph was seventeen years old. Here, the Scripture is drawing to our attention, I suppose, the fact that he was just a youth. Yet we say too that Emmanuel himself was the youngest with respect to certain others, since we may ascribe a seniority in regard to time to those who came before him [297], such as Moses and the prophets. So, examining the meaning of those things written, we shall consider that something else is signified by them. For the number of years will also perhaps portray to us somehow the profound mystery of the economy of the Incarnation. And the way in which it does this I will try to explain as clearly as I am able, recalling what I have already said elsewhere.

4. It is customary for the sacred Scripture, with respect to numbers that are repeated after reaching their prescribed end, that they be taken as symbols of perfection. This is what I mean: if one counts up to ten, and wishes to extend his calculation further, he will begin again with a single unit, and so he will continue all the way to the end.[45] Likewise with a series of seven days.[46] Beginning at the first day, he will count in order up to the seventh. Accordingly, when one has reached the end of the number of days, one comes back again to the first.

So then, the sacred word deems that numbers like this should be taken by us as symbolic. With regard to the distribution of the talents, for instance, and the future allotment of rewards in proportion to one's industriousness in the work of God, it says that the one who had received ten talents should also be appointed over ten cities. That the gifts are given in equal proportion to the total perfection of those thus honored, Christ, the distributor of these things, here shows. Also, a certain one of the saints said that the barren woman would give birth to seven children.[47] Seven is here put in the place of many, and would be reckoned as a perfect number by those who like to work out the significance of numbers.

---

45. Cyril appears to be referring here to the decimal counting system, in which, after reaching a tenth, the number one is reintroduced followed by a sequence leading back up to a tenth.

46. *hebdomas*, "a heptad, group of seven."

47. For "ten cities," Lk 19.17; "seven children," 1 Sm 2.5.

When, therefore, it states concerning Joseph that he was *ten and seven years old*,[48] we grant that Emmanuel consisted of one Christ and Son, composed of two perfections—of both deity and humanity. For we do not accept the opinion of some who consider that the divine temple, which the divine Logos[49] possessed from the holy Virgin, was void of a rational soul. But as he was perfect in his deity, so also in his humanity, while existing as a single being in a way that is ineffable and beyond understanding. The number ten, then, indicates to us in a hidden manner[50] perfection of deity. This being so, seven further indicates perfection of humanity, being less than the ten relating to perfection in the Trinity, yet being added to it and, as it were, attached to it. For the seven comes after the number ten.[51] The divine Logos[52] from the Father exists within the excellence of the Trinity, that is, the Godhead. But the human element is inferior to and less than the glory of God. The divine Logos is understood to be preexisting, while that which is human is joined to him. Therefore, the number ten is necessarily placed first, and seven is added on. This is what it means, then, when it says Joseph was *ten and seven years old.*

Note my concern for both that which is temporary and that which is without beginning, with respect to the age of Emmanuel that is. For as regards the matter of counting his years, he was in fact just like Joseph, yet he had eternal past existence in addition. For he was indeed called to a manner of birth which is to be understood as being just like ours, and on account of his humanity he was assigned a number of years, even though as the Word he is God, and eternal past existence is wholly applicable to him. For he is also to be understood as being truly coeternal with God the Father, as the divine John said [300], "In the beginning was the Word, and the Word was with God, and the Word was God."[53]

---

48. In Gn 37.2 the LXX literally phrases Joseph's age as "ten seven." The Hebrew text, however, has "seven ten."

49. See n. 52 below.

50. Lit. "in a riddle," "in a puzzle."

51. Cyril is still speaking of the sequence of the numerals as appearing in the LXX text.

52. *Theos Logos*, "the God-Word"; also two sentences later.

53. Jn 1.1.

So I say once again, the divine Joseph was seventeen years old, and he tended his father's flocks with his brothers, the sons of Zilpah and Bilhah, that is, the sons of the maidservants. So it was that the Word came from God, and as a human being he walked up and down the land of the Jews, restoring the lost sheep of the house of Israel to the love of God the Father. For as the blessed Paul writes, "God was in Christ, reconciling the world to himself."[54]

Now Emmanuel acted as shepherd for those who were born to bondage, those who were in a way like the sons of the two maidservants, of illegitimate birth, whose lot was not to be freeborn. For after the reign of Jeroboam, the ten tribes were no longer content with Jerusalem, and so they went off and dwelt in Samaria, with Jeroboam leading them on in this matter. Yet there they went astray and worshiped the golden calves. For this reason, God brought charges against them as being two women who played the harlot. This is what he said through the mouth of Ezekiel: "Son of man, there were two women, daughters of the same mother. They played the harlot in Egypt, acting immorally in their youth. There their breasts fell, there they lost their virginity. The older one was named Oholah, and her sister was named Oholibah. They became mine, and they gave birth to sons and daughters. As for their names, Oholah is Samaria, and Oholibah is Jerusalem."[55]

So the Son,[56] having taken on our nature, became a shepherd along with those born in bondage and harlotry. For those of Israel who were preeminent in the matters of the law taught the people, and yet Christ too taught those who came to him, instructing them in the mysteries and bringing them into the path of truth. And that path was himself. That is why he said, "I am the way."[57] The scribes and Pharisees, however, who gloried in their code of laws, fed the people upon thorns and thistles, upon error, on the doctrines and commandments of men. But Christ fed them upon good pasture, on fresh grass, as it were,

---

54. 2 Cor 5.19.
55. Ezek 23.2–4.
56. Var. add "of God, the Word."
57. Jn 14.6.

this being the most excellent and wonderful knowledge of the gospel teachings. Those other shepherds were unconcerned and defective, and what is more they were slaves to unjust gain, insane with boundless greed. They consumed the milk, clothed themselves in the wool, and slaughtered the fatlings, as stated by the prophet.[58] They were uncaring hirelings, considering it not the least bit worthwhile to exert themselves on behalf of the sheep.

As the sons of Zilpah and Bilhah found fault with Joseph, so also that cantankerous bunch of godless Pharisees brought false accusations against Emmanuel, even daring to impugn his glory. Impiously, they called him a Samaritan and a drunkard. They said, moreover, that he was influenced by demonic forces, empowered by the working of Beelzebul to drive [301] the evil spirits out of the afflicted.

Therefore, speaking through the mouth of the prophet, Emmanuel himself cries out against the prating of the Jews, saying, "Woe to them, for they have turned away from me. They are wretched, because they have sinned against me. Though I redeemed them, they spoke lies against me."[59] And again it says, "Their rulers will fall by the sword, because of their unbridled tongue."[60] So then, that horde of insolent and narrow-minded Pharisees prated against Christ. And this, I believe, corresponds to the brothers bringing false charges against Joseph.

It says that Joseph was beloved by his father, because he was the son of his old age. Now even before our Savior manifested himself in the world in flesh, there were other shepherds who were good and noble. First of all, there was the divine Moses, and then following him a succession of those who tended the spiritual flocks. The Father, however, had an especial love for the Son, even though he was after the others, having come in the latter times of the world. While it is quite appropriate that Jacob should have Joseph as a son of his old age, God himself does not grow old. He has no beginning, nor does he increase in age, but he is ever perfect. Seeing it is wise for our remarks

---

58. Cf. Ezek 34.3.
59. Hos 7.13.
60. Hos 7.16.

not to stray far from our proper subject matter, we only say that Emmanuel was like a son born to God the Father in old age, since he came at the end times of the world, namely the present age, and after him there is no other. We expect to be saved by no one else. Indeed, he alone is sufficient, because we say that the salvation and life of the world lie in no other. He will shepherd us forever, as the psalmist says,[61] and we will be placed under the care of this beloved one. He appeared, as I just mentioned, in the latter times of the world, and in flesh, although he preexisted as God. We say in fact that he is coeternal with the Father.

Joseph, then, was especially loved by his father. He gave him a multicolored coat as a special gift, something that stands as a clear indication of his affection. For his brothers, however, this was a provocation to jealousy and a cause of envy, as the outcome of these matters demonstrates. The Pharisees likewise were enraged at the one who was beloved, that is, at Christ, because of the manifold[62] glory from God the Father with which he had been clothed. For, I believe, he became a cause of wonder in many ways—as the giver of life, as light and illuminator of those in darkness, as he who cleanses lepers, who raises the dead when they are already decomposing, who rebukes the sea, and who by his authority is carried upon its waves. The Jews, then, being so perplexed and consumed with an insufferable and burning envy, said to one another, "What shall we do? This man is performing many signs."[63] The multicolored coat, therefore, is a representation[64] to us of the manifold glory with which God the Father is said to have clothed the Son when he became human like us. Yet, with regard to his own proper nature, he is himself the [304] Lord of glory, even though, because of his likeness to us in the economy of his Incarnation, he might say, "Father, glorify your Son."[65]

---

61. Cf. Ps 48.14 (47.15 LXX).
62. Lit. "multiform." The word is intended to echo the description of Joseph's coat.
63. Jn 11.47.
64. Lit. "puzzle," "hint."
65. Jn 16.1.

So, for the reasons I have just stated, those sons born to the maidservants were induced to vexation. In addition to this, they became suspicious at the telling of the dreams. For having learned ahead of time how they themselves would later become subject to their brother and bow down to him, and that he would be greatly superior to them and exalted to such a glory so that even those who had given them birth would bow to him, they gnashed their teeth and resolved to murder him.

The Jews, too, were incited and not a little vexed when they learned that Emmanuel would be superior to the holy patriarchs themselves, and that all the people, or rather the whole world, would bow down to him. When they understood this, they said, "This is the heir. Come, let us kill him and take possession of his inheritance."[66] They spoke like this even though the blessed David plainly says to the incarnate Only-Begotten, "All the nations that you have made shall come and bow down before you, Lord."[67] On another occasion also, he makes evident the envy and unholy wrath of the people of Israel against Christ when he says, "The Lord reigns, let the people rage."[68]

Having, then, sufficiently demonstrated the cruel and unrestrained envy of the Jews, it is the appropriate time for us now to speak of their intolerable and murderous undertakings. Here we shall concentrate throughout upon the literal account and yet also bring out the intent with respect to the Only-Begotten becoming man. The account, in fact, brings us again to this subject.

5. So the divine Joseph was impelled by the command of his father to go to Shechem, that he should pay a visit to his brothers to see if they were well, and how they were managing in tending to the flocks. And so he went, but he was not able to find them, at least not in Shechem, as they had left there for Dothan. When the brothers saw him coming, they gave a bitter and disdainful laugh, and said, *"Behold, here comes that dreamer."* Reuben tried to forestall their determination to kill him, but they put Joseph down one of the pits, disregarding Reuben's ad-

---

66. Mt 21.38.
67. Ps 86.9 (85.9 LXX).
68. Ps 99.1 (98.1 LXX).

vice. After a short space of time they drew the youngster up out of the pit and sold him to the Ishmaelites, who took him down to Egypt. When Reuben returned to the pit and did not find the boy there, he supposed that he was already dead, the victim of a godless deed done by murderers, one that was grievously heavy to bear. So while Joseph was carried down to Egypt, his father mourned, and continued to do so with great lamentation.

Now our Lord Jesus Christ was sent from God the Father to come and visit the people of Israel, to see if they continued to enjoy good health, with regard to their spiritual condition that is, and whether the sheep under their care were faring well, being treated reasonably by the shepherds.

The shepherds, however, were not found in Shechem, but in Dothan. Shechem means "shoulder." This signifies hard work. For the inspired Scripture makes use of the shoulder sometimes as a figure of strength, and sometimes of work. Thus we say, "Put your heart into your shoulders," that is, to do hard work. As for Dothan, this means "great lack."[69] For the people of Israel were deficient, not in [305] the virtue of being hardworking, nor in having good repute with respect to the law, but they were evidently greatly lacking in righteousness and all goodness. For not one of them was righteous; there was no one doing good, not even one.[70] Rather, as God says through the prophet, they only honored him with their tongues, while their minds were elsewhere,[71] and though they sought to comply with the regulations given through Moses, their hearts had removed themselves far away, for they devoted themselves only to the teachings and commandments of men.

Despite this, they did in fact recognize the Beloved, the spiritual Joseph, when he came to them in human flesh.[72] For the blessed evangelist John said, "Yet even many of the rulers believed in him. But because of the Pharisees they did not confess it."[73] So, since they recognized him, they maltreated him. For

69. It is unclear how Cyril, or his source, arrives at this meaning.
70. Cf. Rom 3.10, 12; Ps 14.1, 3 (13.1, 3 LXX).
71. Cf. Is 29.13.
72. Var. omit "in human flesh."
73. Jn 12.42.

those wretched men killed him and, as it were, put him down into a pit—the deep, dark pit of death, which is Hades. For this is what the divine David, as though adopting the role of Christ, indicates to us when he says to God the Father in heaven, "Lord, you brought my soul up out of Hades; you saved me from among those going down into the pit."[74]

Observe the import[75] of the words of the sacred Scriptures, and their great exactness. *The pit,* it says, *was empty; there was no water in it.*[76] By this means it indicates to us most clearly that Hades is here being symbolized. And how is this, I ask? Because water in actual fact represents life, since it sustains life. So it says that there was no water in the pit, for Hades is not unreasonably understood to be a dwelling place that lacks life. Yet the youth was brought up. So also Christ came back to life from the dead, for the pit could not hold on to him. Neither did Christ remain in Hades, but rather he emptied it out, for to those who were in bonds God says, "Come out!"[77]

After the divine Joseph was brought up and sold to the Ishmaelites, who were spice merchants, he came to Egypt, not far away. Likewise, Christ came back to life and rose up out of the pit. Leaving Judea, he passed through the lands of the Gentiles, being conveyed there by those who were spiritual Ishmaelites, that is, those who obey God, for that is what the word means.[78] And who are these? They are the blessed disciples, whose ear is inclined to the teachings of Christ, who are the firstfruits of those greatly approved in matters of obedience and faith, and in the glory that surpasses the law. Such might also aptly be understood to be merchants of spices, spreading the fragrance of the mystery of Christ, and having every kind of virtue applied to their souls. After a certain fashion, these had bought Jesus, forsaking all the wonders present in the law, and they purchased that one most precious pearl which the Savior himself spoke

---

74. Ps 30.3 (29.4 LXX).
75. Var. "soberness."
76. Gn 37.24.
77. Cf. Is 49.9.
78. The name Ishmael is derived from the Hebrew word for "hear" (cf. Gn 16.11), which can also have connotations of obedience.

of in the parable.[79] These took Christ to the nations, serving as ministers of the gospel, everywhere [308] under the sun proclaiming him as God and Lord, as the choice stone, rejected by those spiritual builders under the law, yet choice and precious to God, having become the chief cornerstone.[80]

It was the case, however, that Reuben prevented the brothers from murdering Joseph, and Judah too was extremely troubled over the affair. Reuben was the firstborn, and the kingship was called forth from the tribe of Judah. And so, as many who were privileged to share in the likeness of the firstborn, even though they were of the Jews, these were called into the kingdom of heaven, devoting themselves to the message given through Christ. These were not a little troubled over the outrageous acts done against him. For there were a good many at that time, both in Jerusalem and in the rest of Judea, who were grieved and sympathetic towards Christ over the shameful way he was treated.

The father mourned Joseph, and it says, *he did not wish to be comforted.* In this we see how the rage and bloodthirsty scheming of the Jews against Christ exceedingly grieved God the Father in heaven. They caused such great offense that no comfort could be accepted, and it was as if no one could make appeals on their behalf. The prophets had indeed made frequent appeals to Israel, beseeching them to be saved, and yet they had done things to the prophets that are too indescribable for words. God had often shown his forbearance, for it was members of his own household who were exposing themselves to danger. But when they vented their rage against Christ himself, the Father could not be comforted. His wrath was implacable. For it was no longer just any prophet who suffered maltreatment, but the Savior of all, the Master of the prophets, namely Christ, through whom and with whom be glory to God the Father, together with the Holy Spirit, for ever and ever. Amen.

---

79. Cf. Mt 13.45–46.
80. Cf. Is 28.16; Ps 118.22 (117.22 LXX).

Concerning Judah and Tamar

1. It is the intent of inspired Scripture to indicate to us the mystery of Christ through innumerable objects. Someone might compare it to a magnificent and illustrious city that does not have just one image of its king, but very many, set up everywhere and visible to all. Observe how Scripture does not fail to fulfill this purpose in any single account, but it is present in all. Even if the literal record should seem to contain something inappropriate, this in no way prevents such a purpose being achieved, and what is present in it may be suitably unfolded. For it is not the purpose of Scripture to bring accusations against the lives of the saints. Not at all. Rather, it is to portray[81] to us the knowledge of this mystery, that the message spoken concerning it may be both clear and true, unable to be censured in any way, as though it were perverting the truth. So too the mystery of the economy relating to the Savior is depicted to us in the affair of Judah and Tamar.

It says, *It happened at that time that Judah left his brothers and went down to a certain Adullamite, whose name was Hirah. There Judah saw the daughter of a Canaanite, whose name was Shua,*[82] *and he took her and went into her. She conceived and* [309] *gave birth to a son, and she*[83] *called his name Er. She conceived again, and gave birth to a son, and called his name Onan. Then once more she bore a son, and called his name Shelah.*[84] So these three children were born to Judah.

When the boys had become young men, Judah took Tamar as a wife for his firstborn son, Er. But as Er was evil in the sight of God, before they had produced any children, he died. For it says, *God killed him.*[85] Then the father enjoined Onan to sleep with his brother's wife and to raise up offspring for the deceased. But since the child would not be his own, he violat-

---

81. Or "represent figuratively."
82. Cyril called her Saba.
83. Or "he."
84. Gn 38.1–5. For this last name Cyril follows the LXX in transcribing it as *Sêlôm*.
85. Gn 38.7.

ed the law of procreation, spilling his semen on the ground so that no seed was imparted. Immediately, he too was destroyed by the divine wrath.[86] When this happened, Judah was then afraid to give his third son, Shelah, to Tamar in marriage. The cause of his fear was that perhaps this son should likewise perish. As a reason for not proceeding with the marriage, he made the excuse that the child was not quite fully grown. *He said to his daughter-in-law, "Remain as a widow in your father's house until Shelah my son has grown up." For he thought, "Lest this son also die, like his brothers." So Tamar went and stayed in her father's house.*[87]

When some time had passed, Tamar could no longer bear the delay in marriage. By now she had somehow come to realize that her father-in-law would not fulfill what had been promised her. Rather, the delay was a pretense, and there was no hope of what she expected coming to pass. And what plot was it that she devised in response to this? It says, *Tamar his daughter-in-law was told, "Behold, your father-in-law is going up to Timnah to shear his sheep." So she removed her widow's clothing, and put on a veil, she made herself look attractive, and sat by the gates of Enaim, which is on the way to Timnah. For she had seen that Judah's son Shelah was now grown up, but he had not given her to him as his wife.*[88]

When Judah saw her, he supposed her to be a prostitute, since she had covered her face and he did not recognize her. Then he was seized by lust, and when the woman asked for payment, he promised to send her a goat, and as a pledge of the promise he gave her his staff, his ring, and his signet-cord, that is, an ornament worn around the neck.[89] (One might suppose, and quite appropriately so, that Judah was a Chaldean, since he was inclined to be adorned in a particular way. For the Chaldeans were lovers of ornaments, bedecking their hands and necks with gold, and sometimes even adorning their hair with it. For it was considered by them to be manly, a token of very high birth and of the praises due to manliness.) So these things being done, Judah carried on with his original intentions.

86. Cf. Gn 38.9–10.
87. Cf. Gn 38.11.
88. Gn 38.13–14.
89. Cf. Gn 38.15–18.

Now Tamar was brought to the home of her father [312], and later had the good fortune to find out that she was pregnant. When Judah learned of this, he said it was necessary for the woman to die, since she had committed an act of immorality. Finally, however, she showed him the staff and the other objects, *saying, "I am carrying a child by the man to whom these things belong."* She said, *"See if you recognize who it is that this ring, signet-cord, and staff belong to."* Judah recognized them and said, *"Tamar is more righteous than I am, inasmuch as I would not give her to Shelah my son."* And he did not sleep with her again.[90]

Then it says, *When she came to give birth, there were twins in her womb. As she was giving birth, one of them put out his hand, and the midwife tied a scarlet thread around it, and said, "This one will come out first." But then he drew back his hand, and immediately his brother came out. She said, "What a breach you have made for yourself!" So she called his name "Perez."*[91] *After this his brother, who had the scarlet thread on his hand, came out, and she called his name Zerah.*[92]

This is all I need to relate of the literal account. Yet, hidden within this, once again there is an important spiritual meaning. What this might be, we shall presently examine.

2. First of all, I think it needful to say that though there might be those in the inspired Scripture who distinguish themselves by doing extremely irreverent deeds, since God is well able to provide what is necessary for our profit, we shall be far removed from the harm that can come from stumbling at these offenses. If we take into account the need for us to be wise and prudent, then those things most profitable with respect to the divine economy will not escape our notice.

For let us consider that even the blessed prophet Hosea once obtained for himself a prostitute as a wife. He did not shy away from such a scandalous marriage, and he became known as the father of abominable children whose names were "Not my people" and "Not shown mercy."[93]

---

90. Cf. Gn 38.24–26.

91. This name in Hebrew means "break out" or "break through."

92. Gn 38.27–30. In Hebrew Zerah denotes "brightness," possibly referring to the color of the thread.

93. Cf. Hos 1.2–3, 6–9.

What this matter was all about and for what reasons it was done we will not shrink from discussing. For since those considered to be most prominent persons opposed the preaching of Israel's prophets and refused to accept the divine word, actions like this were performed by those holy men at that time. The reason for this was so that, seeing in what was enacted matters to be fulfilled in the future as though visibly and clearly written on a tablet, the Israelites might apply their minds to the discovery of what was beneficial, and that they themselves might pass on what was profitable and important to understand, and that others might also be persuaded to respond. For they learned that at some future period they would no more be God's people nor be classed among those shown mercy, but they would be hardened and unloved. Had they not become sick of such things and shown to be thoroughly guilty? So the prophet cohabiting with the prostitute was a representation of God, who, after a fashion, was living together with the immoral and utterly defiled woman of the Jewish synagogue, from whom he brought forth children.

Seeing, therefore, that we now understand the way in which things are accommodated to the times in which they took place, we shall willingly cease, I say, from all outcry and finding fault with the immorality of Tamar and indeed of Judah too, but [313] rather we shall say it was a union that occurred by way of accommodation. In fact, Tamar longed for the offspring appropriate to a free woman and yet had been deprived of a legal spouse. Nor was Judah greatly at fault, since he only chose to go with another woman after the death of his first wife. To us this relationship was really a matter of spiritual union and spiritual generation, the physical act of giving birth in itself showing the outlines of the types. The human mind can in no other way be directed to the truth.

3. So then, Judah went down to a certain man, whose name was Hirah. This man was a herdsman and one skilled in handling flocks. While he was there, Judah saw Shua and married her, and he made her the mother of three children, namely Er, Onan, and Shelah. Now Er means "leathery," that is to say, fleshly. Onan was "one whose heart was struck." The third was "pull-

ing out," that is to say, one who brings about a relaxation and who makes peace.[94]

Likewise, the Only-Begotten Word of God came down from heaven, as though from a certain holy country, he being the one who is truly to be praised, and who naturally possesses the glory of the kingdom. For this is what the person of Judah represents to us. The meaning of his name is evidently "praise."[95] And also the tribe of Judah was the most royal of all, and was assigned the highest preeminence. Accordingly, the divine Jacob pronounced this blessing upon him, saying, "Judah, your brothers will praise you."[96] The most-wise Paul also testified that Christ, the one worthy of praise above all creation, originated from the tribe of Judah.[97]

So the Only-Begotten Word of God came down and paid a visit to the blessed Moses as he was tending the sheep in the wilderness of Midian, for he appeared to him in the bush in the form of fire. Also, after a fashion, he was united through Moses to the synagogue of the Israelites in Egypt, as though to a foreign Canaanite woman, just as Judah, when he was tending the sheep, was joined to Shua, whose name means "highness" or "lifting up."[98] For the synagogue of the Jews, having been called, as it were, into a relationship with God, was no longer humbled and downtrodden. Whereas she had been in a mean estate of servitude, she now became lifted up and prominent, for she was redeemed as though from a furnace for smelting iron, and from a house of bondage, as it is written.[99] In Egypt, in that synagogue which belonged to a foreign land and which was devoted to the worship of idols, there were then three peoples that held the place of sons with respect to God, and that were born, so to speak, from the same mother, though their births were separated in time. And how this is so, we shall presently explain.

Then Judah gave Tamar to Er, his firstborn, in marriage. But

94. While it is possible that in Hebrew Er might be related to leather and Shelah to the idea of relaxation, the other meanings are doubtful.
95. Cf. Gn 29.35.
96. Gn 49.8.
97. Cyril seems to be referring to Heb 7.14.
98. The name is, in fact, of uncertain meaning.
99. Cf. Ex 13.3; Dt 4.20.

as he was evil God killed him, and Onan, the second in order of birth and age, immediately succeeded him by marrying Tamar. He, however, did not wish to raise up offspring for his brother, and so being the object of divine wrath, he was killed like the first son. Then the father did not hand over the third son, Shelah, to join Tamar in marriage, fearing that he also might perish as well as the first two sons. [316]

What this matter is about I will try to explain as God gives me wisdom.[100] As for the first synagogue in Egypt, which we have established to be one that is foreign, because it had then become totally unrestrained in adopting both Gentile manners and customs, God reformed it. This he did through the conduct prescribed by the law. It was as though he had appointed a new synagogue, one that was quite different from the first. It is this that is indicated by Tamar.

Observe how the mystery is to be found in the meanings of names. For Tamar means "abandonment" or "shaken."[101] So also the synagogue of the Jews was in actual fact shaken and abandoned. In what way? Well, the ministration according to the law did not continue unshakeable for ever, but gave way to the ministration in the Spirit. And when this ministration through Christ was introduced, it found fault with the former, since this new one was without fault. Now Christ betrothed the church to himself, as a pure virgin, and in doing so left the older, first bride. Therefore, the synagogue of the Jews can be fairly interpreted as abandoned and shaken.

Now the fact that "no one is justified before God by the law"[102] and that in the Jewish synagogue there was no share in the peace of God (for, according to what is written, "the law produces wrath")[103] is figuratively portrayed by the birth of the sons of Judah who were united with Tamar. For Er the firstborn was "leathery," that is, earthly. As he was evil, he was condemned to death. The first people of God also showed themselves to be evil with respect to the truth. They grumbled against God and

---

100. Var. omit "as God gives me wisdom."
101. In Hebrew the name Tamar in fact means "date palm."
102. Cf. Gal 3.11.
103. Rom 4.15.

said, "Can God prepare a table in the wilderness? Though he struck the rock, and waters flowed forth and streams ran abundantly, can he also give bread?"[104] Furthermore, when the spies who were sent to the promised land came back, they at once began to wail like children about being completely undone, and by their disbelief they insulted the God who can do all things. Consequently, they perished, and none of them entered the promised land, but their corpses fell in the wilderness, as it is written.[105] So, the firstborn Er, namely the one who was evil and carnal, perished first, as he bore no fruit of godliness. This further shows us childlessness in the form of a type, for the sensible things are, as it were, images of spiritual things.[106]

After the first, there came a second people, being those who were born, so to speak, as God's son when he redeemed them and brought them out from the house of bondage. These were brought through the Jordan under the leadership of Joshua, and they inherited the promised land. After this they were ruled by judges. Yet they too fell under the disapprobation of heaven. This people were indeed Onan, that is, one who was struck in his heart. For remarkably they turned to polytheism, forsaking the one, true Being. And so this people were also ruined and made subject to foreigners, which is what the book named after those called judges teaches us.

So also did this people die in a state of childlessness, just like Er, because they had sown nothing upon the land. This, then, was a picture of complete failure to produce fruit, or to raise up offspring[107] for his brother. [317] This people coming in the middle, that is, the second in order of time, shrank back from their duty. They did not, through virtuous behavior in accordance with the law, raise up for God, as it were, any offspring in the place of those who had disobeyed him, who would show themselves through their actions to be those now growing up to be the new people of God. For this, I believe, is the figurative meaning of raising up offspring for his brother.

104. Ps 78.19–20 (77.19–20 LXX).
105. Heb 3.17; cf. Nm 14.29.
106. Or "of things in the mind."
107. Lit. "seed."

Two sons had now been taken away and could no more be the source of any blessings (for one was evil, the other was struck in his heart). The father then kept back his third son from being united to Tamar, fearing lest somehow he too would perish, just like those who had already died. Likewise, God did not permit the third and newest people, coming in the last times spoken of by the holy prophets (along with whom also the divine Baptist, their fellow, pointed out the one coming from heaven, namely Christ), to be held, so to speak, in the arms of the Jewish synagogue. Nor did he wish to have offspring from her, lest somehow that too should perish. "For the law produces wrath," and no one can ever be justified by it.

Note, then, how Shelah is especially shown to be a type of this last people, those who are a people through faith. For his name means "pulling out," or "releasing." For when the divine wrath was expended, as it were, upon those of the race of Israel on account of their profane acts and their insufferable raging against Christ, those who believed were pulled out, as though from the mouth of a wild beast. They were released, in a way, from the bonds that had seized hold of those for whom punishment was necessary. For, according to the Scriptures, "a remnant will be saved."[108] And so God said in a certain place through the mouth of the prophet, "As a shepherd pulls out from the mouth of a lion two legs or a piece of an ear, thus will the people of Israel be pulled out."[109] For this reason, then, Shelah is named "pulling out."

It is not difficult to discover, then, that those who believe are excused[110] from union with Tamar, which is in order to bear fruit by the law, and they have been pulled out from the multitude of those who are perishing. As the blessed Paul said concerning the things he could boast of under the law, "But whatever gains I had, these things I counted as loss for the sake of Christ."[111] For he did not desire to have his own righteousness, by which I

---

108. Is 10.22; Rom 9.27.
109. Am 3.12.
110. Or "exempt."
111. Phil 3.7.

mean that coming through the law, but the righteousness which comes by faith in Christ Jesus.

So Shelah, the youngest son, was not united with Tamar. For this reason, she remained a widow, continuing in this state for a long time. For when God no more allowed the Jewish synagogue to be fruitful, this widow, the spiritual bride, was called one who is childless and without husband, and she was in fact so, for in one place Christ said, "She is not my wife, and I am not her husband."[112]

Is this widow then completely disregarded after this? Is she no longer worthy of God's attention? Do not think so. Even though she was condemned for the acts of ungodliness that she had done last of all, because of his innate goodness God will show mercy to her in the final ages of the world, and she herself will also bear the fruit of the tokens of Christ. That she will later follow suit after the Gentiles, we learn through nothing other than those things written themselves. For when Judah went up to shear his sheep, he had intercourse with her on the way, [320] and let her have his staff, ring, and signet-cord, promising also to send her a goat. For Christ too, giving his own most serious attention to receiving, as it were, the fruit of the spiritual flock, meaning those who believe and who have been sanctified in the Spirit,[113] will at some future time bring the Jewish synagogue, though being somewhat indifferent and not entirely willing, into the fellowship of the Spirit. Then he will show her to be fruitful, being pregnant, as it were, with the wisdom she will receive from him. He will present himself to her, just as he did to us, as a staff of power, as the image and likeness of God the Father, which is what is signified by the ring, and as the most beautiful among the sons of men, for this, I believe, is the meaning of the signet-cord. In fact every item used as an ornament may be interpreted spiritually as a symbol of beauty. And he will also send her a goat; that is, he will freely grant forgiveness of her sinful deeds. For according to the law a goat was slain as a sin offering and is a figure of the forgiveness of transgressions.

So Tamar was saved, even though death fell to her lot and she

112. Hos 2.2 (2.4 LXX).
113. Or "in spirit."

was subject to the ultimate penalty, for Tamar was condemned as one who had played the harlot. Nevertheless she was saved, because she showed the staff, the ring, and the signet-cord. Further, she openly admitted that she had become pregnant through Judah, that she might produce his offspring.[114] Christ likewise will one day deliver the Jewish synagogue from the punishment that is due, when she brings the tokens of communion to him, showing clearly that she has conceived what is from him. For thus those who have sought to be approved through faith in Christ declare in a certain place, "Out of fear for you, O Lord, we have conceived and been in labor; we have brought forth the breath of your salvation, which we have produced upon the earth."[115]

Then the time came to give birth, and Tamar was in labor with twin babies. The firstborn put out his hand, but then drew it back in again, though it already had the scarlet thread attached to it. The second then came out first, having broken through the breach, as it were. Then the first child came out last. Now this is a clear indication to us that the Gentiles would be called before those of the race of Israel, and that those coming in the end times would be honored with the glory of the firstborn. There can be no doubt that the one which has received the sacrifice of God will also follow on later, for the scarlet thread is a figure of the sacred blood.

Who, then, is it that has made a breach through the dividing wall,[116] and who called the second in place of the firstborn, putting the first last? Evidently it is Christ, through whom and with whom be glory to God the Father, together with the Holy Spirit,[117] for ever and ever. Amen.

More Concerning Joseph

The intervening account about Judah and Tamar having reached a suitable end, we must now come to the rest of the

---

114. Lit. "fruit."
115. Is 26.18.
116. Cf. Eph 2.14.
117. Var. "be glory with his Father, who is without beginning, and together with the all-holy Spirit of life."

matters concerning Joseph, some of which we have already mentioned.

When the divine Joseph was thrown into the pit by his brothers, we have taken him to be a figurative representation of Christ [321]. This was also the case when he was brought up from the pit and sold to the Ishmaelites, merchants of fragrant spices, distributing them to those who did not have them. And we previously said that by these merchants Joseph was brought into Egypt.[118] For the Only-Begotten condescended to empty himself, becoming like one of us, and was called a brother to those upon the earth. In the presence of the rest of the people of Israel he suffered death, endured the cross, and descended into Hades, of which the pit was a figure. Yet he came back to life again, and was separated from those of the race of Israel. He was given, as it were, to the merchants of spiritual spices, that is, to the holy apostles. These went into the lands of the Gentiles, spreading the fragrance of his myrrh, conveying through the proclamation of the gospel to those who did not know him the form of servanthood that he took upon himself. For he is preached as having become flesh on our account, and as having come in the form of a servant.[119] This, I believe, is the significance of Joseph being brought by the Ishmaelites into Egypt. Now what sufferings befell him there and what he had to do as a result, let us investigate, if it so please.

Joseph, still being young and in his adolescence, overcame the wantonness of the Egyptian woman, though he was forcefully incited to desire to commit an unlawful act. For she shamelessly took hold of his garments and he was not a little pressured to engage in an unacceptable sin. But he abandoned his garment and escaped her wild lustfulness, being unconquered by passion. Afterwards he was falsely accused when the woman brought charges against him, yet in these shameful accusations he was both temperate and longsuffering. All the same, it says that he was put in prison.

Christ, too, was among the Gentiles, I mean in the persons of

---

118. Var. add "Then, when we were interpreting this, we taught that the following is the case."
119. Cf. Phil 2.7.

the holy apostles, who said that they bore his scars in their own bodies.[120] They refused to be conformed to the things of which the world is mindful, but distanced themselves from fleshly lusts. For such always is the life of the saints. Yet for this reason they were plotted against and falsely accused by those in the habit of deeming burdensome those wishing to live in Christ, and they met with severe testing and imprisonment. They remembered, however, what Christ said: "If you were of the world, the world would love its own. But since you are not of the world, for this reason the world hates you."[121] It was in this same way that the lustful woman did not care about Joseph.

When, however, the troubles increased, their effect was softened by the grace of God, making them more reasonable to bear, for, as it says,[122] the jailer was greatly pleased with Joseph.[123] When Pharaoh's eunuchs, namely the cupbearer and the baker, were imprisoned, he explained their dreams. And for this reason, it says, the divine Joseph was the cause of considerable wonder. Then Pharaoh himself also dreamed that in the not-too-distant future there would be a time of fruitfulness and a hard time of famine, which was first seen as cows that were fat and strong, and later as ears of corn. [324] The wise men of Egypt had nothing to say, as they were completely without the knowledge required to be able to explain what was revealed through the dreams. It was testified of Joseph, however, that he was such a one who could do this, and so he came and gave the interpretation. Then Pharaoh too was amazed, and appointed him chamberlain and governor over his dominion.

Now Christ suffered persecution, as it were, in the persons of the holy apostles, as I just said. Yet when these men of whom we speak were undergoing such troubles, they were like those given great wisdom and the ability to explain matters beyond words. They were shown to be among those having dominion in the world, and those having authority over the earth. They also

---

120. Cf. Gal 6.17.

121. Jn 15.19.

122. Cyril actually wrote "as I said," although he has not mentioned this detail before.

123. Cf. Gn 39.21.

believed that they had knowledge of future events through the revelation of God by the Spirit. They agreed to become stewards and rulers of the Gentiles, and to disseminate teachings in the time of famine, teachings which concern life incorruptible, that is, the divine and heavenly word, and they gave the instruction that leads to everything most noble. These men also took possession, or rather Christ did through them, of the lands of the Gentiles for God the Father, just as Joseph in fact did for Pharaoh with the land of Egypt.

Furthermore, two sons were born to Joseph, namely Manasseh and Ephraim, whose mother was Asenath, the daughter of Potiphera the priest. Manasseh means "forgetting" the bad things that had happened, while Ephraim means a "growing" or a "producing" that leads to something better.[124] They were the offspring, so to speak, of a sacred mother, namely the church. Also, those called out from the Gentiles are, through faith in Christ, counted among the sons of God, who likewise will be caused to forget their troubles. "For their former affliction will be forgotten," it says, "and it will not come into their mind. Everlasting praise will be upon their heads, and gladness and joy will overtake them; pain, sorrow, and groaning will flee away."[125] Therefore, they will in due course arrive at that time when their evils will be forgotten. They will also come to grow, hastening to the sweet goal of their hope. For they will be translated from earthly things into the heavenly, passing from temporal things to those that transcend time, from corruption to incorruption, from shame to glory, from weakness to strength.

As the famine was harsh and protracted, the sons of Jacob went down to Egypt to buy food. In the brief account that is presented at this point, Joseph was in effect playing with them, for he claimed that it was not at all for grain that they had come into that land, but rather to act as spies. So he did not permit them to leave the land of Egypt without obligation, but he demanded that they should bring down Benjamin, his younger

---

124. Cyril here is not far off the mark in both instances. The Hebrew name Manasseh resembles the verb form for "causing to forget," while Ephraim relates to the word for "fruitful."

125. Is 65.16; cf. 51.11.

brother, something which their father scarcely allowed them to do. When they came with the boy, Joseph summoned the family, who washed in water and had their fill of bread and wine.

So too the Jews, having been so afflicted and oppressed by an unbearable famine, a spiritual one that is, will eventually forsake their haughtiness and arrogance, and they will come to Christ, desiring to be fed by him [325] with holy and spiritual food that gives life. Yet he will not receive them unless they are accompanied by the new[126] people of God, of which Benjamin was a type. But when they come with one soul and in one accord, as it were, he will happily receive them and bring them into his own household, which is the church. Then he will wash them in pure water, in the washing of regeneration, and will feed them upon bread and wine, which spiritually signify God's word.

Besides this, we also note that when the brothers came with Benjamin and were honored at his table, as I just stated, Joseph was recognized by them. Yet he allotted them no portion of land, but ordered them to hurry back and bring his father Jacob down to him. After he had come down and Joseph now saw him there together with his children, then he assigned to them the best of all the land. This is a clear indication that Christ will receive the people of Israel when they turn to him in the last times of the world. Then they will evidently be joined, as being of one soul, with the new people of God. This latter, as I said, is signified by Benjamin. Further, the allotted portion that we hope for will not be given to us separately from the holy fathers.[127] For although they died in faith, as the wise Paul said, "they did not receive what was promised, because God had provided something better for us so that they would not be made perfect without us."[128] Thus we wait for the fathers, so that we will not be made perfect without them. Then, together with the holy fathers, we—the first, middle, and last people of God together—will receive the most excellent and inalienable inheritance of the kingdom of heaven in Christ, through whom and

---

126. The adjective "new" may also be translated "young."
127. That is, the patriarchs of Israel.
128. Heb 11.39–40.

with whom be glory to God the Father, together with the Holy Spirit, for ever. Amen.

Concerning Joseph and his sons, Ephraim and Manasseh

1. It is indeed the case that, "Every good thing given and every perfect gift is from above, coming down from the Father of lights."[129] I mean that there is no good thing so noble or excellent that we do not gain through Christ. For he has become, it says, "mediator between God and men,"[130] and "through him we have access in one Spirit to God the Father in heaven."[131] Accordingly, he also said, "No one comes to the Father, except through me."[132] In him and through him is the whole fullness of grace and a marvelous inheritance. For although as God he was rich, for our sakes he became poor, in order that by his poverty we might become rich,[133] and so ascending to the same degree of glory as the holy fathers, we shall be able to share in that most attractive hope that they had.

Consider, then, the true account of these matters, and let the eyes of your mind enter into the sacred Scriptures. Here it reads as follows: *It happened after these things that Joseph was told his father was ill. So taking his two sons, Manasseh and Ephraim, he went to Jacob.* [328][134] *When Jacob was told, "Behold, your son Joseph has come to you," Israel summoned his strength and sat up in bed. Jacob said to Joseph, "My God appeared to me at Luz in the land of Canaan. He blessed me, and said to me, 'Behold, I will increase you and multiply you, and I will make you a multitude of nations. I will give this land to you and to your offspring after you as an everlasting possession.' Now then, your two sons who were born to you in Egypt, before I came to you in Egypt, are mine. Ephraim and Manasseh shall be mine, just as Reuben and Simeon are mine. The offspring born to you after them*

---

129. Jas 1.17.
130. 1 Tm 2.5.
131. Cf. Eph 2.18.
132. Jn 14.6.
133. Cf. 2 Cor 8.9.
134. The numbering in the Migne text omits 326 and 327, although text is not missing.

will be yours; they will be called by the name of their brothers in their inheritance. As for me, when I came back from Mesopotamia of Syria, Rachel your mother died in the land of Canaan as I was nearing the highway[135] *of Chabratha on the way to Ephratha. And I buried her by the highway, in Bethlehem."*[136]

The blessed Jacob reached a good old age, as it is written. As he was removed from everyday human concerns, he had it in mind to bless the sons of Joseph who were born to a foreign mother, Asenath the daughter of Potiphera the priest. His intention was that none of the people of Israel should despise them, deeming them to be of a strange and foreign race. With much wisdom and prudence the divine Jacob sought to teach Joseph himself and the other sons that, in keeping with the divine decree, all those born from them should be considered as belonging to their own family. For he said, *"God appeared to me in the land of Canaan and expressly promised that I would be the father of very many peoples, and that I would be enlarged to become nations and multitudes of nations."* So by this means he both persuades them to honor God with judgments that accord with the truth, and teaches that next of kin should be counted as belonging to the same family, even though they might have been born from a foreign mother.

2. These things we have stated briefly, drawing them out of the earthy literalness of the text. So it is also the case that we who have been justified by faith in Christ are sons of God, belonging to the household of the saints. In this, Christ acts as our mediator, and it is through him that we are united both to him and to the Father, and also to the assembly[137] of the saints. This is actually how it was with respect to Joseph, who was like one set in the middle, when he made Ephraim and Manasseh the sons of his own father, and so they too were entered in the register[138] of the patriarchs. For it says, *"Now your two sons who were*

---

135. Cyril retains the LXX term *hippodromos,* denoting a racecourse or a roadway for horses. There is nothing in the Hebrew text corresponding to this.
136. Gn 48.1–7.
137. Lit. "choirs."
138. *katalogos,* "list," "enrollment."

born to you in Egypt are mine. Ephraim and Manasseh shall be mine, just as Reuben and Simeon are mine." That is to say, they would be among the firstborn sons, and also be placed with those who render obedience, for Reuben was the firstborn, and Simeon means "obedience."

Through faith we who are last have become the first, and the people taken from among the Gentiles have inherited the glory of the firstborn. They have been honored on account of their obedience and willing service. For Christ himself has testified concerning them, saying, "A people I did not know served me; as soon as they heard, they obeyed me."[139] For though we have come from a mother of a different race [329] in that the church has been called out of the nations, yet Emmanuel is well able to act as intermediary, and through himself to unite us to God the Father. He assigns to us the inheritance of the saints, bringing upon us a fitting glory, and declaring us to be a holy race.

Consider how, out of love for him, Jacob placed the blessed Joseph's sons among his own. Now we too have become beloved in Christ, and since through him we have been brought forth by a spiritual birth, we have become precious to the Father, as I just said, and placed alongside the saints who went before us. If we are called sons of God the Father, we will be under the care of the one who brought us and united us to him, who is Christ. See how the blessed Jacob incorporated Ephraim and Manasseh among his own children. Yet he says, *"the offspring which are born to you after them will be yours."*[140] So you understand that even though we are called sons of God the Father, we shall no less belong to Christ. And this, I believe, is the very thing he is talking about when he says to the Father, "Those you have given me out of the world, they were yours, and you gave them to me, and I have been glorified in them."[141]

Jacob said that he buried Rachel in Bethlehem. We have mentioned several times that Rachel serves as a picture and

---

139. Ps 18.43–44 (17.44–45 LXX).

140. The words "after them" were omitted by Cyril, but as they are found in both MT and LXX (of Gn 48.6) they have been included here.

141. Jn 17.6, 10.

a type of the Gentile church. Now we would not, in my opinion, be speaking falsely if we wished to say that the church has passed into another manner of life, one that is evidently better and more beneficial than this worldly life. For the church has died to the world since she is no more mindful of the things of the world, but spiritually she is alive to God in Christ through her conduct that is in accord with the gospel. For while she is in the world on account of her life in the flesh, it is as though she is hidden, not possessing any splendor in the world. She has in effect been buried with Christ. This, I believe, is what the most-wise Paul meant when he said to us, "For you have died, and your life is hidden with Christ in God."[142] Understand that when Rachel was buried in Bethlehem, and was no longer seen, it was as though Emmanuel himself was hidden with her, for he was later to be born through the holy Virgin. Let us, then, commend such a death of the church which brings forth the principles of a holy life, a life that is in Christ.

The foregoing is, I believe, something necessary to speak of further. When the father received Joseph's sons as his own children after their mother had died, he also gave instructions about her. He indicated the plot of land in which she had been buried so that, being sure it was not in some other place, Joseph should give her the proper attention that was her due. So too God the Father instructed the Son concerning the church, and assured him that, though she had been overcome by death on account of the ancient curse, she was worthy of care and attention, The divine David therefore cried out to God the Father in heaven for us, "Command, O God, your power; strengthen, O God, what you have wrought among us."[143] He was in effect indicating the body overcome by death so that through the power of God the Father, that is, through the Son, it might be delivered from corruption and be restored again to its original condition, namely to the blessed and incorruptible life in Christ. [332]

3. Israel, being the firstborn and therefore honored with privileges befitting its seniority, fell away from the glory it then had, and the grace of such a splendid glory passed on to the

142. Col 3.3.
143. Ps 68.28 (67.29 LXX).

new people of God coming from the Gentiles. Then we, in our turn, will be in no way inferior. For it says, *When Israel saw the sons of Joseph, he asked, "Who are these?"*[144] *Joseph said to his father, "They are my sons whom God has given to me here." Jacob said, "Bring them to me that I may bless them." Now his eyes were failing with old age, and he was hardly able to see. So Joseph brought them near to him, and he kissed them and embraced them. Israel said to Joseph, "Behold, I have not been deprived of seeing your face, and God has even shown me your offspring too." Then Joseph took them off his knees, and they bowed down to Israel with their faces to the ground. Taking his sons, Joseph set Ephraim on the right, to Israel's left, and he set Manasseh on the left, to Israel's right; and so he brought them near to him. Israel then stretched out his right hand and placed it upon the head of Ephraim, the younger one, and placed his left upon the head of Manasseh, thus crossing his hands. He blessed them and said, "May the God before whom my fathers, Abraham and Isaac, were well-pleasing, the God who has sustained me from my youth until today, the angel who has delivered me from all evils, bless these children."*[145]

So the boys were presented, and the old man inquired whose they were. To this Joseph replied, *"My two sons."* Then, when they were brought near, he honored them with kisses and embraces. You see, then, how it is as though we who were unknown to God the Father have become known and brought near in Christ. He too welcomes us gladly, as the Son testifies of our relationship with him. He thus counts us worthy of his love, and invites us into union, which is a spiritual union, with himself. The kiss also is very plainly symbolic of love, and the embrace of receiving into union. So likewise the most-wise Paul writes to those who believe in Christ, saying, "Now you who were once far off have been brought near,"[146] that is, brought by Christ.[147] And again he says, "Now that you have come to know God, or rather be known by him."[148] For God the Father counts worthy of his attention and recognizes only those who have a spiritual

144. Lit. "Who are these to you?" (LXX).
145. Gn 48.8–16.
146. Eph 2.13.
147. Var. "the Son."
148. Gal 4.9.

relationship with the Son, who by him[149] have been born again through the Spirit, and who have been richly blessed through him. This is, in actual fact, similar to the way in which God recognized those in Egypt who were anointed with the blood of the lamb, when he said, "I will see the blood and I will protect you, and there will be no plague among you to destroy you when I strike the land of Egypt."[150]

Now Jacob was extremely pleased at seeing his son Joseph. *He said, "Behold, I have not been deprived of seeing your face, and* [333] *God has even shown me your offspring too."* So it was that when Christ came to the Jews, the Father was deprived of his Son. For they encompassed him with death, supposing that he would be held down by the gates of Hades, and that he would lie down dead with the rest. But the Author of life did not allow himself to be overcome by death. He therefore came back to life, and the Father saw him again, and also the generation that was born from him and in him, meaning those who believe, the holy nation, the royal priesthood, the people belonging to God.[151] It is over these that Christ himself also rejoices when he says, "Here I am, and the children God has given me."[152]

Joseph brought the sons to his father and they bowed down. Then Manasseh, the firstborn, stood on the right, and Ephraim, the younger one, stood on the left. But when Jacob placed his hands upon them, he crossed them. He honored Ephraim by placing his right hand upon him, and it was as if he was then treating Manasseh as of secondary importance by placing his left hand on him. Thus he commenced his blessing for them. We likewise have been received as the first among those who worship,[153] and as the people of God coming after those others, though it was neither Moses nor the prophets who brought us near (for the law lacks the ability to bring one to salvation), but the Son himself, for through him we have obtained access,[154] as

---

149. Or "at his direction."
150. Ex 12.13.
151. Cf. 1 Pt 2.9.
152. Is 8.18; Heb 2.13.
153. The Greek term "worship" here is related to the verb "bow down" at the beginning of the paragraph.
154. Cf. Rom 5.2.

I said. His aim was in fact to give the flock of those gathered out of the nations priority over Israel. For although Joseph placed Manasseh at the right hand of his father, since they acted toward him profanely beyond measure, the Father gave greater honor to those who came second in time, that is, the Gentiles. So the last were first, and the first last.

Jacob blessed the boys, speaking of the God who sustained him and the angel who delivered him, here completely uniting God the Father and the Son, who through the mouth of the prophets is described as "the Angel of great counsel."[155] Accordingly, all grace and every manner of blessing and provision comes to us in no other way except from the Father through the Son. And so the divine Paul says, "Grace be to you and peace from God our Father and the Lord Jesus Christ."[156]

The divine Joseph was troubled when he saw that the firstborn had been placed, as it were, after the younger. Then his father explained the import of this mystery, *and he said, "He also will become a people and be exalted, but his younger brother will be greater than he, and his offspring will become a multitude of nations,"*[157] and then after other things it says, *he put Ephraim before Manasseh.*[158] Yet, inasmuch as it seemed good to Christ, Israel did not miss out on its own glory. And so Christ plainly stated, "I was sent only to the lost sheep of the house of Israel."[159] Since, however, Israel was hardened, as is written,[160] and ill-treated him who extended the offer of salvation, continuing in a state of disobedience, it was placed at the left hand, the place of lesser glory. Israel itself is indeed blessed and exalted, in the portion of those who have been saved. This is the remnant, in accordance with what the prophet says.[161] But the church taken from among the Gentiles is so much more privileged. It has been enlarged so as to become a multitude of peoples, and it is greater than Israel as it exceeds in having an immeasurably

---

155. Isa 9.6 (9.5 LXX). The Hebrew here lacks the term "angel."
156. Rom 1.7; 1 Cor 1.3; 2 Cor 1.2; etc.
157. Gn 48.19.
158. Gn 48.20.
159. Mt 15.24.
160. Cf. Rom 11.7, 25.
161. Cf. Is 10.22.

more numerous multitude of believers. Yet both those of Israel and those of the Gentiles have been crowned with one and the same grace for sanctification, that is, we who believe and have been justified in Christ, through whom and with whom be glory to God the Father, together with the Holy Spirit, for ever and ever. Amen.

BOOK SEVEN: GENESIS 49

Concerning the blessing of the twelve patriarchs

HE AIM OF THIS present discourse is to explain each of the things spoken by Jacob the forefather about what would later happen to the sons who were born to him. But we first bear witness to the obvious fact that the interpretation of what is said is altogether difficult. The meaning is inaccessible to many,[1] as it is revealed obscurely in figures. The blessing is expressed through diverse manners of speech,[2] though were this not so, it would be even harder to understand. For here the divine Jacob declares to his sons predictions of things pertaining to later times. Yet he makes mention, in addition, of past events and enumerates the misconduct, firstly of Reuben, then immediately after this, of Simeon and Levi. Who, then, would be so bold as to say in what manner the blessing and the remembrance of former sins should be expressed, and would not be thought a speaker of error and one who has drifted away from the proper interpretation? So the discourse concerning these matters is profound and is not readily accessible to those who wish to comprehend it.

What can we say, then, is an admissible yardstick for us to lay down in these matters of contemplation set before us, but that of the Jewish synagogue?[3] In sum, it is speaking of the whole race of the Jews; that is to say, each tribe is a type of what they would be like in the future—being condemned over some matters, while perhaps approved in certain others—and how things would turn

---

1. Or "in many respects."
2. Or "in a mixed manner."
3. The translation incorporates at this point an addition from the Harleian manuscript, which seems to be required to give the complete sense.

out for them in the end. It is such things, no doubt, that the recounting of this prophecy will in some way convey to us.

Note how the description of events that would take place in later times arises out of things that had already happened. Also note the interpretation of names, that is to say, their meaning. These, after a certain fashion, speak of the things that would come to pass and give a distinct portrayal of them in advance.

Now this is what is written here: *Jacob called his sons and said, "Assemble yourselves that I may tell you what will happen to you in the latter days. Gather together and listen, O sons of Jacob, listen to Israel your father."*[4]

Concerning Reuben

"Reuben, you are my firstborn, you are my strength and [337] *the first of my children, hard to endure and unbearably self-willed. You were as unruly as water—do not overflow! For you went up to your father's bed, then you defiled the couch to which you went up."*[5]

Reuben did indeed violate his father's marriage. He did things that were not lawful and was evidently found out. The matter was condemned as evil by Jacob, for it says, "it appeared evil in the sight of Jacob."[6] I do not, however, to any degree suppose that an event that is already past should happen in the last times. To consider such a thing would be utterly foolish. But if we transform, as it were, the figure of the transgression into one that corresponds to it, we will then see the sin of God's firstborn people, Israel.

When God brought the synagogue[7] out of Egypt, it was as though he were taking a young woman to himself through a spiritual union according to the law. He accepted her into his presence, deeming her worthy of a close relationship, and thus he made her a fertile mother of children. In this the all-wise Moses was in effect acting as the one who brings the bride to her husband, with the angels mediating in the formation of

4. Gn 49.1–2.
5. Gn 49.3–4.
6. Gn 35.22.
7. Or "congregation," here a collective term for the Jews.

the union. Yet the synagogue that was brought into this union by God repudiated the law that established the legitimate relationship. It was, in a way, as if she lay with the sons of the one who had married her and played the harlot with them. She no longer bore offspring for the one she was joined to through the law, but her inclination was rather to produce offspring by conceiving with others, by which I mean spiritual conception through instruction. Disdaining the fact that she had been set before God, as though it were something of no consequence, she turned to the commandments and teachings of men. She paid no heed to heavenly instruction, having a merely superficial regard for the law.

For this reason the prophet Isaiah said, "How the faithful city of Zion, once full of justice, has become a harlot! Righteousness once lodged in her, but now murderers! Your silver is worthless. Your wine peddlers mix the wine with water."[8] For righteousness, that is, God, did indeed lodge and abide in her. But she took in murderers, adulterers, and the corrupt, who gave her worthless silver, and who mixed the wine with water. The word of those who persuaded her to respect the teachings and commandments of men was truly worthless. The doctrine of those men was peddled, as it were, mixed with inferior teaching. This, I believe, is the meaning of the wine mixed with water.

That this matter grieved the God of all, who brought a just accusation against Jerusalem as one who had played the harlot, we plainly learn when he says through Jeremiah, "Lift your eyes to look straight ahead, and see where you have become mingled. You sat for them by the wayside like a desolate crow, and you defiled the land with your harlotry.[9] You had many shepherds[10] who were a cause of stumbling for you. You had the face of a harlot, acting shamelessly towards all. You did not call me your companion, your father, and the one who guided you in the time of your virginity."[11] He also says, "If a man divorces his wife, and she departs from him and becomes another man's,

---

8. Is 1.21–22.
9. Var. add "and with your wickedness," as found in the LXX.
10. See n. 12 below.
11. Jer 3.2–4.

will she indeed return to him again? Will not that woman be utterly defiled? [340] But you have played the harlot with many shepherds,[12] and would you return to me? says the Lord."[13]

The Savior himself also clearly showed us their harlotrous manner. For the Pharisees, men without understanding who were always finding fault, came to him, saying, "Why do your disciples transgress the tradition of the elders? For they do not wash their hands when they eat food."[14] Christ said to them, "Why do you transgress the commandment of God for the sake of your tradition? For God said, 'Honor your father and your mother in order that it might go well with you.' But you say, 'Whoever says to his father or mother, "Whatever profit you would have received from me is *korban*," then he need not honor his father or his mother.' And so you have nullified the commandment of God by means of your tradition."[15] Note how it can readily be seen that, being under the direction of other instructors, they chose to observe and perform other things beyond what was given in the law. So the synagogue of the Jews played the harlot. The pure and spotless virgin, however, who was freed from every stain and wrinkle, that is to say, the church, engages to maintain the noble and most excellent form of union with Christ, saying, "My kinsman is mine, and I am his."[16]

Let us, then, maintain that Jacob's concubine Bilhah, whom Reuben, representing the people who were the firstborn, defiled, is a picture of the Jewish synagogue. This is especially seen to be the case as the meaning of Bilhah is "grown old" and that of Reuben is "son of defilement."[17] For when the synagogue of the Jews became old and wrinkled, there arose that new peo-

---

12. The translators of the LXX have misread a Hebrew term (*rē'îm*) meaning "friends," "companions." The same seems to apply to the foregoing Jeremiah citation, though in that particular clause the LXX differs widely from the Hebrew.
13. Jer 3.1.
14. Mt 15.2.
15. Mt 15.3–6; cf. Mk 7.11.
16. Song 2.16.
17. The name Bilhah may indeed be associated with the Hebrew verb for "grow old," "wear out," yet Reuben clearly means "see, a son."

ple of God, those who are so through faith. David rejoiced over this in the Psalms, singing, "The people yet to be created will praise the Lord."[18] For, according to the Scriptures, everything in Christ is a new creation.[19]

Yet Israel was deemed filthy and defiled, having rejected the cleansing offered through Christ. And why do I say this? Because they even laid their hands upon him who spoke to them of cleansing. Accordingly, it was once said through the mouth of the holy prophets, "If the Ethiopian could change his skin, or the leopard its spots, then you who have learned evil would be able to do good."[20] Again, to Jerusalem represented as a woman, it says, "Though you wash with lye, and use much soap on yourself, you will still be stained before me by your iniquities, says the Lord."[21]

Now Jacob said of Reuben, *"You are my firstborn, you are my strength and the first of my children."* To that firstborn people who were brought out of Egypt great strength was displayed by God. For the land of Egypt was punished in many different and wondrous ways—through the waters being turned into blood, swarms of gnats, frogs coming up on the land, the fall of hail, and the death of the firstborn, and besides this the redeemed passed through the sea as though on dry land.

Reuben, then, was called the "strength" of God.[22] Yet he conducted himself harshly [341], and was hardened in stubbornness; that is to say, he was obstinate and rigid, wild and impetuous. Corresponding to this, the Jews were hostile to the truth and unrestrained. Therefore, they were justly told, "You stiff-necked people, uncircumcised in heart and ears! You always resist the Holy Spirit."[23] And Christ himself said in a certain place, "Which of the prophets did your fathers not kill?"[24] and "Fill up the measure of your fathers."[25]

---

18. Ps 102.18 (101.19 LXX).
19. 2 Cor 5.17.
20. Jer 13.23.
21. Jer 2.22.
22. Var. "received the strength of God as his portion."
23. Acts 7.51.
24. Cf. Acts 7.52, where similar words are attributed to Stephen.
25. Mt 23.32.

Israel was also impulsive and quick to anger, having an extreme impetuousness, being *"as unruly as water,"* that is to say, borne by an unrestrained recklessness in whatever they wished. This is what the rushing of water is like. Yet it says, *"Do not overflow."* And what does this mean? When water boils over, it flows away somewhere, as when it overflows from a boiling pot, and there somehow seems to be a great deal of it. So having conferred upon him the nature of flowing water, it continues the metaphor and says, *"Do not overflow,"* which means, "Do not increase in quantity or become many." For those of the race of Israel who have been saved through faith in Christ are few in number compared to the multitude of those saved from among the Greeks.

Then Jacob gives the reason why this would happen, and says, *"For you went up to your father's bed, then you defiled the couch to which you went up."* For as I said before, the Jews no longer sought out the things contained in the law and the heavenly oracles, but they rather devoted themselves to the words of adulterers[26] and to the teachings of men, and so completely strayed from the knowledge of Christ. For this reason he himself said, "You search the Scriptures because you think that in them you have eternal life, and it is they that testify of me. Yet you do not wish to come to me that you may have life,"[27] and again, "If you believed Moses, you would believe in me, for he wrote about me."[28] He also brought serious charges against the teachers of the Jews, saying, "Woe to you, scribes and Pharisees, hypocrites, because you shut up the kingdom of heaven from before men. You yourselves do not enter, nor do you allow those who are entering to go in."[29] Again he said, "Woe to you, scribes and Pharisees, hypocrites, because you cross over sea and dry land to make a single proselyte; and when he becomes one, you make him twice as much a son of hell as yourselves."[30] But this person

---

26. This clause has been added from the Harleian Codex as the sense is confused without it.
27. Jn 5.39–40.
28. Jn 5.46.
29. Mt 23.13.
30. Mt 23.15.

would not have become a son of hell if he had not consented to the words of those adulterers. So then, those of the race of Israel went up to their father's bed. Rejecting the will of the Lawgiver as being irrelevant, they forced their own words into their disciples, and so the seeds of impurity entered into them.

Concerning Simeon and Levi

1. *"Simeon and Levi are brothers; in their seditiousness they carried out wrongful acts.*[31] *Let not my soul come into their counsel, let not my heart be joined to their conspiracy. For in their wrath they killed men, and in their passion they hamstrung a bull. Cursed be their wrath, because it was willful, and their anger, because it was cruel. I will disperse them in Jacob, and scatter them in Israel."*[32]

When Jerusalem played the harlot, and gave her mind over to the godless deceits of strange teaching [344], the God of all was justifiably severe. He said very plainly through the mouth of Isaiah, "This people honor me with their lips, but their heart is far from me. In vain do they worship me, teaching as doctrines the commandments of men."[33]

Since profane Jerusalem was going recklessly astray and behaving as one in a drunken frenzy, so to speak, God the Father determined to train her up in a better way. He sent his own Son from heaven, who became one of us, that is, a human being, so that while the multitude of holy prophets were ineffective in numerous respects (for they said, "Lord, who has believed our report?"),[34] the Jews might at least have regard for the Son himself when he came. They, however, descended into such foolishness that they even thought it possible to take possession of the Lord's inheritance. Having killed the saints, they went to even greater lengths of impiety and also mistreated the Son himself in a way that was inconceivable, for they said among themselves, "This is the heir. Come, let us kill him and take possession of

---

31. Or "they carried out an unjust course of action."
32. Gn 49.5–7. The Harleian Codex omits the final sentence of the citation.
33. Mt 15.9.
34. Is 53.1.

his inheritance."[35] Yet their folly was not limited to these things, but to their actions against the holy prophets they added their treatment of the holy apostles, whose blood they did not spare.

An approach such as this to the prophecy set before us produces its interpretation. So it was indeed appropriate that the divine Jacob should mention again the deeds done among the Shechemites. In this way the import of that righteous man's words is found to be in accordance with the truth. How should one here take what had already occurred as an indication of what would later happen? Well, through what had happened in Shechem it is referring to the same manner of sin that would be enacted against Christ, just as was in fact the case also in the matters relating to Reuben the firstborn.

What, then, did Simeon and Levi do in Shechem? When their sister Dinah had gone out from the tent of their father, and was taking a look at the daughters of the local inhabitants, Shechem son of Hamor forcibly raped her, so deflowering her. At this, Simeon and Levi were greatly displeased and plotted murder through deception. First they persuaded the local men to receive the patriarchal rite of circumcision, so that, if they chose to do this, they would instantly become a kindred people. Yet having done this, they then killed them without warning. They thought they could avail themselves of an excuse for their actions by saying, "Should they have treated our sister like a harlot?"[36]

2. So one must now go on to present an appropriate explanation of the spiritual sense,[37] which we will do as we are able, bringing together all those various elements that contribute towards the interpretation. Let us then broaden our study concerning Jacob and describe the way in which he lived, which women he married, and how he is shown to be the father of so many children.

We said that Jacob took to himself Leah, the eldest of Laban's daughters, and not long after that the younger Rachel as a second wife. We have also established that Leah is a type of

35. Mt 21.38.
36. Gn 34.31.
37. *theôrêma*, denoting the sense derived from spiritual contemplation.

the synagogue of the Jews, and Rachel a type of the church of the Gentiles. Then Leah was interpreted as meaning "weary," and she did indeed have eyes that were extremely weak and unappealing [345]. So the Jewish synagogue became exceedingly weary, being burdened with the law given through Moses, and not seeing the mystery of our Savior with good eyes. "But Rachel was fine-looking with an extremely beautiful face."[38] So too the Gentile church was most attractive.

Now Dinah was the daughter of Leah that was born last. And she herself was also a type of the assembly of the circumcised, those who were born in later times when the Only-Begotten took on human nature among them. This latter assembly of the circumcised went out a short way from the father's tent, that is, from the customs pertaining to the law, and fell in with the local people, which is to say, she had dealings[39] with the holy apostles, through their teaching, and no longer lived according to Jewish customs, but assumed the customs of other nations. When this happened, she was in a spiritual manner deflowered, receiving from the apostles the seed of the gospel teachings and lifestyle which are in Christ.

Certain of the sons of Jacob, however, namely Simeon and Levi, became indignant at this. These were those who were classed as the obedient, and with them the kind that were consecrated and chosen, for Simeon means "obedience," and Levi "accepted" or "chosen."[40] How can it be doubted that it was those having received the honor of the priesthood under the law who fiercely attacked the holy apostles (though the people also went along with them)? They gnashed their teeth at them, calling their conversion of others destructive, and brought against them many such extraordinary accusations. "For behold," they said, "you have filled Jerusalem with your teaching."[41] But when they had reproached them for no longer living according to

---

38. Gn 29.17.

39. The term used here (*epemisgeto*) has strong connotations of sexual intercourse.

40. While the name Simeon may be related to the idea of obedience, Levi in Hebrew is understood to mean "joined" (cf. Gn 29.34).

41. Acts 5.28.

Jewish customs, they discovered that circumcision was esteemed by them. Yet this did not distinguish them in any way at all from the Gentiles, since they chose to interpret the customs of Moses according to their proper sense. For it says, "He is not a Jew who is one outwardly, nor is circumcision that which is outward in the flesh. Rather, he is a Jew who is one inwardly, and circumcision is that of the heart, by the Spirit, and not by the letter."[42] Note how those of the Gentiles who are of good repute have conformed to the customs of the Jews by receiving circumcision by the Spirit, so bearing Jewishness inwardly.

The Jews, however, had also earlier killed the prophets, and even Emmanuel himself. That is why it says, *"in their seditiousness Simeon and Levi carried out wrongful acts."* For Simeon and Levi, that is, both people and priests, were in agreement and conspired together to commit wrongful acts against the saints. So *"in their seditiousness"* here stands for their conspiracy and determination. For those terrible things that befell the saints did not simply happen spontaneously, neither were the outrageous and extraordinarily audacious deeds of the Jews without prior planning, but it was through their counsel to take action that these things which surpassed all evil came to be done.

Therefore, the divine Jacob rejected such conspiracy, base counsel, and plotting, for he said, *"Let not my soul come into their counsel, let not my heart be joined to their conspiracy."* It is as though he were saying, "May I not look upon such counsels with the eyes of my mind, nor may I ever receive [348] such grievous schemes of the ungodly into my heart." Thus the prophet Isaiah also denounced the people of the Jews, saying, "Woe to their souls, because they have devised an evil counsel, saying to themselves, 'Let us bind the righteous one, for he is burdensome to us.'"[43] David, too, in the Psalms said, "Blessed is the man who does not walk in the counsel of the ungodly, and who does not stand in the way of sinners."[44] And again, "I hate the assembly of evildoers, and I will not sit with the ungodly."[45]

42. Rom 2.28–29.
43. Is 3.9–10 LXX.
44. Ps 1.1.
45. Ps 26.5 (25.5 LXX).

So the divine Jacob rejects the scheming of the Jews and states his reason, saying, *"For in their wrath they killed men, and in their passion they hamstrung a bull."* For they did indeed kill the saints, as I stated, being directed by an unholy wrath to cruel and inhuman behavior. And when those wretches admitted into their hearts a wild and uncurbed desire, they hamstrung a bull, which is Christ. What their intention was, we have previously said. Recognizing that he was the heir, they desired to have his inheritance.

3. Note, too, the precise meaning of the words: *"For they killed men, and they hamstrung a bull."* For they encompassed the saints with death, and they remain dead awaiting the time of the resurrection. But like a calf that is hamstrung by an eagle, Christ in a way slumped to the ground, willingly enduring the death of his flesh. Yet he was not held down by death. Although he was dead as a human being, he remained alive in the nature of his Deity. So the bull, a creature that is especially strong, clean, and sacred, is Christ. The Son is the powerful Lord, who committed no sin, but rather offered himself up for us as a pleasing aroma to God the Father.

So now, let those give heed who have hamstrung such a noble bull. *"Cursed be their wrath, because it was willful, and their anger, because it was cruel."* What did they experience as a result? They were removed from their land and left their home country behind. They were scattered and, living everywhere as strangers and aliens, were fearful. For it is true to say that when a man is uprooted from his own place, he is like a bird when it is thrown out of its own nest.

I think it right to say further that for those who hamstrung the bull this matter will result in a curse, while for those who were troubled over this, and who denounced such a terrible crime, there will be redemption, cleansing, and the putting away of sin. We shall find that this very thing I have said is recorded, expressed through the shadows of the law. For in Deuteronomy it reads as follows: "If someone is found slain in the land which the Lord your God is giving you as an inheritance, fallen in the field, and it is not known who struck him down, then your elders and your judges shall go out and measure the distance to the towns around the slain man. And the elders of the town that is nearest to the body shall take a heifer from the herd, which has not labored [349] and which has not pulled with a yoke. The elders of that town shall bring the heifer down to a rough valley, which has not been cultivated nor sown, and they shall slaughter[46] the heifer there in the valley. Then the priests, the Levites, shall come, for the Lord your God has chosen them to stand before him, and to pronounce blessings in his name, and by their word every dispute and every assault[47] shall be settled. And all the elders of that town who come near to the slain man shall wash their hands over the head of the heifer that was slaughtered[48] in the valley. Then they shall answer and say, 'Our hands did not shed this blood, nor did our eyes see it happen. Be gracious, O Lord, to your people Israel, whom you redeemed from the land of Egypt, that innocent blood may not be laid upon your people Israel, and that atonement shall be provided on their behalf for the shed blood.' So you shall remove the guilt of innocent blood from your midst."[49]

Though we make mention of this passage now, it will be discussed in detail at a later occasion. Yet you can see how, when we take the heifer as prefiguring Emmanuel, certain of those falling under the charge of shedding blood acquit themselves. For it was, I believe, necessary for them in acquitting themselves to say, "Our hands did not shed this blood." The people of the Jews, however, will not be found ever to have exclaimed these words. On the contrary, those who hamstrung the calf were bold enough to say, "Our hands shed this blood." For this, I consider, is nothing other than what they foolishly said with regard to Christ, "His blood be upon us and upon our children."[50]

---

46. It is important to note that the precise meaning of the Greek verb is in fact "hamstring."

47. The Greek noun *aphê* literally means "touch." The Latin translator in Migne understood this as "leprosy." In this he departed from the Vg text, which took the reference to be to the determination of clean and unclean.

48. See n. 46 above.

49. Dt 21.1–9.

50. Mt 27.25.

Concerning Judah

"Judah, your brothers will praise you. Your hands will be upon the neck of your enemies. Your father's sons will bow down to you. Judah is a lion's whelp; from the sprouting plant,[51] my son, you have gone up. You crouch down, lying like a lion, and as a whelp. Who will rouse him? A prince shall not be lacking from Judah, nor a ruler from his loins, until there come the things stored up for him; he is the expectation of the nations. He ties his foal to the vine, and his donkey's colt to its branch. He will wash his robe in wine, and his garment in the blood of grapes. His eyes will sparkle more than wine, and his teeth will be whiter than milk."[52]

We see the manner of this blessing to be especially clear—how it expressly presents to the hearers the prediction of the economy of our Savior. At the beginning of the blessing the significance of the name is set forth, and also the preeminence in glory of the tribe of Judah over the others. If one wished to explain the name Judah, he might interpret it as "praise," or "hymn," or "praised with hymns."[53] And this has reference to Christ, who according to the flesh was from the tribe of Judah. The Virgin also, who was chosen for the birth of his flesh, came from Judah, Jesse, and David. The prophet, therefore, looking ahead to the one to come from [352] the tribe of Judah, says, "Your name is true, as your power over matters also shows. You shall be praised, and you shall bear the glory that is due to God."[54] For it is not fitting to ascribe glory to any other except to him alone who truly exists and is known as God. It is as if to say, "Even though you have come as a man, and have emptied yourself, you shall be renowned, reverenced, and celebrated. Those who were your brothers with respect to your human nature will not relate to you as to a man. Though they were made your brothers, they will laud you as Master, they will sing to you

---

51. Cyril here, as expected, follows the LXX, where the Hebrew reads "from the prey."

52. Gn 49.8–12.

53. The Hebrew name "Judah" is clearly related to the idea of praise (cf. Gn 29.35).

54. There is no identifiable biblical source for this citation.

as Maker. Although you were reckoned with them among creatures, they will recognize you, though veiled in the form of a servant, as King and Lord of all."

When Jacob says, *"Your hands will be upon the neck of your enemies,"* he is foretelling that Emmanuel would exercise rule over all those who opposed him, overwhelming his enemies with ease. Christ himself, speaking through the mouth of David, foretold the same thing. He said, "I will pursue my enemies and seize them; I will not turn back until they are consumed. I will crush them, and they will not be able to stand. They will fall under my feet."[55] Jacob therefore says, *"His hands will be upon the neck of his enemies,"* as hands of one pursuing rather than fleeing,[56] not as those of one being struck but of one striking. What is sung in the book of Psalms is true: "The enemy shall not have the advantage over him, and the son of iniquity shall no longer harm him."[57] If he grants us authority to tread upon snakes and scorpions and upon all the power of the enemy, are we not obliged to acknowledge that he himself first has under his authority those wishing to resist him and rise up against him in a profane manner? So then, he does not know what it means to flee, but only to pursue. He intends to exercise his rule over these enemies, and this without effort, for he has in fact conquered the world! The divine Jacob spoke of these things ahead of time, when he said, *"Your hands will be upon the neck of your enemies. Your father's sons will bow down to you."*

How should we interpret the distinction between the *"brothers"* who praise him, and the *"father's sons"* who join with them in bowing down to him? Is it not necessary to say how they differ? Now the blessed Joseph, though he was not the actual father, is ascribed with being the father of Christ. Joseph had sons and daughters from his first marriage, who were also, one may suppose, members of the same family as Christ. These saw him performing signs, and saw how he was utterly unwilling to observe the regulations of the law with respect to the distinc-

---

55. Ps 18.37–38 (17.37–38 LXX).
56. The word here translated as "neck" is literally "back" in the LXX, which allows the idea of approach from behind.
57. Ps 88.23 LXX.

tion between foods, and that he did not choose to honor the Sabbath rest—for he said, "It is not what goes into the mouth that defiles a man,"[58] and that "the Son of Man is Lord of the Sabbath."[59] In seeing these things, they were divided in their opinion about him. They neither wished to honor him completely, as he seemed to disagree with matters concerning the law, but neither did they want to let such a remarkable person remain unadmired. And so they came to him on one occasion and expressly said, "If you do these things, show yourself to the world. For no one does anything in secret while [353] he himself seeks to be known openly,"[60] to which the evangelist added, "For even his own brothers did not believe in him."[61] Nevertheless, though they said such things at first, they did believe later. For they were convinced that he was also in very nature God, and that he had become flesh and appeared as a man. This situation the blessed prophet Jeremiah foreknew in the Spirit and, addressing Emmanuel himself, said, "For even your brothers, and the house of your father, even these have rejected you, and they have cried out and gathered together in pursuit of you. Do not trust them, even though they speak fair words to you."[62] For those who once cried out against him together with others were brought together in faith, and they spoke fair things about him. Accordingly, the blessed James, when he wrote to the twelve tribes, said, "James, a servant of God and of the Lord Jesus Christ."[63] So then, also those who through faith and sanctification have been called to become brothers will praise him as God, yet the father's sons will not bow to him any the less. It is evident, then, that those who bow down to him shall praise him, and those who offer praise will in no way less bow down to him.

Christ, being the all-powerful Son of God, is *"a lion's whelp"* from Judah, who can conquer without a fight, and who is able to strike down those who oppose him by his word alone, for as the

58. Mt 15.11.
59. Mt 12.8.
60. Jn 7.4.
61. Jn 7.5.
62. Jer 12.6. Here we read "fair" (*kala*) with the LXX, rather than Cyril's probable misreading "evil" (*kaka*).
63. Jas 1.1.

prophet says, "The lion will roar, and who will not be afraid?"[64] Christ, then, is *"a lion's whelp,"* and it is as though he had grown up *"from a sprouting plant"* and from a noble root, namely from the holy Virgin.

Christ is also the rod of power that God sent us from Zion,[65] the staff that comforts and sustains all,[66] the scepter of uprightness and of the kingdom,[67] the staff that, on the one hand, justly and gently tends the flock of the saints, and that, on the other, shatters like a potter's vessel those who cannot bear to be governed by him.[68] He is the rod of Aaron that was placed in the divine tabernacle and brought into the holy of holies, the almond rod that blossomed, which is a symbol of resurrection, for the wood of the almond tree somehow causes wakefulness. So the mystery of the resurrection is revered among the churches of God. For this reason the blessed Jacob, describing Christ as *"a sprouting plant,"* immediately made mention of those things to happen at the fulfillment of the divine economy. He said, *"You crouch down,*[69] *lying like a lion,"* that is to say, you were not unwilling to submit to death, but like a lion you were able to seize and terrify all others, to escape the clutches of the hunters. You lay down voluntarily, yet you were not, as those who intended to crucify you supposed, overcome by death, but you were like someone in need of sleep, who closed his eyes momentarily.

"Who will rouse him?" it then says. It is as though it said that he lay down willingly, yet he did not need the help of any other to bring about his resurrection. For he is all-powerful, himself being the power of the Father, capable of all things, so that he is even able without any difficulty whatsoever to restore life to his "temple."[70] This, we note, is what he said when speaking to the Jews: "Destroy this temple, and in three days [356] I will raise it

---

64. Am 3.8.
65. Cf. Ps 110.2 (109.2 LXX).
66. Cf. Ps 23.4 (22.4 LXX).
67. Cf. Ps 45.6 (44.7 LXX).
68. Cf. Ps 2.9.
69. Lit. "fall down."
70. Here "temple" refers to the body of Jesus, as is clear from the context of the following citation.

up."[71] So then, the word makes absolutely clear that there was nobody who worked together with him in this matter, and that he alone was sufficient to do this, having been born with such power.

Now it reveals when the time of his coming will be when it says, *"A prince shall not be lacking from Judah, nor a ruler from his loins, until there comes what is stored up for him; he is the expectation of the nations."* For Jews exercised authority, and there were rulers of Israelite descent among them until the time of Herod son of Antipas, a native of Palestine, who claimed the right to rule and was called a tetrarch. It was in his days that Christ, *"the expectation of the nations,"* was born. It is not necessary to demonstrate that the multitude taken from the nations were saved when he was born, since the matter is patently obvious.[72]

That the new and recently born Gentile people of God, however, were admitted through faith and that Israel will be called in after them, it directly teaches when it says, *"He ties his foal to the vine."* Christ the true vine bound to himself through faith, so to speak, the people of the Gentiles,[73] who are likened to a foal. And he bound to the branch of the vine, that is to say, to his love, *"his donkey's colt,"* meaning those originating from the more ancient mother of the Jews, namely the people of the synagogue who have come to believe. How could one doubt that practically the whole of inspired Scripture speaks to us of this mystery?

That he would make his flesh red with his own blood when he was nailed to the tree and pierced by a spear, it makes manifest when it says, *"He will wash his robe in wine, and his garment in the blood of grapes."* And so, the divine Isaiah also, in speaking of Christ ascending into heaven, says that the holy angels, the powers on high, ask, "Who is this that comes from Edom, with red garments from Bozrah?"[74] And again he says, "Why are your garments red, and your robes like those of someone who has trodden the winepress?"[75]

71. Jn 2.19.
72. Lit. "shouts out."
73. Var. "the people who were saved from among the Gentiles."
74. Is 63.1.
75. Is 63.2.

Though he had been among the dead, and though he had endured the raging of the Jews, the blows and the insults, he who suffered for us and who brought salvation to all under heaven did not reckon such things of any great account. Rather, he ever feels the most cordial and hearty joyfulness. This is shown when it says, *"His eyes will sparkle more than wine."* These words may be interpreted, in my view, as meaning his pleasure, and the eternal joyfulness and exuberance of his Godhead. For the joyful mind is always inclined to gentleness and especially disdains those having the tendency to sorrowfulness.

When the passage continues to speak of *"his teeth,"* saying that they are white, it means that the words of his mouth are pure and bright. For certainly Christ says nothing without purpose, but rather he speaks what is plain and true. Everything he utters is sacred and of great value, and produces such a great illumination of soul and mind in those who listen.

Concerning Zebulun

"Zebulun will dwell by the seashore, and he will be a haven for ships; his border will extend as far as Sidon."[76]

Earlier [357] we said that when investigating the text of the prophecy set before us—its character, and how it might best be described when we study it carefully—we should state both that which is similar to those things already done previously, and we should also especially explain the meaning of the names. In this way the passage is in effect reshaped, indicating the manner in which things to come are foreshown and, I believe, what their interpretation is.

This very thing can in fact clearly be seen again in the case of Zebulun, and the following material. For by those whose practice it is particularly to explain such things, Zebulun is taken as signifying "prosperity" and "blessing."[77] So we find that certain of the people of Israel were indeed blessed, and were made rich and prosperous in all things pleasing to God. Those who have

---

76. Gn 49.13.

77. In Hebrew the name appears to be related to the idea of giving a gift (cf. Gn 30.20).

been justified through faith in Christ and enlightened by the grace of the Holy Spirit are truly able to cry out, "We are blessed[78] by the Lord, who made heaven and earth."[79] The blessed prophet Isaiah, I believe, also concurs with this when he said, "The way of the godly has been made straight, and the way of the godly has been prepared; for the way of the Lord is justice."[80] And so the God of all has commanded that the illumined and the blessed should be invited into the sacred and divine court, saying, "Open the gates, let the people that observes righteousness and preserves truth enter, maintaining truth and keeping peace."[81] Moreover, so that those who fall over the obstructing stumbling blocks are not kept back from good things, he has commanded that a good way,[82] as it were, should be made and that the entrance-way should be laid open, as he says to his holy ministers, "Go through my gates, and cast the stones out of the road."[83] Surely then, those people of Israel who valued faith in Christ were blessed and made prosperous.

It is clearly affirmed that the people of Zebulun would inhabit the region beside the sea. It is as though it was saying that Israel would later on be mingled with the Gentiles, as if the two peoples were brought together into one flock, and were placed under the care of him who is by nature the one good chief shepherd, that is, Christ. That this figure is true the word of inspired Scripture readily proves when it assigns the area beside the sea to the Gentiles. For this is what it says, "The region of Zebulun, the land of Naphtali, the way of the sea, and the rest who inhabit the coastland, Galilee of the Gentiles, the people living in darkness, behold a great light."[84] You see how it refers to the region of Zebulun as belonging to the Gentiles, who also have seen a great light, through Christ that is.

78. Or "May we be blessed."
79. Ps 115.15 (113.23 LXX).
80. Is 26.7–8.
81. Is 26.2–3.
82. Cyril is here punning on the fact that the noun for "prosperity" (*euodia*), used earlier, may be broken down into the two components approximating to "good way."
83. Is 62.10.
84. Is 9.1–2 (8.23–9.1 LXX).

So Israel, as a fellow inhabitant, has been illuminated along with those who dwell in the coastland. This means, I believe, to be made to prosper by God. For in being thoroughly illuminated, one is necessarily caused to prosper as well. This we also understand when the Savior says to the people of the Jews, "While you have the light, walk in the light, so that darkness will not overtake you."[85]

The people, therefore, who once dwelt by themselves, and who [360] avoided mixing with the Gentiles, will be fellow inhabitants with them, being in no way different from them. For the dividing wall has been broken down by Christ, and the law with its commandments and decrees[86] has been annulled. Henceforth the two peoples are set forth as one new man in Christ through the Spirit.

It then says, *"he will be a haven for ships,"* as though he would be in a place of safe refuge, unbeaten by the waves, fastening his cables to the hope that is in Christ. For as if coming out of a great storm, by the grace of Christ he will enter the harbor, just like a merchant ship reaching its haven.

In saying that his borders would even *"extend as far as Sidon,"* it seems to imply that there will be such a great spiritual gathering of the two peoples into one, as though the people from the race of Israel would occupy those cities also. These cities were very much guilty and blameworthy before God since they once led astray and in a way plundered those who worshiped him. For he said in a certain passage through the mouth of the prophet, "And what are you to me, O Tyre and Sidon, and all Galilee of the Gentiles? Are you rendering me a recompense, or do you bear malice against me? Quickly and speedily I will return your recompense upon your own heads, because you have taken my silver and gold, and have brought my fine treasures into your temples. Also, you have sold the children of Judah and the children of Israel to the Greeks, that you might remove them from their territory."[87]

---

85. Jn 12.35.
86. Here reading *en dogmasi* for *endeigmasi,* the latter meaning "with proofs."
87. Jl 3.4–6 (4.4–6 LXX).

Note, then, how those cities that in the past were fearsome and hostile, assisting in the ruin of the people of Israel, will welcome those who believe, giving them no cause to fear. These two peoples of Christ our Savior will be united in peace and oneness of spirit, Christ bringing an end to the enmity, making Israel to live together with the Gentiles in love. In such a way then, I consider, and not in any other, does Zebulun dwell by the seashore.

Concerning Issachar

"Issachar desired that which is good, resting in the midst of his inheritance. Seeing that his resting place was good and that the land was fertile, he bowed his shoulder to labor and became a farmer."[88]

Now the meaning of Issachar is "reward."[89] From what the name signifies we obtain a certain type and a distinct representation of those who are allotted to Christ, being in the nature of a reward, as it were, from God the Father. "Ask of me," says David, "and I will give you the nations as your inheritance, and the ends of the earth as your possession."[90] In another psalm he again indicates, it seems to me, those who are given to Emmanuel: "Behold, children are an inheritance from the Lord, the reward of the fruit of the womb."[91] It says believers from the race of Israel, and also from the other multitude, namely that of the Gentiles, were given to Emmanuel as a kind of reward. Having designated Jesus as Lord, it also says that he himself was "the fruit of the womb," on account of his having the same nature as ourselves. For he was born from a woman, and was shown to be the fruit of a virgin womb.

Christ, therefore, has acquired those who believe, and to God the Father in heaven he says of them, "Those you have given me out of the world [361], they were yours, and you gave them to me."[92] These, then, are those who have desired what

---

88. Gn 49.14–15.
89. This would seem to be close to the Hebrew meaning (cf. Gn 30.18).
90. Ps 2.8.
91. Ps 127.3 (126.3 LXX).
92. Jn 17.6.

is good, that is to say, everything whatsoever that might be said to be truly excellent and especially pleasing to God. This they esteem greatly and diligently perform, as though proclaiming from a good heart, "The judgments of the Lord are true and altogether justified, more desirable than gold and many precious stones."[93] One good thing besides this is the desire to be under Christ himself. This is what the bride also says in the Song of Songs, "I delighted in his shade and sat down."[94]

So then, the people who are so inclined first give careful consideration to those things allotted to them by God, that is, the good things promised to the godly in hope, concerning which the divine David said, "My allotted portions are in your hands."[95] They will, as it were, wholly and utterly stay and rest upon these, because they expect them to come to pass. Having commended, therefore, their own counsel and judgment, esteeming the rest to be found in these things as the cause of immeasurable wonder, that is, eternal honor, life in perfect sanctification, unending glory, a permanent kingdom, and things also which transcend both mind and speech, they will then exercise endurance.

In this way Issachar, having seen that the land was fertile, *"bowed his shoulder,"* it says, and took a liking to labor. He follows the example here of those used to tilling the ground, regarding it as a most noble task, who are most industrious and lovers of digging, keen to labor hard at farming. It is as though they would receive from a rich land, by which we are to understand, I believe, abundant fruit and the things that the land would produce. The wise Hosea also entreats us in this matter, saying, "Sow for yourselves righteousness, gather in the fruit of life, enlighten yourselves with the light of knowledge; seek the Lord until the fruit of righteousness comes upon you."[96] The blessed Paul adds to this when he says, "Now he who provides seed to the sower and bread for food will provide and multiply your supply of seed, and increase the fruit of your righteousness, so

---

93. Ps 19.9–10 (18.10–11 LXX).
94. Song 2.3.
95. Ps 31.15 (30.16 LXX).
96. Hos 10.12.

that always having all sufficiency in everything you may have an abundance for every good deed."⁹⁷

Concerning Dan

*"Dan will judge⁹⁸ his people, as also being one of the tribes in Israel. And let Dan be a snake by the roadside, lying upon the path, biting the horse's heel so that the rider falls backwards, waiting for salvation from the Lord."*⁹⁹

Once again the content of the oracle corresponds to the etymology of the name, for Dan means "judge" or "judgment."¹⁰⁰ In itself this tribe depicted, as it were, that glorious and prominent band of holy apostles, who were placed in authority over believers, and who obtained the exercise of judgment, as Christ himself assigned to them. And so the divine Paul said, "Do you not know that we will judge angels? How much more matters of this life?"¹⁰¹

Now, according to the Scriptures, Christ is the one Judge and Lawgiver. But since the apostles are Christ's ambassadors, and they have been commissioned with the message of reconciliation, it is no contradiction for them to be understood as judges in the same way [364] as Christ. The great Isaiah set forth both the sacred kingship of Christ and the instatement of the holy apostles when he declared to us in a certain passage, "Behold, a righteous king will reign, and rulers will rule with judgment."¹⁰² For in the past those kings of the tribe of Judah reigned in Jerusalem, while those serving at the holy tabernacle, having obtained the lot of the priesthood, were ordained to exercise judgment, for "the lips of a priest should preserve judgment, and people should seek the law from his mouth."¹⁰³

When the shadow of the law receded, so to speak, and the

---

97. 2 Cor 9.10, 8.
98. Here "judge" is meant in the Hebraic sense of "provide justice for" or "govern."
99. Gn 49.16–18.
100. This is correct (cf. Gn 30.6).
101. 1 Cor 6.3.
102. Is 32.1.
103. Mal 2.7.

worship in spirit and truth was introduced through Christ, the most eminent judges were needed for the world. To this end the divine disciples were summoned and took the place of those who taught according to the law. The mother of the Jews, which is Jerusalem, was therefore addressed by God through the psalmist, saying, "In the place of your fathers, your sons have been born to you,"[104] which is to say, "Those who are called your sons have assumed the place of your fathers." And then to our Lord Jesus Christ he says, "You shall appoint them as rulers over all the earth."[105]

One can see how this attained its fulfillment, for we have been assigned rulers and we have been given judges in all places, these being the holy disciples. Through them the mystery of Christ is explained, since they themselves are also keepers of the saving word and the ones who prescribe what deeds ought to be done. They determine what is unprofitable for those being instructed and what is impure, yet at the same time counseling them to embrace that which is suitable for producing some benefit.

So Dan, meaning those who would later be appointed to judge peoples and nations, will exercise dominion with power and great glory, just as one tribe ruled over the Israelites. By this I mean that Judah only was the ruling tribe and no other.

That those appointed by the Savior to be leaders throughout the world were highly honored and attained supreme glory in the sight of those who worship him, who is able to doubt? Yet for them to rule would not in any way be an easy task. They would undergo numerous severe trials and encounter obstacles, and so they would not at all find the exercise of apostleship to be free from danger. This is indicated figuratively when it says, *"Let Dan,"* in the place of which we are to put the people who persecute, *"be like a snake by the roadside, lying upon the path, biting the horse's heel,"* that is, putting forth fearful and unyielding doctrines.[106]

---

104. Ps 45.16 (44.17 LXX).
105. This is a direct continuation of the foregoing citation.
106. We note Cyril's manner of double interpretation, which sees Dan firstly in a positive light as the apostles who are entrusted with judgment, then sec-

How hard it is to avoid the bite of the viper, even though it only be in the heel. For it says, "He shall watch[107] your head, and you shall watch his heel."[108] Thus certain men lay in wait for the holy apostles in order to bring about the death of their bodies. When we say, then, that they endured such a thing, it was like what happens to a rider when his horse stumbles and he falls backwards. Now when the rider has toppled backwards and has fallen to the ground, he waits for one to rescue[109] him. [365] So the divine disciples await the time of their glory and salvation, since they have been called to an unshakable and everlasting kingdom, as Christ proclaims to them, "Come, you blessed of my Father, inherit the kingdom prepared for you from the foundation of the world,"[110] and "I have finished the race, I have kept the faith."[111] Surely then, they will receive the unfading crown of glory.[112]

Now if one took it to mean that there would not be those like snakes lying in wait for Dan by the roadside, but that Dan himself would lie in wait for others, to this we say that the scribes and the Pharisees, occupying the place of those who judge and instruct the people, attacked Christ like the most terrible of vipers. He was like a horseman galloping along a smooth and level path when they, overcome by impiety, struck out and bit at him. And although the horseman fell, willingly suffering the death of his flesh, he did in fact come back to life again, accounting the Father to be his helper. For the Son, being the power of God the Father, himself restored to life his own "temple."[113] So, having exposed himself to peril as a man, he may be said to have been saved by the Father, though he is in nature God, himself maintaining for good the whole of creation, both

---

ondly and negatively as those who, corresponding to the *"snake"* of the oracle, persecute both the apostles and Christ himself.

107. Or "give attention to."
108. Gn 3.15. The Hebrew verb appearing twice in this verse is generally understood to mean "wound" or "crush."
109. Or "save."
110. Mt 25.34.
111. 2 Tm 4.7.
112. Cf. 1 Pt 5.4.
113. See n. 70 above.

visible and invisible. This you may understand when the divine Paul says of him, "For though he was crucified in weakness, yet he lives by the power of God."[114]

Concerning Gad

"Gad, a band of raiders will attack him, but he himself will attack them, pursuing them closely."[115]

Again, the name Gad evidently has an intended meaning, which is either "testing" or "band of raiders."[116] This, in my opinion, is an appropriate meaning, from which is to be understood that God-hating and prideful swarm of scribes and Pharisees who rejected the divine gospel message. These men, deeming the most essential matters to be unprofitable, gnashed their teeth at Christ, who was teaching those things hidden in the shadows of the law. Yet he was extremely popular with the people and highly esteemed, and he equally astounded those throughout all Judea with the excellence of the miracles he performed, presenting to them also those wonderful teachings that result in pleasing God in every respect.

And so, according to what the prophet says, when Christ left Bethany and entered Jerusalem, he was "lowly, riding on a donkey, even on a young foal."[117] While the children going ahead of him proclaimed, "Hosanna to the Son of David! Blessed is he who comes in the name of the Lord!"[118] certain of those going along with him spread their garments on the road, and thought the manner of his entrance to be wonderful. But these others were enraged, smitten with the piercing sting of envy. They conversed together, even alleging, in effect, that there was the need to commit murder. For they said, "Look, you can do nothing. Behold, the whole world has gone after him!"[119] So, since they feared the multitude of those who had already come to believe,

114. 2 Cor 13.4.
115. Gn 49.19.
116. The Greek words relating to "test," "trial," on one hand, and "raider," "plunderer," "pirate," on the other, are similar. See Book 4, n. 136.
117. Zec 9.9.
118. Mt 21.9.
119. Jn 12.19.

they restrained their actions for the time being and held the proposed attack in check.

Then, in order that Christ might give offense to the Roman commanders, they sent some of their own disciples with others of those called Herodians, who said [368], "Teacher, we know that you are true, and defer to no one, for you do not regard people with partiality. Is it lawful to pay tax to Caesar, or not?" But they were instantly rebuked, and when the denarius had been shown, Christ said to them, "Render to Caesar the things that are Caesar's, and to God the things that are God's."[120] At this they were greatly embarrassed and did not pursue this test any further but set about planning another means of testing him.

Later, when he made a whip out of cords and drove from the temple all those selling sheep and cattle, saying, "Take these things out of here! Do not make my Father's house a house of merchandise!"[121] those men were there and became indignant. "By what authority do you do these things?" they asked. "And who gave you this authority?" What, then, did Christ say to this? He said, "I will also ask you a question, and you answer me. The baptism of John—where was it from? From heaven, or from men?" They reasoned among themselves, saying, "If we say, 'From heaven,' he will say to us, 'Then why did you not believe him?' If we say, 'From men,' we fear the crowd, for they all hold that John was a prophet." So they said, "We do not know." What did Christ say to this? "Neither will I tell you by what authority I do these things."[122]

Gad, therefore, indicates a band of raiders, or testers, meaning the Pharisees who were constantly testing. Yet they themselves were immediately[123] tested in return.[124] For, according to the words of the prophet, Christ was the one "who catches the

---

120. Cf. Mt 22.16–21.
121. Cf. Jn 2.15–16.
122. Cf. Mt 21.23–27.
123. The term "immediately" here picks up the idiom from the citation of Gn 49.19 (there translated "closely") that opens this section.
124. We observe here again, as was noted also in the previous section with regard to Dan (see n. 106), Cyril's contrasting double interpretation. The meaning given for "Gad" is applied to the Pharisees, yet the action ascribed to him in the latter part of the opening citation is here ascribed to Christ.

wise in their wisdom, and who cleverly turns the sophistry of schemers into a question against them."[125]

Concerning Asher

"Asher's bread is rich, and he will provide food for rulers."[126]

Now Asher signifies "riches," for that is what the name means.[127] This might, I believe, be understood of him "in whom are hidden all the treasures of wisdom and knowledge,"[128] that is, Christ, who is the treasure hidden in a field, the pearl of great value, and the one who, in the person of Wisdom, expressly says, "Riches and glory are mine, abundant possessions and righteousness."[129] He himself is the one who visited the earth, and, as David says, "you have enriched it abundantly."[130] The most-wise[131] Paul also writes to us about him in a certain passage, saying, "I give thanks to my God always concerning you for the grace of God given to you in Christ Jesus, for in every way you have been enriched in him, in all speech and all knowledge."[132]

For even though he was rich, in that he was God, yet for our sakes he shared in our poverty, in order that by his poverty we might become rich.[133] This is evidently what is meant by the *"bread is rich,"* that is, full of fatness and nourishment. For our Lord Jesus Christ feeds us, descending not as physical manna like that given long ago to the people of Israel, but by making himself to dwell in the souls of believers through the Holy Spirit. That is why he said to the people of the Jews, "Truly [369], truly, I say to you, it was not Moses that gave you the true bread from heaven. For the bread of God is he who comes down from heav-

---

125. Cf. Jb 5.13; 1 Cor 3.19.
126. Gn 49.20.
127. The name Asher (*'āšēr*) would appear to be related to the idea of happiness (cf. Gn 30.13). The Hebrew term for "rich" (*'āšîr*) is not dissimilar, but is an altogether different word.
128. Col 2.3.
129. Prv 8.18.
130. Cf. Ps 65.9 (64.10 LXX).
131. Var. omit "The most-wise."
132. 1 Cor 1.5.
133. Cf. 2 Cor 8.9.

en and gives life to the world,"[134] and again, "I am the bread of life."[135]

This life-giving bread might also be understood in another way, that is, in a more mystical manner.[136] It says, *"he provides food for rulers."* Now I would say that thrones and dominions, principalities and powers, angels and archangels, even the entire holy and spiritual creation, make Christ their food. So the matter might suitably be interpreted. To those, however, who are leaders of the flock on earth, he also distributes food. This is obviously food of a spiritual nature—the revelation of divine mysteries and the knowledge of all virtue—so that these leaders may also feed those people under their authority with teachings that lead to life. Christ therefore says to these men, "Freely you have received, freely give."[137] And elsewhere he says, "Who, then, is the faithful and wise servant whom his Lord will put in charge of his household, to give out their allowance of food at the proper time? Truly, I say to you, blessed is that servant whom, when his Lord comes, he will find him doing these things. Truly, I say to you, that he will put him in charge of all his possessions."[138]

We shall find the teachers of the churches engaged in this task, and before them the holy apostles especially did so. The blessed[139] Paul, for instance, wrote to certain believers, "I desire to see you, that I may impart some spiritual gift to you to strengthen you."[140] So these could also say that they had been comforted by God since he obviously filled them with good things from above and richly nourished them by means of the provisions granted through the Spirit.

Asher, then, is Christ, or those who have been made rich in

---

134. Jn 6.32–33.
135. Jn 6.35, 48.
136. The adjective employed by Cyril has a range of possible equivalents, such as, "secret," "esoteric," "ineffable." What is to be understood from this is immediately explained in the following sentences.
137. Mt 10.8.
138. Mt 24.45–47.
139. Var. omit "The blessed."
140. Rom 1.11.

Christ, with reference to whom the rich bread may also be understood.

Concerning Naphtali

"Naphtali is a spreading stem, imparting beauty to its fruit."[141]

I would think it appropriate, and not off the mark, to apply this again to Emmanuel himself and, if one wished, also to those justified by faith and sanctified in the Spirit. For it was in fact said to the mother of the Jews, Jerusalem, through the mouth of Jeremiah, "The Lord called your name Fair Olive Tree, appearing good for shade. At the sound of it being cropped, fire was kindled against it. Great is the affliction coming against you. Its branches have become worthless, and the mighty Lord who planted you has pronounced evil against you."[142] For when it was necessary to show the olive tree the attention due to it (for this, and nothing else, I believe, is what it "being cropped" signifies), it then also says that it was ruined and set on fire, because it chose to disregard the presence of the vinedresser. He, as it were, with the sharpest of pruning hooks, namely by the working of the Spirit, removed us from among the worthless branches, that is, those which were the most earthly and carnal, so that we might bear forth the desire and eagerness for those things which are of more value than all else.

We may hear, then, what Christ the Savior of all plainly says [372]: "I am the true vine, and my Father is the vinedresser. Every branch in me that does not bear fruit he takes away, and every branch that bears fruit he prunes, so that it may bear more fruit."[143] For Jesus Christ, the Lord of us who are brought to newness of life, is like the root and stem of a vine firmly embedded in the ground. And we are like branches that, through our union with him in the Spirit, grow in him and are dependent upon him. Being united in a bond of love, and becoming lux-

---

141. Gn 49.21.

142. Jer 11.16–17. The interchange of pronouns between second and third persons and the poor translation of the LXX make this citation awkward to render in good English. The Greek has been followed fairly closely.

143. Jn 15.1–2.

uriant through the goodness received from him, we are nourished on the divine grace so as to bear the fruit of virtue.

So God the Father himself cares for our needs together with the Son. It is evident, however, that even though Christ is understood to be a vine, and the Father the vinedresser, he nevertheless cuts off the branch that is completely unproductive in Christ. And he considers worthy of his attention, as being something most excellent, the one that is effectual and fruitful in Christ.

When, therefore, the mother of the Jews, described by the prophet as a fair olive tree that was good for shade, ought to have been found in a better condition, it was then that God destroyed her, and a fire was kindled in her. So the wise John says, "Even now the axe is laid at the root of the trees. Every tree, therefore, that does not bear good fruit is cut down and thrown into the fire."[144]

That the celebrated city would meet its end through coming disasters, the prophet Zechariah expressed beforehand in an oracle, saying, "And the mourning of Jerusalem will be like the mourning for a pomegranate orchard cut down in the plain."[145] Again he said to her, "Open your doors, O Lebanon, and let fire consume your cedars. Let the pine tree wail, because the cedar has fallen, because the mighty trees have been greatly afflicted. Wail, O oaks of Bashan, because the thick forest has been torn down."[146] For Mount Lebanon is luxuriant in cedar trees. Its trees are fragrant and especially valued for their excellence. Lebanon, therefore, represents Jerusalem, which had a much-admired multitude of priests, that is to say, she had a dignified status derived from the law. For these men were appointed rulers, and were like the strongest and most excellent trees in the forest, having a stature above all others, with many people under their authority. Yet Jerusalem, that is, Lebanon, was set on fire. Those illustrious men within her, those who were most prominent, possessing much glory, bewailed one another as they fell and perished, being brought down at the hands of

---

144. Mt 3.10.
145. Zec 12.11.
146. Zec 11.1–2.

those who were in a way like woodcutters, namely the powerful Roman generals.

Yet our Lord Jesus Christ, since those evil men perished so dreadfully, has become *"a spreading stem."* For he always enjoys the infinite supply of heavenly provisions, and spreads, one might say, throughout the whole earth. This very thing God plainly declared beforehand through the mouth of Ezekiel, saying, "And I will take from the choice branches of the cedar, from its very top, and I will crop off one from their midst, and I will plant it upon a lofty mountain, and hang it on a mountain height of Israel. Yea, I will plant it, and it will bring forth shoots and bear fruit, and it will become [373] a great cedar. All kinds of animals will rest under it, and every kind of bird will rest in its shade; and its branches will be restored. And all the trees of the field will know that I, the Lord, am he who brings down the high tree, and raises up the low tree, who withers the green tree, and makes the dry tree flourish. I, the Lord, have spoken, and I will do it."[147]

See, then, that God the Father, taking the choice branches of the cedar, planted for us the tree of life, that is to say, Christ. By the choice branches of the cedar it means the tribe of Judah —that which always had the rule and which was more noble than the others. From this tribe there came forth Jesse, and David, and the holy Virgin, who gave birth to Jesus. That the branch taken from the choice cedar was also hanged upon a cross[148] on our account, and became a goodly and flowery tree, how can one doubt?

Moreover, we, who were formerly dry trees without any fruit, have sprouted forth by the will of the Father, while they who received only the sap and life of the law, namely the people of Israel, in a way became dry and withered. They were once exalted, yet we were lowly and cast down. We, however, have now been exalted in Christ through faith, while they have fallen from their former glory and have become lowly. Therefore, God, the Lord of all, is he who by a mere command humbles the exalted

---

147. Ezek 17.22–24.
148. The word *xulon* has the sense of "wood," "tree," "gallows."

and raises up the lowly, the one who withers the green tree and makes the dry tree flourish.

Because those of the ancient synagogue were no better than thorns and brambles, they were, in effect, cut off from the holy land, while the multitude of those with faith grew up, as it were, in their place. These, we learn, can be likened to the most fragrant of trees, as God says, "And I will turn the desert into pools of water, and the land[149] into watercourses. I will put the cedar in the land without water, and also the box tree, the myrtle, the cypress, and the white poplar."[150] Also later it says, "And instead of the thornbush, the cypress will come up, and instead of the nettle the myrtle will come up."[151]

By the cedar we are to understand the hope of incorruption held by those who believe. For the cedar is not liable to decay. By the box tree we are to understand that frivolous or trivial thoughts are inappropriate to the mind of those in Christ. For they are all people of intelligence, since they have Christ for their understanding. The wood of the box tree is also solid and has considerable sturdiness. By the myrtle we are to understand the fragrance found in sanctification and the perpetual flourishing caused by grace. By the cypress we are to understand height and sweetness of smell. When I say "height," I mean with respect to virtue and eminence as regards doctrines. And by the white poplar we are to understand the splendor and whiteness of righteousness. For those in Christ are splendid, made glorious by the grace they receive from him. So then, *"Naphtali is a spreading stem,"* whether speaking of Christ himself, or of those who are friends of Christ.

When it says, *"imparting beauty to its fruit,"* it likewise hints at such a thing as this, in my opinion. For when at the beginning Christ appeared in the same form as ourselves, it was not believed that he was God by nature, and that he had become flesh. And so, the Jews made so bold as to try to stone him [376], making the accusation against him, "You, though you are a

---

149. LXX: "the thirsty land."
150. Is 41.18–19.
151. Is 55.13.

man, make yourself God."[152] We find that even the holy apostles themselves, for the reason that they did not yet clearly understand the mystery concerning him, were amazed at him, since he could work miracles. So, when Christ commanded it to happen, the sea was calmed, and the wild blowing of the wind was stopped. And it says that the apostles reasoned in themselves, saying, "What kind of man is this, that even the sea and the winds obey him?"[153]

Do you see how he who is God by nature, though he had become flesh, was not yet known to those in the world, and had not yet attained his majestic glory? But when knowledge of him increased among us, then it was eventually believed that he was God by nature, and that to him every knee should bow, and that the whole world should worship him. Surely then, when that knowledge of him was brought to perfection among us, he was then perceived by the sons of men to be most beautiful.

Now if the words *"imparting beauty to its fruit"* are understood with reference to us, their meaning is apparent. For since we are always increasing in virtue, and attaining to better things, namely those things that lie ahead, as the blessed Paul said,[154] then our beauty is becoming more and more evident. By this beauty I mean spiritual beauty, so that it might also be said to us, "The king desired your beauty."[155]

Concerning Joseph

"Joseph is a son who has increased.[156] My imitable[157] youngest son has increased; return to me. Those who plotted against him reviled him,

152. Jn 10.33.
153. Mt 8.27.
154. Cf. Phil 3.13.
155. Ps 45.11 (44.12 LXX).
156. Or "has grown."
157. Here we follow the original word appearing in the LXX, the adjective *zêlôtos*, rather than the cognate noun *zêlôtês* used by Cyril at this point. This is necessary better to understand Cyril's subsequent discussion, which in fact deals with the former of these two. For this term a range of meanings is possible. Most suitable to this present context would perhaps be the sense of "attractive," "desirable." In the following exposition, however, Cyril takes it in its

and the archers[158] *pressed him hard. But their bows were mightily shattered, and the sinews of their arms were made weak by the Mighty One of Jacob* (by which we are to understand *'the God of your father who strengthened Israel'*). *My God has helped you, and he has blessed you with the blessing of heaven above, and with the blessing of the earth that possesses all things, on account of the blessing of the breasts and of the womb, the blessing of your father and of your mother. He has exceeded the blessings of the abiding mountains, and the blessings of the everlasting hills. These will be upon the head of Joseph, and upon the head of the brothers over whom he has ruled.*"[159]

Again the words of the prophecy point us to Emmanuel himself. What is revealed by the prophecy here might, I believe, be nothing other than what I said just now on the matter of *"imparting beauty to its fruit."* When it says that he had *"increased,"* it actually indicates his moving on from how he was at first and the advancement of his glory with respect to his physical nature, as may rightly be understood. For when the Only-Begotten Word of God, being also God from God, emptied himself, as the Scriptures say, and willingly came down to be that which he was not, he was clothed with this most inglorious flesh, and appeared in the form of a servant, becoming obedient to God the Father until death.[160] It then says that he was exalted, and that by way of a reward he received the name above every name (which he did not in any way have from his human nature), according to the words of the blessed Paul.[161] Yet the truth of the matter was [377] that nothing was given to him which was not naturally his in the first place—far from it. Rather, it ought to be understood as an ascent and return to that first estate, which was essentially and inseparably his. So it is that, having put on the lowly nature of

---

other sense of "worthy of imitation." In order to appreciate Cyril's treatment of the term, therefore, both here and in the exposition it has been rendered "imitable." The word has yet a further meaning, that of "enviable," "provoking to jealousy," which Cyril will also explore.

158. Hebrew here employs the idiomatic phrase "masters [or 'lords'] of arrows," which has been preserved in the LXX. Cyril will draw upon this literal sense during the course of his interpretation.

159. Gn 49.22–26.
160. Cf. Phil 2.7–8.
161. Cf. Phil 2.9.

humanity through the Incarnation, he said, "Father, glorify me with the glory which I had with you before the world was."[162] For he always coexisted in his own divine glory with the Father[163] before all ages and all time and before the foundation of the world. So when speaking of Christ, the increase is to be understood as an advancement in glory, which in a sense God most abundantly and most evidently always has. This is because he is increasingly being apprehended according to his nature by those who are in the world, and is being confessed and worshiped as Lord of all along with God the Father.

While Christ himself, however, was the one who made the world, he might appropriately be understood as also being the *"youngest."* For he appeared in the last ages of the world after that glorious and admirable band of holy prophets, and, generally speaking, after all those before his visitation who were considered to enjoy the status of sons on account of their virtue.

That Emmanuel was *"imitable,"* how could one doubt? He is imitated by the saints, who diligently follow in his footsteps and are transformed into his divine beauty. Making him the pattern of their deeds, they acquire the most excellent glory of all.

Zêlôtos[164] might, however, be understood in another way by those who do not care to practice love, by which I mean the leaders of the Jews, the scribes and Pharisees, who suffered the pangs of bitter envy within themselves. These, by making Christ's incomparable glory a cause of jealousy, were very much overcome by it. For Christ raised the dead who were already odorous and decaying, and showed himself to be greater than death itself. But they, though they ought to have marveled and come to believe in him, no longer doubting anything, this they did not do. Rather, they gnashed at him in envy, and felt bitter vexation in their hearts. He healed a man who was blind from birth, and they called him a sinner. A horde of unclean demons was driven out, and they falsely claimed him to have been under the direction of the power of Beelzebul. They made to cast stones at him, declaring impiously, "We are not stoning you for any good deed,

---

162. Jn 17.5.
163. Lit. "Begetter" (*gennêtôr*).
164. See n. 157 above.

but for blasphemy, because you, though you are a man, make yourself God."[165] They were cut to the heart and said, "This is the heir. Come, let us kill him."[166]

Christ was, then, for those who chose to be hateful, the cause of envy,[167] yet he was not in any way overcome by them. For although he suffered the cross, since he was God he came back to life, having trampled upon death, as though God the Father were summoning him and in effect saying, *"Return to me."* He ascended into heaven so that he might also hear the words of him saying, "Sit at my right hand, until I make your enemies a footstool under your feet."[168] That these men did in fact become subject, even though they were so greatly enraged against him, it teaches when it says, *"Those who plotted against him reviled him, and the archers pressed him hard.* For these *"masters of arrows"*[169] gathered in council and plotted harsh things [380]. This means the leaders of the people, who sharply attacked Christ, as though wounding him, and all but transfixed him with nails themselves, even though they dared not do that which was unlawful, and they sprang up against him like wild beasts. Yet *"their bows were shattered, and the sinews of their arms were made weak by the Mighty One of Jacob,"* that is, by God the Father, who is the Lord of power.

God also ordained that the Son should be blessed[170] both in heaven and upon the earth. For the divine Paul writes, "When he brings the firstborn into the world, he says, 'And let all the angels of God worship him.'"[171] In another place the great David declares to us, "May all the earth worship you, and may they sing praises to you."[172] This, we say, indicates *"the heavenly blessing above,"* and also *"the blessing below on the earth that possesses all*

---

165. Jn 10.33.
166. Mt 21.38.
167. *zēlōtos*.
168. Ps 110.1 (109.1 LXX); cf. Mt 22.44; Mk 12.36; Lk 20.42–43; Acts 2.34; Heb 1.13.
169. See n. 158 above.
170. Or "be praised," as the noun "blessing" in the following discussion may also be rendered "praise."
171. Heb 1.6; cf. Dt 32.43 LXX.
172. Ps 66.4 (65.4 LXX).

things," that is to say, in which there is through Christ every kind of goodness and the abundant fruits of devotion to God. For in one passage it says to the Son, "You have visited the earth, and you have watered it and enriched it abundantly."[173] It clearly affirms that the heavenly blessing and the earthly have been given to him, when it says, *"on account of the blessing of the breasts and of the womb, the blessing of your father and of your mother."* Through these words both the birth of the Only-Begotten from God the Father and his birth through the holy Virgin, by which it is also to be understood that he became a man, are very plainly signified. For although he truly was the Son of God the Father by nature, for our sake he underwent birth through a mother, a woman, and suckled at her breast. For it is surely not the case, as is the opinion of some, that he became a man in appearance only,[174] but that he actually did come as a man, the very same thing that we ourselves are, complying with the laws of nature and being sustained by food, even though it was he himself who gave life to the world. Thus the blessed Isaiah, in a certain manner, likewise speaks of the fact that the Lord truly became human in that he needed food suitable for an infant, when he says, "He will eat butter and honey."[175]

So then, Christ was blessed *"on account of the blessing of the breasts and of the womb."* For as I said before, since he became man and was obedient to the Father, he has inherited the name above every name, and to him every knee shall bow, of those in heaven, those on earth, and those under the earth, confessing that Jesus Christ is Lord, to the glory of God the Father.[176]

Yet, although he came as one of us, he has a place higher than every saint, and, as is fitting for one who is God, he stands above all the renowned fathers from the beginning of the world. For the psalmist says, "Who in the heavens can be compared to the Lord? Or who among the sons of God can be likened to him?"[177] This is what the blessed Jacob teaches when he says,

---

173. Ps 65.9 (64.10 LXX).
174. Here referring to the false teaching of Docetism.
175. Is 7.15.
176. Cf. Phil 2.8–11.
177. Ps 89.6 (88.7 LXX).

"He has exceeded the blessings of the abiding mountains, and of the everlasting hills." For the eternal and abiding mountains, as well as the everlasting hills, mean the saints, since they are lifted up from the earth, and think nothing of those things that are base. Rather, they seek the things that are above, and reach up to attain especially the highest of virtues. Even the most notable of the fathers, therefore, reach a measure of virtue that is less than the glory of Christ. [381] For they were servants of the household, even though they obtained a place among the children. But it is the Lord who, being a Son, has provided them with those things by means of which they have become so eminent. Thus it is said, "From his fullness we have all received, grace upon grace."[178]

So the crown of glory will rest essentially upon the head of our Savior. But it will also certainly be the case that a reward will be given to the saints under his authority, who will wear the unfading crown of glory. Having been partakers of his sufferings, they will share in his glory. For he is pleased that, having suffered with him, they should also reign with him.[179]

Concerning Benjamin

"Benjamin is a ravening wolf; in the morning he will eat further, and in the evening he will divide the food."[180]

Rachel first gave birth to the divine Joseph, and then to Benjamin after him. Joseph, however, was called the *"youngest"* son by his father.[181] We grant that this is the case. So we are saying that Benjamin was younger than the youngest. Now Benjamin was in fact the youngest son, and may reasonably be understood as a picture and a type of the youngest people of God, those who were called through the holy disciples after Christ came back to life from the dead and returned to God the Father in heaven.

Benjamin is compared to *"a ravening wolf,"* the reason for

---

178. Jn 1.16.
179. Cf. Rom 8.17; 2 Tm 2.12.
180. Gn 49.27.
181. Referring to the description in the earlier citation of Gn 49.22.

which, I think, is his rapacious appetite for receiving instruction. He is always leaping up and down, being especially desirous, as certain wild animals are, for any kind of food that is good for bodily strength, here to be taken in a spiritual sense. These animals are terrible to behold when they are fulfilling their desire for what they need, and when they seize hold of what is good for them. Yet they are swift to seek refuge from those things that tend towards their harm. They are not easily made to fear, not even if they are surrounded by those who are like dogs, who seek to keep them away from good works and words, and who are intent on attacking them. For they have learned, and that most forcibly, what it means when it says, "What shall separate us from the love of Christ? Shall tribulation, or distress, or famine, or persecution, or nakedness, or danger, or the sword?"[182] Moreover, false shepherds—who, as it is written, "aim at the heart, without pity"[183]—are not at all able to turn them away from the path they love to follow. For people such as this, for whom life means suffering, possess considerable endurance,[184] and so they proclaim, "For me to live is Christ, and to die is gain."[185]

Even if the way in which we have shown the saints to be compared to ravenous wolves were not correct, no harm would be done, it seems. For surely the Savior also calls himself a lion and a leopard, or a panther, saying, "For I am like a panther to Ephraim, and like a lion to the house of Judah. I will come,[186] and I will go; I will take away, and there will be no deliverer."[187] And those who believe in him he calls "wild animals,"[188] as he says [384] through the mouth of Isaiah, "The wild animals will bless me, the owls[189] and the young ostriches, because I have

182. Rom 8.35.
183. Jb 16.13. In both the Hebrew and LXX of this citation the term here rendered "heart" is literally "kidneys," signifying the inward parts.
184. Or "patience."
185. Phil 1.21.
186. LXX: "I will seize."
187. Hos 5.14.
188. Or "beasts of the field."
189. The precise kind of bird intended by this Greek word (*seirênes;* lit. "Sirens") is uncertain. Other possibilities are the "ostrich" or the "nightin-

given water in the wilderness, and rivers in the waterless land, to provide drink for my chosen race, the people I acquired to declare my praises."[190] See, then, how he called the chosen people "wild animals" and "owls," that is, the most melodious of birds. They are wild animals, because they do not, one may suppose, readily let themselves be tamed by Satan, nor can they be made subject to him. Rather, they leap up against him, in effect causing injury also to those who seek to compel them to do unlawful acts. And they are owls, because they call out most beautifully, speaking of the perfections of Christ, and singing to his honor.

Benjamin, the new people of God by faith, is a wolf that is very determined to accomplish what is needful and, what is more, is able also to give what will benefit others. This is indicated when it says, *"In the morning he will eat further, and in the evening he will divide the food."* The one who learns is in a way like one who is being fed. For he allows the teachings entrance into his mind, just as the other obviously does with food into his stomach. So the one who is teaching can be equated with the one who is feeding. Thus the divine Paul also compares the manner of teaching to food, for he said, "Solid food is for the mature, for those whose faculties have been trained by practice to distinguish between good and evil."[191]

So then, *"Benjamin is a ravening wolf; in the morning he will eat further, and in the evening he will divide the food."* It is as though it said, "Although he is one who wishes to learn further, and who has not yet reached perfection, he may benefit others, and just a short time may prove that even those who have recently come to faith may teach what is profitable." For concerning the people of Israel, on account of their great ignorance, I suppose, and their inner dullness[192] of mind, it is said, "Behold, a foolish people without any sense; who have eyes but do not see, and ears but do not hear,"[193] and also, "You who have been borne

---

gale." The latter suits Cyril's discussion best, yet it is doubtful that this is what was intended in the LXX citation from which the term is derived.

190. Is 43.20–21.
191. Heb 5.14.
192. Lit. "roughness."
193. Jer 5.12.

by me from the womb, and taught until your old age."[194] But to those in the faith, who are in Christ, the wise John writes, "You do not need anyone to teach you, but his anointing teaches you about all things."[195] For those who have the mind of Christ know all things, and they are not incapable of teaching and exhorting one another.

Now if one relates the prediction concerning Benjamin to the blessed Paul, saying that it was also fulfilled in him, then such would be proper and true. For he who persecuted the church, running like a wolf after those who loved Christ, in just a short time was transformed into the complete opposite. For he began to proclaim the faith that he had once sought to destroy, and being appointed to the office of apostle he offered up a thank offering, even though he had formerly been a blasphemer, persecutor, and man of violence. He himself said that he was also of the tribe of Benjamin.[196] I would further say that the divine David made clear mention of what would happen with regard to Paul, when he said in the Sixty-seventh Psalm, "There is Benjamin, the younger one, in a state of elation, the princes of Judah, their rulers, the princes of Zebulun, the princes [385] of Naphtali."[197] For the blessed disciples, who were Jews from the race of Israel, became leaders of those justified by faith in Christ, among whom also was the one from the tribe of Benjamin who wrote and said, "For if we are beside ourselves, it is for God; if we are of sound mind, it is for you."[198] For both to Gentiles and to Jews Paul proclaimed the good news of our Lord Jesus Christ, through whom and with whom be glory to God the Father, together with the Holy Spirit, for ever and ever. Amen.

194. Is 46.3–4.
195. 1 Jn 2.27.
196. Cf. Phil 3.5.
197. Ps 68.27 (67.28 LXX).
198. 2 Cor 5.13.

RECENT VOLUMES IN THE FATHERS
OF THE CHURCH SERIES

ST. MAXIMOS THE CONFESSOR, *On Difficulties in Sacred Scripture: The Responses to Thalassios*, translated by Fr. Maximos Constas, Volume 136 (2018)

EUSEBIUS OF CAESAREA, *Against Marcellus and On Ecclesiastical Theology*, translated by Kelley McCarthy Spoerl and Markus Vinzent, Volume 135 (2017)

TYCONIUS, *Exposition of the Apocalypse*, translated by Francis X. Gumerlock, with introduction and notes by David C. Robinson, Volume 134 (2017)

RUFINUS OF AQUILEIA, *History of the Church*, translated by Philip R. Amidon, SJ, Volume 133 (2016)

DIDYMUS THE BLIND, *Commentary on Genesis*, translated by Robert C. Hill, Volume 132 (2016)

ST. GREGORY OF NYSSA, *Anti-Apollinarian Writings*, translated by Robin Orton, Volume 131 (2015)

ST. EPHREM THE SYRIAN, *The Hymns on Faith*, translated by Jeffrey T. Wickes, Volume 130 (2015)

ST. CYRIL OF ALEXANDRIA, *Three Christological Treatises*, translated by Daniel King, Volume 129 (2014)

ST. EPIPHANIUS OF CYPRUS, *Ancoratus*, translated by Young Richard Kim, Volume 128 (2014)

ST. CYRIL OF ALEXANDRIA, *Festal Letters 13–30*, translated by Philip R. Amidon, SJ, and edited with notes by John J. O'Keefe, Volume 127 (2013)

FULGENTIUS OF RUSPE AND THE SCYTHIAN MONKS, *Correspondence on Christology and Grace*, translated by Rob Roy McGregor and Donald Fairbairn, Volume 126 (2013)

ST. HILARY OF POITIERS, *Commentary on Matthew*, translated by D. H. Williams, Volume 125 (2012)

WORKS OF ST. CYRIL OF ALEXANDRIA
IN THIS SERIES

Letters 1–50, translated by John I. McEnerney,
Fathers of the Church 76 (1987)

Letters 51–110, translated by John I. McEnerney,
Fathers of the Church 77 (1987)

Commentary on the Twelve Prophets, Volume 1, translated by
Robert C. Hill, Fathers of the Church 115 (2007)

Commentary on the Twelve Prophets, Volume 2, translated by
†Robert C. Hill, Fathers of the Church 116 (2008)

Commentary on the Twelve Prophets, Volume 3, translated by
†Robert C. Hill, Fathers of the Church 124 (2012)

Festal Letters 1–12, translated by Philip R. Amidon, SJ, and
edited with introduction and notes by John J. O'Keefe,
Fathers of the Church 118 (2009)

Festal Letters 13–30, translated by Philip R. Amidon, SJ,
and edited with notes by John J. O'Keefe,
Fathers of the Church 127 (2013)

Three Christological Treatises, translated by Daniel King,
Fathers of the Church 129 (2014)

Glaphyra on the Pentateuch, Volume 1: Genesis, translated by
Nicholas P. Lunn, with introduction by Gregory K. Hillis,
Fathers of the Church 137 (2018)

FORTHCOMING IN 2019

Glaphyra on the Pentateuch, Volume 2: Exodus through Deuteronomy,
translated by Nicholas P. Lunn, Fathers of the
Church 138 (2019)